GOVERNOR WILLIAM H. ELLERBE

HISTORICAL
ROSTER AND ITINERARY

OF

SOUTH CAROLINA VOLUNTEER TROOPS

WHO

SERVED IN THE LATE WAR BETWEEN THE

UNITED STATES AND SPAIN,

1898,

Coupled with Brief Sketches of their Movements from the Beginning to the Ending of the Conflict.

Compiled and Published by J. W. FLOYD, Adjutant and Inspector General.

Southern Historical Press, Inc.
Greenville, South Carolina

This volume was reproduced from
An 1901 edition located in the
Publisher's private library,
Greenville, South Carolina

All rights reserved. No part of this publication may be reproduced,
stored in a retrieval system, transmitted in any form, posted
on to the web in any form or by any means without
the prior written permission of the publisher.

Please direct all correspondence and orders to:

www.southernhistoricalpress.com
or
SOUTHERN HISTORICAL PRESS, Inc.
PO BOX 1267
375 West Broad Street
Greenville, SC   29601
southernhistoricalpress@gmail.com

Originally published: Columbia, SC. 1901
Reprinted by: Southern Historical Press, Inc.
Greenville, SC
ISBN #0-89308-781-5
All rights Reserved.
Printed in the United States of America

Dedication

To the Officers and Enlisted Men of the First and Second Regiments of Infantry, the Heavy Battery of Artillery, and the three Divisions of Naval Militia composing South Carolina's quota of Troops contributed to the Volunteer forces of the United States Army for service in the late War between the United States and the Kingdom of Spain, and to their children, and to all of the people of our beloved State, this volume is dedicated.   *J. W. F.*

INDEX

	PAGE.
Introductory	7
W. H. Ellerbe, War Governor	9
Remarks by Compiler, General Floyd	11
The Heavy Battery	14
First Regiment Infantry	15
Colonel Jos. K. Alston's Career	17
Tribute to His Memory by Wm. Banks	18
Pathetic Eulogy by N. G. Gonzales	22
Second Regiment Infantry	23
Presentation Sword to Colonel Jones	24
The Men Who Went to Cuba	26
Colonel Jones' Address at the Reunion of His Old Regiment	27
August Kohn, War Correspondent "News and Courier"	32
William Banks, Correspondent "The State"	35
Field and Staff Officers First Regiment	36
Historical Sketch First Regiment, Colonel Frost	40
Itinerary First Regiment, by Colonel Frost	48
Roster Field Officers First Regiment	53
Line Officers and Enlisted Men, Company A, First Regiment	55
Company B, First Regiment	60
Company C, First Regiment	66
Company D, First Regiment	72
Company E, First Regiment	78
Company F, First Regiment	84
Company G, First Regiment	90
Company H, First Regiment	98
Company I, First Regiment	103
Company K, First Regiment	109
Company L, First Regiment	115
Company M, First Regiment	121

INDEX.

	PAGE.
Historical Sketch of Second Regiment, by Colonel Jones	128
Sketch Independent Battalion, by Colonel Henry Thompson	142
Itinerary Second Regiment by Companies	150
Field and Staff Officers Second Regiment	155
Roster of Field and Staff Officers Second Regiment	157
Company A, Second Regiment, Roll Officers and Men	160
Company B, Second Regiment, Roll Officers and Men	167
Company C, Second Regiment, Roll Officers and Men	173
Company D, Second Regiment, Roll Officers and Men	180
Company E, Second Regiment, Roll Officers and Men	186
Company F, Second Regiment, Roll Officers and Men	191
Company G, Second Regiment, Roll Officers and Men	195
Company H, Second Regiment, Roll Officers and Men	200
Company I, Second Regiment, Roll Officers and Men	205
Company K, Second Regiment, Roll Officers and Men	211
Company L, Second Regiment, Roll Officers and Men	216
Company M, Second Regiment, Roll Officers and Men	221
Officers of the Heavy Battery Artillery	226
Heavy Battery Artillery, Historical Sketch by Captain Ed. Anderson	227
Itinerary Heavy Battery Artillery	235
Roll of Officers and Men Heavy Battery	237
Officers of Naval Militia	245
Historical Sketch of the Naval Militia, by Commander R. H. Pinckney	247
Report to Adjutant General by Commander Pinckney	250
Roll of Officers and Men Naval Militia	255
End of War and Peace Declared	263

Introductory

The many inquiries reaching the office of the Adjutant General from this State, and from almost every section of the Union, asking information as to kinsmen and friends that were members of various commands of South Carolina troops during one or more of the several wars in which the nation has been involved with foreign powers (as well as the "War between the States"), and the utter impossibility of ascertaining anything definite in one case out of ten, owing to the imperfect, unintelligible and badly kept records—and in many cases no records at all—has induced me, while the data are at hand and the facts so recent, that errors and mistakes can be avoided, to compile and publish in book form an historical record of the Volunteer Troops furnished by South Carolina in the late war between the United States and Spain. Believing that such a publication distributed through the State would be valuable, if for nothing more than to preserve from oblivious neglect a true and correct Roster of every man that composed the rank and file of the various commands South Carolina contributed.

The fact that no appropriation has been made, or is likely to be made at present, to cover the expense of compiling a more elaborate and substantial volume that would be creditable to the archives of a great State like ours—and especially valuable in the future for ready and reliable information—presents a still further incentive to publish this book, relying for indemnity for the cost I incur upon the generous and substantial support of all who cherish and love the history, heroism and statesmanship of our grand old State, as practically demonstrated throughout the life of our Republic, and in every department of her service.

The full scope of the object attending this publication renders it necessary that a brief review or sketch of events leading up to the enlistment, the mustering in and the mustering out of the forces South Carolina furnished, be accurately and impartially recorded. With that aim before me as of paramount importance, the most careful pains have been exercised, and while the work of collecting and arranging the tabular matter has been tedious, difficult and laborious, nevertheless it is correctly accomplished, and here I confidently rest. Believing and trusting that results obtained will not only meet the approval of those whose deeds and doings it is specially intended to perpetuate, but will likewise attract the attention and gain the favor of every citizen of the State that believes in the timely preservation of every particle of information that may assist the future historian to give a correct and impartial story of the part South Carolina bore in the Spanish-American War.

In conclusion, I desire to express my high appreciation for valuable information and assistance rendered me in the preparation of the book by Col. Jno. D. Frost, Major in the 1st Regiment, Col. Wilie Jones, Colonel of the 2d Regiment, Lieut. Col. Henry T. Thompson, of the Independent Battalion, Capt. Edward Anderson, of the Heavy Battery Artillery, and Commander R. H. Pinckney, of the Naval Militia. And especially am I indebted to them for the interesting narrative of their commands, which appear in the book, and which should greatly enhance its value, from the fact that they were actors in the drama from the beginning to the end. J. W. F.

Spanish-American War Governor of South Carolina.

William Haselden Ellerbe was born in Marion County, of the Pee Dee section of South Carolina, on the 7th day of April, 1862. Both parents were of English extraction, his ancestors having emigrated direct from England to America over a century and a half ago, first settling in Virginia and afterwards removing to the Pee Dee section of this State, where Thomas Ellerby and John Ellerby bought large landed estates and where the family has since resided. The Ellerbes were large slaveholders before the "War between the States," and have always been wealthy and influential citizens of the Pee Dee section. The name is still extant in England, and is spelt "Elerby." William H. Ellerbe was a great-great-grand-son of Capt. Thomas Ellerbe, of the Revolution, who served with Gen. Francis Marion's brigade. William H. Ellerbe's father, Capt. William S. Ellerbe, was one of the largest and most successful planters of the State, and widely known as a citizen of sterling integrity and influence. On the maternal side, William H. Ellerbe's ancestry were equally distinguished; his mother was a daughter of Major James Haselden (who was closely identified with the politics and progress of the State), and grand-daughter of Gen. Thomas Godbold, of Revolutionary fame, and great-great-grand-daughter of James Godbold, the original settler of Marion County. William H. Ellerbe was prepared for college by L. B. Prince, a well known educator of the Pee Dee section, and entered Wofford College in 1880, afterwards entered Vanderbilt University; but in a short while, owing to failing health, and upon the advice of his physician, he left the University and returned to his father's plantation, where he engaged in planting and merchandising. At the time of his death he was one of the largest landowners in the eastern part of the State, owning a portion of his father's ancestral estate, as well as a large plantation of his own purchase. In 1888 he became interested in the politics of the State, and joined vigorously into the "Farmers' Movement," which culminated in the birth of the Reform Faction of the Democratic party, led by Senator B. R. Tillman; and upon that ticket, without solicitation on his part, he was nominated for Comptroller General in 1890, and elected, being the youngest man ever elected to a State office in South Carolina. He served the State for two terms as Comptroller and ran for Governor in 1894, but was defeated, after which he retired, and for two years gave his attention to his large planting interests. In 1896 he was elected Governor by the largest majority ever received by a candidate for that office; was re-elected in 1898, but served only a short while of his second term, when he finally succumbed to a disease that he had so heroically resisted for many years, and died at the "Old Ellerbe Homestead," June 2d, 1899, just as he reached his thirty-seventh year.

As Comptroller General of the State for two terms, he gave eminent and faithful service, and his first administration as Governor gave such entire satisfaction to the people, that he was again nominated by the primary of 1898, and re-elected for another term. However able, however pure, however conscientious, it is "the common fate of all" public officers to suffer the stings of adverse and ofttimes bitter criticisms, and Governor Ellerbe was no exception to the rule. But justly and beautifully some one has said: "Governor Ellerbe never shrank from responsibilities, and faithfully endeavored to do his duty as a man and as a public servant. He was conscientious in what he did, and in honesty of heart did what he deemed right and best."

Gen. J. W. Floyd

Remarks of the Compiler, General J. W. Floyd

As stated in the Introductory, the paramount purpose of this publication was simply to carry to record and preserve for future history a correct account of South Carolina's contribution to the Spanish-American War, which should include an exact roster of every officer and enlisted man; their age, residence, occupation, date of enlistment and discharge, and to be interspersed with brief sketches or narratives of the various commands, from the beginning to the end of their service, and by authors who were constantly amid the scenes, and actors therein. The foregoing purpose having been accomplished, there appears little room for further elaboration, other than to briefly remind the reader of what the State could have confidently expected had her troops been called upon to face the terror and fury of actual battle.

While the war was of short duration, and never reached the proportions at first anticipated, and was practically decided by two naval engagements, and therefore gave no opportunity for "our boys" to show of what stuff they were made, nevertheless we knew them "to the manor born;" bone of the same bone; flesh of the same flesh; sons and brothers of the same blood that from Eutaw Springs to Yorktown in the Revolution, in the War of 1812, and throughout the Mexican War from "Contreras" (where the gallant Butler said to Gen. Shields, "There is not a South Carolinian here who will not follow you to death." "Aye to death," said Private Whitfield Brooks,) to the planting of the Palmetto flag upon the walls of the City of Mexico; and in the "War between the States" from Sumter to Appomattox have by their indomitable courage, unswerving devotion to principle, and patriotic love of State and country, proudly maintained the prestige of South Carolina from the birth of the republic to the dawn of the twentieth century.

In the Spanish-American War, as in every other that has involved the nation, South Carolina did her whole duty. And it may be well to note the fact, that in the President's call for 125,000 volunteer troops, it was understood, and so ordered, that each State's quota be proportioned to population.

South Carolina's population was forty-one per cent. white and fifty-nine per cent. black, and according to the last census she stood thirtieth in the column of States in white population, from which her quota of troops were to be drawn, although her assessment was based upon the total white and black. It is easily seen, therefore, and should not escape our attention, but be passed to coming generations, that South Carolina furnished more volunteer troops in proportion to white population than did any one of twenty-nine other States of much larger white population, and in addition thereto, furnished two independent colored companies of immunes.

Under a joint resolution of Congress, passed April 22d, 1898, the President of the United States was authorized to call into service, if necessary, the entire land and naval forces of the country, which forces were also declared by Congress to consist of the regular army and the militia of the various States of the Union. Immediately following the action of Congress, on the 23d of April, 1898, the President issued a call upon the States of the Union for 125,000 volunteers—the two forces to be known as the Regular and Volunteer Armies of the United States. Under that call, the Governors of the various States were at once advised, through the War Department, of the respective quotas of volunteers that each State would be expected to furnish. From that advisement, South Carolina was to be represented in three branches of the service, viz: Infantry, Artillery and Naval. Governor Ellerbe immediately issued his proclamation, and almost at once the machinery was set in motion to raise as promptly as possible South Carolina's quota of troops. Many of the States, as soon as the call was promulgated, in a few days had solid regiments of their State militia at rendezvous and ready for muster into the United States service. Very much unmerited and harsh criticism was indulged in all over our State because (as was charged) the organized militia was exhibiting so little interest. Before admitting the charge there are very many extenuating reasons and conditions that controvert it, so far as the rank and file of the service are concerned. While a rupture between our country and Spain was thought probable and perhaps looked for by those high in authority, nevertheless, to the masses, the declaration of war came like "a peal of thunder from a clear sky." It came, too, at a season of the year when men with families dependent upon them for their living had entered into business engagements and were beyond the threshold of the year's work. To cast aside family ties and to cancel or ignore business alliances and promises would demand greater and more serious causes for war than then existed. For such sacrifices it may be that even their own liberties and the defense of their own firesides should be at stake. And it may be remarked that the pivotal cause, and perhaps as future history will have it, the one and only cause, "the overt act," the sinking of the Maine in Havana harbor, aroused in an instant the ire and patriotism of the whole nation and at least made the war possible. It must be remembered, too, that various causes had existed for years tending to disintegrate our militia service, and among them none more fatal or certain to destroy its efficiency than illiberal support by the State. In fact, when the war came, our system was regarded (even by the men that composed it) more as a home guard to quell riots and neighborhood disturbances of the public peace, rather than (as it should be) an auxiliary or national reserve force to supplement the regular army whenever the nation required it. Under the system that prevailed then, and had prevailed for several years before the past war in the military department of the State, it was, nevertheless, gratifying to note that fully thirty per cent. of the enlisted men, and about the same of the commissioned and non-commissioned officers which completed the State's quota, were from the rank and file of the State militia. And I may here state that the Colonel and Lieutenant Colonel of the 1st and 2d Regiments, the Captain of the Heavy Artillery Battery and of the Naval Reserves, were all at the time they received their commissions from the National Government active members of the State militia.

It is true that a month or more elapsed from the day Governor Ellerbe received notification through the Secretary of War of the number of troops South Carolina was to furnish, to the day the 1st Regiment and Battalion of Infantry and the Heavy Battery of Artillery had enlisted the full complement of men required and were ready to be mustered into the service of the United States. But it must be remembered that delays, hindrances and obstacles of innumerable number, which the State authorities had little or no power to remove, were constantly arising to retard the haste so much desired, and still the volunteers poured into Columbia, the place of rendezvous, on almost every arrival of a train. A prominent officer of the 1st Regiment has calculated, and declares, that fully 2,500 men went through the medical examination before the 1st Regiment and Heavy Battery of Artillery had secured their complements of men, and were ready to be mustered into the service. The rigorous requirements of the government in the medical examination were, beyond doubt, the source of greatest annoyance and delay. The rules were as strictly followed as in the examination of a recruit for the regular army in times of peace, when as a usual thing only men of the finest physique offer for enlistment.

Although the attention of the government was called to the situation, the authorities remained inflexible to every appeal, and only in a few cases were any accepted into the service after refusal by the medical examiner, and only those few by special efforts of our Senators and members of Congress. There should have been some latitude allowed a medical examiner in times of war, for in a war of any length or magnitude, modification of the present rules would appear imperative. In the "War between the States," it was proverbial that the small, wiry men who, for lack of weight and height, were refused in the late enlistment, were the very men that could stand and did stand the greatest fatigue and hardships of army life, and were equally as effective as the heavy weight man for all the duties that belong to a soldier's life in peace or war.

After all the unfortunate annoyances enumerated, the time-known pluck and persistency of Carolinians prevailed, and the State's quota under the first call of the President was complete and ready for service.

THE HEAVY BATTERY.

The Heavy Battery of Artillery, under command of Capt Edward Anderson, a military man of known ability and graduate of the South Carolina Military Academy, was mustered into the service on May 21st, 1898—twenty-six days from the date of the President's call. But in less than ten days from date of said call, he had raised the number of men required for a Heavy Battery and had reported at State rendezvous for enlistment, but when the trial came more than fifty per cent. of his men were rejected by the medical examiners, and before the final complement of men required for a Battery of Artillery (166) were secured, more than three hundred had undergone the examination. Great credit is due Capt. Anderson for the energy and perseverance he quietly displayed, and especially is he to be commended for the untiring zeal and patriotism he exercised throughout, which led him to declare, "I am full of anxiety that my native State should quickly raise her quota of troops, and thus maintain our prestige and history of the past, so eminent for readiness and action in every emergency of State or country."

The number of men secured, the Heavy Battery of Artillery was ready to move, and immediately following their muster in at Columbia, Capt. Anderson received orders to proceed with his company to Sullivan's Island, one of the defences of Charleston harbor, where his command remained until hostilities ceased, and he and his company were mustered out and honorably discharged from the service of their country. It was a matter of comment by Regular Army officers that no finer body of men, none better drilled or disciplined, could be found in any of our seacoast defences superior to Capt. Anderson's company. And just prior to the muster out of the company, Lieut. Col. J. B. Rawls, Post Commander, under whom Capt. Anderson served, in a letter to Adj. Gen. Corbin, Washington, D. C., said: "As an organization, Capt. Anderson's South Carolina Battery has done valuable, and in the line of many duties most efficient and needed service to their country." The war over, Capt. Anderson and his company were mustered out of the service April 4th, 1899.

1ST REGIMENT.

Immediately following the departure of the Heavy Battery of Artillery for duty upon the coast, the 1st Regiment of Infantry was mustered in on June 2d, about 1,000 strong, and without invidious comparison it may be truthfully said that a nobler, truer, finer looking body of men were never marshalled together than South Carolina's 1st Regiment of Volunteer Infantry, which under its intrepid leaders stood ready and eagerly waiting to hear the order, "Forward to the front." The field officers of the regiment were Joseph K. Alston, Colonel; James H. Tillman, Lieutenant Colonel, and Majors Marcus B. Stokes and John H. Earle; Capt. Jno. D. Frost, Adjutant; Capt. J. E. Jarnigan, Quartermaster; Major Julius A. Mood, Surgeon; Lieuts. Jno. M. Lawson and J. E. Young, Assistant Surgeons. Most of the field and staff of this Regiment were in the service of the State militia when war was declared, and several were graduated in the finest military schools of the country, and all were true and tried Carolinians, men of high character and pedigree, in whose ability and courage the men of the Regiment had confidence, and in whom the whole State had implicit faith, believing that whatever the ordeal or danger they might face, that the honor and reputation of the State was safe and secure in their hands. Col. Joseph K. Alston, the courtly citizen and gallant soldier, died lamented and mourned by the whole State before his regiment was mustered out. As an active and prominent figure in the stirring scenes I am seeking to perpetuate, I have thought proper to here insert as a memorial to his memory the splendid sketch of his life written by Mr. Wm. Banks, the talented reporter of The State newspaper, and which appeared in the daily edition of said paper the day after Col. Alston received his appointment from Governor Ellerbe as Colonel of the 1st Regiment:

Col. Joseph K. Alston.

JOSEPH K. ALSTON'S CAREER.

Col. Joseph K. Alston's scores of friends were delighted yesterday when they heard of his appointment. A military man had this to say of him: "A lifetime study and a superb collegiate and military education has made Mr. Alston the most available man in South Carolina for high wartime responsibility. The Governor has never made a more fitting appointment. Joseph K. Alston has every qualification for a regimental commanding officer, and I predict that he will soon be first in the hearts of every member of his command. He is a strict disciplinarian, and will command a regiment whose tactics and morale and esprit de corps will be second to none in the army of Cuban occupation."

Joseph Kirkland Alston was born November 6, 1860, in Fairfield County, S. C., near Monticello. He was the only child of William F. Alston and Susannah Cook, daughter of Gen. Philip Cook, C. S. A. His nearest kinsman is a half brother, now living in Greenville, S. C., William F. Alston. His father died in 1869, his mother in 1870, leaving him with his half-brother, who became a father to him and has always been his truest friend. Col. Thomas Woodward, of Rockton, was his guardian, and many of his younger days were spent with him. On both sides he is descended of Revolutionary ancestors, celebrated on the field of battle for gallantry, valor and discretion. In every conflict in which his State and nation have been engaged his forefathers bore a distinguished part, and South Carolina sends to Cuba—if there the regiment goes—as her chief officer a man native and to the manor born.

Col. Alston loves the flag under which he is to fight and the flag of the troops he is to lead. His training and education have been military almost entirely. The first school he attended was Porter's, in Charleston. He went from there to the preparatory department of Sewanee University. The next two were at Col. Coward's at King's Mountain, and the Carolina Military Institute at Charlotte. At this place he was a Corporal, and among his classmates were Senator John L. McLaurin and the Hon. John P. Thomas, Jr. From the Carolina Military Institute he went to the Virginia Military Institute, generally known in those days as the West Point of the South. The military education furnished by this institution is not inferior to West Point. The curriculum is high, the members numerous and the discipline as strict as any military school in the country. Col. Alston commenced here as a private and rose gradually during his four years' course through every grade of office, graduating as senior

Captain, the recognized head and leader of the student body. Among his classmates, 1882, is the present leader of the Alabama troops.

Col. Alston's first choice of profession was the army, but at the time of his graduation, although promised it, he failed to get a Second Lieutenancy. His next choice was the law, and after a residence of two years on his plantation, he read law under Henry Gaillard, Esq., of Winnsboro, and was duly admitted to the bar. He then moved to Columbia and for two years further pursued his studies as law clerk in the office of Judge Samuel W. Melton, who at that time had one of the largest practices ever held in this State. The firm of Alston & Patton was then established, and has ever since existed and flourished, commanding to-day a most lucrative practice.

Col. Alston immediately upon his return from school enlisted in the Gordon Light Infantry as private and was shortly afterwards made Sergeant. Immediately upon his coming to Columbia he was elected Junior Second Lieutenant of the Richland Volunteers. At that time Mr. L. D. Childs was Captain, Charles Newnham, First Lieutenant, and Henry Thompson, Second Lieutenant. In 1888 he was elected First Lieutenant, 1889 was regimental Adjutant, 1890 Captain of the Volunteers, 1897 Major, and in 1898 Colonel commanding troops from South Carolina in the United States Volunteer Army.

In 1888 he was happily married to Miss Belle McCaw, of Yorkville, a great-grand-daughter of William and Martha Bratton, of Revolutionary fame. She has been the guiding star of his useful life, that priceless pearl, a worthy wife, and a worthy descendant of the noble womanhood of South Carolina. When a discussion was had in her presence as to the propriety of South Carolina furnishing troops for the Cuban cause, she spoke for it, and said: "I heartily approve Joe's action, and if necessary will accompany him to Cuba."

And I also insert the following very touching eulogy and description of Col. Alston as he appeared and acted with his men in the daily activities of camp life, written by the same author a few days after Col. Alston's death:

He sleeps in the village church yard. Wake him not, for it is best; his voice is mute in command; his ears are deafened to the music he loved so well, the staccato of the bugle, the roll of the drum; his eyes are dimmed to the martial array which set his heart aglow, but he passes in review under the omnipotent eye of the Commander of all armies. He would have inhaled with joy the fumes of battle smoke, but now he breathes the perfumes on eternal altars. He sleeps.

Wake him not. He is dead. Restore him not. For he died with a broken heart.

Few there be who, knowing Joe Alston, knowing him as a man, knowing him as a friend, knowing him as a soldier, few there be who, knowing him as he was, did not love him. But genius is rarely appreciated until the human tenement has fallen, and many did not know him aright. My acquaintance with my dead friend was confined to a few short months before he laid aside the sober garb of a lawyer for the regalia of the commander of the 1st Regiment. In those few months I learned to know him well and to love him better.

Quiet and unobtrusive, he was hard to know, despite his grace and courtliness. But deep down below the placid surface of his life were fountain springs which sent up bubbles of humor, which poured out streams of manliness and common sense. In private life he was first of all a gentleman, which implies the highest type of manhood. A splendid conversationalist, he could for hours keep one interested in those things upon which his mind had fed—the love of the State he loved, her history and her glorious record in by-gone days, for he loved his State intensely. But he had too many friends for me to speak of him as a student, as a citizen, as a man. It is of Joseph Alston as commander of the regiment of whom I love to tell.

When our government was brought face to face with the Cuban question his soul burned within him. Born a patriot and a soldier, with a soldier's name for a heritage, he studied the grave questions of the day as few men did. When our State was still in apathy, he was full of fire and zeal. Not to be commander of a regiment, not to draw a Colonel's pay, but to go as a soldier, in any capacity, to serve his country, to fight for the oppressed. He had aspirations to command a company, with never a thought of higher honors, and I was the first, I think, who suggested to him the possibility of a Colonel's commission. I do not know that he ever applied for the position which he bore so well, but I do know that when he received his appointment he was the happiest man in South Carolina. He would not have exchanged places with the President of our nation. What a magnificent future spread before him. To smell the smoke of battle, to raise his strong arm in defence of his country, to ride at the head of the first regiment from the proudest State in the Union. But he came back without the battle stain upon his brow, and he died broken-hearted.

There came the trying ordeal of organization. He was worried with a most momentous question, he was harassed with a thousand cares. But bravely did he meet the issue, and quietly but firmly doing his duty, he worked incessantly to raise the quota for his regiment—not for his own glory, but for the honor of his State. These men whom he commanded came from homes of comfort and of love. It was hard indeed to inflict upon them the cold hand of discipline, and I think his heart ached as he gave the orders which guided the men, some away from home for the first time, all unaccustomed to the restraint of military discipline.

The day we arrived at Chickamauga he was quite unwell, but so were his men. He refused the offer of a horse, and marched over the hot, dusty road with his men. Oh, the load he had to bear in Chickamauga. High-strung as an Arabian steed, sensitive as the gentlest maiden, he was made to suffer the whispered derision of northerners for his ragged, starved, unarmed regiment. He battled against the red tape fortifications of the supply department, and obtained clothing and guns for us. We were proud when we came from Snodgrass Hill with praises ringing in our ears, but his heart was full of joy, not personal pride, but pride for his State, pride for the regiment which was his very life.

A halo seemed to surmount his brow the night we thought we were goint to Puerto Rico to stand up before death. He was transfigured. But when we got to Jacksonville, there to stay, his spirit was in a measure broken. It was battle for which he yearned. In those trying days when we were faced with the question of dissolution, he took a firm and manly stand, a stand for what he thought was right. Nor could an army have changed him. I saw him when first he knew we would be mustered out. I saw the great, strong man shed bitter tears, not for the loss of his commission, but because he had been denied the honor which he had long dreamed of, long hoped for—the honor of a battle won—promotion.

I watched him when we came home and dissension came among us. No matter what others may say, I know that dissension was not born of his brain, nor was it fostered in his heart. I anxiously watched his last sickness, so very brief. I waited for the tidings from his bedside, and, when they were reassuring, I was glad. The shock of the news of his death I can never feel again. They said that his heart was affected. I knew that it was. I knew that it was broken.

The historian of the future, in looking over the pages of the glorious history of the men of our mother State, will find one page on which is written simply this, "Joseph Kirkland Alston; he tried to do his duty." Ah, what a glorious page that would have made had his life desire been granted. No figure in South Carolina's history would have been more symmetrical. If he had been permitted to see hard fighting in Cuba and to come back to his State, his name would have been on every lip, the choicest laurels would have crowned the brow now wreathed in cedar and immortelles.

He tried to do his duty. Being but human, I sometimes wondered if he were right in some things which he did. I know that he had his faults. I know that he had weaknesses, weaknesses which have been exaggerated by maligning tongues. There never was a mountain without its outlying valleys, with the impotent streamlets seemed striving to tear away the grandeur of the pile thrown up in nature's throes. There never was a life which had graces rising above the common level, without the feeble encroachments of an occasional weakness. Alston's graces were never properly realized by his friends, his weaknesses were too vividly pictured by those who did not know him, and that is why he died broken-hearted.

I have seen him order men under arrest, and have seen the evidences of pain in his face, but it was his duty. I have seen him release men from arrest, not to gain their favor, as others did, but because he grieved for them and hoped to see them bettered. I have seen him in cold, precise and decided tones censure men for whom he had the highest regard, and have seen him pained because they thought that he had overstepped the bounds of his duty, or had let personal feeling decide his course. I have seen him, mistaken, censure those under his charge, and when convinced of his mistake humbly and manfully make restitution. I have seen him slip off to the hospital with tempting broths. I have seen him without display working for the sick in his command; I have seen him dismount on the march to give his canteen to a poor sick fellow on the wayside; I have seen many evidences of the human kindness which he shielded from the public gaze, hoping to do good and not to appear as one who expected a return from his acts of kindness. Poor fellow, it might have been better had he made a display of gentleness and tenderness of the man which was hidden under the cold reserve of the commander. Long after taps have been sounded and his men were peacefully sleeping, I have watched him studying his text books of war, or have heard him discussing what was best for his men. Some might have thought him cold and selfish, but he was full of heart and soul and intellect. He loved his regiment, he loved his men, and had he lived long enough they would have idolized him.

But what was noblest of all in Joe Alston was his love for his sweetheart wife. No courtier could have been more deferential to his queen, no lover more considerate of his mistress, than was he of her happiness and comfort during the months when she so bravely faced the sickness and suffering, the toil and trouble of camp life.

I did not know that I loved him so until he was dead, and I but speak the thought of him dead which he living created in my heart. I was close to him in his administration, but he was the same toward me that he was toward other private soldiers. I had my duties, and he exacted faithful performance, and that uncompromisingly. Should I be prone to ask unnecessary favors, he would kindly but firmly refuse. For that I now admire him the more. This is not mere praise of the man, but an encomium which is his due, on account of the peculiarly trying circumstances which surround his last few broken days. WILLIAM BANKS.

As a fitting close to what has been said in memory of a noble man and gallant soldier, the following pathetic and lofty tribute is added. It is the product of the gifted pen of Mr. N. G. Gonzales, editor of The State, Col. Alston's true friend, and was written and published a few days after his death:

"DIED IN THE SERVICE—JOSEPH K. ALSTON.

Died in the service! As truly a sacrifice to patriotism as if he had fallen at the head of his regiment in the charge up the hill of San Juan or met his fate in a Santiago hospital, Joseph K. Alston, Colonel of the First South Carolina, died yesterday morning. For he brought with him from the camp where duty had held him the seeds of the disease from which he sunk, still a soldier, still in the service.

The State which went out yesterday was freighted with sorrow for the thousand friends that Joe Alston had in South Carolina, for he was widely known and widely loved. His warm, magnetic character drew to him hearts wherever his hands clasped with other hands, and the hope and promise of his life had many kindly watchers.

He was a soldier by nature. To that career both taste and training drew him. He had the ambition to do brave deeds and to win for himself a name in the annals of his State. More than a year ago he had in thought the raising of a company in South Carolina with which to take service in the Cuban army, in whose cause he deeply sympathised, and he was only restrained in this project by proof of the fact that such reinforcement was not needed and would not be accepted. When he was appointed Colonel of the First South Carolina he came radiantly into the office of The State and declared with emphasis that he would rather have that post than hold any civil office in the gift of the people.

Had it been his fortune to reach his goal, the bloody soil of Cuba, we all well knew how proudly he would have led his men to the charge, with what coolness and courage he would have met the crises of the campaign. There he would have preferred to fall under the blue banner of his State and with the shout of triumph to tell him as he passed away that he died for South Carolina, for his country and for the world-wide cause of humanity.

It was not to be. In suffering, but in the peace of home he was to give up his spirit; yet none the less did he die in the good cause and none the less will his people honor his memory."

The reminiscent sketch and itinerary of the movements of the 1st Regiment throughout its period of service is minutely and vividly pictured by Col. John D. Frost (who was first appointed Adjutant, and afterwards promoted to Major in the regiment), and I feel sure will prove of special interest to his brother comrades of the First. The regiment was mustered out of the service November 10th, 1898, at Columbia, S. C.

SECOND REGIMENT.

What has been said all through the annals of American history of the courage and patriotism of South Carolina troops may justly be applied to the 2d South Carolina Regiment furnished by the State in the Spanish-American War: "No truer, nobler, braver, more devoted and self-denying body of men" ever marched to war in defence of their State and country than that gallant band of South Carolinians commanded by Col. Wilie Jones.

The sketch and reminiscences written by Col. Jones are replete and interesting, covering in detail every movement of the regiment from the beginning to the ending of its career in the national service, and, therefore, leaves the writer without a text to elaborate further than to see that certain incidents and writings of compliment to the officers and enlisted men of the regiment be preserved in this book as of special interest to the men that composed the regiment, and to their friends and relatives, more than to the casual reader. The 2d Regiment was the only portion of our troops that had the distinguished honor of treading foreign soil. As a part of the 7th Army Corps, commanded by Gen. Fitz. Lee, the 2d Regiment was ordered to break camp at Savannah about January 1st, 1899, and on January 6th, it arrived at the harbor of Havana, where the troops were disembarked the following day, January 7th, 1899. The career of the regiment during its stay in Cuba, a period of nearly two months, was no doubt full of interest to the boys, and if the tales of interest treasured in the memory of each member of the regiment, and no doubt told o'er and o'er again to eager listeners around the family fireside since their return, could be gathered together, a larger book than this will be would not contain them. I regret that a more exhaustive account of the regiment's Cuban experience does not appear in the book. It was while the regiment was in Cuba that the officers and men were thrown in direct presence and daily contact with the commander of the corps, Gen. Fitzhugh Lee, and it was there that the acquaintance of commander and men ripened into the greatest respect and friendship. Could it be otherwise with men who were descendants of sires that fought with Lee and Jackson? The fact that Gen. Lee had led many of their fathers in the Confederate struggle and had lived (the hero of two wars) to command their sons, was sufficient to establish that patriotic confidence and love for each other that counts when the battle is on, far beyond the slavish fear inculcated by a discipline of military tyranny. Gen. Lee's praise of the 2d Regiment was the subject of remark on many occasions, and to show the confidence he imposed in their grit and courage should the crucial test arise, he was heard to remark just before their departure from Cuba as the regiment passed him in review for the last time, "I know those boys. I was in the Confederate Army for four long years with the fathers of the men who compose that regiment; I know of what stuff they are made, and you may depend upon their fighting at any time and under any circumstances." It may be said with perfect fairness and truth that the love and respect entertained by the men of the 2d Regiment for their field officers was almost phenomenal, and especially was it constantly in evidence as to their Colonel. It was the reciprocation of love, care and admiration of the commanders for the men and the men for the commanders that proved the mighty force of Lee, Jackson, Hampton, Butler and others in the great struggle of the States, and caused the most remarkable record of wars to be written in the whole history of the world—a people of 7,000,000 population overcome in a war of four years duration, the most terrific struggle of modern times, and yet never suffered a complete defeat in a single important battle from Sumter to Appomattox.

As an evidence of the warmth and admiration the men of the 2d Regiment had for their Colonel and the ties of love that had been cemented by his vigilance for their care and comfort, I am led to insert the following happy incident, taken from "The State:"

Col. Jones' Magnificent Sword.

Yesterday afternoon, exercises which were quite interesting occurred in the camp of the 2d South Carolina Regiment, in front of Col. Jones' tent. The occasion was the presentation of a beautiful gold-mounted, embossed sword to Col. Wilie Jones by the enlisted men of the regiment. On the handsome scabbard were the words,

"Presented to
Col. Wilie Jones,
Second South Carolina, U. S. V. I.,
by the
Enlisted Men of His Regiment,
April 17th, 1899."

The beautiful steel blade also bore the Colonel's name.

Sergeant Major Frank Frederick, of Orangeburg, made the presentation speech in the following appropriate words:

"Col. Jones, in behalf of the enlisted men of your regiment, it gives me the greatest pleasure to extend their heartfelt thanks to you for their kindness to them. We know that the hardships of the soldiers fell heavily on your shoulders. You have ever treated us as soldiers and gentlemen, and more than this, you have been a friend to every man in your regiment. We present you this sword as a token to ever show that a thousand hearts beat in gratitude for your kindness."

Col. Jones thanked the men for their token, saying it was the handsomest blade and scabbard he had ever seen, and that never before had he appreciated anything as he did this gift. That since the enlistment of the men he had done all in his power for the men and the regiment, and to know that his efforts had ever been appreciated was well worth any trouble he had undergone. When the regiment left for Cuba he had made a promise to himself to try and bring it safely back to Columbia to be mustered out, and although he had failed in this, he had brought it to the next best place, here in Augusta.

Several days ago he saw Governor Ellerbe and the Governor congratulated the regiment on the record it had made. This was natural that the men of the regiment, who were nearly all the sons of veterans, should make a record not excelled by any in the 7th Army Corps. He then read letters from Gen. Keifer and Gen. Douglass complimenting the regiment. He said that he was glad that not once had he been compelled to use harsh words to a man in the regiment, and not once had a man hesitated to obey one of his commands.

He concluded by saying: "When I return to my home, and you all know where it is, I intend to ask my wife to fix up a room and put over the door a sign, 'For the boys of the 2d South Carolina.' This will be meant for you, every man in the regiment, and whenever you come to stay with us we will be glad to see you. If a few come, they can use the room, and if the whole regiment comes, we can go out in my old field and camp again like we have for the last ten months. Remember, boys, I want you to come and see me."

After the ceremonies of the presentation of the sword, the 2d South Carolina Survivors' Association was formed, and the following officers elected for the first term:

President—Col. Wilie Jones.
First Vice-President—Lieut. Col. Henry T. Thompson.
Second Vice-President—Major Havelock Eaves.
Third Vice-President—Major J. J. Wagener.
Fourth Vice-President—Corp. Owen, of Co. C.
Secretary—Sergt. Major Frank Frederick.
Treasurer—Capt. J. L. Perrin.
Executive Committee—Co. A, Lieut. E. R. Cox; Co. B, Lieut. R. Lawton Dargan; Co. C, Lieut. H. L. Spahr; Co. D, Lieut. J. Kelly; Co. E, Lieut. J. W. Culler; Co. F, Lieut. Houze; Co. G, Lieut. Dukes; Co. H, Lieut. Jas. C. Cheatham; Co. I, Lieut. C. J. Epps; Co. K, Sergt. J. A. Berry; Co. L, Lieut. T. S. Moorman; Co. M, Lieut. W. T. Ellerbe; Staff, Capt. L. M. Haselden; Hospital Corps, Dr. J. E. Poore; Band, Sergt. Eskew.

At a subsequent meeting held in April, 1899, at Columbia, S. C., the first meeting to occur after its formation, the same officers were re-elected for another year. The admirable address of Col. Jones on that occasion will be of interest to the survivors, as well as the details also included.

The Men who Went to Cuba—Reunion of the 2d South Carolina Regiment Volunteers, U. S. A.

The meeting was called to order by Col. Jones, who commanded the regiment, and who delivered the following address:

Fellow-soldiers: In accordance with the resolution passed at the mass meeting of the regiment in Augusta, Ga., a few days before we were mustered out of the service of the United States as soldiers, you are assembled here to-day.

It is for you to say what shall be done to perpetuate the memories of the past and keep up the touch of the elbow, and to keep alive the strong friendships we all formed with each other while in the army. It gives me the greatest pleasure to welcome you all to this city, and to say to you that I have not words to express to you the great pleasure it gives me to look into your brave and honest faces, and to shake you by the hand.

On June 27, 1898, I had the distinguished honor of being appointed your Colonel, and I say without hesitation that I consider it the greatest honor ever conferred on me. When the call was made by the President in the spring of 1898 you responded promptly and entered the United States army to help the down-trodden and much-abused Cubans, and I honor you for it. You have been faithful in all your duties as soldiers. No soldiers ever stood to their commanding officer better than you did to me, and it is for you to say whether I did all I could for you. I certainly tried to do all in my humble power to make your service in the army as agreeable as possible. I never issued an order to you that you did not quickly obey, and you always obeyed my orders in such a way as to make it a pleasure to issue them to you. I do not think there is a man in this regiment who doubts for one moment that I ever issued an order which was unpleasant or hard to execute unless I was compelled to do so by superior authority. I felt towards you all just the same as if you had been my children, and did all in my power for your good. I am satisfied you appreciated what I tried to do for you. Now that it is all over I can speak plainly to you about my anxiety for your health before leaving Savannah for Cuba. From what I had always heard of Cuba I thought that perhaps one-half of the regiment would die of yellow fever before returning to this country, and a friend of mine said to me in Savannah that he was satisfied the anxiety in the regiment about yellow fever was so great that when the order should be issued for the regiment to go to Cuba that hundreds would desert. But, my fellow-soldiers, let me tell you that when that order came to board the transport Roumanian for Havana, on January 3, 1899, I marched the regiment on the boat eight hundred and forty strong, and not a single man deserted. I am sure this record cannot be beaten by any regiment in the world, and I am proud of it.

Now let us form ourselves into a regular organization, elect officers and appoint such committees as we may need. Let us contribute annually to a fund to be kept for the purpose of assisting such of us as may become unable to get along in the world—no man can tell when want may strike him. Let us accumulate a fund to erect a monument on the Capitol grounds to the sixteen noble young men who lost their lives by disease while members of the regiment, and while performing their duty to their country. Let us have inscribed upon that monument that no man ever lost his life in a holier or grander cause than that of volunteering to help drive the Spaniards from that down-trodden and much-abused Island of Cuba.

Three of our members died in Cuba, namely: Epting, Trevett and McKay, from disease contracted in the hot, burning sun of that country. Their bodies are buried in the military graveyard just a half-mile north of Marianao. I think that a committee should be appointed to see to it that their bodies are brought home in the near future by the government and buried in their native soil. The thirteen other members of the regiment who died, namely: Griffin, Epton, Mooney, Covington, Smith, Bluer, Lyles, Hopkins, Ward, Meetze, Barton, Finley and Kitchen, are buried in the United States. The bodies of all these were sent to their parents.

On January 17, 1899, we buried a boy fifteen years old, named Bertie Eastman, who was drowned the day before in the little river near our camp in Cuba. He could not swim, and rode a mule into deep water and was drowned. He was not an enlisted member of the regiment, but had left Savannah with us as a camp follower. I have never to this day been able to find his parents, and his body is now in the military graveyard north of Marianao, with the bodies of the other three members of our regiment. I think we should make an effort to find the parents of this poor boy and let them have his body brought home. I doubt if his parents have ever heard how he died. It was one of the saddest acts I had to perform while in the army—burying this poor, unknown boy.

The death rate in our regiment was less than in almost any other regiment in the 7th Army Corps, and this was due in a large measure to our faithful and efficient Surgeon, Dr. Wannamaker; his able assistants, Drs. Griffith and Poore, and our ever faithful hospital corps. They were untiring in their attention to the sick. I feel that I am in a position to tell of their faithful performance of duty, as I made it a rule to go to the hospital almost daily. The boys always told me they had everything they wanted. The parents of those of our men who died can always rest assured that they had every attention that could be given them.

After we had been at Panama Park about three weeks our sick list reached the alarming number of two hundred and four. I became very much troubled about it, and I at once had a conference with Dr. Wannamaker. We sent a telegram to Governor Ellerbe telling him of the alarming condition of the regiment and asking him to telegraph to the Secretary of War to have us moved at once. The Governor telegraphed the Secretary of War and I was ordered to take the regiment to Savannah in ten days afterwards. Our regiment was the first to arrive at Savannah. The men of this regiment should always have the kindest feelings for Governor Ellerbe, for he was always a great friend to us. On my return from Cuba I called on Governor Ellerbe and he said to me: "I congratulate you and your regiment on the splendid record the regiment has made in the United States Army." I thanked him and told him I agreed with him so far as the regiment was concerned.

In conclusion, I beg leave to extend my most heartfelt thanks to all the officers and enlisted men of the regiment for their uniform kindness and courtesy to me while I had the honor of commanding them.

Col. Jones' address was liberally punctuated by outburts of applause, and at its conclusion the comrades assembled gave three hearty cheers for their gallant Colonel and the regiment.

On motion of Adjt. Haselden, it was resolved that the members, in order to keep alive the memories and fires of patriotism of the regiment, meet annually in social reunion in the city of Columbia on Wednesday of every Fair Week and participate in a grand banquet. This motion was adopted amid intense enthusiasm.

On motion of Capt. Herbert, of Co. C, the officers of the association who were elected at the meeting in Augusta were re-elected for the ensuing year. They are as follows: President, Col. Jones; Vice-Presidents, Major Eaves, Major Wagener, Lieut. Col. Thompson, Corp. Owens; Secretary, Sergt. Major Frank Frederick; Treasurer, Capt. Perrin.

On motion of Sergt. King, Co. A, the address of Col. Jones will be made a part of the permanent record of the association.

On motion of Capt. Herbert, the President was authorized to appoint an Executive Committee to consist of five members, the President to be Chairman, to make arrangements for carrying out the scheme of annual reunion, and that said committee be empowered to appoint sub-committees to arrange the details of the banquet, &c.

On motion of Capt. Herbert, a committee was appointed, consisting of Col. Jones, Major Eaves and Capt. Haselden, to confer with the Governor and make arrangements to bring home the bodies of the members of the regiment who died in Cuba.

On motion of Private W. M. Carter, of Co. B, a committee was appointed, consisting of Major Eaves, Capt. Haselden, Capt. Herbert and Private Carter, to draft resolutions of respect to the memories of the late Governor Ellerbe and the members of the regiment who died in service, said committee to report at the next annual meeting.

Capt. Haselden announced that on the day the regiment was mustered out in Augusta, a brigade officer had turned over to him $33, the same being accrued profits of the regimental bakery. He was at a loss to know what disposition to make of the money, and asked for instructions.

On motion of Major Eaves, the money was ordered turned over to the committee on annual reunion and banquet, which committee Col. Jones will appoint later.

During the meeting informal, but felicitous, remarks heartily endorsing the idea of the annual reunion and banquet were made by Major Eaves, Capt. Moss, Capt. Haselden, Capt. Herbert, Lieut. Cox, Sergt. Parrott and others.

The entire occasion was a very happy one. The exchange of greetings between the assembled comrades in arms was extremely cordial, and friendships formed in the camps in South Carolina, Florida, Cuba and Georgia were renewed and cemented.

The meeting adjourned with three hearty cheers for the gallant 2d South Carolina Regiment and its popular and beloved Colonel.

The regiment was mustered out of the service April 19, 1899.

August Kohn,
Special Detailed "War Correspondent" of

The News and Courier.

Charleston, S. C.

August Kohn, War Correspondent for "The News and Courier."

When the 1st Regiment left Camp Ellerbe, Columbia, for Chickamauga, preparatory to being ordered to Cuba for service, as the regiment believed it would be, it was accompanied by Mr. August Kohn, Columbia representative of The News and Courier, as war correspondent for that paper. Though the regiment never actually experienced the carnage of battle nor many of the hardships of war, it would have made a glorious record if it had. Though Mr. Kohn's duty under such circumstances would not have led to the attainment of military renown, no one who knows him doubts that he would have achieved lasting fame as a war correspondent, and would have ranked far above some men who to-day through the constant self-advertisement of their achievements hope to be considered successors of the great correspondents of the first and latter parts of the century. Though the opportunity was not given him of thus distinguishing himself, nevertheless he won equally as much glory, in one sense, in reporting fully and accurately the life of the soldier boys in camp—for the dear ones at home cared not so much just then as to what was happening in Cuba, as to how their loved ones were faring in camp—how they were enduring the hard life which patriotism called upon them to undergo; whether if sick they were receiving kind attention, or if well whether really they would in the end have to face the bullets of the Spanish army. It was in keeping the people at home so well informed as to all these matters, often in the smallest particulars, that won for Mr. Kohn the heartfelt gratitude of hundreds of families in South Carolina. Mr. Kohn was not a member of any company, yet he was a member of all, paradoxical as it may seem—for he was here, there and everywhere in the camp of the regiment, keeping in touch night and day with officers and men. It was in such a manner that he secured data for his letters and telegrams in The News and Courier, which were looked for daily by the home folk, because they soon realized that what he wrote was a complete account of the happenings in the camp. And it was no easy task, but with indefatigable zeal and amid many discomforts Mr. Kohn pursued his work, expecting no reward, though he did receive one greater than riches, the benediction of his fellow-citizens.

Mr. Kohn went fully prepared to go to Cuba, and had a permit from the Secretary of War to accompany the regiment to the front as correspondent. When the regiment left Chickamauga for Jacksonville he returned to his work at Columbia, awaiting orders for the regiment to go to Cuba or elsewhere, but such orders did not come. But Mr. Kohn's reputation as a newspaper man was made long before the opening of the Spanish War, for though young in years, he is recognized as one of the ablest journalists in the State. That has been his life work, and the signature "A. K." in The News and Courier is a familiar one all over the State. He has aptly and justly been described as "a journalist worthy of all praise and a model for emulation."

Mr. Kohn was born in Orangeburg, February 25, 1868. He is a son of Mr. Theodore Kohn, a well known merchant of that city, and who is a Confederate veteran, having served with the Edisto Rifles, Twenty-fifth S. C. V. He was wounded in the service of his country. Mr. Kohn's early life was spent in his native city. His primary education was received in the celebrated school of Prof. H. G. Sheridan. After leaving that school he spent one year in New York, and entered in 1885 the South Carolina College, taking a literary course. In 1888 he won the debater's medal in the Clariosophic Society. Even while at school in Orangeburg he had won prizes for debating and declamation, carrying on his victories to the higher institution. His first newspaper work was done on The Carolinian, the college magazine, of which he was first managing editor, becoming in 1889 the editor-in-chief. He graduated in June, 1889, receiving the degree of B. A., with distinction.

It was his original intention to be a lawyer, but circumstances prevented, and it was in the year of his graduation that he did his first work for The News and Courier. Mr. N. G. Gonzales, then manager of the Columbia bureau, was attacked with typhoid fever. Recognizing Mr. Kohn's ability he secured him to take charge of the bureau, which he conducted most acceptably until college opened in October. Instead of studying law he accepted a position in Charleston with The News and Courier as one of the local reporters. He gradually rose in his profession and on February 14, 1892, he took charge of the bureau of The News and Courier in Columbia.

Mr. Kohn will always be remembered by the officers and soldier boys of the 1st (as well as by their wives and mothers), for the correct and truthful way in which he conducted his correspondence as reporter for the regiment. Mr. Kohn is now a Lieutenant Colonel on Governor McSweeney's staff, and in him the Governor has a competent aide, and the military an ardent supporter. His honesty and accuracy as a newspaper man is acknowledged throughout the State, as well as his integrity and worth as a citizen and true Carolinian.

William Banks (Co. G),
Correspondent

Columbia, S. C.

William Banks, War Correspondent for "The State."

Mr. William Banks, the war correspondent of The State, was also a member of the Catawba Rifles, of Rock Hill. He was City Editor of The Columbia Register when the war with Spain was declared. Mr. Banks immediately resigned his position as City Editor and enlisted as a private in the Catawba Rifles, one of the crack companies of the 1st Regiment. This company was the first company in the State to volunteer, and was awarded a silk flag for the most popular company in two regiments. It is also claimed that it carried a larger number of members of the State militia into the service than any other company in the State.

Mr. Banks was elected Corporal in his company, and a few days afterwards appointed chief clerk at Col. Alston's headquarters; he preferred, however, to remain with his company and refused the appointment until his ill health forced him to change his decision and accept the place. Mr. Banks' letters in The State while the regiment was at Chickamauga will never be forgotten by those who read that paper, and many an issue of The State has been filed away in the family archives by the wives and parents of the men of the 1st Regiment. Mr. Banks, as correspondent, chief clerk at headquarters and soldier in the ranks, necessitated the greatest display of keenness of judgment and skillful manœuvring that by his letters he would not give offense, and still write true and correct accounts of the situation and happenings in camp as they daily occurred; but Mr. Banks proved fully equal to the task, although on several occasions by his outspoken, independent way of expression in his home papers, he was on the verge of arrest and court martial. It is said that Mr. Banks' trenchant and truthful letters in the home papers, along with those of his friend, Private Emory Holler (who was also a newspaper correspondent), was the great impetus that led to the muster out of the regiment. Mr. Banks' brilliant and pathetic letters to The State were of general comment, and his glowing tribute to the memory of Col. Joe Alston, which will be found in this book, is a gem of composition of the first waters. Mr. Banks will be long remembered after the buoyant soldier boys have become the old survivors of the 1st.

Mr. Banks is now a member of the editorial staff of The State. His brilliancy as a writer is shown by his army letters; and being a graduate of Davidson College, he is thoroughly equipped by education as well as hard common ability and the gift of expression to fully meet the expectation of his friends and those who know him best in the chosen field of his profession.

Col. James H. Tillman

Field and Staff Officers, First Regiment

Lieut. Col. M. B. Stokes.

Maj. J. H. Earle.

Maj. J. D. Frost.

Maj. J. A. Mood.

Field and Staff Officers, First Regiment

Capt. J. H. Grant.

Capt. J. E. Jarnigan.

Lieut. J. M. Lawson.

Dr. G. W. Nevils.
(Assistant Surgeon.)

Field and Staff Officers, First Regiment

Lieut. J. H. Hardin.
(Battalion Adjutant.)

Lieut. F. G. Tompkins.
(Battalion Adjutant.)

Lieut. Wyatt Aiken.
(Battalion Adjutant.)

Capt. G. W. Bussey.
(Chaplain.)

Historical Sketch and Itinerary of the First S. C. V. I.

(PREPARED FOR GEN. J. W. FLOYD, ADJUTANT GENERAL.)

While resting calmly at anchor in Havana harbor on the night of the 13th of February, 1898, the U. S. Battleship Maine was blown up by a cowardly foe, who after a careful investigation proved to be citizens of the Kingdom of Spain. Congress being in session at the time, the report of the Committee was carefully examined by that august body, and as a result war was declared between the United States and Spain. The President immediately issued a call for volunteers, consisting of 125,000, and South Carolina's quota was fixed at one regiment of infantry, one battalion of infantry, and one battery of heavy artillery. Gov. Wm. H. Ellerbe, Commander-in-Chief of the military forces of South Carolina, in compliance with orders from the President, issued a call for the aforesaid organizations, and only a short lapse of time intervened before the companies that were destined to form the 1st S. C. V. I. were on their way to the place of rendezvous. The question of mobilization was now at fever heat between Gov. Ellerbe, who insisted that the troops would be assembled at Columbia, S. C., and the Secretary of War, who announced Charleston, S. C., as the objective point. Gov. Ellerbe stubbornly held to his first idea—Columbia being the centre of the State and easily accessible by railroad, and in a few days the Washington authorities yielded to his wishes. About two miles from the city of Columbia, at a beautiful suburban village known as Hyatt's Park, which is connected by the electric street railway and a broad macadam road with Columbia, was established the main camp known as "Camp Ellerbe," in honor of Gov. Ellerbe, where the troops composing the 1st South Carolina, were to be assembled and mustered into the U. S. service by Capt. Ezra B. Fuller, 7th U. S. Cavalry, chief mustering officer. On the third day of May, 1898, the Governor appointed the officers of the 1st S. C. V. I., comprising the field and staff, and the rendezvous having been selected at Columbia, things began to put on a more warlike appearance; and on the afternoon of May 3, 1898, the first three companies arrived in Columbia and were soon quartered at Camp Ellerbe. The three companies were the Abbeville Volunteers, the Johnson Rifles, and the Newberry Guards, commanded by Capts. Milford, Hunter, and Langford, respectively. Following in rapid succession came the remaining companies of the

1st S. C. V. I. as follows: the Catawba Rifles, of Rock Hill, Capt. Frel Mobley; the Lee Light Infantry, of Chester, Capt. Jos. S. Hardin; the Greenville Guards, Capt. A. D. Hoke; the Butler Guards, Capt. O. K. Mauldin; the Anderson Volunteers, Capt. H. H. Watkins; the Richland Volunteers, Capt. Chas. Newnham; the Sumter Light Infantry, Capt. L. S. Carson; the Governor's Guards, Capt. B. B. McCreery, and the Palmetto Rifles, Capt. Claude E. Sawyer. Col. Jos. K. Alston assumed command of all the volunteers troops assembled at Columbia, S. C., by the issuing of the following order:

HEADQUARTERS CAMP ELLERBE,
Gen. O. No. 1.   May 7, 1898.

In pursuance of orders received from his Excellency the Governor, I hereby assume command of all volunteer State troops assembled in Columbia, in accordance with the proclamation of the Governor.

Jos. K. ALSTON,
Col. 1st S. C. V. I.

Official:

JNO. D. FROST, Capt. and Adjutant.

Camp Ellerbe being headquarters, there was established a camp at the Fair Grounds, in command of Lt. Col. Jas. H. Tillman, which served as an auxiliary camp for the recruiting and mustering of companies before being sent to Camp Ellerbe. There emanated from the camp at the Fair Grounds an order known as Gen. Order No. 1, which would have caused consternation had it been promulgated before the troops were mustered in, particularly paragraph two, which reads as follows: "All Captains are further ordered to give each and every man in his command a shower bath at one of the hydrants in either of the barracks, at least once a day." "Cleanliness being next to godliness," this was a good order if carried out, and, besides, a very amusing one when read.

The 1st S. C. V. I. volunteered their patriotic services to fight for their country wherever the Stars and Stripes floated, and should they have received the chance, they would have grasped the first favorable opportunity, and by their pluck, heroism, and fighting qualities, instilled and bred in them by their fathers, would have won their laurels and spurs on any battlefield, and would have merited the praise well done. The hardest and most severe battle we had to contend with was the U. S. Surgeons, who had the eyes of an eagle, and facing them was like bringing the ox to the slaughter—as many as fifty men being rejected out of a hundred. One very witty Irish lad, whose eyes and head were being examined, looked up pleadingly at the surgeon and said, "Say, pard, I thought you were examining me for fighting and not butting." The lad was rejected at once without further examination. The battle with the surgeons lasted for several days, and some of the boys eager to obey their country's call, and knowing that their comrades had passed examination, were so intent on being mustered in, that they placed lead and such articles in their pockets, in order that they would not be turned down on weight.

The first man to be accepted and mustered into the service of the United States was Adjt. Jno. D. Frost, Jr., on the morning of the 4th of May, 1898. And in quick succession the officers and companies were made a part of the volunteer army of the United States until June 2d, 1898, when Col. Jos. K. Alston was mustered into service, thus completing the 1st S. C. V. I. The men were then clad in citizen's dress and anxiously awaiting the issuing of uniforms, in order that they might present a more soldierly appearance. The regiment was fed by contract up to the day of muster, and at times the meals were good and at other times very scant, but the officers did all in their power to make things as comfortable as possible. Drilling was immediately commenced, and it was but a short time before material progress was clearly demonstrated. Excellent bathing pools were erected at Hyatt's Park, which were a great source of comfort and pleasure to the men after a hard day's drilling or guard duty, and it is needless to say that they were liberally patronized. During the concentration of troops at Columbia, smallpox was raging, and compulsory vaccination had to be enforced, and in a short while the soldiers of the 1st S. C. were carrying their arms in slings, and for several days drills, etc., were practically suspended; some of the soldiers' arms were a pitiful sight from the effects of vaccination. Evening parades were started in the 1st S. C. camp on the 29th of May, and were largely attended by the ladies of Columbia, which was enjoyed to the fullest extent by all the troops at "Camp Ellerbe," and in the short interval of time that the soldiers had been drilling, it was easy for the officers as well as spectators to see that the 1st S. C. V. I. bid fair to be one of the most efficient regiments in the volunteer service. On the 3d day of June, 1898, Mr. A. G. Knebel had a large tent erected in camp, to be known as the Y. M. C. A. tent, which proved to be one of the greatest benefits in camp, on account of the reading and writing facilities furnished by Secretary Knebel, who was untiring in his efforts to promote the comfort of the soldiers. Mr. Knebel was twenty-five years old, and was born in Texas; the whole regiment became attached to him for his gracious acts of kindness, his indefatigable work, and his gentlemanly conduct to all whose pleasure it was to meet him. The 1st S. C. V. I. was also well provided for in the way of war correspondents, viz: Mr. August Kohn, of *The News and Courier,* and Mr. Wm. Banks, of *The Columbia State.* Mr. Kohn is a son of Mr. Theodore Kohn, a Confederate soldier, of Orangeburg, S. C., and was furnished with a correspontdent's pass signed by R. A. Alger, Secretary of War, May 17, 1898, and countersigned by Maj. Gen. Brooke, 1st Army Corps. Mr. Wm. Banks is a son of Mr. A. R. Banks, of Rock Hill, S. C., a Confederate soldier, and was enrolled as a Corporal in Co. G, 1st S. C. V. I. All honor is due these correspondents, who were with the regiment, and by their careful and diligent work kept the parents, wives, sisters, brothers, and sweethearts in close touch with the boys who went forward to fight for their country wherever duty might call them. Messrs. Kohn and Banks having the distinguished pleasure of representing two of the best and ablest journals in the Southern States, viz: *The News and Courier* and *The State.*

Constant daily drills and guard duty at Camp Ellerbe worked to great advantage towards perfecting the soldiers in the task they had volunteered to perform, and the regiment being mustered in, everybody now rested on the anxious bench, awaiting the orders to move. Telegraphic instructions from the War Department, ordering the moving by rail of the 1st S. C. V. I. from Camp Ellerbe, Columbia, S. C., to Camp Thomas, Ga., had the effect of pouring oil on the troubled sea. The men had long been waiting and anxiously expecting the orders to move, and at parade on the evening of the 5th of June, a General Order was published by Col. Jos. K. Alston, whereby the regiment left Columbia on the 6th day of June, 1898, in four sections, for Chickamauga Park, Ga. The 1st S. C. V. I. left Camp Ellerbe on the afternoon of June 6th, 1898, and marched to the Union depot, where trains awaited their arrival. Along the march the crowds who lined the streets gave the regiment prolonged cheers, and at the depot the crowd was so dense that the soldiers could scarcely board the trains. Two sections left by the South Carolina and Georgia Railroad and the remaining two by the Southern, and arrived at Camp Thomas June 7, 1898. People turned out *en masse* to greet the soldiers as they passed the depots on their way to the front, and at several stations eatables and refreshments were served them by the thoughtful and admiring public. As soon as we reached Chickamauga Park, which would be one of the finest camping grounds in the world if only a few feet higher, the signs of war prevailed on all sides. First was a corral of young mules, branded U.

S., numbering 1,800 or more, and wagons in proportion. Upon reporting to Gen. Brooke, our regiment was assigned to the 1st Brigade, 3d Division, 1st Army Corps, and we marched about two and a half miles through the park to our camp, and were received with vociferous cheers by the regiments already in camp along the route we passed. One regiment, which was stationed close to the turnpike road, yelled out, "Where are you from?" and some of the boys said "South Carolina," in a rather calm voice; when the boys, our neighbors in blue, yelled in a voice that made the welkin ring, "Why don't you say South Carolina?" and you could have heard it for miles. We arrived in our camp late in the afternoon, some of the sections not reaching camp before midnight—consequently everything was "topsy-turvey" until the morning of the 8th of June, when a beautiful camp was laid off and all the tents were pitched, under the directions of Adj. Frost, and the 1st S. C. V. I. was then quartered in a new home among the tall and battle-scarred oaks of Chickamauga Park.

When the regiment arrived at Camp Thomas it had comparatively no equipments, but received many praises for its discipline, etc., as the following quotation from the Chattanooga *Times* will show, in speaking of the 1st S. C. V. I.: "Whatever this regiment may have lacked in the way of equipment, they make up for in discipline, which was far better than that of any other volunteer regiment now at the park. Their manner of leaving the train and receiving coffee reminded one of the regulars, if not better than the regulars. The companies act like parts of a machine, responding readily and easily to every command."

On the 10th day of June, uniforms were issued to the 1st S. C. V. I., and they never came too soon. The boys were elated over the fact that they had only been here three days before a complete uniform was furnished them; and when clad in the regulation blue, they were as fine looking a regiment as any stationed at Camp Thomas, or in the service.

On the 17th of June, 1898, Adj. Frost was talking of the thousand questions asked him a day, when Lieut. Jack Harvard, of Co. K, walked up and consolingly said: "Say, look here, if you don't have anything to do, my friend, just come down my way some time, and see what I have to contend with. They begin just after reveille, with lightning-like rapidity, and here are some of the questions continually asked: 'Do I have to go back on that water detail this morning?' 'How long before breakfast?' 'I never had any supper last night; can't the cook give me a little snack now?' 'I can eat rocks,

I am so hungry.' Then another fellow asks: 'Is that fellow that is going to lend us those three dollars, is he coming over here to Chickamauga?' In a minute another asks: 'Do I have to go on duty?' Another, 'Have you got a stamp?' 'When is the paymaster a coming?' And here is the one that kills: 'Can I resign now, as I did not know what was in those articles of war?' 'Do you have to salute nigger lieutenants?' 'Do you have to dance to every one of those dinky little corporals and sergeants?' And another general question is: 'Do you know who stole my blanket?' This is a sample of the questions propounded before breakfast, and it continues all day until taps at night."

Our regiment had the good fortune to be under the command of excellent officers as brigade commanders—noteworthy among these was General Sanger, who did more to advance the efficiency in drill, etc., than any brigade commander at Camp Thomas. He is considered one of the best soldiers in the United States Army, and clearly proved himself as such in the eyes of the 1st S. C.

The men in our regiment established quite a reputation for themselves at target practice, and when the score was completed stood second at Camp Thomas.

The most welcome visitor of all appeared at camp on the 2d day of July, and left behind him a distribution of $40,000 among the 1st S. C. Regiment, and it goes without saying, that many a soul was made happy and many hearts made glad, as this was our first pay day since the regiment was mustered into service.

The regiment having been thoroughly equipped, it was not long before it was considered the second best at brigade headquarters, and one of the best in the First Army Corps. Gen. Sanger was delighted with the progress made by the 1st S. C., and seemed especially gratified when on division review at Snodgrass Hill, only two of the South Carolina boys had to fall by the wayside, after marching eight miles in the hot sun, while some of the regiments lost as many as 200, from exhaustion. This clearly demonstrates the fact that the largest men do not always make the best soldiers. The quick and wiry step was very noticeable in our regiment, as compared with the others, whose time without warning was caught at 112 to the minute, and that of the 1st S. C. was 121 to the minute, as recorded by Gen. Sanger, while the step required by the regulations is 120 per minute. The 1st S. C. V. I. having worked hard and drilled well at Camp Thomas, and being eager for the fray, were very much gratified when an order came detaching them from the 1st Army Corps and ordering them to Jacksonville, Fla., to join the 7th Army Corps, under Gen. Fitzhugh Lee. The whole camp went wild with enthusiasm, thinking that this move would surely place them on the fighting line in a short while; but, much to their sorrow, they were again sidetracked at Panama Park, Fla. The regiment left Camp Thomas and marched to Rossville, a distance of six miles, and there boarded the trains for Florida on the 28th of July, 1898, and arrived July 29, and in a short while were in camp on the banks of the St. John River—where fishing and bathing were greatly enjoyed after duties were done. Upon our arrival at Camp Cuba Libre, Fla., we were ordered out for parade the next afternoon, and were reviewed by Gen. Hubbard, who proclaimed it the best parade he had witnessed at Panama Park.

The Nebraska regiment was stationed near our regiment, and it was the pleasure of the writer of this article to meet frequently and exchange calls with Wm. J. Bryan, the great statesman, who would draw a figure of stone to him by his personal magnetism. The band of the 1st S. C. V. I. was one of the best in the volunteer service, and was frequently complimented as such. The writer of this article had the honor of commanding the band for a long time, and became very much attached to each member on account of their gentlemanly conduct and general deportment. And I can truthfully say that the 1st S. C. had a band that they might well be proud of and was second to none in the service.

Our regiment remained at Camp Cuba Libre, Fla., until September 21, 1898, when, in compliance with G. O. 130, A. G. O., it was prepared to be mustered out of the service, and left camp in three sections for Columbia, S. C., the place of rendezvous, and arrived on the 22d of September, where we were encamped at "Camp Fuller," named in honor of Capt. E. B. Fuller, until the day of muster-out. The regiment was furloughed for thirty days from September 28 to October 28, inclusive, except a guard and all officers, who were kept on waiting orders, in order that the muster-out rolls might be made out and final settlements made with the Government. Capt. Ezra B. Fuller, in whose hands we were entrusted, was the most gallant soldier and splendid gentleman it has ever been my pleasure to meet; thoroughly competent, courteous, kind and obliging, he won a soft spot in the heart of every soldier. I therefore know that I voice the sentiments of the entire regiment when I say that the 1st S. C. V. I. wishes him a safe and prosperous career, and that our homes are his, whenever he sees fit to again visit the Palmetto State.

The 1st S. C. V. I., who volunteered through patriotic motives to travel the paths emblazoned by their illustrious sires on many a bloody field, and who were deprived of that solemn duty, I know not why, were mustered out of service at Columbia, S. C., on the 10th day of November, 1898, by Capt. Ezra B. Fuller, chief mustering officer. In the writer's opinion, though humble it may be, there never left the borders of the old Palmetto State a regiment more willing to do honor for the cause for which they volunteered, and I am doubly sure that had the chance presented itself the regiment, as a unit, would have merited the praise well done.

Having reached the end of the pleasant task assigned me, of writing a sketch of the 1st S. C. Regiment in the Spanish-American War, of which I was a member, my heart swells with emotion as I retrospect the past, and bring to memory's view the happy scenes, the joyous bivouac, the march, the travels, the sweet associations, the new-made friends grown to be old and true, as only a soldier can understand and appreciate. And still a sadder thought intrudes itself—the Regiment is disbanded, the members scattered here and there, lost in the ever increasing multitude of population, never to be gathered together again as the same old 1st. Some have already "passed beyond the river," and some in distant fields of occupation outside the limits of their native State. Yes, many of us—the large majority, perhaps—will never meet again to grasp the hand, and revive those pleasant memories. But however true the passing reflections, I shall yet hope in this life to meet many of my old comrades of the 1st; and as long as life lasts, I shall never forget the obedience, respect, and deference shown me by all the boys, as Major of the 1st Regiment. And the officers, too, I shall always remember with the deepest respect and friendship, for the courtesy and attention they always extended me. Dear old 1st, a fond adieu! And to officers and enlisted men alike I say, God speed in all the relations of life.

Very truly yours,

JOHN D. FROST,
Major 1st S. C. V. I.

Itinerary First S. C. V. I.

The First S. C. V. I. was enrolled and mustered into service June 2d, 1898. Moved by rail, in compliance with telegraphic instructions from the War Department, from Columbia, S. C., to Chickamauga Park, Ga., a distance of 384 miles, June 6th, 1898. Arriving on the 7th of June, 1898, and was assigned to duty with the 1st Brigade, 3d Division, 1st Army Corps. Moved by rail from Rossville, Ga., to Jacksonville, Fla., July 28, 1898, per Special Order No. 57, A. G. O., 1st Army Corps, Maj. Gen. Wade, a distance of 487 miles, and arrived at Jacksonville, Fla., July 30th, 2 P. M., and was assigned to duty with the 2d Brigade, 3d Division, 7th Army Corps, Gen. Lee. Moved by rail from Jacksonville, Fla., to Columbia, S. C., the place of rendezvous, for muster out, per G. O. 124, A. G. O. Had no casualties in transit, and arriving at Columbia, S. C., September 24, 1898. The regiment was then furloughed for thirty days, per G. O. 130, A. G. O., September 29, 1898—all officers being kept on waiting orders. The regiment was after the expiration of furlough mustered out of service at Columbia, S. C., on November 10th, 1898, by Capt. Ezra B. Fuller, of the 7th U. S. Cavalry, chief mustering officer.

Co. A, 1st S. C. V. I., was organized at Abbeville, S. C., in the month of May, 1898, and mustered into service at Columbia, S. C., June 10th, 1898. Left State Camp at Columbia, S. C., June 6, 1898, by rail for Camp Geo. H. Thomas, Chickamauga Park, Ga., arriving on June 7th, 1898, and remained in camp until July 28, 1898, when company left by rail for Camp Cuba Libre, Panama Park, Fla., arriving July 30th, 1898.

Co. A was detailed on special duty as provost guards at Jacksonville, Fla., from August 13 to August 23, 1898, inclusive. Left Camp Cuba Libre, Fla., September 23, 1898, for Columbia, S. C., by rail, arriving September 24, 1898, where the company was furloughed for thirty days, except a guard, from September 29 to October 29, 1898, per G. O. 130, A. G. O., 1st R. From organization to day of muster-out, this company has not lost a single soldier. At the expiration of furlough, during which officers were on waiting orders, the company was mustered out at Columbia, S. C., November 10, 1898, by Capt. Ezra B. Fuller, Captain 7th U. S. Cavalry.

Co. B, 1st S. C. V. I., was organized May 3d, 1898, at Newberry, S. C., and traveled from thence by rail to Columbia, S. C., where it went into camp, and was mustered into service the 11th of May, 1898. Remained in camp until June 6th, 1898, when it moved by rail, as a part of the 1st S. C. V. I., to Chickamauga Park, Ga., and remained at Camp Geo. H. Thomas, Ga., until July 28th, 1898, when ordered with regiment to Camp Cuba Libre, Panama Park, Fla., and arrived the following day. The company remained in camp at Panama Park, Fla., until September 24, 1898, and then moved by rail with regiment to Columbia, S. C., arriving September 25, 1898. Was then furloughed for thirty days from September 29, 1898, except guard, and all officers on waiting orders. At the expiration of furlough the company was mustered out of service at Columbia, S. C., the place of rendezvous, November 10, 1898, by the chief mustering officer, Ezra B. Fuller, Captain 7th U. S. Cavalry.

Co. C, 1st S. C. V. I., was organized at Anderson, S. C., on April 27th, 1898, and proceeded from thence by rail on May 4th, 1898, to Columbia, S. C., where it was mustered into service May 12, 1898, by Capt. Ezra B. Fuller, chief mustering officer. Remained in camp at Columbia, S. C., until June 6th, 1898, when it proceeded to Camp Thomas, Ga., with the regiment, arriving June 7, 1898, and was attached to the 1st Brigade, 3d Division, 1st Army Corps. Remained at Camp Thomas, Ga., until July 29, 1898, and moved by rail from Rossville, Ga., to Camp Cuba Libra, Fla., and was there attached to the 7th Army Corps, under Gen. Fitzhugh Lee, being in the 2d Brigade, 3d Division. Left Camp Cuba Libre by rail, September 24, 1898, for Columbia, S. C., the place of rendezvous, and was there mustered out of service by Ezra B. Fuller, Captain 7th U. S. Cavalry, on November 10, 1898. Upon arriving at Columbia, the company was furloughed for thirty days from September 29, except a guard and all officers, who were on waiting orders.

Co. D, 1st S. C. V. I., was organized at Chester, S. C., in the month of May, 1898, and left for Columbia, S. C., May 4, 1898, and was there mustered into service May 12, 1898. Moved by rail from Columbia, S. C., to Camp Geo. H. Thomas, Chickamauga Park, Ga., June 6, 1898; and remained in camp until July 29, 1898. From thence moved by rail to Camp Cuba Libre, Fla., and upon arrival was assigned to 2d Brigade, 3d Division, 7th Army Corps. Removed by rail from Camp Cuba Libre, Fla., to Columbia, S. C., September 24, 1898, and was there furloughed for thirty days, from September 29; at the expiration of which the company was mustered out of service by Ezra B. Fuller, Captain 7th U. S. Cavalry. During thirty days furlough the officers were on waiting orders.

Co. E, 1st S. C. V. I., was organized at Union, S. C., and left for Columbia, S. C., May 3, 1898; was mustered into service on the 12th of May, 1898. Left Columbia by rail for Camp Geo. H. Thomas, Ga., June 6th, 1898, and was there assigned to duty with the 1st Army Corps. Left Chickamauga Park July 29, 1898, for Camp Cuba Libre, Fla., and was attached to the 7th Army Corps, under Gen. Lee. Left Florida for Columbia, S. C., the place of rendezvous, September 24, and upon arrival was furloughed for thirty days, except a guard and the officers, who were on waiting orders. At the expiration of furlough, which was from September 20 to October 29, the company was mustered out of service by Ezra B. Fuller, Captain 7th U. S. Cavalry, on the 10th day of November, 1898.

Co. F, 1st S. C. V. I., was organized at Greenville, S. C., April 24, 1898, and left for Columbia, S. C., May 4, 1898, where it was mustered into service May 13, 1898, by Capt. Ezra B. Fuller, chief mustering officer. Remained in Camp Ellerbe, at Columbia, S. C., until June 6, 1898, when it proceeded by rail to Camp Geo. H. Thomas, Ga., and was there assigned to duty with the 1st Brigade, 3d Division, 1st Army Corps. Left Camp Thomas, Ga., July 29, 1898, for Camp Cuba Libre, Fla., by rail, and was assigned to duty with the 7th Army Corps, under Gen. Lee. Left Florida for Columbia, S. C., rendezvous, September 4, 1898. Was furloughed for thirty days from September 29, except guard and officers, who were on waiting orders. Was mustered out of service November 10, 1898, by Capt. Ezra B. Fuller, 7th U. S. Cavalry, at Columbia, S. C.

Co. G, 1st S. C. V. I., was organized at Rock Hill, S. C., and ordered to Columbia, S. C., by rail May 4th, 1898, where it was mustered into service May 14, 1898, by Capt. Ezra B. Fuller, 7th U. S. Cavalry. Moved by rail from Columbia, S. C., to Camp Thomas, Ga., June 6th, 1898, and there remained in camp until July 29, 1898, when it proceeded by rail to Camp Cuba Libre, Fla., and was assigned to 7th Army Corps, under Gen. Lee. Left Florida for Columbia, September 24, 1898, place of rendezvous, and was furloughed for thirty days from September 29, 1898, except guard and officers, who were on waiting orders. At the expiration of furlough the company was mustered out at Columbia, S. C., on November 10, 1898, by Capt. Ezra B. Fuller, 7th U. S. Cavalry, mustering officer.

Co. H, 1st S. C. V. I., was organized at Greenville, S. C., and left for Columbia, S. C., on 4th of May, 1898, where it was mustered into service May 15, 1898, by Ezra B. Fuller, Captain 7th U. S. Cavalry.

On June 6, it proceeded by rail from Columbia to Camp Thomas, Ga., and was assigned to duty with the 1st Army Corps, and remained in camp until July 28, when it proceeded by rail to Camp Cuba Libre, Fla., and was there assigned to 7th Army Corps, under Gen. Lee. Removed to Columbia, S. C., by rail, September 24, 1898, and furloughed for thirty days from September 29, 1898. At the expiration of said furlough the company was mustered out of service, November 10, 1898, by Capt. E. B. Fuller, 7th U. S. Cavalry.

Co. I, 1st S. C. V. I., was organized at Columbia, S. C., and marched to Camp Ellerbe May 3, 1898; was mustered into service May 20, 1898, and remained in camp until June 6, 1898, when it proceeded by rail to Chickamauga Park, Ga., where it was assigned to the 1st Army Corps. Moved by rail, July 28, 1898, from Rossville, Ga., to Camp Cuba Libre, Fla., where it was assigned to the 7th Army Corps. Left Camp Cuba Libre for rendezvous at Columbia, S. C., September 24, 1898, where it was furloughed for thirty days from September 29, 1898, except guards and officers, who were on waiting orders. At the expiration of furlough the company was mustered out of service by Ezra B. Fuller, Captain 7th U. S. Cavalry, chief mustering officer.

Co. K, 1st S. C. V. I., was organized at Columbia, S. C., and mustered into service May 24, 1898, at Camp Ellerbee, by Ezra B. Fuller, Captain 7th Cavalry. Left Camp Ellerbe June 6, 1898, for Chickamauga Park, Ga., with regiment. Remained in camp until July 28, 1898, when it was ordered to 7th Army Corps, under Gen. Lee. Remained at Camp Cuba Libre, Fla., until September 24, 1898, and was then ordered to Columbia, S. C., for muster out. After reaching Columbia by rail, September 25, was furloughed for thirty days from September 29, except guard and officers, who were on waiting orders. At the expiration of furlough the company was mustered out of service by Capt. Ezra B. Fuller, chief mustering officer, November 10, 1898

Co. L, 1st S. C. V. I., was organized at Columbia, S. C., by consolidating two militia companies from Aiken and Bamberg into one company, and on 25th May, 1898, was mustered into service at Columbia, S. C., and remained in camp until June 6, 1898, when it proceeded by rail to Camp Thomas, Ga., where it remained in camp until July 29, 1898, when it was ordered to Camp Cuba Libre, Fla., and arrived there July 30, 1898. On the 2d day of August, a telegram from the War Department announced the muster out of the 1st

S. C. V. I. This company proceeded by rail from thence to Columbia, the place of rendezvous, September 24, 1898. When the company reached Columbia it was furloughed for thirty days from September 29, 1898, except a guard and the officers, who were on waiting orders. At the expiration of the furlough, the company was mustered out of service on November 10, 1898, by Ezra B. Fuller, Captain 7th U. S. Cavalry, chief mustering officer, at Columbia, S. C.

Co. M, 1st S. C. V. I., was organized at Sumter, S. C., May 5, 1898, and mustered into service at Columbia, S. C., May 19, 1898. Left Columbia, S. C., for Camp Thomas, Ga., June 6, 1898. Left Camp Thomas for Camp Cuba Libre, Fla., July 29, 1898. Left Florida for Columbia, S. C., by rail, September 24, 1898. Was furloughed for thirty days from September 29, 1898, except guard and officers, who were on waiting orders. At the expiration of furlough was mustered out of service on the 10th day of November, 1898, by Capt. Ezra B. Fuller, 7th Cavalry, chief mustering officer.

Mr. A. G. Knebel,

Roster of Officers First Regiment

1. Jos. K. ALSTON, 37 years, Colonel, lawyer, Columbia; enrolled May 3, '98; mustered in June 2, '98; died October 21, '98, disease, York.
2. JAS. H. TILLMAN, 28 years, Colonel, lawyer, Edgefield; enrolled May 3, '98; mustered in May 13, '98; promoted to Colonel, *vice* Alston.
1. MARCUS B. STOKES, 30 years, Lieutenant Colonel, First Lieutenant U. S. A., Early Branch; enrolled May 4, '98; mustered in May 12, '98; promoted to Lieutenant Colonel, *vice* Tillman.
1. JOHN H. EARLE, 25 years, Major, lawyer, Greenville; enrolled May 3, '98; mustered in May 15, '98.
2. JOHN D. FROST, JR., 27 years, Major, cotton-buyer, Columbia; enrolled May 3, '98; mustered in May 5, '98; promoted from Adjutant to Major, *vice* Stokes.
3. JULIUS A. MOOD, 44 years, Surgeon, physician, Sumter; enrolled May 6, '98; mustered in May 6, '98.
1. GEO. W. BUSSEY, 52 years, Chaplain, minister, Parksville; enrolled May 7, '98; mustered in June 2, '98.
1. Jos. H. GRANT, 29 years, Adjutant, lawyer, Anderson; enrolled May 4, '98; mustered in May 12, '98; promoted from Lieutenant Co. C to Adjutant, *vice* Frost.
1. Jos. E. JARNIGAN, 46 years, Quartermaster, physician, Toby; enrolled May 3, '98; mustered in May 9, '98.
1. JNO. M. LAWSON, 28 years, Assistant Surgeon, physician, Union; enrolled May 4, '98; mustered in May 4, '98.
2. JOHN P. YOUNG, 28 years, Assistant Surgeon, physician, Richburg; enrolled May 4, '98; mustered in May 4, '98; resigned October 15, '98.
1. JESSE H. HARDIN, 22 years, Battalion Adjutant, merchant, Chester; enrolled May 3, '98; mustered in June 1, '98.
2. FRANK G. TOMPKINS, 23 years, Battalion Adjutant, lawyer, Columbia; enrolled May 5, '98; mustered in May 31, '98.
3. WYATT AIKEN, 34 years, Battalion Adjutant, stenographer, Abbeville; enrolled May 3, '98; mustered in June 2, '98; furloughed to accept Battalion Adjutant from Co. A.
3. GEO. W. NEVILS, 29 years, Assistant Surgeon, physician, Blackville; enrolled May 5, '98; mustered in May 26, '98; promoted Assistant Surgeon, *vice* Young.
1. LUTHER M. HASELDEN, 25 years, Sergeant Major, student, Sellers; enrolled May 6, '98; mustered in June 3, '98; discharged to accept commission.
2. TONY B. LUMPKIN, 35 years, Sergeant Major, railroad agent, Rock Hill; enrolled May 4, '98; mustered in May 14, '98; promoted, *vice* Haselden, discharged.
1. JAS. C. DUNCAN, 27 years, Quartermaster Sergeant, stenographer, Newberry; enrolled May 5, '98; mustered in June 2, '98.
1. EMIL WALD, 27 years, Chief Musician, clerk, Orangeburg; enrolled May 5, '98; mustered in June 2, '98.
1. JOHN M. BLAINE, 22 years, Principal Musician, student, Blackstock; enrolled May 5, '98; mustered in June 2, '98.

2. Jos. J. Trowbridge, 23 years, Principal Musician, salesman, Anderson; enrolled May 4, '98; mustered in May 12, '98; transferred to 2d S. C. V. I.
3. Jos. B. Dodd, 18 years, Principal Musician, clerk, Anderson; enrolled May 11, '98; mustered in May 12, '98; appointed Principal Musician, *vice* Trowbridge.
1. Jas. E. Poore, 22 years, Hospital Steward, physician, Lancaster; enrolled May 6, '98; mustered in June 2, '98; discharged to accept commission.
2. John Fox, 21 years, Hospital Steward, druggist, Batesburg; enrolled May 26, '98; mustered in June 2, '98.
3. Hazard Reeves, 21 years, Hospital Steward, pharmacist, Orangeburg; enrolled May 10, '98; mustered in June 3, '98.
4. Wm. J. Taylor, 26 years, Hospital Steward, druggist, Columbia; enrolled May 6, '98; mustered in May 24, '98; appointed Hospital Steward, *vice* Poore.
1. Dargan Bristow, 21 years, private, printer, Spartanburg; enrolled August 2, '98; mustered in August 2, '98; transferred from Co. F to band.
2. Leon P. Brock, 25 years, private, book-keeper, Anderson; enrolled May 4, '98; mustered in May 12, '98; transferred from Co. C to band.
3. Chas. H. Braswell, 24 years, private, carder, Union; enrolled May 3, '98; mustered in May 14, '98; transferred from Co. E to band.
4. Baylis D. Earle, 21 years, private, clerk, Anderson; enrolled May 11, '98; mustered in May 12, '98; transferred from Co. C to band.
5. Saml. P. Fant, 24 years, private, farmer, Union; enrolled May 9, '98; mustered in May 12, '98; transferred from Co. K to band.
6. Rort. H. Hope, private, photographer, Rock Hill; enrolled June 6, '98; mustered in June 18, '98; transferred from Co. G to band.
7. Jas. C. Hughes, 21 years, private, fireman, Abbeville; enrolled May 3, '98; mustered in May 10, '98; transferred from Co. A to band.
8. John T. Hargrove, 23 years, private, lumberman, Laurens; enrolled May 22, '98; mustered in May 24, '98; transferred from Co. K to band.
9. Reuben C. Moorman, 21 years, private, laborer, Columbia; enrolled May 3, '98; mustered in May 20, '98; transferred from Co. I to band.
10. Hasel McKeown, 20 years, private, farmer, Ft. Lawn; enrolled May 4, '98; mustered in May 12, '98; transferred from Co. D to band.
11. Jacob R. Miller, 18 years, private, student, Anderson; enrolled May 4, '98; mustered in May 12, '98; transferred from Co. C to band.
12. Chas. Poore, 19 years, private, clerk, Anderson; enrolled May 7, '98; mustered in May 12, '98; transferred from Co. C to band.
13. Jno. Y. Richardson, private, Charleston; enrolled July 12, '98; mustered in July 12, '98; transferred from Co. G to band.
14. Edgar M. Scott, 27 years, private, farmer, Bushy Creek; enrolled May 4, '98; mustered in May 12, '98; transferred from Co. C to band.
15. Harry T. White, 28 years, private, painter, Newberry; enrolled May 3, '98; mustered in May 11, '98; transferred from Co. B to band.
16. Jas. L. Evans, 43 years, private, carpenter, Union; enrolled May 3, '98; mustered in May 12, '98; transferred from Co. E to band.

Capt. C. A. Millford.

Lieut. F. W. Glenn.

Lieut. J. S. Cochran.

Company A, First Regiment

1. CHAS. A. MILLFORD, 28 years, Captain, druggist, Abbeville; enrolled May 3, '98; mustered in May 10, '98.

1. FRANK W. GLENN, 31 years, First Lieutenant, merchant, Abbeville; enrolled May 3, '98; mustered in May 10, '98.

1. JAS. L. COCHRAN, 29 years, Second Lieutenant, clerk, Abbeville; enrolled May 3, '98; mustered in May 10, '98.

1. THOS. G. WHITE, 21 years, First Sergeant, clerk, Abbeville; enrolled May 3, '98; mustered in May 10, '98.

1. ROBT. B. CHEATHAM, 23 years, Quartermaster Sergeant, teacher, Abbeville; enrolled May 3, '98; mustered in May 10, '98.

1. ANDREW B. EDWARDS, 27 years, Sergeant, clerk, Abbeville; enrolled May 3, '98; mustered in May 10, '98.
2. WM. J. BRYSON, 27 years, Sergeant, merchant, Abbeville; enrolled May 3, '98; mustered in May 10, '98.
3. WM. G. MOSES, 23 years, Sergeant, broker, Abbeville; enrolled May 3, '98; mustered in May 10, '98.
4. EUGENE O. INGRAM, 30 years, Sergeant, merchant, Abbeville; enrolled May 3, '98; mustered in May 10, '98.

1. JAS. A. ALLEN, 31 years, Corporal, salesman, Abbeville; enrolled May 3, '98; mustered in May 10, '98.
2. FRANK H. COTHRAN, 19 years, Corporal, manufacturer, Greenwood; enrolled May 3, '98; mustered in May 10, '98 .
3. JAS. H. PERRIN, 21 years, Corporal, clerk, Abbeville; enrolled May 3, '98; mustered in May 10, '98.
4. ROBT. S. MCCOMBS, 23 years, Corporal, farmer, Abbeville; enrolled May 3, '98; mustered in May 10, '98.
5. JAS A. CALDWELL, 22 years, Corporal, teacher, Due West; enrolled May 3, '98; mustered in May 10, '98.
6. AUGUSTAS B. COCHRAN, 26 years, Corporal, mechanic, Abbeville; enrolled May 3, '98; mustered in May 10, '98.
7. HOWARD L. DICKSON, 23 years, Corporal, fireman, Abbeville, enrolled May 3, '98; mustered in May 10, '98.
8. ALEXANDER BOWIE, 20 years, Corporal, clerk, Abbeville; enrolled May 3, '98; mustered in May 10, '98.
9. WM. F. PERRIN, 27 years, Corporal, clerk, Abbeville; enrolled May 3, '98; mustered in May 10, '98; transferred from Co. L.
10. ALBERT HENRY, 18 years, Corporal, clerk, Abbeville; enrolled May 3, '98; mustered in May 10, '98; promoted from private September 1, '98.
11. GEO. C. GAMBRELL, 25 years, Corporal, printer, Abbeville; enrolled May 3, '98; mustered in May 10, '98; promoted from private September 1, '98.
12. WM. H. WHITE, 19 years, Corporal, merchant, Abbeville; enrolled May 3, '98; mustered in May 10, '98; promoted from private September 1, '98.

1. FRANK W. GREER, 26 years, private, printer, Abbeville; enrolled May 3, '98; mustered in May 10, '98.
2. WM. F. MCDONALD, 39 years, private, tinner, Abbeville; enrolled May 3, '98; mustered in May 10, '98.
3. JAS. L. PEPPER, 39 years, private, farmer, Abbeville; enrolled May 3, '98; mustered in May 10, '98.

1. ABRAM T. ADAMS, 30 years, private, salesman, Edgefield; enrolled May 3, '98; mustered in May 10, '98.
2. ROBERT L. AMMONS, 20 years, private, farmer, Hester; enrolled May 3, '98; mustered in May 10, '98.
3. WM. E. ANDERSON, private, Hester; enrolled June 20, '98; mustered in June 20, '98.
4. JAS. W. BLAKE, private, Ninety-Six; enrolled July 7, '98; mustered in July 7, '98.
5. HENRY L. BROOKS, 28 years, private, machinist, Abbeville; enrolled May 3, '98; mustered in May 10, '98.
6. JOHN H. BROWN, 19 years, private, machinist, Cross Hill; enrolled May 3, '98; mustered in May 10, '98.
7. WM. BUSSEY, 21 years, private, farmer, Parksville; enrolled May 3, '98; mustered in May 10, '98.
8. SAML. C. CALDER, 19 years, private, clerk, Cokesbury; enrolled May 3, '98; mustered in May 10, '98.
9. CHAS. T. CARR, 19 years, private, clerk, Greenwood; enrolled May 3, '98; mustered in May 10, '98.

10. JNO. R. COCHRAN, 24 years, private, farmer, Abbeville; enrolled May 3, '98; mustered in May 10, '98.
11. FRANK J. COLEMAN, private, Greenwood; enrolled July 8, '98; mustered in July 8, '98.
12. WM. T. COLE, 22 years, private, farmer, Greenwood; enrolled May 3, '98; mustered in May 10, '98.
13. JORDAN H. DEAN, 19 years, private, mechanic, Greenwood; enrolled May 3, '98; mustered in May 10, '98.
14. JNO. A. DICKSON, 23 years, private, fireman, Abbeville; enrolled May 3, '98; mustered in May 10, '98.
15. ARCH B. ELLIS, 36 years, private, farmer, Hodges; enrolled May 3, '98; mustered in May 10, '98.
16. WALTER W. EDGE, private, Mt. Tabor; enrolled July 7, '98; mustered in July 7, '98.
17. ALEX. G. FAULKNER, 34 years, private, clerk, Abbeville; enrolled May 3, '98; mustered in May 10, '98.
18. ASHER J. FORDE, 21 years, private, baker, Abbeville; enrolled May 3, '98; mustered in May 10, '98.
19. LESTER L. FORDE, private, Abbeville; enrolled June 26, '98; mustered in June 26, '98.
20. HENRY H. FREEMAN, private, Plum Branch; enrolled June 28, '98; mustered in June 28, '98.
21. CHAS. S. GIBERT, 23 years, private, farmer, Abbeville; enrolled May 3, '98; mustered in May 10, '98.
22. PATRICK R. HENRY, 45 years, private, farmer, Due West; enrolled May 3, '98; mustered in May 10, '98.
23. LUTHER H. HESTER, 23 years, private, farmer, Hester; enrolled May 3, '98; mustered in May 10, '98.
24. MILLEDGE S. HALLMAN, private, Prosperity; enrolled June 20, '98; mustered in June 20, '98.
25. MANSFIELD E. HOLLINGSWORTH, 44 years, private, magistrate, Due West; enrolled May 3, '98; mustered in May 10, '98.
26. THOS. T. HOLLINGSWORTH, 18 years, private, student, Due West; enrolled May 3, '98; mustered in May 10, '98.
27. FRANK C. HODGES, 23 years, private, clerk, Abbeville; enrolled May 3, '98; mustered in May 10, '98.
28. ROBT. M. JONES, 19 years, private, student; Abbeville; enrolled May 3, '98; mustered in May 10, '98.
29. JNO. F. JOHNSON, 28 years, private, clerk, Abbeville; enrolled May 3, '98; mustered in May 10, '98.
30. SIDNEY J. KINSEY, private, Petersburg, Va.; enrolled June 25, '98; mustered in June 25, '98.
31. WM. H. KERR, JR., 19 years, private, clerk, Abbeville; enrolled May 3, '98; mustered in May 10, '98.
32. CAPERS R. KOHN, 20 years, private, farmer, Greenwood; enrolled May 3, '98; mustered in May 10, '98.
33. THOS. W. LANHAM, 28 years, private, farmer, Plum Branch; enrolled May 3, '98; mustered in May 10, '98.
34. ALFRED LYON, 27 years, private, farmer, Hunters; enrolled May 3, '98; mustered in May 10, '98.

35. FRANK T. MCGHEE, 20 years, private, student, Greenwood; enrolled May 3, '98; mustered in May 10, '98.
36. JNO. C. MCCOMBS, private, Hunters; enrolled July 7, '98; mustered in July 7, '98.
37. WM. T. MCILWAIN, private, Abbeville; enrolled July 22, '98; mustered in July 22, '98.
38. JNO. J. MARTIN, 19 years, private, student, Due West; enrolled May 3, '98; mustered in May 10, '98.
39. JNO. S. MILLER, 21 years, private, farmer, Ninety-Six; enrolled May 3, '98; mustered in May 10, '98.
40. SAML. M. MCCRAVY, 35 years, private, sawyer, Cross Hill; enrolled May 3, '98; mustered in May 10, '98.
41. JNO. M. MCKELLER, 28 years, private, farmer, Abbeville; enrolled May 3, '98; mustered in May 10, '98.
42. EUGENE H. MCMILLAN, 24 years, private, farmer, Abbeville; enrolled May 3, '98; mustered in May 10, '98.
43. JOS. L. MORROW, 22 years, private, clerk, Coronaca; enrolled May 3, '98; mustered in May 10, '98.
44. LUTHER H. NICKLES, 25 years, private, clerk, Abbeville; enrolled May 3, '98; mustered in May 10, '98.
45. JAS. W. PAYNE, 18 years, private, farmer, Epworth; enrolled May 3, '98; mustered in May 10, '98.
46. THOS. C. PERRIN, private, Bradleys; enrolled July 7, '98; mustered in July 7, '98.
47. DAVID E. PENNY, 18 years, private, clerk, Abbeville; enrolled May 3, '98; mustered in May 10, '98.
48. ROBT. L. PHILLIPS, 23 years, private, laborer, Abbeville; enrolled May 3, '98; mustered in May 10, '98.
49. JAS. M. POUNDS, 26 years, private, deputy sheriff, Greenwood; enrolled May 3, '98; mustered in May 10, '98.
50. WM. L. PRICE, 20 years, private, merchant, Greenwood; enrolled May 3, '98; mustered in May 10, '98.
51. MILTON B. REESE, 20 years, private, jeweler, Abbeville; enrolled May 3, '98; mustered in May 10, '98.
52. JNO. P. ROBERTSON, private, Calhouns; enrolled July 7, '98; mustered in July 7, '98.
53. JNO. SIMMONS, private, Hardemont, Ga.; enrolled June 29, '98; mustered in June 29, '98.
54. JAS. L. SCOTT, JR., 24 years, private, farmer, Calhoun Falls; enrolled May 3, '98; mustered in May 10, '98.
55. VERNON C. SEAWRIGHT, 22 years, private, mechanic, Abbeville; enrolled May 3, '98; mustered in May 10, '98.
56. ROBT. Y. SIMMONS, 19 years, private, fireman, Abbeville; enrolled May 3, '98; mustered in May 10, '98.
57. MARSHAL L. SMITH, 25 years, private, reporter, Greenwood; enrolled May 3, '98; mustered in May 10, '98.
58. WALTER H. SPEED, 18 years, private, operator, Lowndesville; enrolle˙ May 3, '98; mustered in May 10, '98.
59. JAS. E. TAGGART, 39 years, private, farmer, Mt. Carmel; enrolled May 3, '98; mustered in May 10, '98.

60. JNO. L. TAGGART, 30 years, private, farmer, Wideman; enrolled May 3, '98; mustered in May 10, '98.
61. EDWIN T. TALLEY, 20 years, private, farmer, Cold Springs; enrolled May 3, '98; mustered in May 10, '98.
62. GREEN S. TENNANT, 19 years, private, fireman, Winder, Ga.; enrolled May 3, '98; mustered in May 10, '98.
63. JAS. T. VAUGHN, 42 years, private, farmer, Vaughnsville; enrolled May 3, '98; mustered in May 10, '98.
64. PERRIN B. WATTS, 27 years, private, farmer, Cross Hill; enrolled May 3, '98; mustered in May 10, '98.
65. MARION J. WILEY, 21 years, private, railroad employee, Calhoun Falls; enrolled May 3, '98; mustered in May 10, '98.
66. WM. A. WILSON, 18 years, private, clerk, Abbeville; enrolled May 3, '98; mustered in May 10, '98.
67. JOS. M. WRIGHT, private, Donnalds; enrolled June 24, '98; mustered in June 24, '98.
68. WM. L. WILSON, 22 years, private, farmer, Widemans; enrolled May 3, '98; mustered in May 10, '98.
69. WYATT AIKEN, 34 years, private, stenographer, Abbeville; enrolled May 3, '98; mustered in May 10, '98; furloughed to accept commission.
70. ROBT. E. BRUCE, 22 years, private, shoemaker, Abbeville; enrolled May 3, '98; mustered in May 10, '98; discharged July 1, '98, S. O. 154, A. G. O.
71. MILLEDGE B. MALONE, private, Abbeville; enrolled June 25, '98; mustered in June 25, '98; discharged August 17, '98, by Gen. Lee, 7 A. C.
72. GEO. W. CHANEY, 18 years, private, weaver, Greenwood; enrolled May 3, '98; mustered in May 10, '98; discharged September 1, '98, S. O. 195, 7 A. C.
73. JAS. T. ROWLAND, 38 years, private, machinist, Donnalds; enrolled May 3, '98; mustered in May 10, '98; transferred 3d Div. Hosp. Corps July 19, '98.
74. JAS. P. BOWERS, 21 years, private, weaver, Abbeville; enrolled May 3, '98; mustered in May 10, '98.
75. JAS. C. HUGHES, 21 years, private, fireman, Abbeville; enrolled May 3, '98; mustered in May 10, '98; transferred to band, S. O. 5, Col. Alston.

Capt. W. S. Langford.

Lieut. R. H. Wearn.

Lieut. T. O. Stewart.

Company B, First Regiment

1. WM. S. LANGFORD, 23 years, Captain, merchant, Newberry; enrolled May 3, '98; mustered in May 11, '98.

1. RICHARD H. WEARN, 33 years, First Lieutenant, banker, Newberry; enrolled May 3, '98; mustered in May 11, '98; Ordnance and Commissary G. O. 1 and 6.

1. THOS. O. STEWART, JR., 20 years, Second Lieutenant, coffin maker, Newberry; enrolled May 3, '98; mustered in May 11, '98.

1. GEO. F. WEARN, 27 years, First Sergeant, salesman, Newberry; enrolled May 3, '98; mustered in May 11, '98.

1. GEO. F. SMITH, 28 years, Quartermaster Sergeant, clerk, Newberry; enrolled May 3, '98; mustered in May 11, '98; promoted from Corporal September 22, '98.

1. ALONZO J. COOK, 20 years, Sergeant, clerk, Newberry; enrolled May 3, '98; mustered in May 11, '98.

2. GEO. P. BOULWARE, 20 years, Sergeant, clerk, Newberry; enrolled May 3, '98; mustered in May 11, '98.

3. JNO. F. LANGSTON, 24 years, Sergeant, weaver, Clifton; enrolled May 3, '98; mustered in May 11, '98.

South Carolina Troops in the War with Spain 61

4. WM. E. BLATS, 24 years, Sergeant, druggist, Newberry; enrolled May 3, '98; mustered in May 11, '98; promoted from Corporal September 3. '98.

1. MILTON C. LANCASTER, 27 years, Corporal, book-keeper, Clifton; enrolled May 3, '98; mustered in May 11, '98.
2. DAVID E. SHEPPARD, 25 years, Corporal, pharmacist, Coleman; enrolled May 3, '98; mustered in May 11, '98.
3. ROBT. NORRIS, 23 years, Corporal, student, Newberry; enrolled May 3, '98; mustered in May 11, '98.
4. JOHN H. DAVIS, 24 years, Corporal, printer, Swain; enrolled May 3, '98; mustered in May 11, '98.
5. WM. W. FARROW, 25 years, Corporal, plowman, Greenwood; enrolled May 3, '98; mustered in May 11, '98; promoted from private September 3, '98.
6. RICHARD J. FULLER, 28 years, Corporal, editor, Newberry; enrolled May 3, '98; mustered in May 11, '98; promoted from private September 3, '98.
7. JNO. P. CANNON, 35 years, Corporal, farmer, Prosperity; enrolled May 3, '98; mustered in May 11, '98; promoted from private September 3, '98.
8. LANDY WOOD, 24 years, Corporal, salesman, Milleys; enrolled May 3, '98; mustered in May 11, '98; promoted from private September 3, '98.
9. SILAS L. MEDLOCK, 25 years, Corporal, teacher, Poverty Hill; enrolled May 3, '98; mustered in May 11, '98; promoted from private Septemper 3, '98.
10. JNO. A. FOSTER, Corporal, Brannon; enrolled August 19, '98; mustered in August 19, '98; promoted from private September 3, '98.
11. EARLE SANDERS, Corporal, Cowpens; enrolled August 19, '98; mustered in August 19, '98; promoted from private September 3, '98.
12. ANDREW J. KILGORE, 25 years, Corporal, copper smith, Tacoma Park; enrolled May 3, '98; mustered in May 11, '98; promoted from private September 3, '98.

1. CHAS. P. MIMS, private, Clifton; enrolled July 27, '98; mustered in July 27, '98.
2. WM. B. WERTS, 21 years, private, painter, Newberry; enrolled May 3, '98; mustered in May 3, '98.
3. CASPER C. STEWART, 22 years, private, cabinet maker, Newberry; enrolled May 3, '98; mustered in May 3, '98.
4. JNO. E. OUTZ, 22 years, private, carder, Newberry; enrolled May 3, '98; mustered in May 3, '98.
5. JNO. W. ABRAMS, 26 years, private, farmer, Whitmires; enrolled May 21, '98; mustered in May 23, '98; transferred from Co. L June 19, '98.
6. WALTER ALLEN, 24 years, private, laborer, Pelzer; enrolled May 3, '98; mustered in May 11, '98.
7. WM. M. BEST, 22 years, private, laborer, Whitney, N. C.; enrolled May 3, '98; mustered in May 11, '98.
8. JNO. A. BLATS, private, Newberry; enrolled July 19, '98; mustered in July 19, '98.

9. MIDDLETON S. BODIE, 31 years, private, weaver, Newberry; enrolled May 3, '98; mustered in May 11, '98.
10. JOS. E. BOYD, private, Clinton; enrolled June 26, '98; mustered in June 26, '98.
11. ALSA D. BROWN, 23 years, private, weaver, Clifton; enrolled May 3, '98; mustered in May 11, '98.
12. JNO. L. BROWN, 20 years, private, engineer, Clinton; enrolled May 3, '98; mustered in May 11, '98.
13. JNO. H. BRUCE, 22 years, private, laborer, Spartanburg; enrolled May 3, '98; mustered in May 11, '98.
14. WALTER B. BULLINGTON, private, Clifton; enrolled July 29, '98; mustered in August 19, '98.
15. JNO. O. BRIGHT, private, Spartanburg; enrolled August 19, '98; mustered in August 19, '98.
16. ED. R. CALDWELL, 19 years, private, spooler, Clifton; enrolled May 3, '98; mustered in May 11, '98.
17. CHAS. O. CANNON, private, Ellis; enrolled June 24, '98; mustered in June 24, '98.
18. JNO P. CANNON, 35 years, private, farmer, Prosperity; enrolled May 3, '98; mustered in May 11, '98.
19. JAS. M. CASSIDY, 20 years, private, student, Newberry; enrolled May 3, '98; mustered in May 11, '98.
20. JEFF. D. CHAPMAN, 37 years, private, clerk, Newberry; enrolled May 3, '98; mustered in May 11, '98.
21. ROBT. T. COCKEREL, 23 years, private, salesman, Newberry; enrolled May 3, '98; mustered in May 11, '98.
22. JOS. B. COOLEY, 20 years, private, clerk, Columbia; enrolled May 3, '98; mustered in May 11, '98.
23. JNO. D. COOLEY, private, Clifton; enrolled July 29, '98; mustered in July 29, '98.
24. WM. O. COPELAND, 25 years, private, farmer, Clinton; enrolled May 14, '98; mustered in May 14, '98; transferred from Co. G June 19, '98.
25. CHARLTON T. CROMER, 20 years, private, student, Newberry; enrolled May 3, '98; mustered in May 11, '98.
26. JULIUS G. DANIELS, 21 years, private, jeweler, Newberry; enrolled May 3, '98; mustered in May 11, '98.
27. EDWARD A. DAVIS, 31 years, private, farmer, Hickory; enrolled May 14, '98; mustered in May 14, '98; transferred from Co. G June 17, '98.
28. ROBT. R. DAWSON, private, Clifton, enrolled July 29, '98; mustered in July 29, '98.
29. JESSE. L. DENSON, 34 years, private, farmer, Newberry; enrolled May 3, '98; mustered in May 11, '98.
30. JNO. E. DREHER, 22 years, private, student, Selwood; enrolled May 3, '98; mustered in May 11, '98.
31. JOS. L. EDWARDS, 24 years, private, carpenter, Coleman; enrolled May 3, '98; mustered in May 11, '98.
32. GEO. C. EZELL, private, Cowpens; enrolled August 19, '98; mustered in August 19, '98.
33. ROBT. FINGER, 20 years, private, laborer, Newberry; enrolled May 3, '98; mustered in May 11, '98.

SOUTH CAROLINA TROOPS IN THE WAR WITH SPAIN

34. LEVI E. FOLK, 20 years, private, farmer, Newberry; enrolled May 3, '98; mustered in May 11, '98.
35. THOS. N. FOLK, 20 years, private, farmer, Newberry; enrolled May 3, '98; mustered in May 11, '98.
36. ROWLAND H. GARRISON, 24 years, private, weaver, Clifton, enrolled May 3, '98; mustered in May 11, '98.
37. JESSE T. GEORGE, private, Spartanburg; enrolled August 19, '98; mustered in August 19, '98.
38. FRANK P. GRAY, private, Atlanta, Ga.; enrolled July 9, '98; mustered in July 9, '98.
39. JNO. E. GRIFFITH, 28 years, private, mechanic, Saluda; enrolled May 3, '98; mustered in May 11, '98.
40. ELIJA S. GRISE, 27 years, private, laborer, Spartanburg; enrolled May 3, '98; mustered in May 11, '98.
41. HENRY H. HINSON, 18 years, private, student, Newberry; enrolled May 3, '98; mustered in May 11, '98.
42. MALCOM D. HIPP, 22 years, private, farmer, Whitmires; enrolled May 3, '98; mustered in May 11, '98.
43. CLAYTON F. HOLMES, 28 years, private, carpenter, Clifton; enrolled May 3, '98; mustered in May 11, '98.
44. JAS. E. HOPPER, 19 years, private, laborer, Spartanburg; enrolled May 3, '98; mustered in May 11, '98.
45. POPE D. JOHNSON, private, Jalapa; enrolled July 1st, '98; mustered in July 1st, '98.
46. JOS. H. KEITH, private, Bath; enrolled June 28, '98; mustered in June 28, '98.
47. DAVID V. KIRKPATRICK, 22 years, private, machinist, Union; enrolled May 3, '98; mustered in May 11, '98.
48. WM. T. LIVINGSTON, 27 years, private, carpenter, Newberry; enrolled May 3, '98; mustered in May 11, '98.
49. JAS. J. LONGSHORE, private, Mudlic; enrolled July 6, '98; mustered in July 6, '98.
50. LAIS S. LOVELACE, 18 years, private, flagman, Newberry; enrolled May 3, '98; mustered in May 11, '98.
51. JAS. S. LYONS, private, Clifton; enrolled August 3, '98; mustered in August 3, '98.
52. CLARENCE E. MATHIS, 21 years, private, farmer, Saluda; enrolled May 3, '98; mustered in May 10, '98.
53. JNO. MAYER, 21 years, private, farmer, Peake; enrolled May 3, '98; mustered in May 10, '98.
54. SAML. P. MCCARTY, 19 years, private, farmer, Newberry; enrolled May 3, '98; mustered in May 10, '98.
55. THOS. S. MITCHELL, private, Dennys; enrolled June 22, '98; mustered in June 22, '98.
56. GEO. MOORE, private, Newberry; enrolled June 18, '98; mustered in June 18, '98.
57. JAS. W. NELSON, 33 years, private, farmer, Clinton; enrolled May 3, '98; mustered in May 11, '98.
58. JNO. C. NICHOLSON, private, Harridsville; enrolled June 25, '98; mustered in June 25, '98.

59. SAML. H. PAYSINGER, 32 years, private, sawyer, Newberry; enrolled May 3, '98; mustered in May 11, '98.
60. VANCE V. PEARSOLL, 21 years, private, blacksmith, Newberry; enrolled May 3, '98; mustered in May 11, '98.
61. THOS. J. PEARSON, private, Clifton; enrolled August 3, '98; mustered in August 3, '98.
62. SAML. D. POTTER, private, Spartanburg; enrolled August 24, '98; mustered in August 24, '98.
63. EDDIE P. REDISH, 18 years, private, student, Williams; enrolled May 3, '98; mustered in May 11, '98.
64. EARNEST M. REEDER, private, Charleston; enrolled July 9, '98; mustered in July 9, '98.
65. WM. C. REEDER, 21 years, private, mechanic, Newberry; enrolled May 3, '98; mustered in May 11, '98.
66. RICHARD L. ROBERTS, private, Bridgeton; enrolled July 9, '98; mustered in' July 9, '98.
67. THOS. M. ROEBUCK, private, Newberry; enrolled June 24, '98; mustered in June 26, '98.
68. WM. M. ROBERSON, private, Union; enrolled August 2, '98; mustered in August 4, '98.
69. AUMERLE SCHUMPERT, 20 years, private, student, Newberry; enrolled May 3, '98; mustered in May 11, '98.
70. HENRY L. SIMMONS, private, Newberry; enrolled July 9, '98; mustered in July 10, '98.
71. EDWIN B. SLIGH, private, Newberry; enrolled July 14, '98; mustered in July 18, '98.
72. THEODORE SPEHL, 20 years, private, blacksmith, Newberry; enrolled May 3, '98; mustered in May 11, '98.
73. GEO. B. SUBER, 23 years, private, farmer, Pomaria; enrolled May 3, '98; mustered in May 11, '98.
74. THOS. W. SWINDLER, 22 years, private, harness maker, Newberry; enrolled May 3, '98; mustered in May 11, '98.
75. WM. O. SWINDLER, private, Newberry; enrolled July 18, '98; mustered in July 18, '98.
76. WM. A. TILSON, private, Pacolet; enrolled August 22, '98; mustered in August 22, '98.
77. JEFFERSON TRIBBLE, 21 years, private, painter, Newberry; enrolled May 3, '98; mustered in May 11, '98.
78. GEO. WALL, private, Spartanburg; enrolled August 21, '98; mustered in August 24, '98.
79. MILES A. WALLACE, private, Newberry; enrolled June 26, '98; mustered in June 26, '98.
80. JAS. K. WEEKS, private, Newberry; enrolled June 16, '98; mustered in June 26, '98.
81. THOS. G. WILLIAMS, 40 years, private, machine agent, Helena; enrolled May 3, '98; mustered in May 11, '98.
82. CARLETON WILLIAMS, private, Anderson; enrolled July 9, '98; mustered in July 10, '98.
83. WM. B. WISE, 29 years, private, cotton buyer, Prosperity; enrolled May 3, '98; mustered in May 11, '98.

84. WM. S. WIX, 19 years, private, weaver, Whitney; enrolled May 3, '98; mustered in May 11, '98.
85. WM. P. YARBOROUGH, private, Denneys; enrolled June 22, '98; mustered in June 26, '98.
86. PERRY M. MARTIN, 20 years, farmer, Clinton; enrolled May 3, '98; mustered in May 11, '98; discharged July 6, 1898.
87. THOS. C. MCGAHEE, private, Augusta, Ga.; enrolled July 9, '98; mustered in July 10, '98; discharged July 17, 1898.
88. MARVIN YEARGIN, private, Laurens; enrolled May 3, '98; mustered in May 11, '98; discharged July 6, 1898.
89. MILES STEVENSON, 20 years, private, printer, Spartanburg; enrolled May 3, '98; mustered in May 11, '98; discharged August 17, 1898.
90. RORT. A. MORRISON, 38 years, private, cotton buyer, Chester; enrolled May 3, '98; mustered in May 11, '98; transferred to Co. G.
91. JNO. A. MCCAFFERTY, 37 years, private, laborer, Spartanburg; enrolled May 3, '98; mustered in May 11, '98; transferred to Ambulance Corps July 28, '98.
92. HARRY T. WHITE, 28 years, private, painter, Newberry; enrolled May 3, '98; mustered in May 11, '98; transferred to band July 10, '98.
93. HERBERT HUGHES, 22 years, private, salesman, Peake; enrolled May 3, '98; mustered in May 11, '98; transferred to Hospital Corps July 28, '98.
94. JNO. M. KINARD, 26 years, private, farmer, Newberry; enrolled May 3, '98; mustered in May 11, '98; died July 19, '98, consumption.
95. RORT. ALDRIDGE, 22 years, private, weaver, Newberry; enrolled May 3, '98; mustered in May 11, '98.
96. FRANK J. CLAPP, 36 years, private, weaver, Newberry; enrolled May 3, '98; mustered in May 11, '98.
97. ANDREW T. MCGEE, 21 years, private, weaver, Clifton; enrolled May 3, '98; mustered in May 11, '98.
98. JAS. L. HENDERSON, 26 years, private, laborer, Spartanburg; enrolled May 3, '98; mustered in May 11, '98.
99. ZACK. R. HENDERSON, 20 years, private, laborer, Spartanburg; enrolled May 3, '98; mustered in May 11, '98.
100. HERBERT A. ROSS, 18 years, private, laborer, Spartanburg; enrolled May 3, '98; mustered in May 11, '98.

Capt. H. H. Watkins.

Lieut. J. N. Brown.

Lieut. W. P. Nicholson.

Company C, First Regiment

1. HENRY H. WATKINS, 32 years, Captain, lawyer, Anderson; enrolled May 4, '98; mustered in May 12, '98.

1. JOS. H. GRANT, 29 years, First Lieutenant, lawyer, Anderson; enrolled May 4, '98; mustered in May 12, '98; promoted Adjutant, *vice* Frost.
2. JOS. N. BROWN, JR., 24 years, First Lieutenant, druggist, Anderson; enrolled May 4, '98; mustered in May 12, '98; promoted from Second Lieutenant, *vice* Grant.

1. WM. P. NICHOLSON, 22 years, Second Lieutenant, merchant, Anderson; enrolled May 4, '98; mustered in May 12, '98; promoted from First Sergeant, *vice* Brown.

1. STEVEN E. LEVERETT, 21 years, First Sergeant, student, Anderson; enrolled May 4, '98; mustered in May 12, '98; promoted from Second Sergeant, *vice* Nicholson.

1. BENJ. M. SULLIVAN, 28 years, Quartermaster Sergeant, teacher, Anderson; enrolled May 4, '98; mustered in May 12, '98; promoted from Sergeant, *vice* Johnson.

1. JOHN C. ACKER, 24 years, Sergeant, student, Anderson; enrolled May 4, '98; mustered in May 12, '98.
2. CHAS. W. GENTRY, 21 years, Sergeant, student, Spartanburg; enrolled May 4, '98; mustered in May 12, '98.
3. RICHARD F. DIVER, JR., 19 years, Sergeant, electrician, Anderson; enrolled May 4, '98; mustered in May 12, '98; promoted from Corporal October 26, '98.
4. MILLEDGE L. BONHAM, JR., 18 years, Sergeant, student, Anderson; enrolled May 12, '98; mustered in May 15, '98; promoted from private June 7, '98.

1. HENRY C. MARTIN, 25 years, Corporal, farmer, Anderson; enrolled May 4, '98; mustered in May 12, '98.
2. GEO. T. BAKER, 22 years, Corporal, teacher, Anderson; enrolled May 4, '98; mustered in May 12, '98.
3. CHAS. F. POWER, 26 years, Corporal, clerk, Anderson; enrolled May 4, '98; mustered in May 12, '98.
4. LUTHER E. TATE, 21 years, Corporal, farmer, Anderson; enrolled May 4, '98; mustered in May 12, '98.
5. PAUL E. AYER, 22 years, Corporal, horseman, Olar; enrolled May 4, '98; mustered in May 12, '98; promoted from private September 3, '98.
6. JAS. C. GILMER, 18 years, Corporal, clerk, Anderson; enrolled May 4, '98; mustered in May 12, '98; promoted from private September 3, '98.
7. THOS. B. LEE, JR., 27 years, Corporal, stock dealer, Anderson; enrolled May 4, '98; mustered in May 12, '98; promoted from private September 3, '98.
8. HERBERT C. DAGGETT, 20 years, Corporal, brakeman, Salisbury, N. C.; enrolled May 12, '98; mustered in May 15, '98; transferred from Co. H; promoted September 3, '98.
9. WALTER B. PRATT, 18 years, Corporal, clerk, Honea Path; enrolled May 4, '98; mustered in May 12, '98; promoted from private September 3, '98.
10. ROMUS D. HENDERSON, 18 years, Corporal, salesman, Anderson; enrolled May 7, '98; mustered in May 12, '98; promoted from private September 3, '98.
11. ALFRED M. FORTUNE, 26 years, Corporal, bricklayer, Anderson; enrolled May 4, '98; mustered in May 12, '98; promoted from private September 3, '98.
12. NOEL B. SHARPE, 30 years, Corporal, salesman, Anderson; enrolled May 4, '98; mustered in May 12, '98; promoted from private October 26, '98.

1. JNO. F. TATHAM, 27 years, private, farmer, Walhalla; enrolled May 4, '98; mustered in May 12, '98.
2. JAS. L. HALL, 21 years, private, student, Anderson; enrolled May 4, '98; mustered in May 12, '98.
3. JAS. A. DILLINGHAM, 27 years, private, liveryman, Anderson; enrolled May 4, '98; mustered in May 12, '98.
4. NEWTON H. ACKER, 22 years, private, farmer, Belton; enrolled May 4, '98; mustered in May 12, '98.

5. SAML. W. ADAMS, 33 years, private, carpenter, Anderson; enrolled May 4, '98; mustered in May 12, '98.
6. ABE BLAKELEY, private, Antietam; enrolled June 28, '98; mustered in June 28, '98.
7. JAS. H. BROWN, 21 years, private, clerk, Anderson; enrolled May 4, '98; mustered in May 12, '98.
8. PRUE H. BURRIS, 21 years, private, farmer, Anderson; enrolled May 4, '98; mustered in May 12, '98.
9. JOHN C. BUSBEY, private, Anderson; enrolled July 12, '98; mustered in July 12, '98.
10. CHAS. A. CLINKSCALES, private, Level Land; enrolled June 24, '98; mustered in June 24, '98.
11. WILL W. COCHRAN, 22 years, private, salesman, Anderson; enrolled May 10, '98; mustered in May 12, '98.
12. DANL. B. COLEY, 24 years, private, farmer, Townville; enrolled May 4, '98; mustered in May 12, '98.
13. JNO. DODD, 19 years, private, cotton mill, Anderson; enrolled May 4, '98; mustered in May 12, '98.
14. GEO. W. DAVIS, private, Anderson; enrolled July 12, '98; mustered in July 12, '98.
15. ADOLPHUS A. DUNCAN, 19 years, private, machinist, Seneca; enrolled May 4, '98; mustered in May 12, '98.
16. PAUL R. EARLE, 19 years, private, Hollands; enrolled August 25, '98; mustered in August 25, '98.
17. RUFUS D. EARLE, private, Broyles; enrolled August 25, '98; mustered in August 25, '98.
18. CLYDE N. FANT, 20 years, private, farmer; Boston, S. C.; enrolled May 4, '98; mustered in May 12, '98.
19. PRESTON C. FANT, 21 years, private, printer, Anderson; enrolled May 4, '98; mustered in May 12, '98.
20. ROBT. T. FELTMAN, 27 years, private, farmer, Hollands; enrolled May 11, '98; mustered in May 12, '98.
21. BOARDMAN H. GETSINGER, private, Hampton; enrolled June 28, '98; mustered in June 28, '98.
22. IRA A. GILES, 18 years, private, clerk, Anderson; enrolled May 4, '98; mustered in May 12, '98.
23. ALINON C. HALL, 25 years, private, farmer, Honea Path; enrolled May 4, '98; mustered in May 12, '98.
24. STEVEN F. HOUGH, 18 years, private, druggist, Kershaw; enrolled May 4, '98; mustered in May 12, '98.
25. WM. W. JOLLY, 24 years, private, weaver, Anderson; enrolled May 4, '98; mustered in May 12, '98.
26. EDWIN L. JOHNSON, 35 years, private, oil expert, Fort Hill; enrolled May 4, '98; mustered in May 12, '98; resigned Quartermaster Sergeant August 7, 1898.
27. JAS. P. KILLEBREW, 23 years, private, printer, Anderson; enrolled May 4, '98; mustered in May 12, '98.
28. GEO. W. KING, 23 years, private, farmer, Anderson; enrolled May 4, '98; mustered in May 12, '98.

29. LOUIS O. KING, 20 years, private, farmer, Anderson; enrolled May 4, '98; mustered in May 12, '98.
30. MAURICE E. KING, private, Walhalla; enrolled August 25, '98; mustered in August 25, '98.
31. WM. A. KING, private, Neal; enrolled July 9, '98; mustered in July 9, '98.
32. WM. E. KING, private, Broyles; enrolled August 25, '98; mustered in August 25, '98.
33. ADAM LOSKOSKIE, private, Mountain Creek; enrolled July 9, '98; mustered in July 9, '98.
34. JAY W. MADDEN, 20 years, private, farmer, Pendleton; enrolled May 4, '98; mustered in May 12, '98.
35. JNO. W. MARTIN, 21 years, private, laundryman, Anderson; enrolled May 4, '98; mustered in May 12, '98.
36. REUBEN M. MARTIN, 21 years, private, student, Anderson; enrolled May 4, '98; mustered in May 12, '98.
37. WADE M. MCGEE, 21 years, private, clerk, Anderson; enrolled May 4, '98; mustered in May 12, '98.
38. CLARENCE MURPHY, Anderson; enrolled June 5, '98; mustered in July 18, '98.
39. BUTLER T. NORRIS, 23 years, private, farmer, Tony Creek; enrolled May 7, '98; mustered in May 12, '98.
40. THOS. M. NORWOOD, 29 years, private, carpenter, Anderson; enrolled May 4, '98; mustered in May 12, '98.
41. BENJ. B. O'SHIELDS, 24 years, private, weaver, Anderson; enrolled May 4, '98; mustered in May 12, '98.
42. THOS. E. PRICE, 24 years, private, carpenter, Greenville; enrolled May 12, '98; mustered in May 15, '98; transferred from Co. H June 17, '98.
43. SAM. W. PAYNE, private, Anderson; enrolled July 9, '98; mustered in July 9, '98.
44. ERNEST H. POORE, 18 years, private, clerk, Anderson; enrolled May 4, '98; mustered in May 12, '98.
45. FRANK J. RHODY, 20 years, private, farmer, Anderson; enrolled May 4, '98; mustered in May 12, '98.
46. JNO. T. ROSE, 20 years, private, farmer, Anderson; enrolled May 4, '98; mustered in May 12, '98.
47. JNO. C. ROBINS, private, Anderson; enrolled May 4, '98; mustered in May 12, '98.
48. THOS. R. ROWLAND, 19 years, private, farmer, Newberry; enrolled May 4, '98; mustered in May 12, '98.
49. ETNA P. RUDISEAL, 19 years, private, farmer, Anderson; enrolled May 4, '98; mustered in May 12, '98.
50. MOSLEY E. SEALEY, private, Walhalla; enrolled June 20, '98; mustered in June 20, '98.
51. MARTIN L. SNELGROVE, private, Anderson; enrolled June 25, '98; mustered in June 25, '98.
52. WM. S. SHARPE, 19 years, private, farmer, Anderson; enrolled May 4, '98; mustered in May 12, '98.
53. SANFORD SIMPSON, private, Anderson; enrolled July 12, '98; mustered in July 12, '98.

54. LUTHER G. SMITH, 26 years, private, farmer, Burdine; enrolled May 4, '98; mustered in May 12, '98.
55. MARCELLUS M. STEWART, 23 years, private, clerk, Anderson; enrolled May 4, '98; mustered in May 12, '98.
56. THOS. J. SOUTH, private, Major; enrolled August 4, '98; mustered in August 4, '98.
57. FREDERICK TAYLOR, 21 years, private, engineer, Belton; enrolled May 4, '98; mustered in May 12, '98.
58. CLARENCE E. TOLLY, private, Anderson; enrolled July 9, '98; mustered in July 9, '98.
59. JAS. R. VANDIVER, JR., 20 years, private, farmer, Anderson; enrolled May 4, '98; mustered in May 12, '98.
60. THOS. M. VANDIVER, 24 years, private, farmer, Anderson; enrolled May 4, '98; mustered in May 12, '98.
61. JNO. E. WOOD, 20 years, private, weaver, Anderson; enrolled May 4, '98; mustered in May 12, '98.
62. FRANK H. MORGAN, private, Roberts; enrolled July 16, '98; mustered in July 16, '98; discharged August 13, '98.
63. WM. A. SINKBEIL, private, Anderson; enrolled June 25, '98; mustered in June 25, '98; discharged August 13, '98.
64. ROBT. B. CHESHIRE, 19 years, private, clerk, Anderson; enrolled May 10, '98; mustered in May 12, '98; discharged June 6, '98.
65. THOS. H. BIGBY, 26 years, private, engineer, Honea Path; enrolled May 4, '98; mustered in May 12, '98; discharged September 28, '98.
66. WALTER C. BURRIS, 21 years, private, farmer, Anderson; enrolled May 4, '98; mustered in May 12, '98; discharged September 28, '98.
67. FREDERICK T. CHAPMAN, private, Cateechee; enrolled July 13, '98; mustered in July 13, '98; discharged September 28, '98.
68. HAMILTON A. MOORE, 25 years, private, machinist, Hollands; enrolled May 4, '98; mustered in May 12, '98; discharged September 28, '98.
69. RUFUS C. SHERARD, 23 years, private, farmer, Moffettsville; enrolled May 4, '98; mustered in May 12, '98; discharged September 28, '98.
70. HERMAN M. SIMPSON, 19 years, private, farmer, Honea Path; enrolled May 4, '98; mustered in May 12, '98; discharged September 28, '98.
71. JNO. T. STEWART, 23 years, private, insurance, Culpepper, Va.; enrolled May 6, '98; mustered in May 12, '98; discharged September 28, '98.
72. EDWARD O. GORDON, 22 years, private, farmer, Belton; enrolled May 4, '98; mustered in May 12, '98; discharged October 18, '98.
73. JOS. J. TROWBRIDGE, 23 years, private, salesman, Anderson; enrolled May 4, '98; mustered in May 12, '98; transferred as Principal Musician June 4, '98.
74. LEON P. BROCK, 25 years, private, book-keeper, Due West; enrolled May 4, '98; mustered in May 12, '98; transferred to band June 28, '98.
75. BAYLIS D. EARLE, 21 years, private, clerk, Anderson; enrolled May 11, '98; mustered in May 12, '98; transferred to band June 28, '98.
76. JACOB R. MILLER, 18 years, private, student, Anderson; enrolled May 4, '98; mustered in May 12, '98; transferred to band June 28, '98.
77. CHAS. POORE, 19 years, private, clerk, Anderson; enrolled May 7, '98; mustered in May 12, '98; transferred to band June 28, '98.

78. EDGAR M. SCOTT, 27 years, private, farmer, Brushy Creek; enrolled May 7, '98; mustered in May 12, '98; transferred to band June 28, '98.
79. JOS. B. DODD, 18 years, private, clerk, Charleston; enrolled May 11, '98; mustered in May 12, '98; transferred to band as Principal Musician July 25,, '98.
80. JNO. PRICE, private, Laurens; enrolled August 2, '98; mustered in August 7, '98; transferred to Co. L August 9, '98.
81. JNO. W. ELLEDGE, private, Austin; enrolled August 3, '98; mustered in August 7, '98; transferred to Co. L August 9, '98.
82. ALTIE T. HOLLEY, private, Augusta, Ga.; enrolled August 13, '98; mustered in August 13, '98; transferred to Co. K August 13, '98.
83. SAML. D. HARPER, 19 years, private, farmer, Anderson; enrolled May 4, '98; mustered in May 12, '98; transferred to Hospital Corps July 20, '98.
84. GUY T. GROVE, 30 years, private, telegraph operator, Walhalla; enrolled May 4, '98; mustered in May 12, '98; transferred to Hospital Corps September 15, '98.
85. JNO. L. POWELL, private, Anderson; enrolled August 5, '98; mustered in August 5, '98; transferred to Hospital Corps September 14, '98.
86. JNO. S. MURRAY, 19 years, Corporal, insurance, Anderson; enrolled May 4, '98; mustered in May 12, '98; promoted Sergeant September 3; died of fever, September 10, '98.
87. JEFFERSON D. GAMBRELL, 35 years, private, farmer, Honea Path; enrolled May 4, '98; mustered in May 12, '98; died of fever on furlough October 29, '98.
88. JOHN W. RODGERS, private, Hartwell, Ga.; enrolled July 7, '98; mustered in July 7, '98.

Lieut. A. L. Gaston.

Capt. J. S. Hardin.

Lieut. J. H. Marion.

Company D, First Regiment

1. Jos. S. Hardin, 29 years, Captain, farmer, Chester; enrolled May 4, '98; mustered in May 12, '98.

1. Arthur L. Gaston, 22 years, First Lieutenant, lawyer, Chester; enrolled May 4, '98; mustered in May 12, '98.

1. Jno. H. Marion, 24 years, Second Lieutenant, lawyer, Chester; enrolled May 4, '98; mustered in May 12, '98; resigned to take effect Nov. 7, '98.

1. Jas. G. McFadden, 25 years, First Sergeant, farmer, Chester; enrolled May 4, '98; mustered in May 12, '98; promoted from Sergeant, *vice* Hardin.

1. Frank M. Durham, 23 years, Quartermaster Sergeant, guard, Blackstock; enrolled May 4, '98; mustered in May 12, '98; promoted from Corporal July 1, '98.

1. Wm. G. Hardin, 19 years, Sergeant, stock dealer, Chester; enrolled May 4, '98; mustered in May 12, '98.

2. Wm. B. Home, 23 years, Sergeant, farmer, Chester; enrolled May 4, '98; mustered in May 12, '98.

3. WM. J. MCDANIEL, 25 years, Sergeant, lineman, Chester; enrolled May 4, '98; mustered in May 12, '98; promoted from Corporal August 1, '98.
4. MARTIN L. CLARK, 29 years, Sergeant, editor, Marion; enrolled May 4, '98; mustered in May 12, '98; promoted from Corporal September 27, '98.

1. ROBT. L. MCCONNELL, 20 years, Corporal, printer, Chester; enrolled May 4, '98; mustered in May 12, '98; promoted from private August 1st, '98.
2. AUGUSTUS T. WILLIAMS, 27 years, Corporal, farmer, Chester; enrolled May 4, '98; mustered in May 12, '98; promoted from private August 1st, '98.
3. JESSIE GRANT, 20 years, Corporal, farmer, Chester; enrolled May 4, '98; mustered in May 12, '98; promoted from private August 1st, '98.
4. ROBT. L. DANIEL, B5 years, Corporal, merchant, Mullins; enrolled May 4, '98; mustered in May 12, '98; promoted from private July 1st, '98.
5. LAURENCE S. BOYD, 20 years, Corporal, farmer, Fort Lawn; enrolled May 4, '98; mustered in May 12, '98; promoted from private September 11, '98.
6. JAS. FUDGE, 23 years, Corporal, printer, Chester; enrolled May 4, '98; mustered in May 12, '98; promoted from private September 1, '98.
7. JOS. H. SIMRILL, 22 years, Corporal, brick maker, Chester; enrolled May 4, '98; mustered in May 12, '98; promoted from private September 1, '98.
8. JNO. K. HINTON, 30 years, Corporal, farmer, Chester; enrolled May 4, '98; mustered in May 12, '98; promoted from private September 1, '98.
9. FRANK HORNE, 19 years, Corporal, clerk, Chester; enrolled May 4, '98; mustered in May 12, '98; promoted from private September 1, '98.
10. EDWARD W. HANNAHAN, Corporal, Winnsboro; enrolled August 29, '98; mustered in August 29, '98; promoted from private September 1, '98.
11. WM. H. COLEMAN, 22 years, Corporal, farmer, Feasterville; enrolled May 4, '98; mustered in May 12, '98; promoted from private September 1, '98.
12. CARROLL C. CHALK, 21 years, Corporal, carpenter, Williamsburg; enrolled May 4, '98; mustered in May 12, '98; promoted from private September 1, '98.

1. THOS. J. ALLEN, 19 years, private, millman, Winnsboro; enrolled May 4, '98; mustered in May 12, '98.
2. JAS. A. BETHEA, 25 years, private, teacher, Latta; enrolled May 4, '98; mustered in May 12, '98.
3. THEO. K. BIRD, 21 years, private, farmer, Chester; enrolled May 4, '98; mustered in May 12, '98.
4. CEPHUS W. BOLICK, private, Winnsboro; enrolled August 29, '98; mustered in August 29, '98.
5. ADOLPHUS B. BONEY, 43 years, private, farmer, Chester; enrolled May 4, '98; mustered in May 12, '98.

6. THOS. BRANHAM, private, Ridgeway; enrolled August 12, '98; mustered in August 12, '98.
7. CLAUDE T. BRAWLEY, 23 years, private, farmer, Wilkesborough; enrolled May 4, '98; mustered in May 12, '98.
8. ARCHIE L. BROWN, 22 years, private, farmer, Latta; enrolled May 4, '98; mustered in May 12, '98.
9. MARION H. BARNES, private, Camden; enrolled August 10, '98; mustered in August 10, '98.
10. WALTER CAPPS, 21 years, private, farmer, Marion; enrolled May 4, '98; mustered in May 12, '98.
11. CHAS. R. CARTER, 21 years, private, farmer, Chester; enrolled May 4, '98; mustered in May 12, '98.
12. EAPHIL W. CARTE, private, Lowrysville; enrolled June 21, '98; mustered in June 27, '98.
13. WM. J. CHESTER, private, Henderson, N. C.; enrolled August 12, '98; mustered in August 12, '98.
14. WM. G. CHISHOLM, 23 years, private, clerk, Chester; enrolled May 4, '98; mustered in May 12, '98.
15. LOUIS M. COOK, private, Rodman; enrolled June 27, '98; mustered in June 27, '98.
16. JNO. F. COOPER, private, Blackstock; enrolled August 17, '98; mustered in August 17, '98.
17. WM. L. CULP, 20 years, private, carpenter, Columbia; enrolled May 4, '98; mustered in May 12, '98.
18. LEROY CUNNINGHAM, 21 years, private, farmer, Winnsboro; enrolled May 4, '98; mustered in May 12, '98.
19. JAS. FARRELL, 18 years, private, farmer, Chester; enrolled May 4, '98; mustered in May 12, '98.
20. JNO. R. FEASTER, 38 years, private, clerk, Feasterville; enrolled May 4, '98; mustered in May 12, '98.
21. JAS. W. FISHER, 20 years, private, druggist, Charleston; enrolled May 4, '98; mustered in May 12, '98.
22. ELIAS E. FRAZER, 23 years, private, farmer, Rodman; enrolled May 4, '98; mustered in May 12, '98.
23. JNO. A. GRAHAM, 44 years, private, book-keeper, Chester; enrolled May 4, '98; mustered in May 12, '98.
24. JOS. B. GWINN, 22 years, private, farmer, Sharon; enrolled May 4, '98; mustered in May 12, '98.
25. LEONIS K. GWIN, 20 years, private, farmer, Chester; enrolled May 4, '98; mustered in May 12, '98.
26. ROBT. B. HAIR, private, Jefferson, N. C.; enrolled August 12, '98; mustered in August 12, '98.
27. WALTER B. HARDIN, 19 years, private, farmer, Chester; enrolled May 4, '98; mustered in May 12, '98.
28. GEE HARELLSON, 28 years, private, farmer, Marion; enrolled May 4, '98; mustered in May 12, '98.
29. DAVID H. HART, 20 years, private, clerk, Charleston; enrolled May 4, '98; mustered in May 12, '98.
30. JAS. A. HAYNE, 26 years, private, physician; Blackstock; enrolled May 4, '98; mustered in May 12, '98.

South Carolina Troops in the War with Spain   75

31. ROBT. A. HERRON, private, Winnsboro; enrolled August 12, '98; mustered in August 12, '98.
32. WM. H. HOWARD, 26 years, private, fireman, Chester; enrolled May 4, '98; mustered in May 12, '98.
33. WALTER W. IRBY, private, Rockton, enrolled August 19, '98; mustered in August 19, '98.
34. THOS. E. JOHNSON, 28 years, private, guard, Chester; enrolled May 4, '98; mustered in May 12, '98.
35. WM. JOHNIKIN, 18 years, private, student, Ridge Springs; enrolled May 4, '98; mustered in May 12, '98.
36. WM. H. LEWIS, 20 years, private, farmer, Blackstock; enrolled May 4, '98; mustered in May 12, '98.
37. DAVID R. MARTIN, private, Monticello; enrolled August 29, '98; mustered in August 29, '98.
38. WM. L. MARTIN, private, Monticello; enrolled August 29, '98; mustered in August 29, '98.
39. WM. H. MACKORELL, private, Blackstock; enrolled August 17, '98; mustered in August 17, '98.
40. CHAS. E. MCLEAN, 19 years, private, printer, Dillon; enrolled May 4, '98; mustered in May 12, '98.
41. THOS. W. MCCALL, private, Chester; enrolled July 20, '98; mustered in July 20, '98.
42. JAS. L. MCCRAVEY, 25 years, private, farmer, Chester; enrolled May 4, '98; mustered in May 12, '98.
43. LONNIE L. MELTON, private, Rockton; enrolled August 25, '98; mustered in August 25, '98.
44. BERRY H. MOBLEY, private, White Oak; enrolled July 20, '98; mustered in July 20, '98.
45. WYLIE W. MOBLEY, private, Fort Lawn; enrolled June 27, '98; mustered in June 27, '98.
46. JAS. E. NARKET, private, Fort Mill, enrolled August 22, '98; mustered in Augest 22, '98.
47. JNO. E. ORR, 18 years, private, millhand, Chester; enrolled May 4, '98; mustered in May 4, '98.
48. GEO. M. PEARSON, private, Rock Hill; enrolled August 30, '98; mustered in August 30, '98.
49. WM. T. PERRY, private, Flint Ridge; enrolled July 20, '98; mustered in July 20, '98.
50. EDDIE T. PORTER, private, Winnsboro; enrolled August 10, '98; mustered in August 10, '98.
51. DIXIE L. POWELL, private, Rockton; enrolled August 25, '98; mustered in August 25, '98.
52. CHAS. C. PROCKTOR, private, Ridgeway; enrolled August 12, '98; mustered in August 12, '98.
53. FRANK B. READ, 21 years, private, plumber, Chester; enrolled May 4, '98; mustered in May 12, '98.
54. GEO. H. RION, private, Winnsboro; enrolled August 29, '98; mustered in August 29, '98.
55. ALONZO SETZER, private, Newton, N. C.; enrolled July 20, '98; mustered in July 20, '98.

56. COLLIER E. SIGMON, 25 years, private, farmer, Chester; enrolled May 4, '98; mustered in May 12, '98.
57. JESSIE SIMS, private, Heaths; enrolled June 27, '98; mustered in June 27, '98.
58. AUGUST M. SMITH, 27 years, horseman, Chester; enrolled May 4, '98; mustered in May 12, '98.
59. AGUSTAS STACKHOUSE, private, Marion; enrolled June 17, '98; mustered in June 17, '98.
60. JAS. H. THOMAS, private, Lenoir, N. C.; enrolled August 12, '98; mustered in August 12, '98.
61. ROSS TRYLETT, private, Hickory, N. C.; enrolled July 20, '98; mustered in July 20, '98.
62. CHAS. N. WALKER, 18 years, student, Appleton; enrolled May 4, '98; mustered in May 12, '98.
63. LAMAR L. WATSON, 19 years, private, farmer, Chester; enrolled May 4, '98; mustered in May 12, '98.
64. CHAS. W. WIGGINS, 32 years, private, farmer, Marion; enrolled May 4, '98; mustered in May 12, '98.
65. HUGH WOODS, 35 years, private, sawyer, Latta; enrolled May 4, '98; mustered in May 12, '98.
66. PAUL A. WORKMAN, private, Rock Hill; enrolled August 25, '98; mustered in August 25, '98.
67. WM. J. WRIGHT, 21 years, private, farmer, Chester; enrolled May 4, '98; mustered in May 12, '98.
68. GEO. C. WRIGHT, 25 years, private, clerk, Chester; enrolled May 4, '98; mustered in May 12, '98.
69. CHAS. M. YOUNGBLOOD, private, Chester; enrolled August 10, '98; mustered in August 10, '98.
70. JESSE H. HARDIN, 22 years, First Sergeant, merchant, Chester; enrolled May 4, '98; mustered in May 12 ,'98; discharged to accept commission.
71. FRANCIS M. MOBLEY, Quartermaster Sergeant, Columbia; enrolled June 17, '98; mustered in June 17, '98; discharged Sept. 26, '98.
72. THOS. C. HOWZE, 30 years, Sergeant, farmer, Bascomville; enrolled May 4, '98; mustered in May 12, '98; discharged to accept commission.
73. CHEEVER S. SESSIONS, 26 years, Corporal, clerk, Latta; enrolled May 4, '98; mustered in May 12, '98; discharged Sept. 27, '98, telegram A. G. O.
74. ROBT. L. HOOD, 22 years, private, farmer, Hoodtown; enrolled May 4, '98; mustered in May 12, '98; discharged Sept. 29, '98; telegram A. G. O.
75. HOLMES MURPHY, 26 years, private, brakeman, Chester; enrolled May 4, '98; mustered in May 12, '98; discharged Sept. 28, '98, telegram A. G. O.
76. WM. J. CARTER, 21 years, private, farmer, Chester; enrolled May 4, '98; mustered in May 12, '98; discharged July 27, '98, S. O.
77. JNO. CHALK, private, Chalkville; enrolled July 20, '98; mustered in July 20, '98; discharged Sept. 29, '98, telegram A. G. O.
78. PINK DEWETTE, 23 years, private, farmer, Woodwards; enrolled May 4, '98; mustered in May 12, '98; discharged Sept. 29, '98, telegram A. G. O.

79. HUGH C. GUMLEY, 23 years, private, farmer, Olive; enrolled May 4, '98; mustered in May 12, '98; discharged Sept. 29, '98, telegram A. G. O.
80. JNO. B. LEWIS, 20 years, private, farmer, Chester; enrolled May 4, '98; mustered in May 12, '98; discharged Sept. 29, '98, telegram A. G. O.
81. THOS. J. LEWIS, 28 years, private, farmer, Dillon; enrolled May 4, '98; mustered in May 12, '98; discharged Sept. 28, '98, telegram A. G. O.
82. JAS. SIMPSON, 28 years, private, farmer, Chester; enrolled May 4, '98; mustered in May 12, '98; discharged Sept. 28, '98, telegram A. G. O.
83. JESSIE C. WOODWARD, 18 years, private, student, Latta; enrolled May 4, '98; mustered in May 12, '98; discharged Aug. 16, '98; disability.
84. SEATON C. YATES, 19 years, private, operator, Chester; enrolled May 4, '98; mustered in May 12, '98; discharged Sept. 28, '98, telegram A. G. O.
85. WALTER H. BRICE, 23 years, Corporal, liveryman, Chester; enrolled May 4, '98; mustered in May 12, '98; transferred Hospital Corps July 19, '98.
86. HENRY B. BROWN, private, Winnsboro; enrolled August 25, '98; mustered in August 25, '98; transferred Ambulance Corps Sept. 25, '98.
87. JNO. H. FREEMAN, private, Columbia; enrolled August 12, '98; mustered in August 12, '98; transferred to Ambulance Corps September 25, 98.
88. WM. H. LUCAS, 20 years, private, farmer, Chester; enrolled May 4, '98; mustered in May 12, '98; transferred to Hospital Corps Sept. 19, '98.
89. HAYES MCKEOWN, 20 years, private, farmer, Chester; enrolled May 4, '98; mustered in May 12, '98; transferred to Ambulance Corps Sept. 25, '98.
90. THOS. M. MORGUE, private, Richburg; enrolled August 12, '98; mustered in August 12, '98; transferred Ambulance Corps Sept. 25, '98.
91. EDWARD H. ROBERTS, private, Chester; enrolled August 12, '98; mustered in August 12, '98; transferred Ambulance Corps Sept. 25, '98.
92. JEPTHA D. TURNER, 21 years, private, farmer, Chester; enrolled May 4, '98; mustered in May 12, '98; transferred Ambulance Corps Sept. 25, '98.
93. HENRY C. WATSON, 19 years, private, lineman, Dillon; enrolled May 4, '98; mustered in May 12, '98; transferred Ambulance Corps Sept. 25, '98.
94. SAML. R. WILLIAMS, 21 years, private, farmer, Dudley; enrolled May 4, '98; mustered in May 12, '98; transferred to Ambulance Corps Sept. 25, '98.
95. CHAS. P. CARTER, 21 years, private, farmer, Chester; enrolled May 4, '98; mustered in May 12, '98.
96. MARION MONEYHAM, 19 years, private, farmer, Latta; enrolled May 4, '98; mustered in May 12, '98.
97. WADE H. YOUNG, 20 years, private, machinist, Chester; enrolled May 4, '98; mustered in May 12, '98.

Capt. J. E. Hunter.

Lieut. Wm. McGowan.

Lieut. C. H. Norman.

Company E, First Regiment

1. JAS. E. HUNTER, 31 years, Captain, editor, Union; enrolled May 3, '98; mustered in May 12, '98.
1. WM. MCGOWAN, 30 years, First Lieutenant, lawyer, Union; enrolled May 3, '98; mustered in May 12, '98; detached as Recruiting Officer.
1. CHAS. H. NORMAN, 30 years, Second Lieutenant, salesman, Union; enrolled May 3, '98; mustered in May 12, '98.
1. REUBEN L. MCNALLY, 23 years, First Sergeant, book-keeper, Union; enrolled May 3, '98; mustered in May 12, '98.
1. JAS. D. FLEMMING, 42 years, Quartermaster Sergeant, farmer, Carlisle; enrolled May 10, '98; mustered in May 15, '98.
1. WM. K. HOUZE, 21 years, Sergeant, clerk, Union; enrolled May 3, '98; mustered in May 12, '98.
2. MACBETH YOUNG, 35 years, Sergeant, lawyer, Union; enrolled May 3, '98; mustered in May 12, '98.
3. JAS. I. VINSON, 31 years, Sergeant, policeman, Union; enrolled May 3, '98; mustered in May 12, '98.
4. HARRY L. GOSS, 20 years, Sergeant, clerk, Union; enrolled May 3, '98; mustered in May 12, '98.

1. AURELIUS RUSSELL, 24 years, Corporal, sailor, Spartanburg; enrolled May 3, '98; mustered in May 12, '98.
2. JAS. CASEY, 25 years, Corporal, electrician, Union; enrolled May 3, '98; mustered in May 12, '98.
3. JNO. P. DAVIS, 21 years, Corporal, clerk, Edgefield; enrolled May 9, '98; mustered in May 12, '98.
4. THOMPSON HARRIS, 19 years, Corporal, clerk, Spartanburg; enrolled May 9, '98; mustered in May 12, '98.
1. CARL A. STOEBER, 21 years, private, printer, Atlanta, Ga.; enrolled May 9, '98; mustered in May 12, '98.
2. JAS. E. MARTIN, 19 years, private, farmer, Spartanburg; enrolled May 3, '98; mustered in May 12, '98.
3. ROBT. FORD, 38 years, private, mechanic, Union; enrolled May 3, '98; mustered in May 12, '98.
4. LEWIS A. SCHOPPAUL, 21 years, private, carpenter, Union; enrolled May 3, '98; mustered in May 12, '98.
5. LON BEAM, 20 years, private, sawyer, Union; enrolled May 3, '98; mustered in May 12, '98.
6. LEE BELUE, 20 years, private, picker, Lockhart; enrolled May 3, '98; mustered in May 12, '98.
7. RATCHFORD BRANNON, 24 years, private, brakeman, Union; enrolled May 3, '98; mustered in May 12, '98.
8. EVERETT BROWN, 23 years, private, farmer, Landrum; enrolled May 3, '98; mustered in May 12, '98.
9. THOS. B. BROWN, 35 years, private, carpenter, Spartanburg; enrolled May 3. '98; mustered in May 12, '98.
10. LEROY BUSBEE, 23 years, private, weaver, Union; enrolled May 3, '98; mustered in May 12, '98.
11. THOS. BRUCE, private, Spartanburg; enrolled June 18, '98; mustered in June 18, '98.
12. BENJ. L. BISHOP, private, Spartanburg; enrolled August 12, '98; mustered in August 12, '98.
13. MARION BRIGGS, private, Spartanburg; enrolled August 11, '98; mustered in August 11, '98.
14. EDWARD A. CAMPBELL, 24 years, private, laborer, Gaffney; enrolled May 3, '98; mustered in May 12, '98.
15. OWEN CANNON, 22 years, private, loom fixer, Columbia; enrolled May 9, '98; mustered in May 12, '98.
16. JETER CORNWELL, 24 years, private, farmer, Union; enrolled May 3, '98; mustered in May 12, '98.
17. GEO. I. CHAMBERS, 19 years, private, mill hand, Gaffney; enrolled May 3, '98; mustered in May 12, '98.
18. MANNING H. CALDWELL, private, Spartanburg; enrolled June 18, '98; mustered in June 18, '98.
19. ROBT. CHAPMAN, 25 years, private, carpenter, Union; enrolled May 3, '98; mustered in May 12, '98.
20. BERTRAND B. CLAYTON, private, Spartanburg; enrolled August 12, '98; mustered in August 12, '98.
21. HENRY E. DILLINGHAM, 21 years, private, mill hand, Fingerville; enrolled May 7. '98; mustered in May 12, '98.

22. THOS. E. DAVIS, private, Union; enrolled July 11, '98; mustered in July 11, '98.
23. JAS. F. EDMUNDS, 19 years, private, clerk, McCormacks; enrolled May 7, '98; mustered in May 12, '98.
24. EUGENE EDWARDS, 18 years, private, clerk, Union; enrolled May 9, '98; mustered in May 12, '98.
25. CHAS. G. ERWIN, 21 years, private, Gaffney; enrolled May 3, '98; mustered in May 12, '98.
26. JAS. L. EVANS, 43 years, private, carpenter, Union; enrolled May 3, '98; mustered in May 12, '98.
27. JAS. H. FANT, 19 years, private, farmer, Santuc; enrolled May 3, '98; mustered in May 12, '98.
28. CHAS. M. FOSTER, 22 years, private, brick mason, Spartanburg; enrolled May 7, '98; mustered in May 12, '98.
29. JNO. F. FOSTER, 26 years, private, stenographer, Union; enrolled May 7, '98; mustered in May 12, '98.
30. ANDREW G. FLOYD, private, Spartanburg; enrolled June 20, '98; mustered in June 20, '98.
31. RUSSELL GAFFNEY, 19 years, private, liveryman, Spartanburg; enrolled May 7, '98; mustered in May 12, '98.
32. WM. W. GREEN, 20 years, private, mail carrier, Spartanburg; enrolled May 7, '98; mustered in May 12, '98.
33. THOS. GREGORY, 19 years, private, mill hand, Union; enrolled May 3, '98; mustered in May 12, '98.
34. DAVID GOSWELL, 20 years, private, mill hand, Union; enrolled May 3, '98; mustered in May 12, '98.
35. ROME GOWAN, private Spartanburg; enrólled June 20, '98; mustered in June 20, '98.
36. JNO. E. GREEN, private, Greenville; enrolled July 11, '98; mustered in July 11, '98.
37. HENRY T. HAMES, 36 years, private, paper hanger, Spartanburg; enrolled May 3, '98; mustered in May 12, '98.
38. WM. J. HAMMETT, 23 years, private, farmer, Gaffney; enrolled May 7, '98; mustered in May 12, '98.
39. CLESTER C. HOPPER, 22 years, private, clerk, Gaffney; enrolled May 7, '98; mustered in May 12, '98.
40. MELVIN C. HOUZE, 19 years, private, clerk, Carlisle; enrolled May 9, '98; mustered in May 12, '98.
41. WM. B. HUDGENS, 30 years, private, carpenter, Spartanburg; enrolled May 7, '98; mustered in May 12, '98.
42. JNO. F. HAMMETT, private, Spartanburg; enrolled July 13, '98; mustered in July 13, '98.
43. JAS. P. HIX, private, Union; enrolled July 11, '98; mustered in July 13, '98.
44. WM. E. HARRIS, private, Union; enrolled July 25, '98; mustered in July 25, '98.
45. SAML. HENDERSON, private, Spartanburg; enrolled June 18, '98; mustered in June 18, '98.
46. CHAS. HENSLEY, private, Greenville; enrolled July 5, '98; mustered in July 5, '98.

47. ANDREW HAWKINS, private, Greenville; enrolled July 11, '98; mustered in July 11, '98.
48. THOS. B. HAYNES, private, Spartanburg; enrolled August 10, '98; mustered in August 10, '98.
49. ROBT. B. HOLLMAN, private, Spartanburg; enrolled August 12, '98; mustered in August 12, '98.
50. KELLY JOHNS, 26 years, private, farmer, Santuc; enrolled May 9, '98; mustered in May 12, '98.
51. BENJ. F. JOLLEY, 21 years, private, clerk, Union; enrolled May 9, '98; mustered in May 12, '98.
52. WM. N. JONES, 24 years, private, farmer, Union; enrolled May 3, '98; mustered in May 12, '98.
53. ALBERT D. JENKINS, private, Spartanburg; enrolled July 13, '98; mustered in July 13, '98.
54. JNO. McJENNINGS, private, Union; enrolled June 28, '98; mustered in June 28, '98.
55. JNO. W. KIMBROUGH, 43 years, picker, Spartanburg; enrolled May 7, '98; mustered in May 12, '98.
56. ALBERT E. LACY, 24 years, private, clerk, Spartanburg; enrolled May 7, '98; mustered in May 12, '98.
57. LEMUEL L. LEVESTER, 20 years, private, farmer, Herbert; enrolled May 9, '98; mustered in May 12, '98.
58. HASKEL MABRY, 21 years, private, laundryman, Spartanburg; enrolled May 3, '98; mustered in May 12, '98.
59. EDWARD W. MAY, private, Spartanburg; enrolled June 18, '98; mustered in June 18, '98.
60. THOS. McDANIEL, 24 years, private, farmer, Union; enrolled May 9, '98; mustered in May 12, '98.
61. WM. T. McDANIEL, 23 years, private, farmer, Santuc; enrolled May 9, '98; mustered in May 12, '98.
62. JNO. M. McDANIEL, 37 years, private, farmer, Santuc; enrolled May 9, '98; mustered in May 12, '98.
63. WM. K. McDOWELL, 32 years, private, farmer, Union; enrolled May 7, '98; mustered in May 12, '98.
64. PERRY L. MORRIS, 24 years, private, weaver, Union; enrolled May 3, '98; mustered in May 12, '98.
65. ROBT. L. NELSON, private, Spartanburg; enrolled July 12, '98; mustered in July 12, '98.
66. FREDERICK M. PARHAM, 20 years, private, butcher, Union; enrolled May 3, '98; mustered in May 12, '98.
67. THOS. PARHAM, 22 years, private, clerk, Union; enrolled May 3, '98; mustered in May 12, '98.
68. ALEX. PEARSON, 22 years, private, mill hand, Union; enrolled May 7, '98; mustered in May 12, '98.
69. ENGLISH PINCKNEY, 21 years, private, mechanic, Union; enrolled May 3, '98; mustered in May 12, '98.
70. JAS. R. PORTER, 31 years, private, printer, Union; enrolled May 7, '98; mustered in May 12, '98.
71. WM. T. POWELL, 24 years, clerk, Union; enrolled May 3, '98; mustered in May 12, '98.

72. WALTER J. TENNY, private, Spartanburg; enrolled July 13, '98; mustered in July 13, '98.
73. BELTON O. PRINCE, private, Spartanburg; enrolled July 13, '98; mustered in July 13, '98.
74. DAVID ROBBINS, 25 years, weaver, Union; enrolled May 13, '98; mustered in July 13, '98.
75. JAS. ROSS, 21 years, private, carpenter, Spartanburg; enrolled May 13, '98; mustered in July 13, '98.
76. THEO. K. ROPER, private, Spartanburg; enrolled June 18, '98; mustered in June 18, '98.
77. JNO. R. RUSSUM, private, Spartanburg; enrolled July 12, '98; mustered in July 12, '98.
79. JNO. ROSEMAN, private, Greenville, enrolled July 12, '98; mustered in July 12, '98.
80. WALLACE S. SIMS, private, Spartanburg; enrolled June 18, '98; mustered in June 18, '98.
81. JNO. K. THOMAS, 27 years, private, farmer, Union; enrolled May 3, '98; mustered in May 12, '98.
82. ALLIVER V. TURNER, 21 years, private, farmer, Spartanburg; enrolled May 3, '98; mustered in May 12, '98.
83. ANDREW TRAIL, private, Spartanburg; enrolled June 24, '98; mustered in June 24, '98.
84. ALBERT TURNER, private, Spartanburg; enrolled August 23, '98; mustered in August 23, '98.
85. FRANK THEODORE, private, Spartanburg; enrolled July 14, '98; mustered in July 14, '98.
86. CLARENCE A. VAUGHN, 22 years, private, farmer, Santuc; enrolled May 3, '98; mustered in May 12, '98.
87. BENJ. H. WILKERSON, 27 years, private, druggist, Union; enrolled May 3, '98; mustered in May 12, '98.
88. DANL. M. WALLACE, private, Union; enrolled May 7, '98; mustered in May 12, '98.
89. EDWARD D. DEAN, private, Spartanburg; enrolled August 9, '98; mustered in August 11, '98.
90. SADLER GILLESPIE, 27 years, private, broker, Charlotte, N. C.; enrolled May 10, '98; mustered in May 12, '98.
91. PAUL A. MCNALLY, 20 years, Corporal, clerk, Union; enrolled May 3, '98; mustered in May 12, '98; discharged September 28, '98.
92. HARLEY A. MADOLE, 18 years, private, civil engineer, Spartanburg; enrolled May 7, '98; mustered in May 12, '98; discharged June 12, '98.
93. MARVIN MCNEACE, 18 years, private, clerk, Union; enrolled May 9, '98; mustered in May 12, '98; discharged June 12, '98.
94. WM. SMITH, 20 years, private, mill hand, Union; enrolled May 7, '98; mustered in May 12, '98; discharged June 24, '98, S. O. 124.
95. MALLIE BRASWELL, 20 years, private, weaver, Spartanburg; enrolled May 24, '98; mustered in May 24, '98; transferred from Co. K; discharged July 26.
96. WALLACE VINCENT, 18 years, private, confectioner, Union; enrolled May 3, '98; mustered in May 12, '98; discharged July 23, '98; S. O. 166, A. G. O.

SOUTH CAROLINA TROOPS IN THE WAR WITH SPAIN

97. PAUL SMITH, 19 years, private, clerk, McCormack; enrolled May 9, '98; mustered in May 12, '98; discharged August 5, '98, G. O. 178, A. G. O.
98. JNO. T. BALDWIN, 22 years, private, farmer, Pinckney; enrolled May 3, '98; mustered in May 12, '98; discharged September 30, '98, telegram A. G. O.
99. CLARENCE HAWKINS, 21 years, private, mill hand, Union; enrolled May 9, '98; mustered in May 12, '98; discharged September 30, '98, telegram A. G. O.
100. SAML. P. FANT, 24 years, private, farmer, Union; enrolled May 9, '98; mustered in May 12, '98; transferred to Co. K June 19, '98.
101. CHAS. E. SLOVER, private, Spartanburg; enrolled June 18, '98; mustered in June, 18, '98; transferred to Co. I July 9, '98.
102. LEWIS A. HENDERSON, private, Gaffney; enrolled July 5, '98; mustered in July 5, '98; transferred to Co. H July 10, '98.
103. CHAS. H. BRASWELL, 24 years, private, carder, Union; enrolled May 3, '98; mustered in May 12, '98; transferred to band June 18, '98.
104. BENJ. F. BENNETT, private, Union; enrolled July 11, '98; mustered in July 11, '98; transferred Hospital Corps September 18, '98.
105. JAS. W. SHEEHAN, 26 years, private, carpenter, Union; enrolled May 3, '98; mustered in May 12, '98.
106. JAS. C. FOWLER, private, Spartanburg; enrolled June 19, '98; mustered in June 19, '98.
107. TOLLIVER A. PHILLIPS, private, Spartanburg; enrolled July 16, '98; mustered in July 16, '98.
108. JOHN COSTINE, private, Spartanburg; enrolled July 13, '98; mustered in July 13, '98.
109. WM. H. SUTTON, private, Spartanburg; enrolled July 18, '98; mustered in July 18, '98.

Capt. A. D. Hoke.

Lieut. J. W. Gray, Jr.

Lieut. W. D. Whitmire.

Company F, First Regiment

1. AUGUSTAS D. HOKE, 28 years, Captain, laundry, Greenville; enrolled May 4, '98; mustered in May 13, '98.

1. JAS. W. GRAY, JR., 23 years, First Lieutenant, planter, Greenville; enrolled May 4, '98; mustered in May 13, '98.

1. WM. D. WHITMIRE, 24 years, Second Lieutenant, deputy sheriff, Greenville; enrolled May 4, '98; mustered in May 13, '98.

1. HARRY A. DARGAN, 28 years, First Sergeant, salesman, Greenville; enrolled May 4, '98; mustered in May 13, '98.

1. CHAS. D. WHITMAN, 22 years, Quartermaster Sergeant, salesman, Spartanburg; enrolled May 4, '98; mustered in May 13, '98.

1. CHAS. A. COOPER, 28 years, Sergeant, printer, Greenville; enrolled May 4, '98; mustered in May 13, '98.

2. JAS. A. MCDAVID, 20 years, Sergeant, salesman, Greenville; enrolled May 4, '98; mustered in May 13, '98; promoted from Corporal June 1, '98.

3. GEO. W. BUBRANKS, 22 years, Sergeant, clerk, Greenville; enrolled May 4, '98; mustered in May 13, '98.

4. JNO. M. STEELE, 23 years, Sergeant, wheelwright, Greenville; enrolled May 4, '98; mustered in May 13, '98.

South Carolina Troops in the War with Spain 85

1. CLIFFORD L. BABB, 20 years, Corporal, cotton buyer, Laurens; enrolled May 4, '98; mustered in May 13, '98.
2. ARTHUR D. MILSTER, 28 years, Corporal, tinner, Spartanburg; enrolled May 4, '98; mustered in May 13, '98.
3. SAML. M. NABERS, JR., 20 years, Corporal, book-keeper, Spartanburg; enrolled May 4, '98; mustered in May 13, '98.
4. CHAS. P. ROBISON, 37 years, Corporal, farmer, Greers; enrolled May 4, '98; mustered in May 13, '98.
5. OSCAR B. WILLIS, 22 years, Corporal, clerk, Spartanburg; enrolled May 4, '98; mustered in May 13, '98.
6. JNO. H. HARRIS, 30 years, Corporal, mill hand, Spartanburg; enrolled May 4, '98; mustered in May 13, '98; promoted from private June 1, '98.
7. WM. L. ORNESBY, 42 years, Corporal, plumber, Laurens; enrolled May 4, '98; mustered in May 13, '98; promoted from private Sept. 4, '98.
8. THOS E. PETERSON, 27 years, Corporal, fireman, Laurens; enrolled May 4, '98; mustered in May 13, '98; promoted from private Sept. 4, '98.
9. WM. W. TRIBBLE, 21 years, Corporal, machinist, Laurens; enrolled May 4, '98; mustered in May 13, '98; promoted from private Sept. 4, '98.
10. SOLOMON C. HARGROVE, 24 years, Corporal, machinist, Laurens; enrolled May 4, '98; mustered in May 13, '98; promoted from private Sept. 4, '98.
11. HARRISON H. FERGUSON, 21 years, Corporal, clerk, Spartanburg; enrolled May 4, '98; mustered in May 13, '98; promoted from private Sept. 4, '98.
12. GEO. W. CHILDRESS, 27 years, Corporal, machinist, Greers; enrolled May 4, '98; mustered in May 13, '98; promoted from private Sept. 4, '98.

1. LUTE C. BRADLEY, 28 years, private, painter, Simpsonville; enrolled May 4, '98; mustered in May 13, '98.
2. ATCHIE WATSON, 22 years, private, telegraph operator, Columbia; enrolled May 4, '98; mustered in May 13, '98.
3. MAGE J. CALLAHAN, 20 years, private, salesman, Spartanburg; enrolled May 4, '98; mustered in May 13, '98.
4. THOS. M. BASWELL, 38 years, private, blacksmith, Greers; enrolled May 4, '98; mustered in May 13, '98.
5. FRANK HOOPER, 22 years, private, wagoner, Columbia; enrolled May 4, '98; mustered in May 13, '98.
6. LEONARD BECKER, private, Spartanburg; enrolled August 8, '98; mustered in August 8, '98.
7. THOS. B. BENNET, 38 years, private, painter, Laurens; enrolled May 4, '98; mustered in May 13, '98.
8. MILES B. BOMAR, 21 years, private, farmer, O'Neal; enrolled May 4, '98; mustered in May 13, '98.
9. VOLNEY B. BOGAN, private, Gaffney; enrolled July 1, '98; mustered in July 1, '98.
10. WM. A. BROWN, private, Spartanburg; enrolled August 2, '98; mustered in August 2, '98.
11. HIRAM T. BURKET, 25 years, private, weaver, Pelzer; enrolled May 4, '98; mustered in May 13, '98.

12. LINDER CARRIER, private, Spartanburg; enrolled August 8, '98; mustered in August 8, '98.
13. JOS. CHANEY, 19 years, private, photographer, Laurens; enrolled May 4, '98; mustered in May 13, '98.
14. JAS. W. CLARK, 19 years, private, mill hand, Spartanburg; enrolled May 4, '98; mustered in May 13, '98.
15. JAS. CLUTTS, private, Spartanburg; enrolled August 6, '98; mustered in August 6, '98.
16. JNO. A. CURETON, 21 years, private, baker, Greenville; enrolled May 4, '98; mustered in May 13, '98.
17. CORVISIE Y. CUNNINGHAM, private, Spartanburg; enrolled August 1, '98; mustered in August 1, '98.
18. WM. DAVIS, private, Holysville, N. C.; enrolled August 9, '98; mustered in August 9, '98.
19. FRED. L. DILLARD, 20 years, private, clerk, Spartanburg; enrolled May 4, '98; mustered in May 13, '98.
20. EARLE DODD, 21 years, private, weaver, Spartanburg; enrolled May 4, '98; mustered in May 13, '98.
21. SIDNEY W. EDWARDS, 20 years, private, mill hand, Laurens; enrolled May 4, '98; mustered in May 13, '98.
22. JAS. C. ELLENBURG, 21 years, private, mill hand, Pelzer; enrolled May 4, '98; mustered in May 13, '98.
23. ROBT. J. FARMER, 27 years, private, farmer, Arlington; enrolled May 4, '98; mustered in May 13, '98.
24. ANDREW FLOOD, private, Spartanburg; enrolled August 8, '98; mustered in August 8, '98.
25. JAS. C. GAFFNEY, 21 years, private, painter, Spartanburg; enrolled May 4, '98; mustered in May 13, '98.
26. BENJ. F. GIBBES, private, Spartanburg; enrolled August 4, '98; mustered in August 4, '98.
27. JNO. M. GOSWELL, 26 years, private, mill hand, Augusta, Ga.; enrolled May 4, '98; mustered in May 13, '98.
28. ALLEN T. GREEN, private, Spartanburg; enrolled August 17, '98; mustered in August 17, '98.
29. MILAS T. HARRIS, 23 years, private, farmer, Clinton; enrolled May 4, '98; mustered in May 13, '98.
30. ANDY P. HILL, 25 years, private, farmer, Greenville; enrolled May 4, '98; mustered in May 13, '98.
31. WM. M. HILL, 35 years, private, mechanic, Spartanburg; enrolled May 4, '98; mustered in May 13, '98.
32. ROME HOLLAND, Pacolet; enrolled August 2, '98; mustered in August 2, '98.
33. HOWELL HOLLINGSWORTH, 19 years, private, printer, Spartanburg; enrolled May 4, '98; mustered in May 13, '98.
34. JESSE A. HUDSON, 26 years, private, farmer, Greenville; enrolled May 4, '98; mustered in May 13, '98.
35. JAS. P. HUSKEY, private, Gaffney; enrolled June 30, '98; mustered in June 30, '98.
36. JAS. J. HENDERSON, 23 years, private, mill hand, Gaffney; enrolled May 4, '98; mustered in May 13, '98.

South Carolina Troops in the War with Spain 87

37. JESSE R. JOLLY, 36 years, private, carpenter, Spartanburg; enrolled May 4, '98; mustered in May 13, '98.
38. WM. L. JONES, 24 years, private, weaver, Piedmont; enrolled May 4, '98; mustered in May 13, '98.
39. SAML. F. LANFORD, 22 years, private, mill hand, Lanford; enrolled May 4, '98; mustered in May 13, '98.
40. ROBT. G. LEMONS, private, Spartanburg; enrolled August 1, '98; mustered in August 1, '98.
41. CLARENCE C. MCGOWAN, 19 years, private, clerk, Spartanburg; enrolled May 4, '98; mustered in May 13, '98.
42. JNO. W. MARTIN, private, Spartanburg; enrolled August 1, '98; mustered in August 1, '98.
43. DAVID L. MELVIN, 31 years, private, mill hand, Greers; enrolled May 4, '98, mustered in May 13, '98.
44. EDWARD R. MILLAN, 20 years, private, insurance, Spartanburg; enrolled May 4, '98; mustered in May 13, '98.
45. ARTHUR W. MILLER, private, Spartanburg; enrolled August 2, '98; mustered in August 2, '98.
46. THOMAS MILLWOOD, private, Spartanburg; enrolled August 6, '98; mustered in August 6, '98.
47. EUGENE W. MOON, 28 years, private, farmer, Greers; enrolled May 4, '98; mustered in May 13, '98.
48. JAS. E. MOON, 28 years, private, carpenter, Greers; enrolled May 4, '98; mustered in May 13, '98.
49. WM. MORGAN, private, Spartanburg; enrolled August 9, '98; mustered in August 9, '98.
50. CHARLIE B. MOTT, 20 years, private, machinist, Laurens; enrolled May 4, '98; mustered in May 13, '98.
51. ARCH. C. OWINGS, JR., 22 years, private, farmer, Rapley; enrolled May 4, '98; mustered in May 13, '98.
52. JNO. S. O'NEALE, private, Spartanburg; enrolled August 4, '98; mustered in August 4, '98.
53. LEM L. POPLIN, 22 years, private, carpenter, Spartanburg; enrolled May 4, '98; mustered in May 13, '98.
54. HUGH L. PEDEN, private, Spartanburg; enrolled August 17, '98; mustered in August 17, '98.
55. GEORGE G. ROBERTSON, 28 years, private, farmer, O'Neale; enrolled May 4, '98; mustered in May 13, '98.
56. JOS. H. ROBINSON, 19 years, private, barber, Greenville; enrolled May 4, '98; mustered in May 13, '98.
57. NIGH P. ROBINSON, 20 years, private, clerk, Spartanburg; enrolled May 4, '98; mustered in May 13, '98.
58. WM. H. ROLAND, private, Spartanburg; enrolled August 9, '98; mustered in August 9, '98.
59. EBBIE F. ROWLEY, 18 years, private, student, Greenville; enrolled May 4, '98; mustered in May 13, '98.
60. EDGAR H. RUSH, 39 years, private, carpenter, Spartanburg; enrolled May 4, '98; mustered in May 13, '98.
61. THAD. G. SAXTON, 30 years, private, merchant, Walterboro; enrolled May 4, '98; mustered in May 13, '98.

62. WM. STEELE, 19 years, private, salesman, Greenville; enrolled May 4, '98; mustered in May 13, '98.
63. JNO. A. SHIPMAN, private, Spartanburg; enrolled August 8, '98; mustered in August 8, '98.
64. ARTHUR R. SHOCKLEY, private, Spartanburg; enrolled August 9, '98; mustered in August 9, '98.
65. BERRY C. SLOAN, 19 years, private, farmer, Spartanburg; enrolled May 4, '98; mustered in May 13, '98.
66. CLAUDE P. SMITH, 21 years, private, farmer, Woodruff; enrolled May 4, '98; mustered in May 13, '98.
67. WM. SINOR, private, Spartanburg; enrolled August 17, '98; mustered in August 17, '98.
68. WM. T. THOMAS, private, Spartanburg; enrolled August 10, '98; mustered in August 10, '98.
69. BISHOP P. THOMASON, 43 years, private, cotton buyer, Greenville; enrolled May 4, '98; mustered in May 13, '98.
70. JAS. TURNER, 19 years, private, mill hand, Spartanburg; enrolled May 4, '98; mustered in May 13, '98.
71. MCDANIEL VAUGHAN, 43 years, private, wood turner, Greenville; enrolled May 4, '98; mustered in May 13, '98.
72. MOULTRIE E. VOISELLE, private, Union; enrolled August 6, '98; mustered in August 6, '98.
73. HENRY H. WARD, 23 years, private, carpenter, Augusta, Ga.; enrolled May 4, '98; mustered in May 13, '98.
74. LON R. WARD, private, Greenville; enrolled July 5, '98; mustered in July 5, '98.
75. ZEBULON WEST, private, Spartanburg; enrolled August 17, '98; mustered in August 17, '98.
76. LEONARD A. WHITMIRE, 18 years, private, student, Greenville; enrolled May 4, '98; mustered in May 13, '98.
77. AUGUSTAS D. KUYKENDALL, 26 years, private, brickmason, Flat Rock, N. C.; enrolled May 4, '98; mustered in May 13, '98; discharged August 13, '98.
78. WAKE SHAVER, 19 years, private, decorator, Spartanburg; enrolled May 4, '98; mustered in May 13, '98; discharged July 1, '98, S. O. 150.
79. JAMES WATERS, 19 years, private, farmer, Enoree; enrolled May 4, '98; mustered in May 13, '98; discharged July 2, '98, S. O. 152.
80. EDWARD NEIGHBORS, 19 years, private, express, Moores; enrolled May 4, '98; mustered in May 13, '98; discharged July 3, '98, S. O. 153.
81. HARLEY L. RODGERS, 20 years, private, mill hand, enoree; enrolled May 4, '98; mustered in May 13, '98; discharged July 9, '98, S. O. 156.
82. CHAS. P. LANFORD, 18 years, private, farmer, Woodruff; enrolled May 4, '98; mustered in May 13, '98; discharged May 19, '98, S. O. 164.
83. ROBT. CARLSON, 18 years, private, carpenter, Spartanburg; enrolled May 4, '98; mustered in May 13, '98; discharged July 23, '98, S. O. 167.
84. THOS. TINSLEY, 18 years, private, salesman, Spartanburg; enrolled May 4, '98; mustered in May 13, '98; discharged August 11, '98, S. O. 188.
85. BRUCE MILLER, 23 years, private, machinist, Charlotte, N. C.; enrolled May 4, '98; mustered in May 13, '98; discharged September 28, '98, telegram.

86. WM. C. REID, private, Spartanburg; enrolled August 9, '98; mustered in August 9, '98; discharged September 28, '98, telegram.
87. JNO. L. RICHARDS, private, Gaffney; enrolled July 2, '98; mustered in July 2, '98; discharged September 18, '98, S. O. 194.
88. ANSELM S. MILLER, private, Greenville; enrolled May 4, '98; mustered in May 13, '98; transferred Hospital Corps.
89. KEITH D. BRISTOW, private, Spartanburg; enrolled August 2, '98; mustered in August 2, '98; transferred to Regiment Band.
90. GARY R. VAUGHN, 24 years, private, farmer, Greenville; enrolled May 4, '98; mustered in May 13, '98; died August 10, '98, typhoid fever.
91. JNO. M. GLENN, 23 years, private, weaver, Piedmont; enrolled May 4, '98; mustered in May 13, '98; died September 6, '98, heart failure.

Capt. Frel Mobley.

Lieut. W. M. Dunlap.

Lieut. H. Dunlap.

Company G, First Regiment

1. FREL MOBLEY, 35 years, Captain, merchant, Rock Hill; enrolled May 4, '98; mustered in May 14, '98.
1. WALTER M. DUNLAP, 22 years, First Lieutenant, book-keeper, Rock Hill; enrolled May 4, '98; mustered in May 14, '98.
1. JAS S. WHITE, 20 years, Second Lieutenant, merchant, Rock Hill; enrolled May 4, '98; mustered in May 14, '98; resigned September 7, '98, S. O. 211, A. G. O.
2. HERBERT DUNLAP, 22 years, Second Lieutenant, book-keeper, Rock Hill; enrolled May 4, '98; mustered in May 14, '98; promoted September 13, '98, *vice* White.
1. FRED. D. MARSHALL, 22 years, First Sergeant, electrician, Rock Hill; enrolled May 4, '98; mustered in May 14, '98; promoted September 13, '98, *vice* Dunlap.
1. TONY B. LUMPKIN, 35 years, Quartermaster Sergeant, railroad agent, Rock Hill; enrolled May 4, '98; mustered in May 14, '98; promoted Sergeant Major, G. O. 7.
2. ROBT. A. MORRISON, Quartermaster Sergeant, Rock Hill; enrolled May 4, '98; mustered in May 14, '98; promoted Quartermaster Sergeant July 31, *vice* Lumpkin.

1. JAS H. BECKHAM, 21 years, Sergeant, clerk, Rock Hill; enrolled May 4, '98; mustered in May 14, '98.
2. JNO. C. WITHERSPOON, 22 years, Sergeant, student, Rock Hill; enrolled May 4, '98; mustered in May 14, '98.
3. ERNEST L. ADAMS, 22 years, Sergeant, railroad clerk, Rock Hill; enrolled May 4, '98; mustered in May 14, '98.
4. WM. S. ADAMS, 20 years, Sergeant, book-keeper, Rock Hill; enrolled May 4, '98; mustered in May 14, '98; promoted from Corporal September 13, '98.

1. ALBERT A. BRADFORD, 21 years, Corporal, clerk, Fort Mill; enrolled May 4, '98; mustered in May 14, '98.
2. WM. D. BOLICK, 28 years, Corporal, painter, Ridgeway; enrolled May 4, '98; mustered in May 14, '98.
3. WADE B. RHODY, 19 years, student, Richburg; enrolled May 4, '98; mustered in May 14, '98.
4. WM. BANKS, 20 years, Corporal, editor, Rock Hill; enrolled May 4, '98; mustered in May 14, '98.
5. JAS. M. IVY, 23 years, Corporal, salesman, Rock Hill; enrolled May 4, '98; mustered in May 14, '98; promoted from private July 8, '98.
6. MORRIS F. COBB, 18 years, Corporal, bank clerk, Rock Hill; enrolled May 4, '98; mustered in May 14, '98; appointed Headquarter's Clerk.
7. BENJ. S. MAY, 31 years, Corporal, painter, Lancaster; enrolled May 4, '98; mustered in May 14, '98; promoted from private September 1, '98.
8. CRAWFORD C. MOORE, 23 years, Corporal, druggist, Yorkville; enrolled May 4, '98; mustered in May 14, '98; promoted from private September 12, '98.
9. FRANKLIN S. LOVE, 21 years, Corporal, clerk, Rock Hill; enrolled May 4, '98; mustered in May 14, '98; promoted from private September 1, '98.
10. ALVA B. CULP, 24 years, Corporal, journalist, Fort Mill; enrolled May 4, '98; mustered in May 14, '98; promoted from private September 1, '98.
11. WM. L. BLACK, 20 years, Corporal, book-keeper, Rock Hill; enrolled May 4, '98; mustered in May 14, '98; promoted from private September 1, '98.
12. JAS. F. TOMPKINS, 19 years, Corporal, book-keeper, Rock Hill; enrolled May 4, '98; mustered in May 14, '98; promoted from private September 1, '98.

1. THOS. L. SHAVER, 39 years, private, carpenter, Rock Hill; enrolled May 4, '98; mustered in May 14, '98.
2. HERBERT M. DAVIS, 20 years, private, cotton buyer, Rock Hill; enrolled May 4, '98; mustered in May 14, '98; appointed Regimental Clerk.
3. MARSHALL A. STEELE, 21 years, private, cotton buyer, Rock Hill; enrolled May 4, '98; mustered in May 14, '98.
4. DICK VARNADORE, private, Kershaw; enrolled June 24, '98; mustered in June 24, '98.
5. JAS. L. ADAMS, 18 years, private, Rock Hill; enrolled May 4, '98; mustered in May 14, '98.

6. CYRUS M. ALEXANDER, private, Charlotte, N. C.; enrolled August 18, '98; mustered in August 18, '98.
7. JAS. D. ALEXANDER, private, Lancaster; enrolled August 22, '98; mustered in August 22, '98.
8. GEO. W. BUTLER, 18 years, student, Vaucleuse; enrolled May 4, '98; mustered in May 14, '98.
9. GENERAL J. BAREFOOT, private, Charlotte, N. C.; enrolled August 11, '98; mustered in August 11, '98.
10. JNO. L. BREWER, private, Mt. Island, N. C.; enrolled August 11, '98; mustered in August 11, '98.
11. HENRY C. BOGGS, private, Charlotte, N. C.; enrolled August 19, '98; mustered in August 19, '98.
12. NEWTON BROOM, private, Rock Hill; enrolled June 24, '98; mustered in June 24, '98.
13. MARION BRUBAKER, student, Rock Mart, Ga.; enrolled June 27, '98; mustered in June 27, '98.
14. GUS BAKER, private, Camden; enrolled July 30, '98; mustered in July 30, '98.
15. WM. H. CAMPBELL, 24 years, private, farmer, Rock Hill; enrolled May 4, '98; mustered in May 14, '98.
16. SAML. B. CARROLL, 18 years, private, loom fixer, Rock Hill; enrolled May 4, '98; mustered in May 14, '98.
17. JESSE B. CLYBURN, 26 years, private, machinist, Rock Hill; enrolled May 4, '98; mustered in May 14, '98.
18. JAS. M. CULLENS, 24 years, private, farmer, Rock Hill; enrolled May 4, '98; mustered in May 14, '98.
19. CHAS. H. CULP, 30 years, private, merchant, Chester; enrolled May 10, '98; mustered in May 14, '98.
20. ROY J. CUNNINGHAM, 19 years, private, student, Lancaster; enrolled May 4, '98; mustered in May 14, '98.
21. WM. J. CURETON, 26 years, private, fireman, Lancaster; enrolled May 4, '98; mustered in May 14, '98.
22. EARLE COUSART, private, Fort Mill; enrolled August 3, '98; mustered in August 3, '98.
23. EMMET G. COOK, private, Old Point; enrolled August 9, '98; mustered in August 9, '98.
24. JACOB A. CROW, private, Kershaw; enrolled June 24, '98; mustered in June 24, '98.
25. BENJ. R. DABBS, private, Rock Hill; enrolled August 17, '98; mustered in August 17, '98.
26. ROLAND P. DOZIER, private, Rock Hill; enrolled June 29, '98; mustered in June 29, '98.
27. KERSHAW B. DUBOSE, private, Camden; enrolled July 30, '98; mustered in July 30, '98.
28. HOUSTON A. ENRY, private, Salisbury, N. C.; enrolled August 18, '98; mustered in August 18, '98.
29. GEO. E. FINCHER, 26 years, private, laborer, Rock Hill; enrolled May 4, '98; mustered in May 14, '98.
30. LEWIS G. FERGUSON, 18 years, private, painter, Yorkville; enrolled May 4, '98; mustered in May 14, '98.

31. CLAUDE H. HOWIE, 18 years, private, weaver, Rock Hill; enrolled May 4, '98; mustered in May 14, '98.
32. EMORY A. HOLLER, 23 years, private, student, Rock Hill; enrolled May 10, '98; mustered in May 14, '98.
33. EUGENE M. HOLLER, 18 years, private, student, Rock Hill; enrolled May 4, '98; mustered in May 14, '98.
34. JNO. P. HAWTHORNE, private, Due West; enrolled June 2, '98; mustered in June 2, '98.
35. GEO. V. JORDAN, 27 years, private, cattle buyer, Fort Lawn; enrolled May 4, '98; mustered in May 14, '98.
36. FRANCIS B. JONES, private, Rock Hill; enrolled July 30, '98; mustered in July 30, '98.
37. RORT. KENNEDY, private, Rock Hill; enrolled August 19, '98; mustered in August 19, '98.
38. ISRAEL P. KLINE, 22 years, private, farmer, Catawba; enrolled May 4, '98; mustered in May 14, '98.
39. CICERO J. KNOTT, 35 years, private, bricklayer, Winston, N. C.; enrolled May 4, '98; mustered in May 14, '98.
40. ROBT. L. KIRBY, private, Fort Mill; enrolled August 8, '98; mustered in August 8, '98.
41. ERNEST B. LOWRY, 29 years, private, student, Yorkville; enrolled May 4, '98; mustered in May 14, '98.
42. RICHARD C. LEWIS, private, Lumberton, N. C.; enrolled August 18, '98; mustered in August 18, '98.
43. VINCENT G. MCFADDEN, 20 years, private, mechanic, Rock Hill; enrolled May 4, '98; mustered in May 14, '98.
44. CHAS. L. MCLEOD, private, Camden; enrolled July 30, '98; mustered in July 30, '98.
45. RORT. E. MCGRAW, 18 years, private, weaver, Rock Hill; enrolled May 4, '98; mustered in May 14, '98.
46. THEODORE MCGRAW, private, Rock Hill; enrolled August 17, '98; mustered in August 17, '98.
47. JNO. M. MAHER, private, Lancaster; enrolled July 6, '98; mustered in July 6, '98.
48. ROBT. J. MISENHEIMER, 21 years, private, mechanic, Rock Hill; enrolled May 4, '98; mustered in May 14, '98.
49. WALTER J. MORGAN, 20 years, private, farmer, Leslies; enrolled May 4, '98; mustered in May 14, '98.
50. PHILLIP L. MOORE, 20 years, private, student, Yorkville; enrolled May 4, '98; mustered in May 14, '98.
51. BART. F. MOTHERSHED, private, Lancaster; enrolled July 2, '98; mustered in July 2, '98.
52. HARRY E. MERRITT, private, Fort Mill; enrolled August 25, '98; mustered in August 25, '98.
53. WM. F. MAYNARD, private, Charlotte, N. C.; enrolled August 12, '98; mustered in August 12, '98.
54. NOEL L. MARLOW, private, Stony Point, N. C.; enrolled August 12, '98; mustered in August 12, '98.
55. THOMAS T. MORRISON, private, Rock Hill; enrolled June 22, '98; mustered in June 22, '98.

56. KENLOCH G. MATHIS, 19 years, printer, Lancaster; enrolled May 4, '98; mustered in May 14, '98.
57. WM. J. NEELY, 19 years, private, farmer, Rock Hill; enrolled May 4, '98; mustered in May 14, '98.
58. JNO. J. ORMAND, private, Fort Mill; enrolled August 8, '98; mustered in August 8, '98.
59. LON. OLIVER, private, Charlotte, N. C.; enrolled August 11, '98; mustered in August 11, '98.
60. LAURENCE L. PARKER, 18 years, private, millman, Ridgeway; enrolled May 4, '98; mustered in May 14, '98.
61. ARTHUR L. PARKS, 21 years, private, weaver, Fort Mill; enrolled May 4, '98; mustered in May 14, '98.
62. ERNEST R. PATTERSON, 18 years, clerk, Fort Mill; enrolled May 4, '98; mustered in May 14, '98.
63. RAYMOND G. PAXTON, 20 years, private, farmer, Rock Hill; enrolled May 4, '98; mustered in May 14, '98.
64. CHARLIE L. PETERSON, 18 years, farmer, Tirzah; enrolled May 4, '98; mustered in May 14, '98.
65. JAS. F. POAG, 22 years, private, clerk, Rock Hill; enrolled May 4, '98; mustered in May 14, '98.
66. DAVID L. POPLIN, 20 years, private, mill hand, Rock Hill; enrolled May 4, '98; mustered in May 14, '98.
67. GEO. POPE, 22 years, private, farmer, Blair; enrolled May 4, '98; mustered in May 14, '98.
68. JNO. R. PURSER, 25 years, mechanic, Charlotte, N. C.; enrolled May 4, '98; mustered in May 14, '98.
69. HUGH A. PENCE, private, Charlotte, N. C.; enrolled August 11, '98; mustered in August 11, '98.
70. JAS. T. QUALLS, private, Burlington, N. C.; enrolled August 18, '98; mustered in August 18, '98.
71. WM. M. RAY, 27 years, private, farmer, Rock Hill; enrolled May 4, '98; mustered in May 14, '98.
72. ALBERT H. SANCKEN, 18 years, private, clerk, Rock Hill; enrolled May 4, '98; mustered in May 14, '98.
73. LOUIS B. SESSIONS, 18 years, private, farmer, Sharps; enrolled May 4, '98; mustered in May 14, '98.
74. SAML. STEELE, 31 years, private, farmer, Rock Hill; enrolled May 4, '98; mustered in May 14, '98.
75. WOODS M. STEELE, 20 years, private, operator, Fort Mill; enrolled May 4, '98; mustered in May 14, '98.
76. JESSE W. SUMMERLIN, private, Rock Hill; enrolled August 17, '98; mustered in August 17, '98.
77. WM. L. TURNER, 21 years, private, engineer, Sharon, N. C.; enrolled May 4, '98; mustered in May 14, '98.
78. ROBT. L. TILLMAN, private, Rock Hill; enrolled June 20, '98; mustered in June 22, '98.
79. ROBT B. WELSH, 27 years, private, miller, Lancaster; enrolled May 4, '98; mustered in May 14, '98.
80. WM. J. WHITENER, 24 years, private, farmer, Yorkville; enrolled May 4, '98; mustered in May 14, '98.

South Carolina Troops in the War with Spain 95

81. WM. A. WHITENER, private, Charlotte, N. C.; enrolled August 18, '98; mustered in August 18, '98.
82. ALVA Y. WILLIAMSON, 21 years, private, farmer, Fort Mill; enrolled May 4, '98; mustered in May 14, '98.
83. RICHARD E. WITHERS, private, Yorkville; enrolled June 22, '98; mustered in June 22, '98.
84. JNO. C. WILLIAMS, 23 years, private, farmer, Ridgeway; enrolled May 4, '98; mustered in May 14, '98.
85. WM. J. WILLIAMS, private, Lancaster; enrolled June 22, '98; mustered in June 22, '98.
86. RUTHERFORD S. WILLIAMS, private, Ridgeway; enrolled July 25, '98; mustered in July 25, '98.
87. JAS. M. WILLIAMS, private, Charlotte, N. C.; enrolled August 18, '98; mustered in August 18, '98.
88. PHILLIP L. WOLFE, private, Yorkville; enrolled August 1, '98; mustered in August 1, '98.
89. HERBERT M. DUNLAP, 22 years, First Sergeant, book-keeper, Rock Hill; enrolled May 4, '98; mustered in May 14, '98; discharged September 13, to accept commission.
90. PRESTON D. BARRON, 21 years, private, teacher, Rock Hill; enrolled May 4, '98; mustered in May 14, '98; discharged July 18, S. O. 18, A. G. O.
91. JULIAN C. WATSON, 18 years, private, student, Sellers; enrolled May 4, '98; mustered in May 14, '98; discharged June 4, S. O. 15, A. G. O.
92. GLENMORE B. BARRON, 18 years, private, student, Rock Hill; enrolled May 4, '98; mustered in May 14, '98; discharged August 16, S. O. 187, A. G. O.
93. JNO. W. TRIPP, 25 years, private, clerk, Blacksburg; enrolled May 4, '98; mustered in May 14, '98; discharged June 30, S. O. 14, A. G. O.
94. JNO. L. PHILLIPS, private, Rock Hill; enrolled June 22, '98; mustered in June 22, '98; transferred Hospital Corps.
95. EDWARD A. DAVIS, 31 years, private, farmer, Fruit Hill; enrolled May 4, '98; mustered in May 14, '98; transferred Co. B June 19, S. O. 2.
96. WM. O. COPELAND, 25 years, private, farmer, Clinton; enrolled May 9, '98; mustered in May 14, '98; transferred Co. B June 19, S. O. 2.
97. AUGUSTAS M. DEAL, 21 years, Corporal, student, Blacksburg; enrolled May 4, '98; mustered in May 14, '98; transferred to 2d S. C. V. I. June 27, S. O. 150, A. G. O.
98. DANIEL M. WALLACE, 18 years, private, surveyor, Union; enrolled May 4, '98; mustered in May 14, '98; transferred to Co. E June 18, S. O. 3.
99. TONY B. LUMPKIN, 35 years, Quartermaster Sergeant, railroad agent, Rock Hill; enrolled May 4, '98; mustered in May 14, '98; promoted Sergeant Major, G. O. No. 7.
100. ROBT. H. HOPE, private, Rock Hill; enrolled June 22, '98; mustered in June 22, '98; transferred to band, July 28, S. O. No. 5.
101. J. Y. RICHARDSON, private, Charleston; enrolled July 12, '98; mustered in July 12, '98; transferred to band July 28, S. O. No. 5.

102. WM. L. ABERNATHY, 21 years, private, clerk, Catawba; enrolled May 4, '98; mustered in May 14, '98; discharged September 28, '98.
103. JUNE J. JACKSON, private, Rock Hill; enrolled July 9, '98; mustered in July 9, '98.
104. GEO. M. MOORE, 21 years, private, farmer, Bellefield; enrolled May 4, '98; mustered in May 14, '98; discharged September 28, '98.
105. CHAS. E. CARTER, 23 years, merchant, Lancaster; enrolled May 9, '98; mustered in May 14, '98; transferred to Hospital Corps, G. O. 29.

Capt. O. K. Mauldin.

Lieut. W. H. Ligon.

Lieut. T. B. Ferguson.

Company H, First Regiment

1. OSCAR K. MAULDIN, 23 years, Captain, lawyer, Greenville; enrolled May 4, '98; mustered in May 15, '98.

1. WADE H. LIGON, 26 years, First Lieutenant, merchant, Greenville; enrolled May 4, '98; mustered in May 15, '98.

1. THOS. B. FERGUSON, 24 years, Second Lieutenant, machanic, Greenville; enrolled May 4, '98; mustered in May 15, '98.

1. EDWARD B. LIGON, 22 years, First Sergeant, mechanic, Greenville; enrolled May 4, '98; mustered in May 15, '98.

1. BENJ. H. KENDRICK, 38 years, Quartermaster Sergeant, mechanic, Greenville; enrolled May 4, '98; mustered in May 15, '98.

1. JAS. E. DYER, 22 years, Sergeant, mechanic, Greenville; enrolled May 4, '98; mustered in May 15, '98.

2. THOS. LESLIE, 19 years, Sergeant, mechanic, Greenville; enrolled May 4, '98; mustered in May 15, '98.

1. NORMAN Z. ABBOTT, 20 years, Corporal, saw mill, Central; enrolled May 4, '98; mustered in May 15, '98; promoted from private.

2. CLAUDE D. PELL, 24 years, Corporal, clerk, Greenville; enrolled May 4, '98; mustered in May 15, '98.

3. KIRK N. ROBINSON, 23 years, Corporal, insurance, Greenville; enrolled May 4, 98; mustered in May 15, '98.
4. EDWIN R. HANEY, 20 years, Corporal, mechanic, Greenville; enrolled May 4, '98; mustered in May 15, '98.
5. JAS. M. BOLDING, 23 years, Corporal, barber, Greenville; enrolled May 4, '98; mustered in May 15, '98.
6. THOS. E. PRICE, 24 years, Corporal, carpenter, Greenville; enrolled May 4, '98; mustered in May 15, '98; promoted from private September 1, '98.
7. JNO. A. MOSELEY, Corporal, Greenville; enrolled June 24, '98; mustered in June 24, '98; promoted from private September 1, '98.
8. HENRY M. SMITH, 26 years, Corporal, guard, Spartanburg; enrolled May 4, '98; mustered in May 15, '98; promoted from private September 1, '98.
9. BUD P. MATTHEWS, 35 years, Corporal, carpenter, Greers; enrolled May 4, '98; mustered in May 15, '98; promoted from private September 1, '98.
10. WM. H. CHARLES, 43 years, Corporal, clerk, Greenville; enrolled May 6, '98; mustered in May 15, '98; promoted from private September 1, '98.
11. JESSE H. HENDERSON, Corporal, Greenville; enrolled June 29, '98; mustered in June 29, '98; promoted from private September 1, '98.
1. WM. T. PRESTON, 18 years, private, carpenter, Spartanburg; enrolled May 14, '98; mustered in May 15, '98.
2. WM. B. ADAMS, private, Greenville; enrolled June 29, '98; mustered in June 29, '98.
3. HERBERT D. TORRENCE, 23 years, private, blacksmith, Greenville; enrolled May 4, '98; mustered in May 15, '98.
4. ANDREW C. LEAGUE, 27 years, private, farmer, Greenville; enrolled May 4, '98; mustered in May 15, '98.
5. ROBT. B. ARTHUR, 20 years, private, clerk, Greenville; enrolled May 4, '98; mustered in May 15, '98.
6. WM. M. BENTON, 29 years, private, laborer, Greenville; enrolled May 4, '98; mustered in May 15, '98.
7. EDWARD BOWEN, 22 years, private, weaver, Greenville; enrolled May 4, '98; mustered in May 15, '98.
8. ERNEST Y. BROOKS, 19 years, private, farmer, Greenville; enrolled May 4, '98; mustered in May 14, '98.
9. EDGAR W. BULL, 23 years, private, stone cutter, Greenville; enrolled May 13, '98; mustered in May 15, '98.
10. WM A. BATES, private, Pelzer; enrolled July 5, '98; mustered in July 5, '98.
11. HENRY C. BURDETT, 30 years, private, carpenter, Greenville; enrolled May 4, '98; mustered in May 15, '98.
12. ROWLAND J. CAHILL, 19 years, private, salesman, Spartanburg; enrolled May 4, '98; mustered in May 15, '98.
13. JNO. M. CROOK, 21 years, private, printer, Greenville; enrolled May 4, '98; mustered in May 15, '98.
14. ROBT. L. CHANDLER, 19 years, private, farmer, Greenville; enrolled May 9, '98; mustered in May 15, '98.

SOUTH CAROLINA TROOPS IN THE WAR WITH SPAIN 99

15. GEO. A. COX, 21 years, private, farmer, Greenville; enrolled May 4, '98; mustered in May 15, '98.
16. CHAS. R. CRUMLEY, 20 years, private, brakeman, Greenville; enrolled May 4, '98; mustered in May 15, '98.
17. DAN'L P. CUNNINGHAM, private, Danville, Va.; enrolled June 18, '98; mustered in June 18, '98.
18. ANDREW S. CURETON, private, Greenville; enrolled July 10, '98; mustered in July 10, '98.
19. FRANCES G. EARLE, 38 years, private, farmer, Holland; enrolled May 4, '98; mustered in May 15, '98.
20. JAS. W. FOSTER, private, Greenville; enrolled June 29, '98; mustered in June 29, '98.
21. WM. M. FOSTER, private, Greenville; enrolled June 29, '98; mustered in June 29, '98.
22. JAS. M. GARNER, 22 years, private, weaver, Greenville; enrolled May 4, '98; mustered in May 15, '98.
23. JAS. M. GRIFFITH, 21 years, private, farmer, Greenville; enrolled May 4, '98; mustered in May 15, '98.
24. BEN. A. GRIFFITH, private, Camden; enrolled July 28; mustered in July 28, '98.
25. ROBT. T. GUNNELLS, private, Greenville; enrolled July 5, '98; mustered in July 5, '98.
26. WHITFIELD A. HAYES, 20 years, private, weaver, Pelzer; enrolled May 12, '98; mustered in May 15, '98.
27. WM. S. HUNNICUTT, 22 years, private, carpenter, Murphy, N. C.; enrolled May 9, '98; mustered in May 15, '98.
28. MEMMUS W. HUDGENS, 20 years, private, farmer, Laurens; enrolled May 4, '98; mustered in May 15, '98.
29. JNO. P. HAWKINS, private, Greenville; enrolled May 20, '98; mustered in May 20, '98.
30. LEWIS A. HENDERSON, private, Gaffney; enrolled July 5, '98; mustered in July 5, '98.
31. LELAND A. HOPKINS, private, Greenville; enrolled June 24, '98; mustered in June 24, '98.
32. JNO. H. JONES, private, Greenville; enrolled July 20, '98; mustered in July 20, '98.
33. PLEASANT A. JENKINS, 25 years, private, carpenter, Greenville; enrolled May 4, '98; mustered in May 15, '98.
34. THOS. B. KENNEMORE, 18 years, private, student, Greenville; enrolled May 4, '98; mustered in May 15, '98.
35. MANLEY E. KENNEMORE, 19 years, private, farmer, Greenville; enrolled May 4, '98; mustered in May 15, '98.
36. JNO. F. KENNEDY, 18 years, private, millman, Pelzer; enrolled May 4, '98; mustered in May 15, '98.
37. WM. S. LAND, 29 years, private, carpenter, Greenville; enrolled May 4, '98; mustered in May 15, '98.
38. JULIAN E. LANE, 23 years, private, clerk, Greenville; enrolled May 4, '98; mustered in May 15, '98.
39. JNO. S. LUPO, 19 years, private, farmer, Greenville; enrolled May 4, '98; mustered in May 15, '98.

40. ABE C. LYNN, 23 years, private, farmer, Greenville; enrolled May 4, '98; mustered in May 15, '98.
41. JAS. LOONEY, private, Greenville; enrolled June 29, '98; mustered in June 29, '98.
42. JNO. R. LENDERMAN, private, Ready River; enrolled July 5, '98; mustered in July 5, '98.
43. GEO. D. MCALISTER, 21 years, private, farmer, Spartanburg; enrolled May 15, '98; mustered in May 15, '98.
44. JNO. L. MCCLELLION, 21 years, private, farmer, Williamston; enrolled May 4, '98; mustered in May 15, '98.
45. WM. H. MCGAHA, 26 years, private, weaver, Greenville; enrolled May 4, '98; mustered in May 15, '98.
46. AUSTIN L. MAHAFFY, 23 years, private, clerk, Williamston; enrolled May 4, '98; mustered in May 15, '98.
47. GEO. W. MANLEY, 38 years, private, upholsterer, Greenville; enrolled May 4, '98; mustered in May 15, '98.
48. MOORE MURPHY, 20 years, private, farmer, Greenville; enrolled May 4, '98; mustered in May 15, '98.
49. JULIUS H. MANCKE, private, Columbia; enrolled June 11, '98; mustered in June 11, '98.
50. WOODFIN L. MCLANE, private, Greenville; enrolled July 5, '98; mustered in July 5, '98.
51. ALBERT C. MCCREARY, private, Pelzer; enrolled June 29, '98; mustered in June 29, '98.
52. JAS. V. NABERS, private, St. Allans; enrolled July 5, '98; mustered in July 5, '98.
53. GEO. B. PATTERSON, 19 years, private, miller, Greenville; enrolled May 4, '98; mustered in May 15, '98.
54. JNO. J. PINSON, 23 years, private, plumber, Greenville; enrolled May 4, '98; mustered in May 15, '98.
55. ISHAM W. PINSON, private, Greenville; enrolled July 16, '98; mustered in July 16, '98.
56. GEO. PIERCE, private, Greenville; enrolled July 5, '98; mustered in July 5. '98.
57. ROBT. L. RICHARDSON, 27 years, private, weaver, Greenville; enrolled May 4, '98; mustered in May 15, '98.
58. SANFORD SCRUGGS, 20 years, private, expressman, Greenville; enrolled May 4, '98; mustered in May 15, '98.
59. LUTHER A. SEAY, 30 years, private, farmer, Inman; enrolled May 14, '98; mustered in May 15, '98.
60. ROBT. C. SIMPSON, 19 years, private, millman, Pelzer; enrolled May 12. '98; mustered in May 15, '98.
61. ROWLEY H. SMITH, 23 years, private, carpenter, Greenville; enrolled May 4, '98; mustered in May 15, '98.
62. JNO. L. STROUD, 23 years, private, millman, Pelzer; enrolled May 12, '98; mustered in May 15, '98.
63. GEO. W. SERRATT, 21 years, private, millman, Greenville; enrolled May 4, '98; mustered in May 15, '98.
64. ANTHONY STOWE, private, millman, Greenville; enrolled July 28, '98; mustered in July 28, '98.

South Carolina Troops in the War with Spain 101

65. BENJ. M. STRADLEY, private, Greenville; enrolled August 30, '98; mustered in August 30, '98.
66. GEORGE E. TURPIN, 45 years, private, carpenter, Greenville; enrolled May 13, '98; mustered in May 15, '98.
67. GEO. M. THACKSTON, private, Sterling; enrolled July 20, '98; mustered in July 20, '98.
68. FRANK VAUGHAN, private, Greenville; enrolled June 24, '98; mustered in June 24, '98.
69. FOREST N. WAKEFIELD, 19 years, private, weaver, Greenville; enrolled May 4, '98; mustered in May 15, '98.
70. GUY L. WATSON, 21 years, private, clerk, Greenville; enrolled May 4, '98; mustered in May 15, '98.
71. JNO. A. WILSON, 23 years, private, farmer, Landrums; enrolled May 13, '98; mustered in May 15, '98.
72. LOUIS W. WILSON, 20 years, private, carpenter, Greenville; enrolled May 4, '98; mustered in May 15, '98.
73. ROBT. C. WILSON, 23 years, private, weaver, Greers; enrolled May 10, '98; mustered in May 15, '98.
74. COLUMBUS M. WATSON, private, Willis; enrolled July 12, '98; mustered in July 12, '98.
75. CLAUDE E. CHAPMAN, 21 years, private, farmer, Greenville; enrolled May 6, '98; mustered in May 15, '98; discharged July 23, '98.
76. HENRY L. TRIPP, private, Landrums; enrolled July 5, '98; mustered in July 5, '98; discharged September 22, '98.
77. HERBERT M. GAINES, 26 years, Sergeant, mechanic, Gaffney; enrolled May 4, '98; mustered in May 15, '98; discharged September 29, '98, telegram.
78. WM. A. WALLACE, 23 years, Sergeant, book-keeper, Greenville; enrolled May 9, '98; mustered in May 15, '98; discharged September 28, '98, telegram.
79. HAYNE Y. SMITH, 38 years, Corporal, kiln-man, Greenville; enrolled May 4, '98; mustered in May 15, '98; discharged September 28, '98, telegram.
80. WM. B. LEAGUE, 26 years, private, carpenter, Greenville; enrolled May 4, '98; mustered in May 15, '98; discharged September 29, '98, telegram.
81. HENRY POLLARD, private, Greenville; enrolled July 20, '98; mustered in July 20, '98; discharged September 29, '98, telegram.
82. SAML. R. PRESTON, private, Greenville; enrolled July 28, '98; mustered in July 28, '98; discharged September 29, '98, telegram.
83. HERBERT C. DAGGETT, 22 years, private, painter, Anderson; enrolled May 12, '98; mustered in May 15, '98; transferred to Co. C June 17, '98.
84. THOS. PAIGE, 28 years, private, decorator, Anderson; enrolled May 12, '98; mustered in May 15, '98; transferred to Co. C June 17, '98.
85. MILLEDGE L. BONHAM, JR., 18 years, private, student, Anderson; enrolled May 12, '98; mustered in May 15, '98; transferred to Co. C June 17, '98.
86. SAML. FRANKLIN, 31 years, machinist, Macon, Ga.; enrolled May 11, '98; mustered in May 15, '98; transferred to Co. K July 5, '98.

87. WM. W. WELLS, 20 years, Corporal, railroad agent, Greenville; enrolled May 4, '98; mustered in May 15, '98; transferred to Hospital Corps July 21, '98.
88. LON WARD, private, Greenville; enrolled July 13, '98; mustered in July 13, '98; transferred to Co. F July 13, '98.
89. REUBEN R. HOLLINGSHEAD, 41 years, private, jeweler, Spartanburg; enrolled May 13, '98; mustered in May 15, '98; transferred Hospital Corps, G. O. 158.
90. JNO. H. BEARD, private, Greenville; enrolled June 29, '98; mustered in June 29, '98; transferred Hospital Corps September 11, '98.
91. MEREDITH COX, 27 years, private, clerk, Greenville; enrolled May 4, '98; mustered in May 15, '98; transferred Hospital Corps September 13, '98.
92. AVERY F. HIGHTOWER, private, Greenville; enrolled June 29, '98; mustered in June 29, '98; transferred Hospital Corps September 13, '98.
93. WM. MATHEWS, private, Greenville; enrolled July 5, '98; mustered in July 5, '98; died of fever August 6, '98.
94. THOS. J. STEINS, private, Greenville; enrolled June 24, '98; mustered in July 24, '98; died of meningitis August 17, '98.
95. LAURENCE L. TURNER, 38 years, private, farmer, Greenville; enrolled May 4, '98; mustered in May 15, '98; died heart failure September 25, '98.
96. SANDERS W. PATTERSON, 21 years, private, millman, Pelzer; enrolled May 12, '98; mustered in May 15, '98.
97. DANL. M. SHIPMAN, 30 years, private, farmer, Greenville; enrolled May 12, '98; mustered in May 15, '98.
98. LEE M. WALKER, 22 years, private, weaver, Augusta, Ga.; enrolled May 10, '98; mustered in May 15, '98.
99. WM. L. WALKER, 24 years, private, blacksmith, Greenville; enrolled May 10, '98; mustered in May 15, '98.

Capt. Chas. Newnham.

Lieut. C. B. Smith.   Lieut. W. N. Kirkland.

Company I, First Regiment

1. CHAS. NEWNHAM, 48 years, Captain, contractor, Columbia; enrolled May 3, '98; mustered in May 20, '98.

1. CLARENCE B. SMITH, 23 years, First Lieutenant, reporter, Columbia; enrolled May 3, '98; mustered in May 20, '98; A. D. C. to Gen. Barkley, S. O. No. 3.

1. WALTER N. KIRKLAND, 23 years, Second Lieutenant, farmer, Florence; enrolled May 3, '98; mustered in May 20, '98.

1. ELBERT M. BROWN, 25 years, First Sergeant, clerk, Columbia; enrolled May 3, '98; mustered in May 20, '98.

1. WM. B. MOORE, 28 years, Quartermaster Sergeant, book-keeper, Columbia; enrolled May 3, '98; mustered in May 20, '98.

1. PERCY S. NORRIS, 22 years, Sergeant, salesman, Batesburg; enrolled May 3, '98; mustered in May 20, '98.

2. HENRY W. HOLLOWAY, 22 years, Sergeant, detective, Columbia; enrolled May 3, '98; mustered in May 20, '98.

3. WM. H. GLENN, 22 years, Sergeant, salesman, Columbia; enrolled May 3, '98; mustered in May 20, '98.

4. BENJ. T. HARRISON, 20 years, Sergeant, painter, Columbia; enrolled May 3, '98; mustered in May 20, '98.

1. WM. L. ALLEN, 27 years, Corporal, clerk, Columbia; enrolled May 3, '98; mustered in May 20, '98.
2. ROBT. R. JACKSON, 28 years, Corporal, clerk, Columbia; enrolled May 3, '98; mustered in May 20, '98.
3. CHAS. T. GOODWYN, 25 years, Corporal, farmer, Columbia; enrolled May 3, '98; mustered in May 20, '98.
4. CHAS. H. EVANS, 22 years, Corporal, farmer, Marion; enrolled May 3, '98; mustered in May 20, '98.
5. WM. W. ROBERTSON, 28 years, Corporal, clerk, Columbia; enrolled May 3, '98; mustered in May 20, '98.
6. JNO. M. DOZIER, 19 years, Corporal, guard, Boykins; enrolled May 3, '98; mustered in May 20, '98.
7. WM. D. CHRISTOPHER, 22 years, Corporal, carpenter, Easley; enrolled May 18, '98; mustered in May 20, '98; promoted from private September 1, '98.
8. ELBERT H. DAWKINS, 21 years, Corporal, clerk, Columbia; enrolled May 5, '98; mustered in May 20, '98; promoted from private September 1, '98.
9. CHAS. W. GEORGE, Corporal, Spartanburg; enrolled June 17, '98; mustered in June 17, '98; promoted from private September 1, '98.
10. RUFUS A. JOHNSON, 24 years, Corporal, farmer, Boykin; enrolled May 3, '98; mustered in May 20, '98; promoted from private September 1, '98.
11. JOS. S. JOHNSON, 21 years, Corporal, student, Florence; enrolled May 10, '98; mustered in May 20, '98; promoted from private September 1, '98.
12. ALEX. N. TALLEY, 20 years, Corporal, clerk, Columbia; enrolled May 5, '98; mustered in May 20, '98; promoted from private September 1, '98.

1. MURDOCK F. DAVIS, 23 years, private, jeweler, Marion; enrolled May 3, '98; mustered in May 20, '98.
2. ROBT. L. WILLIAMS, private, Spartanburg; enrolled June 18, '98; mustered in June 18, '98.
3. JNO. W. CARTER, 43 years, private, farmer, Marion; enrolled May 15, '98; mustered in May 20, '98.
4. WM. H. STRICKLAND, 25 years, private, drayman, Columbia; enrolled May 3, '98; mustered in May 20, '98.
5. JAS. H. ADAMS, 24 years, private, salesman, Leesville; enrolled May 15, '98; mustered in May 20, '98.
6. THEO. M. ALLEN, 24 years, private, operator, Sycamore; enrolled May 10, '98; mustered in May 20, '98.
7. WM. H. BAKER, 18 years, private, operator, Langley; enrolled May 20, '98; mustered in May 20, '98.
8. RICHARD M. BALLARD, 18 years, private, laborer, Hagood; enrolled May 3, '98; mustered in May 20, '98.
9. CLEVELAND E. BRYANT, 20 years, private, liveryman, Spartanburg; enrolled May 18, '98; mustered in May 20, '98.
10. JNO. M. CLEMENTS, 34 years, private, laborer, Langley; enrolled May 20, '98; mustered in May 20, '98.

South Carolina Troops in the War with Spain 105

11. Jno. M. Cushman, 18 years, private, farmer, Langley; enrolled May 20, '98; mustered in May 20, '98.
12. Ansel P. Dannelly, 23 years, private, farmer, Woodford; enrolled May 3, '98; mustered in May 20, '98.
13. Augustas Day, 23 years, private, farmer, Pickens; enrolled May 18, '98; mustered in May 20, '98.
14. Danl. E. Dunmire, Ruffsdale, Pa.; enrolled August 29, '98; mustered in August 29, '98.
15. Wm. L. Eargle, 22 years, private, farmer, Peaks; enrolled May 3, '98; mustered in May 20, '98.
16. Jno. A. Entzminger, 22 years, farmer, Blythewood; enrolled May 3, '98; mustered in May 20, '98.
17. Robt. Ford, 24 years, private, clerk, Columbia; enrolled May 3, '98; mustered in May 20, '98.
18. Wm. D. Flannigan, 21 years, private, painter, Richmond, Va.; enrolled May 17, '98; mustered in May 20, '98.
19. West B. Fludd, 21 years, private, laborer, Columbia; enrolled May 20, '98; mustered in May 20, '98.
20. Saml. B. Gardener, 21 years, private, farmer, Columbia; enrolled May 3, '98; mustered in May 20, '98.
21. Wm. E. Garren, private, Pacolet; enrolled August 10, '98; mustered in August 10, '98.
22. Chas. P. Green, 21 years, private, laborer, Laurens; enrolled May 3, '98; mustered in May 20, '98.
23. Henry B. Graves, 21 years, private, farmer, Mendon; enrolled May 10, '98; mustered in May 20, '98.
24. Jack T. Green, 20 years, private, farmer, Boykin; enrolled May 3, '98; mustered in May 20, '98.
25. Jno. F. Griffin, private, Spartanburg; enrolled June 17, '98; mustered in June 17, '98.
26. Jas. Hall, private, Spartanburg; enrolled June 18, '98; mustered in June 18, '98.
27. Wm. H. Huntley, private, Spartanburg; enrolled June 18, '98; mustered in June 18, '98.
28. Jno. R. Huffman, 33 years, private, laborer, Blythewood; enrolled May 3, '98; mustered in May 20, '98.
29. Churchill Jackson, private, Spartanburg; enrolled August 17, '98; mustered in August 17, '98.
30. Jno. F. Jeffcoat, 32 years, private, farmer, Witt's Mill; enrolled May 17, '98; mustered in May 20, '98.
31. Clarence A. Johnson, 21 years, private, blacksmith, Williston; enrolled May 20, '98; mustered in May 20, '98.
32. Tillman Kirk, Spartanburg; enrolled August 20, '98; mustered in August 20, '98.
33. Wm. W. Krider, 30 years, private, depot clerk, Greenville; enrolled May 18, '98; mustered in May 20, '98.
34. Loyd C. Kirby, private, Spartanburg; enrolled June 18, '98; mustered in June 18, '98.
35. Robert L. Kirby, private, Spartanburg; enrolled August 24, '98; mustered in August 24, '98.

36. STEPHEN V. LANE, 23 years, private, farmer, Oak Grove; enrolled May 15, '98; mustered in May 20, '98.
37. LESLIE E. LIVINGSTON, 23 years, private, laborer, Woodford; enrolled May 12, '98; mustered in May 20, '98.
38. SIDNEY E. LIVINGSTON, 18 years, private, farmer, North; enrolled May 12, '98; mustered in May 20, '98.
39. CHAS. W. MAY, 23 years, private, operator, Columbia; enrolled May 3, '98; mustered in May 20, '98.
40. MAURICE MANNING, 20 years, private, farmer, Little Rock; enrolled May 3, '98; mustered in May 20, '98.
41. LESTER G. MALONE, 19 years, private, baker, Columbia; enrolled May 20, '98; mustered in May 20, '98.
42. CHAS. L. MCBEE, private, Spartanburg; enrolled June 18, '98; mustered in June 18, '98.
43. FRANKLIN J. MCMAHAN, 18 years, private, clerk, Easley; enrolled May 16, '98; mustered in May 20, '98.
44. JNO. MERCER, private, Greenville; enrolled June 29, '98; mustered in June 29, '98.
45. MALCERN MITCHELL, private, Spartanburg; enrolled June 18, '98; mustered in June 18, '98.
46. WM. L. PARKER, 27 years, private, blacksmith, Columbia; enrolled May 3, '98; mustered in May 20, '98.
47. AUGUSTAS C. PATTERSON, 18 years, private, clerk, North; enrolled May 18, '98; mustered in May 20, '98.
48. RONIE PATTON, private, Spartanburg; enrolled August 23, '98; mustered in August 23, '98.
49. THOS. L. PEACE, private, Spartanburg; enrolled July 12, '98; mustered in July 12, '98.
50. SEWARD PICKENS, private, Spartanburg; enrolled August 23, '98; mustered in August 23, '98.
51. CALVIN PITTMAN, private, Betty; enrolled July 16, '98; mustered in July 16, '98.
52. HENRY POORE, private, Greenville; enrolled July 16, '98; mustered in July 16, '98.
53. ROBT. M. POOLE, private, Spartanburg; enrolled June 18, '98; mustered in June 18, '98.
54. EUGENE B. PRICE, 19 years, private, clerk, Blythewood; enrolled May 3, '98; mustered in May 20, '98.
55. HENRY C. RICHARDSON, 43 years, private, salesman, Columbia; enrolled May 3, '98; mustered in May 20, '98.
56. SAML. M. REEVES, 32 years, private, machinist, Columbia; enrolled May 3, '98; mustered in May 20, '98.
57. BUD REESE, private, Seward, N. C.; enrolled August 24, '98; mustered in August 24, '98.
58. ROBT. L. ROBINSON, 23 years, private, teacher, Gray's; enrolled May 20, '98; mustered in May 20, '98.
59. ALONZO T. RUSHTON, 19 years, private, laborer, Columbia; enrolled May 3, '98; mustered in May 20, '98.
60. DAVID H. ROWELL, 26 years, private, guard, Columbia; enrolled May 5, '98; mustered in May 20, '98.

South Carolina Troops in the War with Spain   107

61. WM. A. ROOK, 20 years, private, guard, Columbia; enrolled May 3, '98; mustered in May 20, '98.
62. CALEB R. RHODES, 25 years, private, weaver, Langley; enrolled May 16, '98; mustered in May 20, '98.
63. ALFRED E. SAMS, private, Spartanburg; enrolled June 18, '98; mustered in June 18, '98.
64. JAS. SHEPARD, private, Clifton; enrolled August 3, '98; mustered in August 3, '98.
65. CALVIN B. SMITH, 20 years, private, farmer, Batesburg; enrolled May 3, '98; mustered in May 20, '98.
66. WM. B. SMITH, 23 years, private, farmer, Gaddy; enrolled May 3, '98; mustered in May 20, '98.
67. REUBEN J. SMITH, private, Spartanburg; enrolled July 16, '98; mustered in July 16, '98.
69. WM. D. SOLSBY, private, Spartanburg; enrolled August 18, '98; mustered in August 18, '98.
70. CHAS. E. STOVER, private, Nevada, Mo.; enrolled June 18, '98; mustered in June 18, '98.
71. WM. R. TABOR, 19 years, private, student, Columbia; enrolled May 3, '98; mustered in May 20, '98.
72. CLARENCE L. TURNER, 20 years, private, clerk, Columbia; enrolled May 3, '98; mustered in May 20, '98.
73. JULIEN E. ULMER, 18 years, private, clerk, Gillisonville; enrolled May 15, '98; mustered in May 20, '98.
74. HENRY T. ULMER, 20 years, private, farmer, Cosawhatchie; enrolled May 16, '98; mustered in May 20, '98.
75. CHAS. T. WALKER, 20 years, private, farmer, Ridgeway; enrolled May 3, '98; mustered in May 20, '98.
76. CLIFTON H. WILSON, 22 years, private, farmer, Blythewood; enrolled May 16, '98; mustered in May 20, '98.
78. WILLIE WOOTEN, private, Greenville; enrolled July 16, '98; mustered in July 16, '98.
79. WILFORD V. WEST, private, Roebuck; enrolled August 18, '98; mustered in August 18, '98.
80. HENRY I. POWER, private, Spartanburg; enrolled June 18, '98; mustered in June 18, '98; discharged September 29, '98.
81. OSCAR PETTY, private, Pacolet; enrolled August 10, '98; mustered in August 10, '98; discharged September 29, '98.
82. REUBEN S. C. MOORMAN, 21 years, private, laborer, Columbia; enrolled May 3, '98; mustered in May 20, '98; transferred to band July 28, '98.
83. WADE H. HANCOCK, 21 years, private, inspector, Bath; enrolled May 20, '98; mustered in May 20, '98; transferred to Co. L July 28, '98.
84. GILBERT G. HARRIS, 21 years, private, clerk, Bath; enrolled May 19, '98; mustered in May 20, '98; transferred to Co. L July 28, '98.
85. WM. H. HILL, 23 years, private, farmer, Langley; enrolled May 20, '98; mustered in May 20, '98; transferred to Co. L July 28, '98.
86. FRED D. HARLEY, 25 years, private, laborer, Vaukton; enrolled May 20, '98; mustered in May 20, '98; transferred to Co. L July 28, '98.

87. ALEXANDER F. BORDERFER, 29 years, private, decorator, Charleston; enrolled May 3, '98; mustered in May 20, '98; transferred to Hospital Corps September 12, '98.
88. ROBT. V. MACON, 22 years, private, nurse, Columbia; enrolled May 16, '98; mustered in May 20, '98; transferred to 3d Div. Hosp. August 5, '98.
89. WM. D. OWINGS, 23 years, private, printer, Marion; enrolled May 10, '98; mustered in May 20, '98 died July 17, '98, fever, Camp Thomas.
90. ARTHUR A. McELRATH, private, Spartanburg; enrolled July 13, '98; mustered in July 13, '98; died September 16, '98, fever, Panama Park, Fla.
91. DAVID W. HOLSTINE, 19 years, private, farmer, Batesburg; enrolled May 8, '98; mustered in May 20, '98; died September 23, '98, fever, Panama Park, Fla.
92. JAS. O. ESKEW, private, Greenville; enrolled July 16, '98; mustered in July 16, '98; died September 29, 98, conjestion of brain, Florida.
93. JOS. A. QUICK, 25 years, private, clerk, Columbia; enrolled May 20, '98; mustered in May 20, '98; died October 3, '98, Columbia Hospital, S. C.
94. THOS. R. LEE, 23 years, private, laborer, Columbia; enrolled May 3, '98; mustered in May 20, '98.
95. CHARLES E. KELLY, 23 years, private, farmer, Columbia; enrolled May 3, '98; mustered in May 20, '98.
96. WARREN D. GERALD, 27 years, private, mechanic, Leesville; enrolled May 15, '98; mustered in May 20, '98.
97. WALKER ALLEN, private, Pacolet; enrolled August 10, '98; mustered in August 20, '98.
98. CHAS. H. GRIMSLEY, private, Spartanburg; enrolled August 18, '98; mustered in August 18, '98.
99. CORNWELL M. WALL, private, Boiling Spring; enrolled August 19, '98; mustered in August 19, '98.
100. GEO. W. CASTLEBURY, 23 years, private, farmer, Columbia; enrolled May 3, '98; mustered in May 20, '98.
101. OSCAR N. SWAYNGHAM, 22 years, private, tailor, Easley; enrolled May 16 '98; mustered in May 20, '98.

Capt. B. B. McCreery.

Lieut. J. D. Lowrance.

Lieut. J. T. Harvard.

Company K, First Regiment

1. BARRY B. MCCREERY, 30 years, Captain, broker, Columbia; enrolled May 6, '98; mustered in May 24, '98.

1. JAS. D. LOWRANCE, 26 years, First Lieutenant, book-keeper, Columbia; enrolled May 6, '98; mustered in May 24, '98.

1. JNO. T. HARVARD, 28 years, Second Lieutenant, bicyclist, Columbia; enrolled May 9, '98; mustered in May 24, '98.

1. WM. A. MOORE, 24 years, First Sergeant, lumberman, Columbia; enrolled May 7, '98; mustered in May 24, '98.

1. WALTER PERDUE, 28 years, Quartermaster Sergeant, hotel clerk, Columbia; enrolled May 6, '98; mustered in May 24, '98.

1. ALEX T. MOORE, 20 years, Sergeant, clerk, Columbia; enrolled May 6, '98; mustered in May 24, '98.
2. GEO. R. REMBERT, 23 years, Sergeant, mail agent, Columbia; enrolled May 6, '98; mustered in May 24, '98.
3. DYER G. MARSHALL, 21 years, Sergeant, clerk, Columbia; enrolled May 6; '98; mustered in May 24, '98.
4. MALCOM M. LANDER, 27 years, Sergeant, postal clerk, Jacksonville, Fla.; enrolled May 14, '98; mustered in May 24, '98.

1. EDWARD C. ADAMS, 22 years, Corporal, merchant, Columbia; enrolled May 6, '98; mustered in May 24, '98.
2. WALTER S. LYNCH, 22 years, Corporal, mariner, Columbia; enrolled May 6, '98; mustered in May 24, '98.
3. GEO. F. PRESTON, 25 years, Corporal, postal clerk, Jacksonville, Fla.; enrolled May 14, '98; mustered in May 24, '98.
4. ARTHUR W. GOOCH, 22 years, Corporal, waterman, Columbia; enrolled May 6, '98; mustered in May 24, '98; promoted from private August 30, '98.
5. JAY R. LYLES, 19 years, Corporal, farmer, Horeb; enrolled May 16, '98; mustered in May 24, '98; promoted from private August 30, '98.
6. JEROME P. STARK, 21 years, private, clerrk, Columbia; enrolled May 6, '98; mustered in May 24, '98; resigned as Sergeant, promoted Corporal August 30, '98.
7. MIMS FOWLER, 21 years, Corporal, electrician, Columbia; enrolled May 7, '98; mustered in May 24, '98; promoted from private August 30, '98.
8. CALEB P. GLAZE, 22 years, Corporal, millman, Edgefield; enrolled May 13, '98; mustered in May 24, '98; promoted from private September 10, '98.
9. CHAS. W. AZMAN, 21 years, Corporal, lumberman, Swansea; enrolled May 6, '98; mustered in May 24, '98; promoted from private September 10, '98.
10. GEO. E. REMBERT, 27 years, Corporal, farmer, Columbia; enrolled May 20, '98; mustered in May 24, '98; promoted from private September 10, '98.
11. JNO. B. CARR, 20 years, Corporal, clerk, Columbia; enrolled May 6, '98; mustered in May 24, '98; promoted from private September 10, '98.

1. VIRGIL D. RUCKER, 38 years, private, machinist, Swansea; enrolled May 24, '98; mustered in May 24, '98.
2. CHAS. B. STONE, 20 years, private, clerk, Columbia; enrolled May 6, '98; mustered in May 24, '98.
3. ALLEN D. CAGLE, 34 years, private, farmer, Spartanburg; enrolled May 24, '98; mustered in May 24, '98.
4. RORT. ALIXIN, 19 years, private, lineman, Augusta, Ga.; enrolled May 19, '98; mustered in May 24, '98.
5. THEO. ANTHONY, private, Charlotte, N. C.; enrolled August 18, '98; mustered in August 18, '98.
6. JNO. A. ARNOLD, 22 years, private, farmer, Greenwood; enrolled May 6, '98; mustered in May 24, '98.
7. CLARENCE M. BERMAN, 21 years, private, railroad employee, Columbia; enrolled May 7, '98; mustered in May 24, '98.
8. WM. O. BALDWIN, private, Pelzer; enrolled July 7, '98; mustered in July 7, '98.
9. JAS. BROWN, private, Pelzer; enrolled July 7, '98; mustered in July 7, '98.
10. JNO. H. BURGIN, private, Marion, N. C.; enrolled August 26, '98; mustered in August 26, '98.
11. JAS. E. BURGIN, private, Marion, N. C.; enrolled August 26, '98; mustered in August 26, '98.

12. JESSE L. CAMPBELL, 28 years, private, farmer, Dover; enrolled May 15, '98; mustered in May 24, '98.
13. ANDREW CONSTANTINE, 23 years, private, expressman, Columbia; enrolled May 14, '98; mustered in May 24, '98.
14. WM. A. CARTLEDGE, private, Columbia; enrolled May 11, '98; mustered in June 10, '98.
15. ROBT. CRAWFORD, private, Sandersville; enrolled July 7, '98; mustered in July 7, '98.
16. ARTHUR DRIGGERS, 22 years, private, farmer, Summerville; enrolled May 16, '98; mustered in May 24, '98.
17. JACOB B. EBERHARDT, private, Columbia; enrolled August 26, '98; mustered in August 26, '98.
18. DOUGLAS EPTON, 19 years, private, millman, Spartanburg; enrolled May 17, '98; mustered in May 24, '98.
19. JOS. GARTMAN, 20 years, lumberman, Gaston; enrolled May 15, '98; mustered in May 24, '98.
20. LEMUEL B. GOOCH, 22 years, private, laborer, Columbia; enrolled May 6, '98; mustered in May 24, '98.
21. PETER GLAZE, 24 years, private, carpenter, Bath; enrolled May 13, '98; mustered in May 24, '98.
22. WM. D. GRAY, 34 years, private, machinist, Bath; enrolled May 9, '98; mustered in May 24, '98.
23. JNO. K. HANE, 18 years, private, money lender, Columbia; enrolled May 6, '98; mustered in May 24, '98.
24. ROBT. H. HARDIN, 19 years, private, blacksmith, Columbia; enrolled May 6, '98; mustered in May 24, '98.
25. WM. J. HARRIS, 21 years, private, farmer, Columbia; enrolled May 5, '98; mustered in May 24, '98.
26. GEO. HASELDEN, 20 years, private, clerk, Lake City; enrolled May 24, '98; mustered in May 24, '98.
27. EDWARD E. HOEY, 20 years, private, flagman, Columbia; enrolled May 6, '98; mustered in May 24, '98.
28. JOS. E. HOLLIS, 23 years, private, hotel clerk, Columbia; enrolled May 6, '98; mustered in May 24, '98.
29. GEO. E. HOLEBOUGH, private, Charlotte, N. C.; enrolled August 11, '98; mustered in August 11, '98.
30. ED. H. HOLLOWAY, 27 years, private, millman, Columbia; enrolled May 6, '98; mustered in May 24, '98.
31. ED. R. HUGHES, 22 years, private, barber, Delta, Pa.; enrolled May 14, '98; mustered in May 24, '98.
32. LAURENCE S. JACOBS, 40 years, private, laborer, Swansea; enrolled May 14, '98; mustered in May 24, '98.
33. THOS. S. JENKINS, 20 years, private, brickmason, Bath; enrolled May 16, '98; mustered in May 24, '98.
34. MARK S. JONES, 27 years, private, machinist, Columbia; enrolled May 6, '98; mustered in May 24, '98.
35. WM. M. JONES, 36 years, private, farmer, Spartanburg; enrolled May 24, '98; mustered in May 24, '98.
36. WM. T. KAIGLER, private, Sandy Run; enrolled August 1, '98; mustered in August 1, '98.

37. ROY A. KOON, 18 years, private, pressman, Columbia; enrolled May 8, '98; mustered in May 24, '98.
38. CHAS. LEE, 21 years, private, farmer, Pacolet; enrolled May 14, '98; mustered in May 24, '98.
39. CHAS. LUNDY, 23 years, private, electrician, Columbia; enrolled May 6, '98; mustered in May 24, '98.
40. JAS. G. MCBEE, private, Mica, N. C.; enrolled August 26, '98; mustered in August 26, '98.
41. ANDREW L. MCCARSON, private, Hendersonville, N. C.; enrolled August 29, '98; mustered in August 29, '98.
42. JAS. A. MCKINSTRY, 21 years, private, farmer, Fairview; enrolled May 23, '98; mustered in May 24, '98.
43. JNO. I. MCGILL, 20 years, private, clerk, Marion; enrolled May 5, '98; mustered in May 24, '98.
44. HENRY L. MEETZE, 21 years, private, millman, Columbia; enrolled May 6, '98; mustered in May 24, '98.
45. HENRY W. MEETZE, 21 years, private, clerk, Columbia; enrolled May 6, '98; mustered in May 24, '98.
46. RAINEY MILLER, private, Burlington N. C.; enrolled August 18, '98; mustered in August 18, '98.
47. GEO. R. NASH, private, Charlotte, N. C.; enrolled August 17, '98; mustered in August 17, '98.
48. WM. M. NELSON, private, Savannah, Ga.; enrolled August 25, '98; mustered in August 25, '98.
49. MIKE A. NICELEY, private, Jacksonville, Fla.; enrolled August 20, '98; mustered in August 20, '98.
50. WM. F. OGBURN, 28 years, private, carpenter, Spartanburg; enrolled May 24, '98; mustered in May 24, '98.
51. JAS. H. PARKS, 23 years, private, farmer, Fairfield; enrolled May 20, '98; mustered in May 24, '98.
52. EARLY A. PATTERSON, private, Pelzer; enrolled July 7, '98; mustered in July 7, '98.
53. JACK M. REYNOLDS, 22 years, private, weaver, Cowpens; enrolled May 6, '98; mustered in May 24, '98.
54. WADE H. RUCKER, 21 years, private, farmer Swansea; enrolled May 24, '98; mustered in May 24, '98; transferred from Co. L June 21, '98.
55. CORNELIUS F. SEE, 25 years, private, millman, Columbia; enrolled May 6, '98; mustered in May 24, '98.
56. MOSES SEIBERT, 24 years, private, blacksmith, Columbia; enrolled May 6, '98; mustered in May 24, '98.
57. SAML. W. SHEELEY, 21 years, private, millman, Brookland; enrolled May 6, '98; mustered in May 24, '98.
58. WM. T. SIMPSON, private, Williamston; enrolled July 7, '98; mustered in July 7, '98.
59. WM. S. SLOAN, private, printer, Columbia; enrolled August 25, '98; mustered in August 25, '98.
60. HENRY B. SMITH, 23 years, private, driver, Columbia; enrolled May 6, '98; mustered in May 24, '98.
61. LEE SPRAUSE, 18 years, private, farmer, Gaffney; enrolled May 14, '98; mustered in May 24, '98.

62. JAS. P. STUDLEY, 19 years, farmer, Copes; enrolled May 24, '98; mustered in May 24, '98.
63. THOS. STOKES, private, Charlotte, N. C.; enrolled August 18, '98; mustered in August 18, '98.
64. CHAS. SWEARINGEN, 22 years, private, moulder, Columbia; enrolled May 6, '98; mustered in May 24, '98.
65. WYLIE D. WARD, 19 years, private, blacksmith, Columbia; enrolled May 6, '98; mustered in May 24, '98.
66. SAML. D. WITHERSPOON, 22 years, private, motorman, Columbia; enrolled May 6, '98; mustered in May 24, '98.
67. WM. M. WESTBERRY, 19 years, private, hotel clerk, Columbia; enrolled May 9, '98; mustered in May 24, '98.
68. ERNEST E. BUTNER, private, Salem, N. C.; enrolled August 28, '98; mustered in August 28, '98.
69. ARTIE E. HOLLEY, private, Augusta, Ga.; enrolled August 18, '98; mustered in August 18, '98.
70. WM. NISSEN, 19 years, private, farmer, Johnson; enrolled May 19, '98; mustered in May 24, '98.
71. WM. H. GINN, private, Pelzer; enrolled July 7, '98; mustered in July 7, '98.
72. BERT. S. CASSELS, 18 years, private, student, Johnson; enrolled May 24, '98; mustered in May 24, '98; discharged June 10, '98, S. O. 34.
73. FRANK A. SLOAN, 18 years, private, laborer, Gadsden; enrolled May 24, '98; mustered in May 24, '98; discharged August 20, '98, S. O. 192.
74. JAS. V. SMITH, 32 years, private, teacher, Swansea; enrolled May 24, '98; mustered in May 24, '98; discharged September 8, '98; disability.
75. WESTON ADAMS, 25 years, private, farmer, Columbia; enrolled May 6, '98; mustered in May 24, '98; transferred to Hospital Corps July 19, '98.
76. MALLIE BRASWELL, 20 years, private, weaver, Spartanburg; enrolled May 24, '98; mustered in May 24, '98; transferred to Co. E June 19, '98.
77. JNO. T. HARGROVE, 23 years, private, lumberman, Laurens; enrolled May 24, '98; mustered in May 24, '98; transferred from Co. E to Co. K June 19, '98.
78. SAML. P. FANT, 24 years, private, farmer, Columbia; enrolled May 24, '98; mustered in May 24, '98; transferred to Hospital Corps July 12, '98.
79. WM. J. TAYLOR, 26 years, private, drug clerk, Columbia; enrolled May 24, '98; mustered in May 24, '98; promoted Hospital Steward July 12, '98.
80. SAML. FRANKLIN, 31 years, private, machinist, Norfolk, Va.; enrolled May 25, '98; mustered in May 25, '98; transferred Hospital Corps August 5, '98.
81. JNO. F. MCDONALD, 31 years, private, fireman, Charleston; enrolled May 20, '98; mustered in May 24, '98.
82. WM. MYERS, 19 years, private, sailor, Columbia; enrolled May 6, '98; mustered in May 24, '98.
83. SIMON J. SHARP, 23 years, private, farmer, Swansea; enrolled May 23, '98; mustered in May 24, '98.

84. CHAS. T. ALLMAN, private, Williamston; enrolled July 7, '98; mustered in July 7, '98.
85. EDWARD C. BALDIN, private, Pelzer; enrolled July 7, '98; mustered in July 7, '98.
86. WM. H. GINN, private, Pelzer; enrolled July 7, '98; mustered in July 7, '98.
87. ALBERT P. GANTT, private, Pelzer; enrolled July 7, '98; mustered in July 7, '98.
88. JEROME P. GLAZE, 26 years, private, mason, Dallas, Tex.; enrolled May 11, '98; mustered in May 24, '98.
89. GEO. PHILLIPS, 19 years, private, farmer, White Plains; enrolled May 14, '98; mustered in May 24, '98.
90. JNO. J. SNELSON, 25 years, private, sailor, Charleston; enrolled May 20, '98; mustered in May 24, '98.

Capt. C. E. Sawyer.

Lieut. W. J. Duncan.

Lieut. J. A. Willis.

Company L, First Regiment

1. CLAUDE E. SAWYER, 46 years, Captain, lawyer, Aiken; enrolled May 7, '98; mustered in May 26, '98.

1. WILLIS J. DUNCAN, 40 years, First Lieutenant, planter, Barnwell; enrolled May 7, '98; mustered in May 26, '98.

1. JAS. A. WILLIS, 20 years, Second Lieutenant, student, Aiken; enrolled May 7, '98; mustered in May 26, '98.

1. GEO. P. ASHLEY, 18 years, First Sergeant, farmer, Aiken; enrolled May 7, '98; mustered in May 26, '98.

1. GEO. W. NEVILS, 29 years, Quartermaster Sergeant, physician, Blackville; enrolled May 7, '98; mustered in May 26, '98; discharged to accept commission October 26.

1. WM. A. COLLETT, 22 years, Sergeant, merchant, Edgefield; enrolled May 5, '98; mustered in May 26, '98.
2. CARROLL D. NANCE, 21 years, Sergeant, student, Cross Hill; enrolled May 26, '98; mustered in May 26, '98.
3. RICHARD G. STONE, 21 years, Sergeant, lawyer, Aiken; enrolled May 7, '98; mustered in May 26, '98.

4. MIKE H. MURRAY, 27 years, Sergeant, railroad conductor, Aiken; enrolled May 7, '98; mustered in May 26, '98; promoted from Corporal September 26, '98.

1. HENRY A. WRIGHT, 28 years, Corporal, merchant, Bamberg; enrolled May 5, '98; mustered in May 26, '98.
2. WM. M. PRITCHER, 26 years, Corporal, farmer, Weymess; enrolled May 7, '98; mustered in May 26, '98.
3. ALLEN M. PERRY, 24 years, Corporal, carpenter, Monetta; enrolled May 5, '98; mustered in May 26, '98.
4. ALBERT E. HILL, 20 years, Corporal, clerk, Aiken; enrolled May 7, '98; mustered in May 26, '98.
5. JOS. E. HARLEY, 19 years, Sergeant, student, Williston, enrolled May 5, '98; mustered in May 26, '98; promoted from Corporal October 26, '98.
6. ALBERT S. BERRIE, 23 years, Corporal, plumber, Charleston; enrolled May 16, '98; mustered in May 26, '98; promoted from private August 14, '98.
7. BENJ. S. MOORE, BI years, Corporal, farmer, Barnwell; enrolled May 5, '98; mustered in May 26, '98; promoted from private August 14, '98.
8. ERNEST JONES, 18 years, Corporal, millman, Langley; enrolled May 7, '98; mustered in May 26, '98; promoted from private August 1, '98.
9. THOS. M. USSERY, 18 years, Corporal, farmer, Baldoc; enrolled May 17, '98; mustered in May 26, '98; promoted from private August 1, '98.
10. RYERSON S. GUESS, 18 years, Corporal, student, Denmark; enrolled May 21, '98; mustered in May 26, '98; promoted from private August 1, '98.
11. WILSON L. SHERIDAN, 20 years, Corporal, farmer, Barnwell; enrolled May 5, '98; mustered in May 26, '98; promoted from private August 1, '98.
12. JAS. M. HUIET, 19 years, Corporal, operator, Johnsons; enrolled May 7, '98; mustered in May 26, '98; promoted from private August 1, '98.

1. JAS. A. PRICE, 22 years, private, farmer, Bamberg; enrolled May 5, '98; mustered in May 26, '98.
2. ELIJA W. FREE, 21 years, private, farmer, Bamberg; enrolled May 5, '98; mustered in May 26, '98.
3. ORRIN ALEXANDER, 24 years, private, engineer, Columbia; enrolled May 16, '98; mustered in May 26, '98.
4. ROPER H. BUSSEY, 18 years, private, farmer, Modoc; enrolled May 5, '98; mustered in May 26, '98.
5. WYATT A. BACKERS, 21 years, private, railroad employee, Savannah, Ga.; enrolled May 17, '98; mustered in May 26, '98.
6. PHROAH J. BOTTOMS, 27 years, private, tobacco factory, Bamberg; enrolled May 5, '98; mustered in May 26, '98.
7. JOS. A. BELL, 21 years, private, book-keeper, Charleston; enrolled May 22, '98; mustered in May 26, '98.
8. PORTIOUS D. BROWN, 21 years, private, laborer, Charleston; enrolled May 14, '98; mustered in May 26, '98.

South Carolina Troops in the War with Spain 117

9. Henry Dempsey, 21 years, private, blacksmith, Hampton; enrolled May 21, '98; mustered in May 26, '98.
10. Clarence Dye, 21 years, private, farmer, Batesburg; enrolled May 15, '98; mustered in May 26, '98.
11. Chas. L. Edwards, 19 years, private, millman, Columbia; enrolled May 23, '98; mustered in May 26, '98.
12. Monroe Fennell, 21 years, private, farmer, Allendale; enrolled May 23, '98; mustered in May 26, '98.
13. Gideon C. Hair, 21 years, private, constable, Williston; enrolled May 5, '98; mustered in May 26, '98.
14. Geo. H. Hope, 26 years, private, carpenter, Denmark; enrolled May 5, '98; mustered in May 26, '98.
15. Edward W. Halman, 28 years, private, farmer, Barnwell; enrolled May 5, '98; mustered in May 26, '98.
16. Jas. J. Jefcoat, 23 years, private, painter, Barnwell; enrolled May 5, '98; mustered in May 26, '98.
17. Henry M. Kirkland, 29 years, private, laborer, Aiken; enrolled May 18, '98; mustered in May 26, '98.
18. June Leonard, 19 years, private, mason, Gaffney; enrolled May 21, '98; mustered in May 26, '98.
19. Jake Lott, 21 years, private, millman, Langley; enrolled May 7, '98; mustered in May 26, '98.
20. Jno. J. Moore, 38 years, private, farmer, Barnwell; enrolled May 5, '98; mustered in May 26, '98.
21. Chas. F. Munn, 19 years, private, millman, Bath; enrolled May 7, '98; mustered in May 26, '98.
22. Jno. L. Neece, 35 years, private, laborer, Swansea; enrolled May 24, '98; mustered in May 26, '98.
23. Robt. Q. Nevils, 21 years, private, wagoner, Barnwell; enrolled May 5, '98; mustered in May 26, '98.
24. Clifton Peake, 19 years, private, farmer, Fairfield; enrolled May 24, '98; mustered in May 26, '98.
25. Wm. Pearson, 25 years, private, millman, Pacolet; enrolled May 16, '98; mustered in May 26, '98.
26. Laurence B. Padgett, 21 years, private, farmer, Montmorenci; enrolled May 19, '98; mustered in May 26, '98.
27. Henry P. Price, Jr., 18 years, private, farmer, Parksville; enrolled May 5, '98; mustered in May 26, '98.
28. Jos. G. Pricher, 37 years, private, lawyer, Weymers; enrolled May 7, '98; mustered in May 26, '98.
29. Jno. H. Prince, 23 years, private, farmer, Modoc; enrolled May 16, '98; mustered in May 26, '98.
30. Jos. S. Redd, 20 years, private, millman, Langley; enrolled May 21, '98; mustered in May 26, '98.
31. Jno. H. Reece, 20 years, private, millman, Augusta, Ga.; enrolled May 7, '98; mustered in May 26, '98.
32. Henry L. Rowell, 23 years, private, wheelwright, Bamberg; enrolled May 5, '98; mustered in May 26, '98.
33. Chas. G. Sontag, 25 years, Corporal, farmer, Denmark; enrolled May 5, '98; mustered in May 26, '98; promoted from private October 26, '98.

34. CHAS. L. STAUBES, 21 years, private, undertaker, Aiken; enrolled May 7, '98; mustered in May 26, '98.
35. GEO. S. TAYLOR, 25 years, private, millman, Columbia; enrolled May 20, '98; mustered in May 26, '98.
36. WM. E. TURNER, 19 years, private, farmer, Cope; enrolled May 23, '98; mustered in May 26, '98; died October 8, '98, at Cope, S. C.
37. SQUIRE W. USSERY, 18 years, private, farmer, Baldoc; enrolled May 17, '98; mustered in May 26, '98.
38. GEO. M. WHITTLE, 21 years, private, millman, Langley; enrolled May 7, '98; mustered in May 26, '98.
39. JAS. L. WHITING, 23 years, private, millman, Pacolet; enrolled May 24, '98; mustered in May 26, '98.
40. JNO. WILLIAMS, 39 years, private, farmer, Barnwell; enrolled May 12, '98; mustered in May 26, '98.
41. STEPHEN M. WIGGINS, 21 years, private, farmer, Pecks; enrolled May 24, '98; mustered in May 26, '98.
42. CHAS. T. WISEMAN, 33 years, private, contractor, Batesburg; enrolled May 26, '98; mustered in May 26, '98.
43. WM. M. YOUNG, 19 years, private, farmer, Camden; enrolled May 26, '98; mustered in May 26, '98.
44. WM. R. WRIGHT, 30 years, private, merchant, Bamberg; enrolled May 5, '98; mustered in May 26, '98.
45. OTIS R. KENNEDY, 20 years, private, farmer, Aiken; enrolled May 8, '98; mustered in May 26, '98.
46. ALLOYD M. SMITH, 22 years, private, mason, Summerville; enrolled May 24, '98; mustered in May 26, '98.
47. WM. A. WINGARD, 21 years, private, printer, Aiken; enrolled May 7, '98; mustered in May 26, '98.
48. JNO. M. AUTLEY, private, Elcove; enrolled July 9, '98; mustered in July 9, '98.
49. HENRY K. FAUST, private, Ola; enrolled July 19, '98; mustered in July 19, '98.
50. LUCIUS B. NEWSON, private, Bamberg; enrolled July 19, '98; mustered in July 19, '98.
51. WALTER L. GREGORY, private, Langley, enrolled July 22, '98; mustered in July 22, '98.
52. THOS. J. ROBERTS, private, Bamberg; enrolled July 19, '98; mustered in July 19, '98.
53. JNO. VINNEMAN, private, Aiken; enrolled July 22, '98; mustered in July 22, '98.
54. ALONZO SIZEMORE, private, Langley; enrolled July 22, '98; mustered in July 22, '98.
55. LEWIS H. PADGETT, private, Springfield; enrolled June 27, '98; mustered in June 27, '98.
56. WARREN M. ANDERSON, private, Dunbarton; enrolled June 21, '98; mustered in June 27, '98.
57. JNO. W. ELLEGE, private, Austin; enrolled August 3, '98; mustered in August 3, '98.
58. ROBT. F. JACKSON, 25 years, private, mechanic, Graniteville; enrolled May 6, '98; mustered in May 20, '98; transferred from Co. D, 2d S. C. V. I.

59. HEDGEMAN B. SIMS, 21 years, private, millman, Graniteville; enrolled May 7, '98; mustered in May 20, '98; transferred from Co. D, 2d S. C. V. I.
60. JAS. L. HAMBURG, private, Denmark; enrolled August 21, '98; mustered in August 21, '98.
61. FRED. D. HARLEY, 25 years, private, laborer, Vaucluse; enrolled May 7, '98; mustered in May 20, '98; transferred from Co. I to Co. L.
62. WADE H. HANCOCK, 21 years, private, inspector, Bath; enrolled May 7, '98; mustered in May 20, '98; transferred from Co. I to Co. L.
63. GILBERT G. HARRIS, 21 years, private, clerk, Bath; enrolled May 7, '98; mustered in May 20, '98; transferred from Co. I to Co. L.
64. WM. H. HILL, 23 years, private, farmer, Langley; enrolled May 7, '98; mustered in May 20, '98; transferred from Co. I to Co. L.
65. LAWSON K. GUNTER, 33 years, private, carpenter, Aiken; enrolled May 7, '98; mustered in May 26, '98.
66. ELIJA R. COLLINS, private, Blackville; enrolled July 9, '98; mustered in July 9, '98.
67. WM. C. DICKINSON, private, Bamberg; enrolled July 19, '98; mustered in July 19, '98.
68. CHAS. NIMMONS, private, Govans; enrolled July 19, '98; mustered in July 19, '98; died at home November 3, '98.
69. WM. F. PERRIN, 27 years, private, clerk, Abbeville; enrolled May 24, '98; mustered in May 26, '98; transferred to Co. A June 19, '98.
70. JNO. P. HAWKINS, 24 years, private, butcher, Greenville; enrolled May 20, '98; mustered in May 26, '98; transferred to Co. A June 19, '98.
71. JNO. W. ABRAMS, 26 years, private, farmer, Whitmire; enrolled May 23, '98; mustered in May 26, '98; transferred to Co. H June 19, '98.
72. WADE H. RUCKER, 21 years, private, farmer, Swansea; enrolled May 24, '98; mustered in May 26, '98; transferred to Co. K June 19, '98.
73. LEWIS H. TROTTI, 21 years, private, clerk, Williston; enrolled May 6, '98; mustered in May 26, '98; transferred to Hospital Corps July 19, '98.
74. RUFUS R. MOORE, 24 years, private, merchant, Barnwell; enrolled May 10, '98; mustered in May 26, '98; transferred to Hospital Corps July 19, '98.
75. JOS. A. BELL, 21 years, book-keeper, Charleston; enrolled May 22, '98; mustered in May 26, '98; transferred to Hospital Corps July 19, '98.
76. JNO. J. HOLMES, 41 years, Corporal, farmer, Charleston; enrolled May 5, '98; mustered in May 26, '98; transferred to Hospital Corps July 19, '98.
77. CHAS. H. PEEPLES, 33 years, private, farmer, Whaley's; enrolled May 5, '98; mustered in May 26, '98; transferred to Hospital Corps July 19, '98.
78. ISRAEL O. EDMUNDS, 33 years, private, salesman, Charleston; enrolled May 23, '98; mustered in May 26, '98; transferred to Co. E, 2d S. C. V. I.
79. LINTON L. KENNEDY, 31 years, private, printer, Denmark; enrolled May 5, '98; mustered in May 26, '98; transferred to Hospital Corps September 13, '98.
80. JNO. PRICE, private, Laurens; enrolled August 3, '98; mustered in August 3, '98; transferred to Hospital Corps September 13, '98.

81. JNO. H. HOLMAN, 34 years, private, brakeman, Denmark; enrolled May 6, '98; mustered in May 26, '98; transferred to Hospital Corps September 13, '98.
82. JNO. A. BEST, 22 years, private, farmer, Ulmer; enrolled May 16, '98; mustered in May 26, '98; died June 9, at Ola.
83. SAML. F. COLGAN, 44 years, private, watchman, Edgefield; enrolled May 21, '98; mustered in May 26, '98; died July 19, '98, Camp Thomas.
84. WM. E. TURNER, 19 years, private, farmer, Cope; enrolled May 5, '98; mustered in May 26, '98; died Cope, S. C., October 28, '98.
85. COKE SMITH, 20 years, private, millman, Spartanburg; enrolled May 24, '98; mustered in May 26, '98.
86. JNO. H. WIGGINS, 25 years, private, farmer, Pecks; enrolled May 24, '98; mustered in May 26, '98.

Capt. L. S. Carson.

Lieut. I. H. Moses, Jr.

Lieut. B. D. Wilson.

Company M, First Regiment

1. LAURENCE S. CARSON, 31 years, Captain, cashier, Sumter; enrolled May 5, '98; mustered in May 19, '98.

1. ISAAC H. MOSES, JR., 27 years, First Lieutenant, insurance, Sumter; enrolled May 5, '98; mustered in May 19, '98; detailed A. D. C. August 9, '98, S. O. 3.

1. BRAINARD D. WILSON, 24 years, Second Lieutenant, teacher, Sumter; enrolled May 5, '98; mustered in May 19, '98.

1. JNO. B. MILLER, 25 years, First Sergeant, printer, Sumter; enrolled May 5, '98; mustered in May 19, '98.

1. ASHBY MOORE, 29 years, Quartermaster Sergeant, expressman, Sumter; enrolled May 5, '98; mustered in May 19, '98.

1. JAS. D. WYNN, 23 years, Sergeant, bank clerk, Sumter; enrolled May 5, '98; mustered in May 19, '98; detailed Sergeant of Band June 28, '98.

2. CALDER B. YEADON, 23 years, Sergeant, agent, Sumter; enrolled May 5, '98; mustered in May 19, '98; promoted from Corporal August 16, '98.

3. CONNIE J. GALLAGHER, 21 years, Sergeant, clerk, Sumter; enrolled May 5, '98; mustered in May 19, '98; promoted from Corporal August 25, '98.
4. JNO. F. JENKINS, 22 years, Sergeant, mechanic, Sumter; enrolled May 5, '98; mustered in May 19, '98; promoted from Corporal August 16, '98.

1. MORDECAI A. STRAUSS, 23 years, Corporal, clerk, Maysville; enrolled May 5, '98; mustered in May 19, '98.
2. ARTHUR W. SCARBOROUGH, 18 years, Corporal, farmer, Providence; enrolled May 5, '98; mustered in May 19, '98.
3. IRVIN A. BROWN, 25 years, Corporal, guard, Sumter; enrolled May 5, '98; mustered in May 19, '98; promoted from private August 15, '98.
4. MANNING B. CLYDE, 23 years, Corporal, teacher, Sumter; enrolled May 5, '98; mustered in May 19, '98; promoted from private August 15, '98.
5. HERBERT A. MOSES, 21 years, Corporal, book-keeper, Sumter; enrolled May 5, '98; mustered in May 19, '98; promoted from private August 22, '98.
6. ROBT. D. SAUNDERS, 23 years, Corporal, guard, Sumter; enrolled May 5, '98; mustered in May 19, '98; promoted from private August 28, '98.
7. JAS. M. MASON, 21 years, Corporal, railroad employee, Sumter; enrolled May 5, '98; mustered in May 19, '98; promoted from private August 28, '98.
8. MIDDLETON D. SCARBOROUGH, 30 years, Corporal, farmer, Bishopville; enrolled May 5, '98; mustered in May 19, '98; promoted from private August 28, '98.
9. ALEXANDER C. THOMPSON, 26 years, Corporal, farmer, Sumter; enrolled May 5, '98; mustered in May 19, '98; promoted from private August 28, '98.
10. WALTER L. NICHOLSON, 26 years, Corporal, farmer, Edgefield; enrolled May 5, '98; mustered in May 19, '98; promoted from private August 28, '98.
11. ELLIE D. LAW, 27 years, Corporal, farmer, Elliotts; enrolled May 5, '98; mustered in May 19, '98; promoted from private August 28, '98.
12. WADE H. FLOWERS, 21 years, Corporal, mechanic, Sumter; enrolled May 5, '98; mustered in May 19, '98; promoted from private August 28, '98.

1. FRED. N. BEECHER, private, Spartanburg; enrolled July 18, '98; mustered in July 18, '98.
2. JNO. J. GILES, private, Hot Springs, Va.; enrolled July 23, '98; mustered in July 23, '98.
3. WALTER M. LENOIR, 18 years, private, carpenter, Hagood; enrolled May 5, '98; mustered in May 19, '98.
4. BENJ. E. GILMORE, 21 years, private, farmer, Columbia; enrolled May 5, '98; mustered in May 19, '98.
5. SAML. T. BARNES, 21 years, private, farmer, Bishopville; enrolled May 5, '98; mustered in May 19, '98.
6. JACKSON BARWICK, 22 years, private, mechanic, Sumter; enrolled May 5, '98; mustered in May 19, '98.

SOUTH CAROLINA TROOPS IN THE WAR WITH SPAIN

7. JNO. P. BISHOP, private, Spartanburg; enrolled August 23, '98; mustered in August 23, '98.
8. WYLIE J. BRADLEY, 26 years, private, guard, Sumter; enrolled May 5, '98; mustered in May 19, '98.
9. EUGENE T. BRAILSFORD, 21 years, private, liveryman, Sumter; enrolled May 5, '98; mustered in May 19, '98.
10. JOS. E. BRAZELL, 21 years, private, farmer, Sumter; enrolled May 5, '98; mustered in May 19, '98.
11. JAS. H. BROWN, 21 years, private, farmer, Spring Hill; enrolled May 5, '98; mustered in May 19, '98.
12. ANTHONY K. BURROWS, 24 years, private, farmer, Providence; enrolled May 5, '98; mustered in May 19, '98.
13. JAS. CURRAN, 23 years, private, laborer, Sumter; enrolled May 5, '98; mustered in May 19, '98.
14. SIMON P. CLAYTON, private, Spartanburg; enrolled July 19, '98; mustered in July 19, '98.
15. SAML. A. CLAYTON, private, Spartanburg; enrolled July 19, '98; mustered in July 19, '98.
16. GEO. CLAYTON, private, Spartanburg; enrolled July 19, '98; mustered in July 19, '98.
17. ROSIER CASTON, private, Darlington; enrolled June 21, '98; mustered in June 21, '98.
18. SEYMORE COCHRANCE, private, Mayesville; enrolled July 23, '98; mustered in July 23, '98.
19. WM. A. CLYDE, 25 years, private, insurance, Sumter; enrolled May 5, '98; mustered in May 19, '98.
20. WM. A. CURETON, private, Clear Springs; enrolled July 23, '98; mustered in July 23, '98.
21. TOM. DENNIS, private, Sumter; enrolled June 27, '98; mustered in June 27, '98.
22. LOUIS W. DECHAMPS, 23 years, private, merchant, Sumter; enrolled May 5, '98; mustered in May 19, '98.
23. WALTER L. DICK, 20 years, private, clerk, Sumter; enrolled May 5, '98; mustered in May 19, '98.
24. TILDEN J. DOBY, 21 years, private, farmer, Providence; enrolled May 5, '98; mustered in May 19, '98.
25. ARTHUR B. DURANT, 20 years, private, clerk, Bishopville; enrolled May 5, '98; mustered in May 19, '98.
26. JOS. EMANUEL, 29 years, private, farmer, Sumter; enrolled May 5, '98; mustered in May 19, '98.
27. KINNEY S. FOSTER, 19 years, private, student, Sumter; enrolled May 5, '98; mustered in May 19, '98.
28. VERNON FOWLER, private, Spartanburg; enrolled July 19, '98; mustered in July 19, '98.
29. MAT. J. GAINES, private, Inman; enrolled August 23, '98; mustered in August 23, '98.
30. LAURENCE O. GILMORE, 23 years, private, railroad employee, Lykesland; enrolled May 5, '98; mustered in May 19, '98.
31. CHARLIE P. HANCOCK, 22 years, private, farmer, Bishopville; enrolled May 5, '98; mustered in May 19, '98.

32. SAML. HAMMOND, 19 years, private, laborer, Camden; enrolled May 5, '98; mustered in May 19, '98.
33. AINSLEY D. HARBEY, 21 years, private, merchant, Sumter; enrolled May 5, '98; mustered in May 19, '98.
34. MADISON L. HARVIN, 25 years, private, farmer, Sumter; enrolled May 5, '98; mustered in May 19, '98.
35. WM. A. HARVIN, 21 years, private, farmer, Sumter; enrolled May 5, '98; mustered in May 19, '98.
36. ROBT. J. HENDRIX, 44 years, private, farmer, Columbia; enrolled May 5, '98; mustered in May 19, '98.
37. MARION M. HUGGINS, 19 years, private, laborer, Providence; enrolled May 5, '98; mustered in May 19, '98.
38. BLUFORD A. HUSSEY, private, Sumter; enrolled June 27, '98; mustered in June 27, '98.
39. GEO. D. JENNINGS, 24 years, private, farmer, Providence; enrolled May 5, '98; mustered in May 19, '98.
40. JNO. K. JENNINGS, 19 years, private, farmer, Providence; enrolled May 5, '98; mustered in May 19, '98.
41. CHARLIE L. JONES, 18 years, private, laborer, Sumter; enrolled May 5, '98; mustered in May 19, '98.
42. HASEL JONES, 19 years, private, laborer, Sumter; enrolled May 5, '98; mustered in May 19, '98.
43. JAS. H. JONES, 24 years, private, farmer, Sumter; enrolled May 5, '98; mustered in May 19, '98.
44. SWINTON P. JONES, 28 years, private, salesman, Spring Hill; enrolled May 5, '98; mustered in May 19, '98.
45. SPAIN KELLY, 20 years, private, farmer, Bishopville; enrolled May 5, '98; mustered in May 19, '98.
46. JNO. W. KILGORE, 19 years, private, farmer, Sumter; enrolled May 5, '98; mustered in May 19, '98.
47. JARRED A. LAW, 21 years, private, farmer, Elliotts; enrolled May 5, '98; mustered in May 19, '98.
48. WASHINGTON L. LEE, 22 years, private, planter, Sumter; enrolled May 5, '98; mustered in May 19, '98.
49. LEONARD B. LESENE, 22 years, private, laborer, Sumter; enrolled May 5, '98; mustered in May 19, '98.
50. GUS. LYNCH, private, Sumter; enrolled June 21, '98; mustered in June 21, '98.
51. PETER MELLETT, private, Sumter; enrolled June 27, '98; mustered in June 27, '98.
52. BURWELL W. MORRIS, private, Sumter; enrolled June 27, '98; mustered in June 27, '98.
53. ROBT. W. McLEOD, 19 years, private, clerk, Scarborough; enrolled May 5, '98; mustered in May 19, '98.
54. MANTON B. McCUTCHEN, 21 years, private, clerk, Bishopville; enrolled May 5, '98; mustered in May 19, '98.
55. BEN. NORMAN, private, Spartanburg; enrolled July 19, '98; mustered in July 19, '98.
56. HAMPTON R. NORRIS, 21 years, private, farmer, Sumter; enrolled May 5, '98; mustered in May 19, '98.

57. HARRY NUNNAMAKER, private, Sumter; enrolled August 15, '98; mustered in August 15, '98
58. JNO. PADGETT, private, Spartanburg; enrolled July 19, '98; mustered in July 19, '98.
59. GEO. B. PHILLIPS, 21 years, private, farmer, Providence; enrolled May 5, '98; mustered in May 19, '98.
60. SAML. J. REAMS, 22 years, private, machinist, Columbia; enrolled May 5, '98; mustered in May 19, '98.
61. CHAS. H. REESE, 22 years, private, farmer, Congaree; enrolled May 5,'98; mustered in May 19, '98.
62. EUSTACE RHAME, 22 years, private, farmer, Magnolia; enrolled May 5, '98; mustered in May 19, '98.
63. FRED F. RICKER, 20 years, private, book-keeper, Sumter; enrolled May 5, '98; mustered in May 19, '98.
64. WILLIS R. SANDERS, 21 years, private, clerk, Sumter; enrolled May 5, '98; mustered in May 19, '98.
65. HALLIE P. SCOTT, 22 years, private, clerk, Sumter; enrolled May 5, '98; mustered in May 19, '98.
66. CLIFFORD SMITH, private, Sumter; enrolled June 27, '98; mustered in June 27, '98.
67. ROBT. F. SMITH, 19 years, private, farmer, Congaree; enrolled May 5, '98; mustered in May 19, '98.
68. JOS. B. SOLSBY, private, Spartanburg; enrolled August 23, '98; mustered in August 23, '98.
69. CHAS. S. SPANN, 18 years, private, operator, Sumter; enrolled May 5, '98; mustered in May 19, '98.
70. ROBT. SPANN, JR., private, Sumter; enrolled June 22, '98; mustered in June 22, '98.
71. WILLIE STEWART, 20 years, private, farmer, Bishopville; enrolled May 5, '98; mustered in May 19, '98.
72. JAS. R. STRICKLAND, private, Spartanburg; enrolled July 18, '98; mustered in July 18, '98.
73. JAS. E. TENNETT, private, Sumter; enrolled June 21, '98; mustered in June 21, '98.
74. WM. D. VINCENT, 21 years, private, farmer, Sumter; enrolled May 5, '98; mustered in May 19, '98.
75. WESLEY WATERS, private, Greenville; enrolled July 23, '98; mustered in July 23, '98.
76. JNO. R. WEATHERS, private, Spartanburg; enrolled August 23, '98; mustered in August 23, '98.
77. JNO. E. WEAVER, 18 years, private, farmer, Sumter; enrolled May 5, '98; mustered in May 19, '98.
78. WADE H. WEAVER, Sumter; enrolled August 15, '98; mustered in August 15, '98.
79. EBBIE WELLS, 21 years, private, clerk, Sumter; enrolled May 5, '98; mustered in May 19, '98.
80. ALLIE W. WELDON, 23 years, private, farmer, Providence; enrolled May 5, '98; mustered in May 19, '98.
81. CHAS. O. WHEELER, JR., private, Sumter; enrolled June 21, '98; mustered in June 21, '98.

82. Jos. S. Wheeler, 23 years, private, farmer, Magnolia; enrolled May 5, '98; mustered in May 19, '98.
83. Wm. N. White, 33 years, private, farmer, Sumter; enrolled May 5, '98; mustered in May 19, '98.
84. Murray Woodward, private, Spartanburg; enrolled July 18, '98; mustered in July 18, '98.
85. David W. Cunningham, 27 years, private, clerk, Sumter; enrolled May 5, '98; mustered in May 19, '98.
86. Willie L. McGhee, 18 years, private, farmer, Providence; enrolled May 5, '98; mustered in May 19, '98; discharged September 3, '98, S. O. 204.
87. Jas. B. Hollman, 20 years, private, clerk, Lexington, Ky.; enrolled May 5, '98; mustered in May 19, '98; transferred June 7, '98, Independent Battalion.
88. Alex. N. Talley, 20 years, private, clerk, Columbia; enrolled May 5, '98; mustered in May 19, '98; transferred June 23, '98, Co. I.
89. Jno. F. Reid, 22 years, Sergeant, book-keeper, Sumter; enrolled May 5, '98; mustered in May 19, '98; transferred August 21, '98, to 2d S. C. V. I.
90. Arthur W. Miller, Spartanburg; enrolled July 18, '98; mustered in July 18, '98; transferred July 23, '98, to Co. F.
91. David W. Cunningham, 27 years, Corporal, clerk, Sumter; enrolled May 5, '98; mustered in May 19, '98; transferred Hospital Corps July 19, '98.
92. Richard Dozier, Jr., 34 years, private, book-keeper, Sumter; enrolled May 5, '98; mustered in May 19, '98; transferred Hospital Corps August 30, '98.
93. Dwight H. Dick, private, Sumter; enrolled June 6, '98; mustered in June 6, '98; died of fever July 9, '98.

Col. Wilie Jones

The Second S. C. V. I.

To General J. W. Floyd, Adjutant General S. C.

Dear General: At your request I have written with much pleasure to me the following narrative of the Second S. C. Volunteer Infantry Regiment, U. S. Army, in the Spanish-American War:

The formation of the Second S. C. Volunteer Infantry was completed on August 23, 1898, by the swearing in on that day at Shandon Hill, near Columbia, S. C., of Wilie Jones as Colonel, and Ben. A. Rogers as Captain of Company M. The Regiment consisting of 1,013 officers and men.

In a short time the Regiment was ordered to report to Gen. Lee at Jacksonville, Fla., and on the 15th of September we took the train for that place and reached there next day, September 16th, 1898. The Regiment was put in camp at Panama Park, four miles from Jacksonville and just across the big road opposite the camp of the 1st S. C. Regiment, then under command of that gallant and splendid soldier, Col. J. K. Alston. The Regiment remained in camp at Panama Park till October 21st, when it was ordered to Savannah, Ga. The camp at Panama Park proved to be a most horrible place, and was utterly unfit for a camp. The water was sulphur and it made almost all of the men sick. We had at one time 204 men sick. A committee came out from Washington to inspect the camp, and I said to them that it was unfit for a camp; that it was no fit place for an American soldier to camp; that I would not sleep in my tent for $100 a night, if I was not compelled to do so. As I was in the army, I had to sleep in the camp and could not help myself. The Committee was very much astonished when I said that. When my sick list reached 204, I became very much alarmed for the safety of my men, and had a consultation at once with my ever faithful, true and competent Surgeon, Dr. E. J. Wannamaker. He was as much alarmed as I was, and we concluded that we would at once telegraph Gov. Ellerbe of the fearful condition of the health of our Regiment. We sent a private telegram to Gov. Ellerbe asking him to have our Regiment moved to any place on earth, just so we left Panama Park. Gov. Ellerbe afterwards told me he had telegraphed the Secretary of War, and in less than one week we received orders to go to Savannah, Ga. My Regiment was the first Regiment of the 7th Army Corps to reach Savannah. We shall always feel grateful to Gov. Ellerbe for what he did to get us out from Jacksonville. Eight of our men died at Panama Park. I am satisfied their deaths were caused by the bad climate and the horrible water we had to drink.

We reached Savannah on the morning of October 22, 1898, and went at once into camp on Dale Avenue, near Thunderbolt. This camp proved to be the finest that we had occupied during our entire term of service, and the water was the best I ever drank. We had not been in camp at Savannah but a very short time before our men commenced to get well and soon we had not a dozen men in the hospital. The people of Savannah treated the Regiment splendidly—they could not do too much for us and we will never forget them for it. On Thanksgiving day the whole 7th Army Corps were treated to a fine dinner by the good people of Savannah. There were nearly 100 ladies to come to our Regiment, and each company had about eight ladies assigned to it, and they set the tables, put on table cloths, and when all was ready, waited on the men. I do not believe that there was ever an army treated so well before, and I have never heard of or read of such magnificent treatment any where. I shall always love the good people of Savannah, and so does every member of the Regiment and of the 7th Army Corps. I heard that the people of several of the States were fixing to send car loads of turkeys for their Regiments for their Christmas dinner, and as I had not heard that the good people of South Carolina were making arrangements to send a car load of turkeys to the 2d Regiment for theirs, I concluded I would treat the Regiment to turkeys at my own expense. So I requested Lieut. Culler, of Co. E, to go up to Savannah and purchase enough turkeys for the Regiment, and he came back and reported to me that he had purchased 130 turkeys, which he thought would be enough for the entire Regiment. I went home on that day to take dinner with my family; when I returned to camp the next day, the boys told me they had a splendid dinner, and all seemed very grateful to me for thinking of them. It was a great pleasure to me to treat the boys of my Regiment, as they had all been so very faithful to me. We had a great deal of trouble in getting lumber in Savannah to fix up floors for our tents, but after repeated demands by our Quartermaster, Capt. G. C. Sullivan, we at last succeeded. At the request of our Chaplain, Capt. P. A. Murray, I made a requisition for 3,000 feet of lumber to fix up the Y. M. C. A. tent, and Gen. Douglass returned it disapproved. We were very much put out about it, but could not help ourselves. It did not make very much difference, because we left for Cuba very soon after that.

On January 1st, 1899, we received orders to go to Havana, Cuba, on the transport Roumanian. On January 3, 1899, I marched the

Regiment through the city of Savannah, 840 strong, counting officers, enlisted men and teamsters. We had 24 wagons and 132 horses and mules. While in Savannah a friend of mine said to me that the anxiety in the Regiment about the yellow fever in Cuba was so great that when we received the order to go to Cuba he thought that hundreds would desert. I told him I had the greatest confidence in my South Carolina boys, practically all of whom were sons of Confederate Veterans, and I thought he was mistaken. I am proud to say that I marched the Regiment on board the boat 840 strong and not a single man deserted. No Regiment in the world can show a better record than that, and I shall always be proud of it.

The Regiment marched through the city of Savannah flying a banner, on which was inscribed the following: "Hurrah for the good people of Savannah, we will never forget them for their kindness to us." One of the men in the 3d Battalion had a little dog leading him with a string, and had a white cotton cloth cover on him, and had marked on it in black letters the following: "Hurrah for Savannah, to hell with Jacksonville." The people of Savannah were very much pleased with what they read on the banner and on the little dog, and cheered us greatly as we marched through the city.

We reached Havana without accident, on the morning of January 6, 1899. Very soon after the ship sailed from the wharf in Savannah, the Quartermaster in charge came to me and said I was in command of the ship, as I was the ranking officer on board. He wished to know what orders I had to give; I said to him that I had but one order to give, and that was that no liquor should be sold on the ship. This order was carried out and we had no trouble at all with our men, they behaved splendidly.

As our transport entered the harbor of Havana, Maj. Eaves and Capt. Wannamaker held our flags on the bridge, and as we passed Morro Castle we were greeted with cheers from the garrison in charge. A great many of the men had sea-sickness very badly, but got well as soon as we reached our camp near Havana. The 1st Battalion, under Lt. Col. H. T. Thompson, was unloaded at once and went straight to their camp. The 2d and 3d Battalions could not be gotten off that day, so had to remain over on the boat till next day. When we reached San Jose wharf, Havana, no one of the Regiment was allowed to go off but the Quartermaster of the ship and myself. I left the boat with him, and left Lt. Col. Thompson in command.

As I came down the long rope ladder alone, the Regiment were all looking at me, and when I put my feet on Cuban soil, a cheer from a thousand throats went up—it seemed loud enough to shake the old boat. I was very proud to be the first man on the boat to step on Cuban soil. I went straight to the telegraph office and sent a telegram to my wife and to Gov. Ellerbe, telling them of our safe arrival. I had a good deal of trouble to find the telegraph office, as I could speak little Spanish; but I went up the street saying to the people I met, "Telegrafo," and they pointed with their fingers to the building in which the office was. I telegraphed my wife the word "Safe," and it cost me $2.40. The telegram I sent to Gov. Ellerbe, I made the Government pay for, so I made it quite long. The weather was so warm when we reached Cuba that we could with difficulty wear our heavy winter clothes. As we marched through the beautiful city of Havana we were cheered on all sides by the people, and the beautiful Cuban senoritas, dressed in white muslin dresses, with black mantillas on their heads, waved United States and Cuban flags at us, and would smile most beautifully. Often we would see a small child standing on a piazza with a Cuban flag in one hand and an American flag in the other, waving them at us and cheering us as we marched along. I told my men that they could bow to all the pretty Cuban girls they saw, but that they must keep in ranks. But, of course, soldiers will be soldiers, and they often fell out to speak to a good-looking girl and get a drink of cool water. My Regiment behaved splendidly in marching through Havana and gave me no trouble at all. The first night we camped in Cuba, there was an awful rain and little sleeping was done. But after that we were not troubled much with rain, and in fact it was very dry all the time. We were soon very comfortably fixed in our Cuban camp, called Camp Columbia, situated on the Havana and Marianao Railroad, just five miles from the city and half a mile from Gen. Lee's headquarters at Buena Vista. We had the most beautiful camp in Havana I ever saw—it was as clean as a parlor. This was due to the great precautions taken by all the officers to keep things clean, and they had the earnest assistance of the enlisted men in this. Soon after we reached Cuba, Gen. Lee ordered that an officer should be appointed for each Regiment to look after the sanitary condition of the camp, and to be excused from all other duty. I appointed to perform this very important duty Maj. J. J. Wagener, of the 3d Battalion. Maj. Wagener kept the camp as neat as a pin and was untiring in his efforts to keep down disease, and he was successful, for we lost only three men in Cuba. I am satisfied our small death rate in Cuba was due to the cleanliness of the camp through the zeal of Major Wagener and the skill of our surgeons. When we left Cuba our entire camp was covered with lime. We were unable to get lumber, so had to sleep on the ground, but each man in the Regiment had a cot furnished by the Government, and said to have been presented to the troops in Cuba by Miss Helen Gould. After being in camp about one month, we were supplied with lumber, and each tent had a nice floor. We found the Cubans very kind and friendly to us. We had little to do with the Spaniards; but those we met were quite polite, and treated us all right. The climate is very delightful at night, quite warm in the day. The average temperature while we were there was about 85. I slept under a blanket every night I was in Cuba. When we first reached Cuba, the orders were so strict that no officer or enlisted man could go to Havana without a pass, approved by our Major General; we had to apply for a pass one day and send it up the next, and you were required to state in your request for the pass your business and how long you wished to stay. In my first request for a pass, I stated that I wished to go to the theatre Saturday night, make some necessary purchases, and go to church Sunday morning, and return at 12 o'clock. We received orders to go on a ten days' march February 19th, and early that morning I had the Regiment ready to move, in marching order. We had a wagon train of 25 wagons, and had to carry barrels of water and wood with which to cook. Wood is very scarce in Cuba, and we did not know what kind of water we would find on the roadside. But we found the water good and healthy. Our Brigade was commanded by Gen. H. T. Douglass, of Baltimore, and was composed of the 9th and 4th Illinois and the 2d South Carolina. The men of these two western regiments were very friendly, and especially were we friendly with the 9th Illinois. This Regiment and our Regiment never passed each other without a cheer or a salute. The first day's march was very hard on the men, owing to the heat, and not being used to long marches. The General told me after the first day's march that the men of the 2d had straggled too much that day, and that we must try to do better hereafter. I was much mortified at this gentle rebuke from the General, and next morning when the Regiment was drawn up in column of fours in the big road ready to march, I rode to the first Battalion and made them a short speech, telling them what the General had said, and that they must remember that they were from South Carolina, and that I hoped and knew that they would do better; I rode to the other two Battalions and made the same talk to them, and they cheered me and said they would do it, and I never had any more trouble. We marched as far as Guines, about fifty miles from Havana, and went in camp on a beautiful little river, and remained there about three days, and then returned to Havana. The heat was very severe on this march and many of our men were made sick by it. I am satisfied we lost one man, R. N. McKay, from the effect of that march, as he was taken sick on the march and died about four weeks after we came back.

As we marched through Cuba the people treated us with the greatest consideration, and whenever we passed the Cuban soldiers, they always gave us a salute, which we returned. The day set for the march to begin happened to be Sunday. I went to my commanding General and reminded him that we had been ordered to move on Sunday, and suggested to him in a very gentle manner that I hoped he would postpone the march till next day, Monday, as I did not see the great importance of moving that day, and I had always been taught not to do anything on Sunday that was not necessary. He laughed at the idea and said it made no difference, and off we went on Sunday. Soon after we arrived in Cuba, several of the Captains in my Regiment reported to me that they had lost their boxes of meat on the boat in going over, and that their men would have no meat for at least a week, the next ration day. I said to the Captains that I would see that they had meat at once, if I had to go to Gen. Lee. I got on my horse and rode up to the headquarters of my Brigadier General, and reported the facts to him. He said he had no authority at all to issue extra rations, that the Captains should be held responsible for the loss of the meat. I said to him that unless rations were at once issued to these Companies that my men would suffer, and he still refused me. I then felt very much hurt about the way he treated us, and asked the General if he could tell me where I could buy some meat for my men, and that I had the money in my pocket to pay for it, and would do so rather than see my men suffer. He told me where I could buy the meat, and I rode back to camp and sent for my Commissary, Lieut. A. C. Davis, and told him to go and buy the meat needed, and that I would pay for it. He went off, and soon reported to me that he had seen the Brigade Commissary, and in some way or another he got the meat without having to pay for it. I am sure the General does not know to this day that we got that meat without paying for it.

About the 20th of March, 1899 (the day Senator Tillman, Congressmen Norton and Latimer and others visited our camp), I received orders from Gen Lee to prepare my Regiment to go home. I heard the night before by a telegram from Maj. J. G. Evans in Havana, that these gentlemen would visit us the next day, and I left camp early next morning to go to Havana to meet them. Before leaving camp I requested Maj. Wagener to have a stand erected in front of my tent from which they might speak. They came as expected, and spoke to us. Most of the men of the 9th Illinois had come over to hear the speaking, and we had a great time. The men did not know that I had the order to go home in my pocket, and when the speaking was all over, I stepped on the platform and said to my men that I had something better to tell them than any of the speakers that had spoken, and I then drew out of my pocket the order from Gen. Lee to go home, and there was the greatest excitement and joy at the idea of going back to America. After reading the order I ordered the Regiment formed at once, as a compliment to our visiting Congressmen and their wives. I gave my horse to Senator Tillman and he reviewed the Regiment. The night before we left Havana, the 9th Illinois Regiment came to our camp in a body with their Band and serenaded us. Officers of both Regiments made speeches, and the two Regiments parted great friends. It certainly will be a great pleasure to us to meet those soldiers in the future. The wives of four of our officers, Mrs. Maj. Eaves, Mrs. Capt. Gonzales, Mrs. Capt. McCaughrin, and Mrs. Lt. Dowling, came to our camp just after we reached Cuba. Their husbands put up a nice settlement of tents and they went regularly to housekeeping. The dining room was made of bamboo wood, and they called the settlement Bamboo Lodge. It was just about three hundred yards from our camp, on a hill. I boarded with them, and certainly enjoyed the fare they gave us very much. I did not have a headache while I was in Cuba, and I am sure the good fare these excellent ladies gave me was the cause of it. We were so much pleased when the ladies came to camp that I ordered the Band to go over and serenade them.

The movements of the Regiment was as follows:

September 15, 1898, left Columbia; arrived at Jacksonville September 16.

October 21, 1898, left Jacksonville; arrived at Savannah October 22.

January 3, 1899, left Savannah; arrived at Havana January 6.

February 19, 1899, left Havana; arrived at Guines February 21.

February 23, 1899, left Guines, Cuba; arrived at Havana February 27.

The Regiment left Havana in four sections for America as follows:

March 22, 1899, Cos. A and B, Col. Thompson commanding; arrived in Augusta March 26th.

March 23, 1899, Cos. C, D, E, F, and G, Major Eaves commanding; arrived Augusta March 27.

March 25, 1899, Cos. H and Band, Col. Jones commanding; arrived in Augusta March 28th.

March 26, 1899, Cos. I, K, L, and M, Maj. Wagener commanding; arrived in Augusta March 29th.

Col. Jones and Col. Thompson went on the Olivette. The others went on the Warmouth.

The following is a correct list of the members of the 2d Regiment who died:

September, 1898, Arthur Epton, Co. K., at Columbia, S. C.
October 21, 1898, M. T. Mooney, Co. G, at Panama Park, Fla.
October 22, 1898, Robt. Covington, Co. C, at Panama Park, Fla.
October 25, 1898, Albert Smith, Co. F, at Panama Park, Fla.
October 26, 1898, J. W. Bluer, Co. E, at Panama Park, Fla.
October 28, 1898, Meek Lyles, Co. L, at Panama Park, Fla.
October 30, 1898, E. A. Hopkins, Co. E, at Panama Park, Fla.
November 3, 1898, R. L. Ward, Co. L, at Panama Park, Fla.
November 7, 1898, E. W. Metze, Co. M, at Savannah, Ga.
November 9, 1898, Golphin Barton, Co. E, at Panama Park, Fla.
November 29, 1898, Wm. Finley, Co. H, at Savannah, Ga.
December 10, 1898, Matthew Kitchen, Co. I, at Savannah, Ga.
February 19, 1899, J. A. Epting, Co. L, at Havana, Cuba.
February 20, 1899, Thos. S. Trivette, Co. F, at Havana, Cuba.
March 30, 1899, R. N. McKay, Co. L, at Havana, Cuba.
April 16, 1899, Walter Griffin, Hospital Steward, at Savannah, Ga.

As soon as we reached camp in Augusta, Ga., the Regiment was ordered to prepare to be mustered out, and we dropped all drilling and dress parades and went to work with a will. I had intended to have a parade through the city before we were disbanded, but a few days after reaching Augusta the Band instruments were taken from us, and, of course, the parade abandoned. The people of Augusta were very kind to us all, and we were reminded of the generous treatment we had received from the people of Savannah. We were in Augusta nearly a month and did not lose a single man from death. When we left Savannah for Cuba, a boy 15 years old, named Bertie Eastman, followed us, and on January 16, 1899, he rode a mule into the little river near our camp, and not being able to swim was drowned. As he was not an enlisted man, we had no means of telling his parents, and do not know who they are to this day. He is buried in the U. S. military graveyard near Marianao, Cuba. Every effort has been made to find his parents without success so far.

While we were in camp in Cuba, Major J. J. Wagener, commanding the 3d Battalion, and Capt. John L. Perrin, commanding Co. H, were presented with beautiful swords by their respective commands, as a token of the high esteeem and affection in which they both were held. Senator Tillman happened to be in camp that day, and he presented the sword to Maj. Wagener and made a very appropriate speeech. Col. Thompson presented the sword to Capt. Perrin on a previous occasion, on behalf of his Company, in a neat and graceful speech. Just two days before the Regiment was mustered out in Augusta, the enlisted men of the Regiment presented me with a most magnificent sword. The presentation was made by Sergeant Major F. W. Frederick, the ranking non-commissioned officer in the Regiment, in a most creditable manner. I shall keep this sword as long as I live, and appreciate it more than anything ever presented to me.

The pay of an enlisted man in time of peace in the U. S. Army is $13.00 a month, in time of war it is $15.60 a month. Those soldiers who went to Cuba were allowed two months extra pay as a bonus. The treaty of peace between the United States and Spain was signed on the 10th day of April, 1899. The 2d S. C. Regiment was mustered out April 19, 1899. The Paymaster in Augusta received orders that our Regiment must be paid on peace footing after April 10th, and also that the two months bonus for going to Cuba must be calculated at $13.00 a month instead of $15.60 a month. I calculated the amount to be paid to the Regiment and found that this outrageous and unfair order from the War Department would cut our Regiment out of at least $6,000. It did not affect the commissioned officers at all, only the enlisted men. I was very much put out about it, and went at once to see the Paymaster, who said that he was very sorry to say that he had gotten orders to that effect. He did not think it was right and fair, but he had to obey orders. I at once concluded that I must have the matter corrected, and I sent a telegram to Senator B. R. Tillman, telling him of the great injustice about to befall the 2d South Carolina. In less than an hour I heard from Senator Tillman, saying that he had telegraphed the Secretary of War. The next morning the muster-out officer came to my tent smiling, and said he had just received orders from Washington to pay on a war footing and not on the basis of $13.00 a month. Had it not been for this prompt action on the part of Senator Tillman, the enlisted men of the Regiment would have lost $6,000 at least.

The members of the 2d S. C. Regiment should always have the kindest feelings to all our Representatives in Congress. They did all they could for us. Senator Tillman and Mrs. Tillman, Congressman Norton and Mrs. Norton, and Congressman Latimer paid us the compliment to come to Cuba while we were there. They all did what they could to have deserving men with families at home honorably discharged. I made it a rule to approve of the honorable discharge of every married man in the Regiment who applied for it, and when we went to Cuba we had very few married men with us. I thought it better to go to Cuba with a small Regiment than to be taking men away from their wives and children against their will, and I am satisfied I acted right and to the best interest of the Government. Senator McLaurin went twice to Washington with Col. Thompson and myself when we were organizing the Regiment, and we would have had a great deal of trouble to have accomplished what we did without his assistance.

I was in constant correspondence with Senator McLaurin, and he did all he could to see that the Regiment was sent to Cuba. I was so anxious, and so were all of the officers and enlisted men, to go to Cuba after we were sent to Savannah, that I wrote to him often on the subject, and he always said he was working to have us sent. I wrote him a letter urging that we be sent to Cuba just one week before we sailed.

The principal amusement in the Regiment was horse-racing in the afternoons, in the Main street of the camp. General Lee came over one evening and witnessed the race, and was very much pleased. A few days before we sailed from Havana, I called on the General and asked him please to give us a good ship to go home on, as we had such an awful old ship to carry us there. He smiled, and said he would write to the Secretary of War to send the largest and longest ship to be had for the use of the 2d South Carolina, so that they could race their horses as they crossed over to Florida. I was riding on horseback with Gen. Lee one afternoon through our camp on an inspecting tour, and I said to him that there was a bar-room near our camp that I wished he would have closed, as the boys were drinking there, and that when South Carolina boys got under the influence of whiskey, they would fight a circular saw. The General turned to me and said, "South Carolina boys will fight a circular saw or any thing else at any time and under any circumstances. He had been in the Confederate Army with the fathers of these boys, and he knew what they would do." A member of our Band heard that his sister was very sick at home, and he came to me to approve an application to go home, which I did. The application for the furlough came back disapproved from Brigade Headquarters. The father of this young man was in the Confederate Cavalry during the Civil War. It was suggested to him to go right up to Gen. Lee's Headquarters, and to tell him about his father being under him in Virginia during the Civil War. He went, and he came back with an order to me from Gen. Lee to let him go.

The 7th Army Corps in Cuba consisted of the following:
1st N. C. Volunteer Infantry.
2d S. C. Volunteer Infantry.
2d Illinois Volunteer Infantry.
9th Illinois Volunteer Infantry.
161st Indiana Volunteer Infantry.
4th Virginia Volunteer Infantry.
49th Iowa Volunteer Infantry.
6th Missouri Volunteer Infantry.
1st Texas Volunteer Infantry.
2d Louisiana Volunteer Infantry.
3d Nebraska Volunteer Infantry.
4th Illinois Volunteer Infantry.
1st Maine Volunteer Artillery.
8th U. S. Infantry.
10th U. S. Infantry.
8 Troops 7th U. S. Cavalry.
2 Batteries 2d U. S. Artillery.
1 Battalion 2d U. S. Volunteer Engineers.

Our Regiment had scarcely gotten settled in their camp at Panama Park before I was very much pressed by different persons to allow them to open a canteen for the Regiment, giving them the right to sell beer, etc. Nearly all the Regiments in the army had canteens. I positively refused to allow a canteen opened in the Regiment, because I was satisfied it would work great harm to our men—I did not think it was right to have such temptation placed in their way; I said that if a canteen was forced on me, I would resign at once and go home. There was no Regiment in the 7th Army Corps more orderly than ours, and I am satisfied not having beer sold within our lines had a great deal to do with it.

Ex-Governor and Mrs. Thompson, the parents of our Lieut. Colonel, came to Savannah to visit their son while we were camped there, and stopped at Thunderbolt. I at once carried the Band over and gave them a serenade. The Governor had prepared a most elegant oyster supper for us, and we certainly enjoyed it. A few days afterwards, the Governor invited all of the officers of the Regiment to dine with him, and we went and enjoyed it very much. I gave the Governor my spirited horse, Dixie, one afternoon, and he reviewed the Regiment on dress parade, and he sat the horse like an Indian warrior.

Col. W. J. Bryan's Regiment was camped just across the road from us in Savannah, and I saw him often and formed a great attachment for him. I do not wonder that so many people in this country want him to be elected President. He is as gentle and kind as a woman, and should be elected President on account of his lovable character if for no other reason.

We were certainly very fortunate in being placed under the command of Gen. Lee. He was as kind as he could be to us, and I do not believe there was ever a General who looked after the welfare of his men more closely than he did. He thought a great deal of the 2d South Carolina, and when he came to our camp we would give him a cheer.

I have not words to express what we all thought of dear old Gen. J. Warren Keifer, of Ohio, our Division Commander. We all loved him because he was so good and kind to us. He was without doubt, after Gen. Lee, the most popular officer in the Corps. He is a man of great ability and a splendid officer. There were two men in our Regiment whose names I will not mention, who would have been disgraced and ruined for life, but for the big heart and the kindness of Gen. Keifer. I went to him and explained their cases, and begged for mercy for them, and he granted it, and they are both all right now and I am glad of it. The mothers of these young men will never forget Gen. Keifer for his kindness. I have never voted a Republican ticket in my life and never expect to, but if I were a citizen of Ohio, and Gen. Keifer, who is a Republican, was running for an office, I do not see how I could resist the temptation to vote for him on personal grounds. The 2d South Carolina will never forget Gen. Keifer, and will always have the greatest respect and affection for him. With such magnificent American citizens as Gen. Lee, of Virginia, and Gen. Keifer, of Ohio, standing shoulder to shoulder in time of war, the people of this grand American Republic need never have any fear of the safety of their country from foreign foes.

All honor to the American Volunteer Soldiers, they have proven themselves the equals, if not the superiors, of the regulars, and they can always be relied upon when the command forward is given!

For a short time while in Savannah, we had the honor of being commanded by that courtly gentleman and gallant officer, Gen. Wheaton, who was a Colonel in the U. S. Army during the Civil War. He told me he had been in the Army nearly forty years. He is now gallantly fighting in the Phillippine Islands.

I wish to take this opportunity to thank all the officers and enlisted men of the Regiment for their many acts of kindness and courtesy to me while I had the honor to command them. to assure them that I shall never forget them in the future, and to assure them further that I consider my appointment as Colonel of the Regiment the greatest honor ever conferred on me. I do not think there ever was a better Regiment than the 2d S. C. V. I. On my return from Cuba, Gov. Ellerbe said to me in his yard that he congratulated the Regiment on the splendid record it had made, and that he was very proud of it. The only regret I have is that the Regiment did not get into a battle. When we consider that this Regiment was composed of the sons of Confederate Veterans almost entirely, I am sure no one will doubt for a moment that they would not have done their whole duty in a fight— I know they would have done it. The Regiment obeyed every order given it promptly and cheerfully, and what more could they have done?

After spending a very pleasant time in Augusta, Ga., and being treated most kindly by the good people of that city, the Regiment was paid off and disbanded, April 19, 1899. I went to Orangeburg with Companies C, E, and L, and we were met at the depot by a great crowd of people and two military companies, and escorted to the Opera House for supper. After the banquet was over, we met in the Opera House and listened to the speeches of welcome. After the speaking, we went to the Ball and met the beautiful ladies of Orangeburg. We certainly had a grand reception, and appreciated it very much indeed. I was entertained at the home of Judge Izlar, and was most royally treated by Mrs. Izlar and Miss Marie—the Judge was away. Next morning, those of us living in the up country took the train for Columbia. There was but one thing for me to do then, and that was to turn over to the Adjutant General our flags, which I did in a short time afterwards.

Thus ends the narrative you have requested me to write of the reminiscences of the 2d South Carolina Regiment in the Spanish-American War. In my own plain style it has been to me a pleasant task, because in pursuing the work I have lived over again those pleasant associations and stirring scenes that marked its career, and my connection as Colonel of that grand and noble body of men— many of them, perhaps, I will never meet again in this life. But whatever the future may bring, my prayers and wishes will always be for the happiness, prosperity and success of each and every member of my old command. WILIE JONES,
Colonel 2d S. C. Vol. Infantry, 2d Brigade, 1st Division, 7th Army Corps, U. S. Army, Gen. FitzHugh Lee Commanding.

LIEUT. COL. H. T. THOMPSON

Historical Sketch of the Independent Battalion, S. C. V. I.

BY LIEUT. COL. HENRY T. THOMPSON.

The Darlington Guards, commanded by the writer of this article, volunteered for the war with Spain on April 27, 1898, and their services were at once accepted. Before they were ordered to Columbia, however, that is, on May 3, Governor Ellerbe promoted their Captain to Major, in charge of the Independent Battalion, and wired him to report in Columbia immediately. On his arrival there, the Governor assigned him to duty in connection with the organization and management of the camp at the Fair Grounds, where, a day or two later, reported the four companies that were designated to form the Independent Battalion, namely, the Darlington Guards, the Sumter Light Infantry, the Edisto Rifles, and the Manning Guards. These companies came from the four contiguous counties of Darlington, Sumter, Orangeburg and Clarendon, respectively, and representing one section of the State, united naturally into a single compact organization. Many of those originally in their ranks were rejected on the physical examination; but as their places became gradually filled by others, the four companies were mustered in, one after another, in the order given above, Darlington Guards, Co. A; Sumter Light Infantry, Co. B; Edisto Rifles, Co. C, and Manning Guards, Co. D. On May 22, the organization was declared by the United States authorities to be complete, and the commanding officer and his Adjutant, First Lieut. W. E. Gonzales, were duly mustered in, as was also Dr. E. J. Wannamaker, whom the Governor had appointed Assistant Surgeon, with the rank of First Lieutenant. Walter Griffin, of Co. A (Darlington Guards), was appointed Hospital Steward of the Battalion by the Governor, and Sergt. N. H. Bull, of Co. C (Edisto Rifles), was detailed by the commanding officer as Sergeant Major. As thus completed, the Independent Battalion was the first organization in the State to be mustered into the service of the United States for the war with Spain.

The United States Regulations called for 84 men to a company. None of the companies in the State had more than half that number prior to hostilities, while many had considerably less than half. To complete the quota up to 84, therefore, it was necessary to use a large number of perfectly "raw" recruits. Add to these the recruits that were accepted in place of those who failed on the physical examination, and the number afterwards necessary to increase each company from 84 to 106, and it is safe to assert that nine-tenths of the Battalion were ignorant of the first principles of military drill before coming to Columbia, while very many of them had never even seen a militia company formed in line.

The camp at the Fair Grounds was commanded by Lieut. Col. Tillman. Besides the Independent Battalion, there were mobilized there several companies of the 1st Regiment and the Charleston Heavy Battery. On May 24, the Battalion left the Fair Grounds and moved to Shandon, a southeastern suburb of Columbia. Being in daily expectation of orders to move to the front, this was regarded at the time as but a temporary abiding place; but it really proved to be the home of the Battalion for several months to come. The commanding officer gave to the Shandon camp the name of "Fitzhugh Lee," in anticipation of the service afterwards to be rendered in Cuba under that distinguished commander. On leaving the camp at the Fair Grounds, Lieut. B. D. Wilson, of Co. B (Sumter Light Infantry), was detailed as Acting Quartermaster of the Battalion; Lieut. A. H. Moss, of Co. C (Edisto Rifles), as Commissary of Subsistence, and Lieut. A. C. Davis, of Co. D (Manning Guards), as Ordnance Officer.

On the day of its removal to Shandon, Col. Jas. D. Blanding, on behalf of the Survivors' Association of the Mexican War, in an eloquent address, presented to the Battalion the historic flag and spearhead of the gallant Palmetto Regiment, highly prized and greatly cherished relics—the first American emblems ever planted upon the walls of the City of Mexico. The commanding officer received them for the Battalion, and publicly placed them in the custody of Sergt. James Blanding Holliman, of Co. B, who had been detailed to act as Color Sergeant. In all of its wanderings thereafter, the Battalion had these colors with it, but on returning from Cuba, delivered them back to the Mexican Survivors' Association. They are thus the only South Carolina colors ever taken to two foreign wars.

Towards the end of May, the Governor was called on by the War Department to forward to Chickamauga the Independent Battalion, as being the only organization which the State had thus far completed. Subsequently, on June 3, the First Regiment was filled up by transferring the Sumter Light Infantry to it from the Independent Battalion. This was done by direction of the Governor, and resulted in leaving the Battalion again in an incomplete condition. Thereupon, the orders of the War Department were changed, so that the

First Regiment was to be sent to Chickamauga instead of the Battalion, greatly to the latter's disappointment, for at that time Chickamauga seemed to mean "going to the front."

The First Regiment left for Chickamauga on June 6, being escorted to the depot by the Battalion. The chagrin which the latter experienced was short-lived, for at the very time that it was passing through Main street on escort parade, the commanding officer received a telegram from Maj. Gen. M. C. Butler, at Camp Alger, Va., stating that the Battalion would be ordered to report to him immediately. The men were wild with delight at hearing this, and the prospect of serving under that gallant officer and distinguished Carolinian, so loved and admired by them all, seemed to fully reconcile them to seeing the 1st Regiment board the trains without them.

Gen. Butler's telegram, however, was never followed by any specific orders from the War Department, though they were anxiously looked for day after day. This was probably due to a series of circumstances which followed, namely, the delay in equipping the Battalion, and in organizing it a second time after the loss of the Sumter Light Infantry; the fact that very soon after such reorganization it was made a part of the 2d South Carolina Volunteer Infantry, for which, in turn, two more battalions had to be organized, and finally, the transfer of Gen. Butler from his command at Camp Alger to the service of the government in an even higher sphere of usefulness in the West Indies.

On June 15, a fourth company, to be known as "B," made up of men from all parts of the State, was organized for the Battalion. The following officers were elected by the members of the company, Governor Ellerbe having agreed to leave their selection to the men: W. G. Sirrine, Captain; T. C. Stone, First Lieutenant; Richard L. Dargan, Second Lieutenant. On the transfer of the Sumter Light Infantry to the First Regiment, Lieut. E. R. Cox, of Co. A (Darlington Guards), was detailed as Acting Quartermaster of the Battalion.

The uniforms for the Battalion arrived on June 15, thus making it the first South Carolina organization that was equipped by the government.

On June 21, the ladies of Columbia treated the Battalion to an elegant banquet at Shandon—a graceful act, which was thoroughly enjoyed by the "soldier boys."

The weary days of waiting at Camp Fitzhugh Lee were spent chiefly in familiarizing the men with their duties, and in perfecting them in military drill; the progress which they made was excellent.

On June 23 (which was just seven weeks from the time they had landed in Columbia), having received their uniforms, a battalion parade, participated in by Companies A, C and D, was given through the streets of the capital. Of this parade, The Columbia Register, on Friday morning, June 24, said:

"Columbia had the pleasure of witnessing a battalion drill yesterday afternoon by the soldiers encamped at Shandon. It was a spectacle that caused every onlooker to feel a kind of pride and opened all eyes in astonished admiration. Those handsome, well uniformed and well disciplined recruits who yesterday executed the difficult battalion manœuvres with veteran-like ease and perfectness, are the same recruits who a short time past did not know the first elements of military discipline and instruction. Experienced military officers say it was a wonderful contrast. They watched the parade with keen interest, and expressed great satisfaction both as to how the men were handled and as to the conduct of the men themselves.

"Major Thompson assembled the Battalion at Camp Lee and began the march about 6 o'clock. The music of Pinckney's band was heard before the troops emerged into Main street. Gervais was chosen as the route, and from there they appeared in Main, marching in columns of platoons. The six double columns of blue tramped with steady step up the main thoroughfare of Columbia. Hundreds of men, women and children lined the streets and peered out eagerly from the windows of the buildings on both sides of the avenue. The officers had the men under perfect control, and as each command was given it was executed without hesitation or confusion. As the lines passed in front of the Jerome Hotel the group of spectators burst into cheers. The enthusiastic yells were taken up and echoed all along the march. At the end of Main street the soldiers executed fours right about and commnced the return. Cheers broke out at intervals as they passed back along the same route. On the whole, the exhibition of what the Battalion can do was enough within itself to put the seal of excellence on both soldiers and commander. Major Thompson was showered with congratulations."

And on the editorial page of that date, the same journal said: "Did you see those sturdy sons of South Carolina last afternoon? Could you ask better? Six weeks ago they came from the field, yesterday they marched like veterans. And, God bless them, they are imbued with that courage and determination that will make them remembered if battles are to be fought, which we hope the good Providence will forefend. There were boys that had never known a harsher note than those of the reeds; their hearts were large, filled with milk of human kindness, and yesterday we saw them in martial array. Their arms were strong—so were their hearts. They simply meant business—trite but true. Major Thompson was made the commander of raw recruits, who have improved so that yesterday the people of this city saw a seasoned, well-drilled, goodly body of men."

On June 27, the Independent Battalion was made the First Battalion of the new 2d South Carolina Volunteer Infantry, and thereafter its history is a part of the history of that regnment. Col. Wilie Jones, of Columbia, was made Colonel of the regiment, and the writer was made Lieutenant Colonel, which position enabled him to retain the command of the First Battalion.

The Battalion gave a second street parade in Columbia on July 4, when it again attracted considerable attention and favorable comment on account of its proficiency in drill. On this occasion (which was exactly two months from the time the first companies had arrived in Columbia), the new B Company was also in line, and made an excellent appearance. The men were completely armed and equipped, and were ready for the field in every respect.

The health of the men during their stay at "Camp Fitzhugh Lee" was remarkably good. Mild epidemics like measles and mumps flourished amongst them almost continuously; yet there was very little fever or serious sickness of any kind, and the men fared very well, but for the long period of weary waiting to which they were subjected.

There were only three deaths in the Battalion up to the time it was incorporated in the Second Regiment. The first of these was that of Private Jos. P. McLeod, Co. D, on June 3. Young McLeod contracted pneumonia in camp, and was transferred to the Columbia Hospital, where everything possible was done for him, but in vain. The remains were interred at the soldier's home in Clarendon County. They were escorted to the train by the entire Battalion, and were sent the rest of the way under a guard of honor.

Private Argyle Gilbert, of Co. A, died suddenly of heart disease on June 27. He was a native of Virginia, and as it was found difficult to communicate with his relatives, he was buried in Elmwood Cemetery, in the city of Columbia, Camp Hampton, United Confederate Veterans, very kindly offering a part of its lot for that purpose. There, at sunrise on the morning of the 28th, in the presence of the whole Battalion, the young soldier, dressed in the complete uniform of the United States Army, was laid to rest by the side of that host of Southern soldiers who had "worn the gray." A handsome monument erected by his comrades of Co. A marks the spot where he sleeps.

Private Jos. F. Stokes, of Co. D, died of typhoid fever on July 27, at his home near Brogden, Clarendon County, whither he had been sent from camp when he was first taken sick. He was buried the following day at Manning.

The organization of the 2d Regiment brought about a number of changes in the Battalion. First Lieut. E. J. Wannamaker, Assistant Surgeon, was promoted to Surgeon of the regiment, with the rank of Major; Hospital Steward Griffin was made the Chief Hospital Steward of the regiment; Adjt. Gonzales was made Captain of K Company; Lieut. A. H. Moss, of C Company, was made Captain of L Company; First Sergt. H. L. Spahr, of C Company, was promoted to Second Lieutenant, *vice* Moss, promoted. Sergt. Major Bull was mustered out to accept the position of Adjutant of one of the new battalions, to which he had been appointed by the Governor, though he never qualified, as the War Department afterwards ruled that no provision had been made for battalion Adjutants for the 2d South Carolina. For the same reason, no successor was appointed to Adjt. Gonzales, though Lieut. T. C. Stone, of B Company, was detailed by the Battalion commander to act in that capacity. Sergt. F. F. Frederick, of Co. C, was detailed as Sergeant Major, *vice* Bull, mustered out. Sergt. R. F. Woods, of A Company, was appointed First Lieutenant of H; Sergt. L. J. Bristow, of A Company, Second Lieutenant of L, and Sergt. C. J. Epps, of D Company, Second Lieutenant of I. R. L. Croswell, Bugler of A Company, was appointed Chief Bugler for the regiment, and J. S. Gibson, of A Company, Regimental Wagon Master. Lieut. Stone, of Co. B, was detailed as Ordnance Officer for the regiment, and Lieut. Davis, of Co. D, as Regimental Commissary.

Prior to the President's second call for troops, the four companies of the Battalion, under orders received from the War Department after its organization, had been recruited up to 106 men each, the "war footing." The department having decided that the companies of the 2d Regiment should consist of only 84 men each, the four companies of the First Battalion were cut down to that number, the difference between 84 and 106, in every case, being transferred to the various companies of the Second and Third Battalions, which were then being organized. There were also transferred to the latter a number of non-commissioned officers and privates from the First Battalion (particularly from the three older companies), who were induced to make the change because they obtained promotion thereby. Thus it was that a number of the most efficient non-commissioned officers of the new battalions received their training in the First; while privates from the latter were scattered all over the rest of the regiment. As a result of all this the imprint of the First Battalion was implanted upon the regiment from the very beginning.

In September, the regiment left Columbia for Jacksonville, to join the 7th Army Corps, under Maj. Gen. Fitzhugh Lee. On the occasion of its first appearance on dress parade there, Gen. Barclay, to whose brigade it had been assigned, rode up to the commander of the First Battalion and publicly complimented him in flattering terms on its appearance and its proficiency in drill.

The 7th Army Corps was moved from Jacksonville, Fla., to Savannah, Ga., in November. Shortly after its arrival in the latter city, the First Battalion of the 2d South Carolina Regiment gave an exhibition drill there, which was witnessed by some 10,000 people, and which was commended in the highest terms by distinguished United States army officers who were present.

In the closing days of the year, when the corps was reviewed by President McKinley in Savannah, shortly before embarking for Cuba, the 2d South Carolina Regiment had the honor of being on the right of the line. As a result, the First Battalion of that regiment was the first organization to pass the President's stand when the march in review began, the men marching in column of companies with their usual accuracy and precision of movement. They occupied a similar position and with the same degree of success, when the 2d Brigade, 1st Division, 7th Army Corps, passed in review before Gen. Gomez in the streets of Guines, Cuba, in March, whither the brigade had been sent by Gen. Lee from its station near Havana, for the purpose of duly impressing the natives in the intervening country.

Shortly before the regiment left for Cuba, Sergt. Major Frederick, of the First Battalion, was promoted to the position of Regimental Sergeant Major, and Sergt. Mabry, of C Company, was detailed to act in his place. The Battalion became a thing of the past on April 19, 1899, when, with the rest of the 2d South Carolina Volunteer Infantry, it was mustered out of the service of the United States in the city of Augusta, Ga. It was made up of a fine body of representative Carolinians, who, had they been called upon to engage in actual hostilities, would have been heard from in no uncertain way. As it was, they discharged, to the fullest extent, every duty that was required of them, and won a name for their organization which, in the opinion of competent military critics, reflected credit on the State.

The successful career of the Battalion was due, in a very great degree, to the ability, soldierly qualities and faithful services of Adj. Gonzales and the company officers. Such a combination, in particular, as that of Capts. Boyd, Herbert, Davis and Sirrine, is rarely to be found in a battalion of volunteers; and it is to their able management, in a large measure, that the Independent Battalion owes the reputation it made.

Walter Griffin, the Chief Hospital Steward of the regiment, who had been with the Battalion since its organization in Columbia, in May, 1898, died in the army hospital in Savannah, Ga., a day or two before the regiment was mustered out. He contracted fever in Cuba, and early in March was sent to Savannah on the hospital ship Missouri. By the time of his service, which was almost exactly coincident with the life of the organization itself; by his unselfish devotion to duty, and his tender and unremitting care of the sick comrades who were entrusted to him, his name is inseparably linked with that of the Independent Battalion and what he did for it must ever form an important part of the history of that organization.

Itinerary Second S. C. V. I.

The 2d S. C. V. I. was formed at Columbia, S. C., and mustered into service August 23, 1898, where it remained in Camp Lee until September 15, 1898, when orders were received by virtue of which the regiment left Columbia, S. C., for Jacksonville, Fla., and arrived at Camp Cuba Libre September 16, 1898. Moved by rail from Camp Cuba Libre, Fla., October 21, 1898, and arrived at Savannah, Ga., October 22, 1898. Left Savannah, Ga., by water for Havana, Cuba, January 3, 1899, arriving January 6, 1899. Left Havana, Cuba, February 19, 1899, and arrived at Guines, Cuba, February 21, 1899. Left Guines, February 23, and arrived at Havana, February 27, 1899. Left Havana, Cuba, for Augusta, Ga., in four detachments, March 22, 23, 25 and 27, 1899, respectively, and arrived at Augusta, Ga., in order named, March 26, 27, 28 and 29, 1899. The first and third detachments sailed on the steamer Olivette, the second and fourth detachments on the steamer Yarmouth. The regiment sailed from Savannah, Ga., for Cuba January 3, 1899, on the U. S. transport Roumanian. While in Cuba the regiment made an eighty mile march. The regiment remained at Camp McKenzie, Augusta, Ga., until April 19, 1899, when it was mustered out of service by Lieut. Ellwood W. Evans, 8th U. S. Cavalry, mustering officer. The officers and men of this command were entitled to two months extra pay, by authority of an Act of Congress, approved January 12, 1899. This regiment was formed under the second call on the Independent Battalion as a nucleus.

Co. A, 2d S. C. V. I., was organized under the first call of the President of the United States, and was mustered into service by Capt. Ezra B. Fuller, May 14, 1898, and assigned to duty as Co. A of the Independent Battalion; was afterwards recruited to the maximum strength of 106 men. August 23, 1898, the enlisted strength was reduced to 80 men, per telegraphic instructions from A. G. O., Washington, D. C. On September 15, 1898, moved from Columbia, S. C., by rail to Camp Cuba Libre, Fla., and was assigned to duty with the 2d Brigade, 3d Division, 7th Army Corps. The movements of this company afterwards conformed with the movements of the 2d S. C. V. I., of which it was a part, until April 19, 1899, when it was mustered out at Augusta, Ga., by Lieut. Ellwood W. Evans, 8th U. S. Cavalry.

Co. B, 2d S. C. V. I., was organized at Greenville, S. C., and mustered into service at Columbia, S. C., June 15, 1898, by Capt. Ezra B. Fuller, 7th U. S. Cavalry. Through recruiting service was increased to maximum strength. By telegraphic instructions the company was reduced to minimum strength, August 23, 1898, by transferring to new companies of 2d S. C. V. I. Remained at Camp Lee, Columbia, S. C., until September 15, 1898, and moved by rail to Camp Cuba Libre, Fla. Moved by rail to Camp Onward, Savannah, Ga., October 21, 1898, and was there equipped with magazine rifles, cal. 30, November 25, 1898. Left Savannah, Ga., for Havana, Cuba, on transport Roumanian, January 3, 1899. Left Havana, Cuba, for Augusta, Ga., March 22, 1899, on steamship Olivette, and was mustered out of service at Augusta, Ga., April 19, 1899, by Lieut. Ellwood W. Evans, 8th Cavalry.

Co. C, 2d S. C. V. I., was organized at Orangeburg, S. C., and mustered into service May 20, 1898, at Columbia, S. C., by Capt. Ezra B. Fuller, 7th U. S. Cavalry, as Co. C of the Independent Battalion, S. C. Volunteer Troops. This company was afterwards placed as Co. C, 2d S. C. V. I., under the second call of the President. Remained in camp at Columbia, S. C., until September 15, 1898; at Jacksonville, Fla., until October 21, 1898; at Savannah, Ga., until January 3, 1899; at Havana, Cuba, until March 23, 1899, when the company sailed for Augusta, Ga., and was there mustered out of the service of the United States April 19, 1899, by Lieut. Ellwood W. Evans, 8th U. S. Cavalry, at Camp McKenzie.

Co. D, 2d S. C. V. I., was organized at Manning, S. C., and was mustered into service May 21, 1898, completing the Independent Battalion. Was, under the second call of the President, assigned to duty with the 2d S. C. V. I. Left Camp Lee, Columbia, S. C., for Camp Cuba Libre, September 15, 1898, and was there assigned to duty with the 7th Army Corps, under Gen. Lee. Left Camp Cuba Libre for Savannah, Ga., October 21, 1898. Left Savannah, Ga., for Havana, Cuba, January 3, 1899, and remained at Camp Columbia, Cuba, until March 23, 1899, when the regiment was ordered to Augusta, Ga., for muster-out. Was mustered out of service at Augusta, Ga., April 19, 1899, by Lieut. Ellwood W. Evans, 8th U. S. Cavalry, mustering officer.

Co. E, 2d S. C. V. I., was organized at Orangeburg, S. C., and mustered into service at Camp Lee, Columbia, S. C., August 15,

1898; and moved from thence by rail for Camp Cuba Libre, Fla., September 15, 1898, and was there assigned to duty with 7th Army Corps, under Gen. Lee. Left Florida for Camp Onward, Savannah, Ga., October 21, 1898, and there remained in camp until January 3, 1899, when it embarked for Havana, Cuba. Returned from Cuba to the United States on March 24, 1899, and arrived at Camp McKenzie, Augusta, Ga., March 27, 1899, and was there mustered out of service by Lieut. Ellwood W. Evans, 8th U. S. Cavalry, on the 19th day of April, 1899.

Co. F, 2d S. C. V. I., was organized at Chester, S. C., and mustered into service at Camp Lee, Columbia, S. C., August 17, 1898. Moved by rail with the regiment to Camp Cuba Libre, Fla., September 15, 1898, and was there attached to the 7th Army Corps, under Gen. Lee. Left Florida with 7th Army Corps for Savannah, Ga., on October 21, 1898, and there remained at Camp Onward until January 3, 1899, when the corps embarked for Havana, Cuba. Left Havana, Cuba, for the United States, March 23, 1899; arrived at Camp McKenzie, Augusta, Ga., on March 26, 1899, and was there mustered out of service by Lieut. Ellwood W. Evans on the 19th day of April, 1899.

Co. G, 2d S. C. V. I., was organized at Newberry, S. C., and mustered into service at Camp Lee, Columbia, S. C., August 19, 1898, by Capt. Ezra B. Fuller, 7th U. S. Cavalry. Moved by rail to Jacksonville, Fla., September 15, 1898, and was assigned to duty with the 7th Army Corps. Moved by rail to Camp Onward, Savannah, Ga., October 21, 1898, and from thence by water to Havana, Cuba, on U. S. transport Roumanian, January 3, 1899. Left Havana, Cuba, for the United States March 2, 1899, and was encamped at Camp McKenzie, Augusta, Ga., until April 19, 1899, when the company was mustered out of service by Lieut. Ellwood W. Evans, 8th U. S. Cavalry, mustering officer.

Co. H, 2d S. C. V. I., was organized and mustered into service August 19, 1898, at Columbia, S. C. Remained at Columbia in camp until September 15, 1898. Moved by rail to Panama Park, Fla., arriving there September 16, 1898. Moved by rail to Camp Onward, Savannah, Ga., October 21, 1898. Left Camp Onward on U. S. transport Roumanian for Havana, Cuba, January 3, 1899. Left Havana, Cuba, March 25, 1899, for the United States, and arrived at Camp McKenzie, Augusta, Ga., March 27, 1899. Remained at Camp McKenzie, Augusta, Ga., until April 19, 1899, when mustered out of service by Lieut. Ellwood W. Evans, 8th U. S. Cavalry, mustering officer.

Co. I, 2d S. C. V. I., was organized at Columbia, S. C., and mustered into service at Camp Lee, August 23, 1898. Moved by rail with regiment for Jacksonville, Fla., September 15, 1898, and was assigned to 7th Army Corps, under Gen. Lee. Left Florida for Camp Onward, Savannah, Ga., October 21, 1898, and there remained in camp until January 3, 1899, when the regiment sailed for Havana, Cuba, on the U. S. transport Roumanian, and arrived January 6, 1899. Left Havana, Cuba, for the United States on steamship Yarmouth, March 24, 1899, and arrived at Camp McKenzie, Augusta, Ga., March 28, 1899, after delay by quarantine. Regiment was there mustered out of service on the 19th of April, 1899, by Lieut. Ellwood W. Evans, 8th U. S. Cavalry, mustering officer.

Co. K, 2d S. C. V. I., was organized and mustered into service at Columbia, S. C., August 23, 1898. Left by rail September 15, 1898, per orders A. G. O., for Camp Cuba Libre, Fla., to join 7th Army Corps, under command of Gen. Lee. Remained at Camp Cuba Libre until October 22, 1898, and moved by rail to Camp Onward, Savannah, Ga. Left Savannah, Ga., January 3, 1899, for Havana, Cuba, on U. S. transport Roumanian. Remained at Camp Columbia, Cuba, until March 25, 1899, when it sailed for the United States for muster-out. Arrived at Augusta, Ga., Camp McKenzie, March 27, 1899, and was there mustered out of service by Lieut. Ellwood W. Evans, 8th U. S. Cavalry, mustering officer, on April 19, 1899.

Co. L. 2d S. C. V. I., was organized and mustered into service at Camp Lee, Columbia, S. C., August 23, 1898. Left Columbia, S. C., with regiment by rail for Camp Cuba Libre, Fla., September 15, 1898. Removed from Camp Cuba Libre, Fla., October 21, 1898, for Camp Onward, Savannah, Ga., as a part of 7th Army Corps, under Gen. Lee. Left Camp Onward for Havana, Cuba, January 3, 1899, on U. S. transport Roumanian. Left Havana, Cuba, for Camp McKenzie, Augusta, Ga., March 25, 1899, for muster-out. Arrived at Camp McKenzie March 28, 1899, and was there mustered out of service by Lieut. Ellwood W. Evans, 8th U. S. Cavalry, mustering officer, April 19, 1899.

Co. M, 2d S. C. V. I., was organized and mustered into service August 23, 1898, at Camp Lee, Columbia, S. C. Moved by rail to Camp Cuba Libre, Fla., September 15, 1898, and there joined the 7th Army Corps, under Gen. Lee. Left Florida for Camp Onward, Savannah, Ga., October 21, 1898, and there remained until January 3, 1899, when the Regiment sailed for Havana, Cuba, on U. S. Transport "Roumanian." Left Cuba for the United States March 26, 1899, for muster-out, and arrived at Camp McKenzie, Augusta, Ga., March 30, 1899. The company remained in Camp McKenzie, where it was mustered out of service by Lieut. Ellwood W. Evans, 8th U. S. Cavalry, mustering officer, April 19, 1899.

Field and Staff Officers, Second Regiment

Maj. Havelock Eaves.

Capt. G. P. Sullivan.

Capt. L. M. Haselden.

Field and Staff Officers, Second Regiment

Maj. E. J. Wannamaker.

J. E. Poore.
(Assistant Surgeon.)

Capt. P. A. Murray.
(Chaplain.)

Roster Officers Second S. C. V. I.

1. WILIE JONES, 47 years, Colonel, banker, Columbia; enrolled June 27, '98; mustered in August 23, '98; brigade commander March 10 to 22, '99.

1. HENRY T. THOMPSON, 39 years, Lieutenant Colonel, lawyer, Darlington; enrolled August 20, '98; mustered in August 20, '98; promoted from Major Independent Battalion.

1. HAVELOCK EAVES, 28 years, Major, agent, Bamberg; enrolled June 27, '98; mustered in August 19, '98.
2. JULIUS J. WAGENER, 51 years, Major, merchant, Charleston; enrolled June 27, '98; mustered in August 23, '98.

1. LUTHER M. HASELDEN, 25 years, Adjutant, lawyer, Sellers; enrolled July 4, '98; mustered in July 5, '98.

1. EDWARD J. WANNAMAKER, 31 years, Major, physician, Columbia; enrolled June 27, '98; mustered in June 27, '98.

1. GEO. C. SULLIVAN, 20 years; Quartermaster, editor, Anderson; enrolled July 13, '98; mustered in July 18, '98.

1. PHILLIP A. MURRAY, 43 years, Chaplain, minister, Beaufort; enrolled June 27, '98; mustered in August 24, '98.

1. LEWIE A. GRIFFITH, 32 years, Assistant Surgeon, physician, Lewiedale; enrolled June 27, '98; mustered in June 28, '98.
2. JAS. E. POORE, 22 years, Assistant Surgeon, physician, Lancaster; enrolled July 4, '98; mustered in July 5, '98.

1. FRANK W. FREDERICK, 36 years, Sergeant Major, civil engineer, Orangsburg; enrolled May 5, '98; mustered in May 7, '98; transferred from Co. C October 15, '98.

1. WM. W. FULLER, 25 years, Quartermaster Sergeant, teacher, Troy; enrolled August 5, '98; mustered in August 5, '98; transferred from Co. B August 5, '98.

1. JOS. W. TROWBRIDGE, 23 years, Chief Musician, salesman, Anderson; enrolled May 4, '98; mustered in May 12, '98; transferred from Co. C, 1st S. C. V. I., July 21, '98.

1. THOS. E. ESKEW, 23 years, Principal Musician, salesman, Pendleton; enrolled July 25, '98; mustered in August 23, '98.
2. SAML. R. TROWBRIDGE, 25 years, Principal Musician, broker, Anderson; enrolled July 18, '98; mustered in August 24, '98.

1. JOS. W. FLOYD, JR., 24 years, Hospital Steward, student, Liberty Hill; enrolled June 27, '98; mustered in August 23, '98.

1. EDWIN R. BACON, private, Spartanburg; enrolled December 27, '98; mustered in December 29, '98.
2. CLINTON E. BARBER, private, Harmony Grove, Ga.; enrolled December 31, '98; mustered in December 31, '98.
3. DAN'L. R. BLACKMAN, 29 years, private, machinist, Darlington; enrolled May 5, '98; mustered in May 15, '98; transferred from Co. I September 2, '98.
4. DAVID R. CLAYTON, 26 years, private, painter, Columbia; enrolled August 10, '98; mustered in August 15, '98; transferred from Co. E September 2, '98.
5. DUGAN HARGROVE, 21 years, private, moulder, Augusta, Ga.; enrolled August 12, '98; mustered in August 15, '98; transferred from Co. G September 2, '98.
6. GEO. HARVEY, 19 years, private, harness maker, Atlanta, Ga.; enrolled June 10, '98; mustered in June 10, '98; transferred from Co. B September 2, '98.
7. JAS. C. HUGHES, private, Abbeville; enrolled January 10, '99; mustered in January 16, '99.
8. CHRISTOPHER C. LOWE, private, Mt. Holly, N. C.; enrolled December 29, '98; mustered in December 29, '98.
9. JNO. E. MCBRYDE, 19 years, private, book-keeper Lamar; enrolled May 14, '98; mustered in May 15, '98; transferred from Co. M September 2, '98.
10. CHAS. MCCANTS, private, painter, Columbia; enrolled August 8, '98; mustered in August 9, '98; transferred from Co. M September 2, '98.
11. BENJAMIN MCGILL, 28 years, private, farmer, Due West; enrolled August 5, '98; mustered in August 15, '98; transferred from Co. M September 2, '98.
12. WM. H. NOLAN, private, Savannah, Ga.; enrolled January 2, '99; mustered in January 2, '99.
13. EDGAR M. SCOTT, private, Bushy Creek; enrolled January 10, '99; mustered in January 16, '99.
14. THOS. M. SEAL, private, Abbeville; enrolled February 1, '99; mustered in February 18, '99.
15. WM. B. SMELTZER, 27 years, private, broker, Columbia; enrolled August 9, '98; mustered in August 9, '98; transferred from Co. E September 2, '98.
16. JEFFERSON SMITH, private, Greenville; enrolled July 27, '98; mustered in July 27, '98; transferred from Co. B September 2, '98.
17. CHAS. S. SPANN, private, Sumter; enrolled February 1, '99; mustered in February 18, '99.
18. ROSWELL R. WALKER, private, Darien, Ga.; enrolled December 21, '98; mustered in December 21, '98.
19. JNO. Y. RICHARDSON, private, Charleston; enrolled January 10, '99; mustered in January 16, '99.
20. EDWARD R. TOMPKINS, 22 years, Sergeant Major, teacher, Rock Hill; enrolled July 15, '98; mustered in July 23, '98; discharged September 9, '98.

21. THOS. H. TATUM, 19 years, Sergeant Major, student, Copes; enrolled May 5, '98; mustered in May 5, '98; discharged Jacksonville, October 15, '98.
23. EDWARD M. OSBORNE, 43 years, Hospital Steward, druggist, Ninety Six; enrolled June 27, '98; mustered in August 22, '98; discharged Havana, February 3, '99.
24. THOS. E. LIGHTFOOT, 26 years, private, laundryman, Orangeburg; enrolled May 19, '98; mustered in May 19, '98; transferred from Co. C September 2, '98.
25. LAVE L. LOUDERMILK, 24 years, private, weaver, Mt. Island, N. C.; enrolled July 29, '98; mustered in July 29, '98; transferred from Co. F, discharged December 17, '98.
26. LUTHER M. PRICE, 26 years, private, millman, Alcolu; enrolled May 5, '98; mustered in May 5, '98; transferred from Co. I, discharged December 22, '98.
27. JAS. A. WALKER, private, Orangeburg; enrolled June 13, '98; mustered in June 13, '98; transferred from Co. C, discharged December 22, '98.
28. JAS. W. WILSON, 21 years, private, farmer, Branchville; enrolled July 19, '98; mustered in July 22, '98; transferred from Co. G, discharged March 15, '99.
29. WALTER GRIFFIN, 24 years, Hospital Steward, student, Darlington; enrolled May 5, '98; mustered in August 23, '98; died of disease April 18, '99.

Capt. J. E. Boyd.

Lieut. E. R. Cox.

Company A, Second Regiment

1. JNO. E. BOYD, 28 years, Captain, physician, Darlington; enrolled May 5, '98; mustered in May 14, '98; acting Major 1st Battalion March 9 to 29, '99.

1. EDWIN R. COX, 30 years, First Lieutenant, merchant, Darlington; enrolled May 5, '98; mustered in May 14, '98; Acting Quartermaster December 9, '98, Savannah, Ga.

1. CHAS. S. MCCULLOUGH, 24 years, Second Lieutenant, liveryman, Darlington; enrolled May 5, '98; mustered in May 14, '98.

1. FRANK R. WINTERS, 21 years, First Sergeant, laborer, Darlington; enrolled May 5, '98; mustered in May 14, '98; promoted from Sergeant September 9, '98.

1. SIMON C. KING, 24 years, Quartermaster, lawyer, Darlington; enrolled May 5, '98; mustered in May 14, '98; promoted from Sergeant September 9, '98.

1. JACOB C. MOONEY, 34 years, Sergeant, salesman, Darlington; enrolled May 5, '98; mustered in May 14, '98.

South Carolina Troops in the War with Spain 161

2. Junius Parrott, 21 years, Sergeant, book-keeper, Darlington; enrolled May 5, '98; mustered in May 14, '98; promoted from Corporal August 26, '98.
3. Eddie T. Rodgers, 21 years, Sergeant, clerk, Darlington; enrolled May 5, '98; mustered in May 14, '98; promoted from Corporal September 9, '98.
4. Robt. E. L. Freeman, 21 years, Sergeant, farmer, Darlington; enrolled May 5, '98; mustered in May 14, '98; promoted from Corporal September 9, '98.

1. Jno. W. Williamson, Corporal, Darlington; enrolled June 24, '98; mustered in June 24, '98; promoted from private July 22, '98.
2. Jere B. Smith, 31 years, Corporal, lumberman, Conway; enrolled May 11, '98; mustered in May 14, '98; promoted from private July 22, '98.
3. Jno. H. Jordan, 21 years, Corporal, farmer, Bennettsville; enrolled May 5, '98; mustered in May 14, '98; promoted from private July 27, '98.
4. Wm. D. Shaw, 24 years, Corporal, printer, Darlington; enrolled May 5, '98; mustered in May 14, '98; promoted from private October 4, '98.
5. Wade H. Abrahms, 21 years, Corporal, carpenter, Conway; enrolled May 5, '98; mustered in May 14, '98; promoted from private October 1, '98.
6. Duncan R. Morris, 19 years, Corporal, student, Darlington; enrolled May 5, '98; mustered in May 14, '98; promoted from private November 12, '98.

1. Benj. Turnage, 21 years, private, farmer, Society Hill; enrolled May 13, '98; mustered in May 14, '98.
2. Abner B. Floyd, 19 years, private, student, Darlington; enrolled May 5, '98; mustered in May 14, '98.
3. Arthur G. Fletcher, 22 years, private, carpenter, McCall; enrolled May 13, '98; mustered in May 14, '98.
4. Saml. R. Chapman, 22 years, private, stone cutter, Chesterfield; enrolled May 5, '98; mustered in May 14, '98.
5. Jno. W. Whittaker, 24 years, private, farmer, Blenheim; enrolled May 13, '98; mustered in May 14, '98.
6. Wm. R. Alford, private, Florence; enrolled July 29, '98; mustered in July 29, '98.
7. Forsythe O. Altman, private, Kingstree; enrolled July 13, '98; mustered in July 13, '98.
8. Lonnie Bristow, private, Dillon; enrolled August 22, '98; mustered in August 22, '98.
9. Jas. H. Bryant, 28 years, private, farmer, Darlington; enrolled May 5, '98; mustered in May 14, '98.
10. Thos. J. Bryant, private, Darlington; enrolled August 13, '98; mustered in August 13, '98.
11. Otto Buchholz, private, Timmonsville; enrolled July 22, '98; mustered in July 22, '98.
12. Jas. H. Burns, private, Walhalla; enrolled August 8, '98; mustered in August 8, '98.

13. CLAUDE M. DEAL, private, Walhalla; enrolled August 8, '98; mustered in August 8, '98.
14. JNO. F. ERVIN, 42 years, private, farmer, Darlington; enrolled May 5, '98; mustered in May 14, '98.
15. EVANDER M. GANDY, private, Darlington; enrolled July 12, '98; mustered in July 12, '98.
16. WM. E. GARRISON, 23 years, private, farmer, Darlington; enrolled May 5, '98; mustered in May 14, '98.
17. NOAH M. GIBSON, 23 years, private, farmer, McCalls; enrolled May 13, '98; mustered in May 14, '98.
18. JAS. L. GIBSON, 22 years, private, clerk, Bennettsville; enrolled June 20, '98; mustered in June 20, '98.
19. JAS. C. GOOSON, private, Darlington; enrolled June 22, '98; mustered in June 22, '98.
20. WM. F. GOODSON, 23 years, private, weaver, Columbia; enrolled June 15, '98; mustered in June 15, '98; transferred from Co. B June 26, '98.
21. HENRY HANCOCK, 19 years, private, blacksmith, Darlington; enrolled May 5, '98; mustered in May 14, '98.
22. CHAS. I. HOFFMAN, private, Hartsville; enrolled August 9, '98; mustered in August 9, '98.
23. WADE H. HOWLE, 21 years, private, farmer, Darlington; enrolled May 5, '98; mustered in May 14, '98.
24. WM. L. HUSBANDS, 28 years, private, farmer, Darlington; enrolled May 5, '98; mustered in May 14, '98.
25. JOS. HUBBARD, 25 years, private, marshal, Bennettsville; enrolled May 13, '98; mustered in May 14, '98.
26. WM. E. HUBBARD, private, Bennettsville; enrolled July 28, '98; mustered in July 28, '98.
27. JACOB B. LAWSON, 20 years, private, farmer, Florence; enrolled May 5, '98; mustered in May 14, '98.
28. JAS. R. LAWSON, 19 years, private, farmer, Florence; enrolled May 5, '98; mustered in May 14, '98.
29. JAS. L. LAYTON, 28 years, private, farmer, Hartsville; enrolled May 5, '98; mustered in May 14, '98.
30. NEWTON F. LEMMONS, private, Oakway; enrolled August 8, '98; mustered in August 8, '98.
31. JAS. W. MARSHALL, 24 years, private, farmer, Stokes Bridge; enrolled May 10, '98; mustered in May 14, '98.
32. ARCHIBALD M. MCBRYDE, private, Davidson, N. C.; enrolled August 2, '98; mustered in August 2, '98.
33. JNO. W. MCELVEEN, private, Kingstree; enrolled July 13, '98; mustered in July 13, '98.
34. RICHARD S. MEELER, private, Oakway; enrolled August 8, '98; mustered in August 8, '98.
35. WM. S. MOORE, 22 years, private, teacher, Charleston; enrolled May 12, '98; mustered in May 14, '98.
36. WADE H. NEAL, 21 years, private, farmer, Darlington; enrolled May 16, '98; mustered in May 21, '98; transferred from Co. D June 17, '98.
37. WM. R. NEWELL, 20 years, private, weaver, Lamar; enrolled May 13, '98; mustered in May 14, '98.

38. JNO. H. NORMENT, 33 years, private, clerk, Darlington; enrolled May 5, '98; mustered in May 14, '98.
39. JNO. ODOM, 20 years, private, farmer, Darlington; enrolled May 16, '98; mustered in May 21, '98; transferred from Co. D June 17, '98.
40. ROLAND PARROT, 19 years, private, farmer, Darlington; enrolled May 9, '98; mustered in May 14, '98.
41. WADE H. PARROTT, 21 years, private, farmer, Darlington; enrolled May 9, '98; mustered in May 14, '98.
42. LAURENCE PEPKIN, 22 years, private, farmer, Darlington; enrolled May 5, '98; mustered in May 14, '98.
43. WM. B. REYNOLDS, 21 years, private, farmer, Darlington; enrolled May 5, '98; mustered in May 14, '98.
44. JOSIE D. SHAW, private, Fayetteville, N. C.; enrolled December 22, '98; mustered in December 22, '98.
45. BLANCHARD H. SMITH, 22 years, private, stenographer, Bennettsville; enrolled May 10, '98; mustered in May 14, '98.
46. RASMUS STEVENS, 21 years, private, farmer, Walterboro; enrolled August 8, '98; mustered in August 23, '98; transferred from Co. M September 18, '98.
47. HUGH STRONG, private, Kingstree; enrolled July 13, '98; mustered in July 13, '98.
48. JNO. A. STUCKEY, 20 years, private, farmer, Darlington; enrolled May 5, '98; mustered in May 14, '98.
49. LAWRENCE E. WEATHERFORD, private, Darlington; enrolled July 15, '98; mustered in July 15, '98.
50. FRANK G. WELLS, private, Charleston; enrolled June 20, '98; mustered in June 20, '98.
51. JOS. B. WELLS, private, Darlington; enrolled June 24, '98; mustered in June 24, '98.
52. WALTER WILLIAMS, 22 years, private, farmer, Darlington; enrolled May 5, '98; mustered in May 14, '98.
53. ALBERT L. WILLIAMSON, private, Darlington; enrolled June 24, '98; mustered in June 24, '98.
54. SUMMER M. WILLIS, 22 years, private, paper finisher, Kingstree; enrolled May 5, '98; mustered in May 14, '98.
55. REESE L. WYSE, private, Kingstree; enrolled July 14, '98; mustered in July 14, '98.
56. CLYDE WILSON, private, Darlington; enrolled August 16, '98; mustered in August 16, '98.
57. DOUGLAS A. YOUNG, 23 years, private, baker, Darlington; enrolled May 5, '98; mustered in May 14, '98.
58. LOUIS J. BRISTOW, 22 years, Sergeant, editor, Kingstree; enrolled May 5, '98; mustered in May 14, '98; discharged to accept commission.
59. EDWIN J. BRODIE, 35 years, private, mariner, Darlington; enrolled May 5, '98; mustered in May 14, '98; discharged January 16, '99.
60. JNO. C. CARMICHAEL, private, Marion; enrolled June 11, '98; mustered in June 11, '98; discharged October 13, '98.
61. ROBT. L. CROSWELL, 27 years, private, soldier, Darlington; enrolled May 5, '98; mustered in May 14, '98; discharged March 4, '99.

62. RICHARD L. DARGAN, 23 years, private, clerk, Abbeville; enrolled May 5, '98; mustered in May 14, '98; discharged to accept promotion, June 18, '98.
63. JAS. S. GIBSON, 22 years, Corporal, clerk, Darlington; enrolled May 5, '98; mustered in May 14, '98; discharged September 30, '98, telegram.
64. WM. J. HOLLEMAN, private, Kingstree; enrolled July 13, '98; mustered in July 13, '98; discharged December 17, '98.
65. JNO. N. MCCALL, 29 years, private, clerk, Clio; enrolled May 14, '98; mustered in May 14, '98; discharged November 3, '98.
66. JNO. S. MCCULLOUGH, private, Indiantown; enrolled July 13, '98; mustered in July 13, '98; discharged February 6, '99.
67. JNO. MOODY, private, Darlington; enrolled July 15, '98; mustered in July 15, '98; discharged February 18, '99, at hospital.
68. CLARENCE S. NETTLES, 34 years, Quartermaster Sergeant, lawyer, Darlington; enrolled May 5, '98; mustered in May 14, '98; discharged August 8, '98.
69. JAS. E. PLOWDEN, 20 years, Corporal, student, Gibson, N. C.; enrolled May 5, '98; mustered in May 14, '98; discharged August 8, '98.
70. CHAS. RHODES, 28 years, private, farmer, Society Hill; enrolled May 5, '98; mustered in May 14, '98; discharged November 3, '98.
71. MAXCY J. SPEARS, 19 years, private, clerk, Lamar; enrolled May 5, '98; mustered in May 14, '98; discharged June 28, '98.
72. FRANK R. SMITH, private, Gibson, N. C.; enrolled June 9, '98; mustered in June 9, '98; discharged December 20, '98.
73. JOS. D. WEST, 29 years, private, teacher, Socaste; enrolled May 12, '98; mustered in May 14, '98; discharged September 9, '98.
74. RALPH E. WINDHAM, 19 years, private, farmer, Lamar; enrolled May 5, '98; mustered in May 14, '98; discharged March 9, '99.
75. ROBT. F. WOODS, 27 years, Sergeant, student, Darlington; enrolled May 5, '98; mustered in May 14, '98; discharged August 25, '98.
76. HENRY APPELT, private, Darlington; enrolled May 5, '98; mustered in May 21, '98; transferred from Co. D June 17, '98.
77. DANL. R. BLACKMAN, 29 years, private, mechanic, Darlington; enrolled May 5, '98; mustered in May 14, '98; transferred to Co. I August 23, '98.
78. CULL BRASINGTON, 18 years, private, clerk, Darlington; enrolled May 5, '98; mustered in May 14, '98; transferred to Co. I August 23, '98.
79. GEO. A. BRISTOW, 20 years, private, printer, Darlington; enrolled May 12, '98; mustered in May 14, '98; transferred to Co. I August 32, '98.
80. THOS. P. BROWN, 22 years, private, farmer, Packsville; enrolled May 5, '98; mustered in May 14, '98; transferred to Co. D June 17, '98.
81. ABRAM E. BRUNSON, 23 years, private, agent, St. Stevens; enrolled May 5, '98; mustered in May 14, '98; transferred to Co. I August 23, '98.
82. JNO. R. COX, private, Kingstree; enrolled July 14, '98; mustered in July 14, '98; transferred to Co. I August 23, '98.
83. TIM G. DARGAN, 21 years, Corporal, horseman, Darlington; enrolled May 5, '98; mustered in May 14, '98; transferred to Battery June 17, '98.
84. MICHAEL A. GARDENER, 21 years, private, hostler, Manning; enrolled May 5, '98; mustered in May 14, '98; transferred to Co. D June 17, '98.

South Carolina Troops in the War with Spain 165

85. FRED. E. GIBSON, 20 years, private, printer, Bennettsville; enrolled May 12, '98; mustered in May 14, '98; transferred to Co. M August 23, '98.
86. WALTER GRIFFIN, 24 years, private, student, Columbia; enrolled May 5, '98; mustered in May 14, '98; promoted Hospital Steward, May 21, '98.
87. JOS. W. HANNA, private, Chesterfield; enrolled June 24, '98; mustered in June 24, '98; transferred to Co. L August 23, '98.
88. WM. J. HANNA, JR., 26 years, Corporal, farmer, Chesterfield; enrolled May 5, '98; mustered in May 14, '98; transferred to Co. L August 23, '98.
89. NEIL R. HATCHEL, private, Florence; enrolled July 12, '98; mustered in July 12, '98; transferred to Co. I August 23, '98.
90. EVAN E. HODGE, 30 years, private, farmer, Alcolu; enrolled May 5, '98; mustered in May 14, '98; transferred to Co. D June 17, '98.
91. JAS. A. KING, 19 years, private, millman, Manning; enrolled May 5, '98; mustered in May 14, '98; transferred to Co. D June 17, '98.
92. FRED. W. KLINTWORTH, 22 years, private, farmer, Laurens; enrolled May 5, '98; mustered in May 14, '98; transferred to Hospital Corps October 25, '98.
93. ROBT. J. LUMNEY, 20 years, private, student, Darlington; enrolled May 5, '98; mustered in May 14, '98; transferred to Co. M August 23, '98.
94. DAN'L M. MCCALL, 26 years, private, clerk, Clio; enrolled May 14, '98; mustered in May 14, '98; transferred to Co. M August 23, '98.
95. CHAS. A. MCCLUNG, private, Columbia; enrolled July 22, '98; mustered in July 22, '98; transferred to Co. I August 23, '98.
96. WILLIE ODOM, 18 years, private, farmer, Hartsville; enrolled May 5, '98; mustered in May 14, '98; transferred to Co. I August 23, '98.
97. SIMON F. PARROTT, 24 years, private, editor, Darlington; enrolled May 5, '98; mustered in May 14, '98; transferred to Co. M August 23, '98.
98. ELBERT R. PLOUDEN, 19 years, private, clerk, Gibson, N. C.; enrolled May 5, '98; mustered in May 14, '98; transferred to Co. H August 29, '98.
99. OBIDAE S. PATE, private, Mars Bluff; enrolled July 29, '98; mustered in July 29, '98; transferred to Co. I August 23, '98.
100. LUTHER M. PRICE, 26 years, private, millman, Columbia; enrolled May 5, '98; mustered in May 21, '98; transferred from Co. D June 17, '98.
101. GEO. W. STOKES, 23 years, private, farmer, Stokes Bridge; enrolled May 5, '98; mustered in May 14, '98; transferred to Co. M August 23, '98.
102. FRANK P. SWAN, 28 years, private, farmer, Effingham; enrolled May 13, '98; mustered in May 14, '98; transferred to Co. I August 23, '98.
103. ARCHIE M. THOMPSON, 43 years, private, farmer, Georgetown; enrolled May 5, '98; mustered in May 14, '98; transferred to Co. D June 17, '98.
104. WALTER K. WEST, 25 years, private, farmer, Socaste; enrolled May 12, '98; mustered in May 14, '98; transferred to Co. M September 10, '98.

105. WALTER M. WILSON, 21 years, Corporal, clerk, Florence; enrolled May 5, '98; mustered in May 14, '98; transferred to Co. I August 23, '98.
106. ARGUILE GILBERT, 23 years, private, farmer, Darlington; enrolled May 5, '98; mustered in May 21, '98; transferred from Co. D, and died June 27, '98.
107. SAM'L A. MCLENDON, private, Hartsville; enrolled July 5, '98; mustered in July 5, '98.

Capt. W. G. Sirrine.

Lieut. R. L. Dargan.

Lieut. T. C. Stone.

Company B, Second Regiment

1. WM. G. SIRRINE, 27 years, Captain, lawyer, Greenville; enrolled June 7, '98; mustered in June 15, '98.

1. RICHARD L. DARGAN, 23 years, First Lieutenant, clerk, Abbeville; enrolled May 3, '98; mustered in June 18, '98; promoted from private June 17, '98.

1. THEO. C. STONE, 23 years, Second Lieutenant, merchant, Greenville; enrolled June 7, '98; mustered in June 15, '98.

1. AUGUSTAS M. DEAL, 21 years, First Sergeant, student, Blacksburg; enrolled May 4, '98; mustered in May 27, '98; transferred from Co. G, 1st S. C. V. I.

1. CHRISTIE J. B. DECAMPS, 19 years, Quartermaster Sergeant, student, Greenville; enrolled June 8, '98; mustered in June 15, '98.

1. JOS. E. LEACH, 20 years, Sergeant, clerk, Greenville; enrolled June 13, '98; mustered in June 15, '98.

2. WM. P. LIGON, 22 years, Sergeant, clerk, Greenville; enrolled June 11, '98; mustered in June 15, '98.

3. CLAUDE M. CRAWFORD, 23 years, Sergeant, laborer, Richardsonville; enrolled June 8, '98; mustered in June 15, '98; promoted from Corporal June 30, '98.

4. ROBT. E. HOUSTON, 18 years, Sergeant, student, Greenville; enrolled June 8, '98; mustered in June 15, '98; promoted from Corporal March 1, '99.

1. HENRY THOMPSON, 22 years, Corporal, laborer, Lowell, Mass.; enrolled June 6, '98; mustered in June 15, '98.
2. RANDOLPH W. SHANNON, 20 years, Corporal, farmer, Camden; enrolled June 15, '98; mustered in June 15, '98; promoted from private August 5, '98.
3. JNO. D. TATE, 23 years, Corporal, carpenter, Gaffney; enrolled June 8, '98; mustered in June 15, '98; promoted from private August 5, '98.
4. HENRY G. CARROLL, Corporal, Bennettsville; enrolled July 30, '98; mustered in July 30, '98; promoted from private August 5, '98.
5. ROBT. H. POLLARD, 24 years, Corporal, farmer, Laurinburg, N. C.; enrolled June 6, '98; mustered in June 15, '98; promoted from private December 20, '98.
6. HENRY P. MCLENDON, Corporal, Camden; enrolled June 12, '98; mustered in June 12, '98; promoted from private March 1, '99.
7. WARREN W. CRENSHAW, private, Greenwood; enrolled August 8, '98; mustered in August 8, '98.
8. CHAS. F. MCGREGOR, private, Pacolet; enrolled July 27, '98; mustered in July 27, '98.
9. JOS. N. CAUSSEE, 24 years, private, farmer, Conway; enrolled June 8, '98; mustered in June 15, '98.
10. ROBT. M. WRAY, 27 years, private, farmer, Blacksburg; enrolled June 14, '98; mustered in June 15, '98.
11. ADAM H. JENKINS, JR., 32 years, private, Greenville; enrolled June 8, '98; mustered in June 15, '98.
12. WM. H. CAPELL, 18 years, private, laborer, Greenville; enrolled June 15, '98; mustered in June 15, '98.
13. NATHANIEL C. CARSON, 18 years, private, lineman, Greenville; enrolled June 13, '98; mustered in June 15, '98.
14. WM. M. CARTER, 18 years, private, student, Columbia; enrolled June 6, '98; mustered in June 15, '98.
15. BEVERLY P. COBB, 23 years, private, farmer, Blacksburg; enrolled June 14, '98; mustered in June 15, '98.
16. JAMES COBB, 20 years, private, farmer, Blacksburg; enrolled June 7, '98; mustered in June 15, '98.
17. GEO. W. DYER, private, Walhalla; enrolled August 8, '98; mustered in August 8, '98.
18. RICHARD EVETT, private, Greenville; enrolled July 27, '98; mustered in July 27, '98.
19. JAS. O. GLENN, 24 years, private, farmer, Newberry; enrolled June 14, '98; mustered in June 15, '98.
20. WALTER W. GOUDELOCK, 23 years, private, laborer, Pacolet; enrolled June 13, '98; mustered in June 15, '98.
21. GEO. HAITHCOCK, private, Bennettsville; enrolled July 30, '98; mustered in July 30, '98.
22. JNO. P. HILL, 21 years, private, weaver, Asheville, N. C.; enrolled June 8, '98; mustered in June 15, '98.

23. Chas. W. Hudson, 20 years, private, tinner, Atlanta, Ga.; enrolled June 5, '98; mustered in June 15, '98.
24. Jno. M. Jeter, private, Santuc; enrolled July 21, '98; mustered in July 21, '98.
25. Jos. A. Johnson, 19 years, private, farmer, Charleston; enrolled May 30, '98; mustered in June 15, '98.
26. Thos. O. Lee, private, Camden; enrolled August 22, '98; mustered in August 22, '98.
27. Robt. Ligon, private, Greenville; enrolled July 19, '98; mustered in July 19, '98.
28. Fred T. Logan, private, Atlanta, Ga.; enrolled July 30, '98; mustered in July 30, '98.
29. Robt. H. Lupe, 20 years, private, student, Greenville; enrolled June 14, '98; mustered in June 15, '98.
30. Peter J. Mack, private, Columbia; enrolled June 25, '98; mustered in June 25, '98.
31. Ernest L. McCall, private, Bennettsville; enrolled July 30, '98; mustered in July 30, '98.
32. Geo. B. McCombs, private, Columbia; enrolled July 27, '98; mustered in July 27, '98.
33. Stanmore Y. Morris, 24 years, private, farmer, Prosperity; enrolled June 15, '98; mustered in June 15, '98.
34. J. T. Nalley, private, Easley; enrolled August 8, '98; mustered in August 8, '98.
35. Jas. S. Norris, private, Briggs; enrolled July 27, '98; mustered in July 27, '98.
36. Edward R. Parker, 23 years, private, laborer, Columbia; enrolled June 13, '98; mustered in July 15, '98.
37. Wm. Platt, Columbia; enrolled August 5, '98; mustered in August 5, '98.
38. Frank Y. Sammons, private, Greenville; enrolled July 21, '98; mustered in July 21, '98.
39. Sam'l C. Sessions, 18 years, private, clerk, Columbia; enrolled June 5, '98; mustered in June 15, '98.
40. Wm. R. Sprouse, private, Blacksburg; enrolled July 5, '98; mustered in July 5, '98.
41. Jas. P. Strong, 23 years, private, laborer, Gaffney; enrolled June 14, '98; mustered in June 15, '98.
42. Geo. D. Suttles, 21 years, private, laborer, Greenville; enrolled June 8, '98; mustered in June 15, '98.
43. Chas. H. Terry, 20 years, private, farmer, Greenville; enrolled June 13, '98; mustered in June 15, '98.
44. Jno. H. Tork, private, Greenville; enrolled July 19, '98; mustered in July 19, '98.
45. Thos. M. Wakefield, private, Andrews, N. C.; enrolled August 8, '98; mustered in August 8, '98.
46. Albert P. Ward, private, Georgetown; enrolled June 21, '98; mustered in June 21, '98.
47. Milton A. Ward, 18 years, private, weaver, Greenville; enrolled June 8, '98; mustered in June 15, '98.

48. JNO. W. WARE, 20 years, private, farmer, Abbeville; enrolled June 8, '98; mustered in June 15, '98.
49. HARLEY WEST, 18 years, private, clerk, Greenville; enrolled June 8, '98; mustered in June 15, '98.
50. JAS. L. WHITMAN, 21 years, private, farmer, Abbeville; enrolled June 8, '98; mustered in June 15, '98.
51. WYLIE T. WOOD, 23 years, private, weaver, Gaffney; enrolled June 9, '98; mustered in June 15, '98.
52. JONATHAN BYERS, 19 years, private, farmer, Blacksburg; enrolled June 6, '98; mustered in June 6, '98; discharged July 12, '98.
53. BROOKS EASTERLING, private, Bennettsville; enrolled July 30, '98; mustered in July 30, '98; discharged September 21, '98.
54. ALTER T. HOLLEY, 18 years, private, laborer, Augusta, Ga.; enrolled June 8, '98; mustered in June 15, '98; discharged July 30, '98.
55. LORING P. LYDE, 21 years, private, farmer, Orangeburg; enrolled June 15, '98; mustered in June 15, '98; discharged December 7, '98.
56. BENJ. H. LITTLEJOHN, 22 years, private, weaver, Danville, Va.; enrolled June 8, '98; mustered in June 15, '98; discharged March 15, '99.
57. SAM'L E. MABERY, 29 years, Sergeant, musician, Jonesville; enrolled June 13, '98; mustered in June 15, '98; discharged February 9, '99.
58. ROBT. M. MEEKS, 19 years, Sergeant, lineman, Greenville; enrolled June 13, '98; mustered in June 15, '98; discharged December 21, '98.
59. WM. J. VARNER, 20 years, Corporal, farmer, Spartanburg; enrolled June 13, '98; mustered in June 15, '98; discharged December 10, '98.
60. JOS. ALFORD, private, Ashboro, N. C.; enrolled July 27, '98; mustered in July 27, '98; transferred to Co. I August 23, '98.
61. HERMAN P. AULL, 20 years, Corporal, farmer, Newberry; enrolled June 14, '98; mustered in June 15, '98; transferred to Co. G August 23, '98.
62. JOS. N. AUTIBUS, 19 years, private, plumber, Charleston; enrolled June 15, '98; mustered in June 15, '98; transferred to Co. I August 23, '98.
63. McPHERSON B. BROOKS, 19 years, Corporal, clerk, Ninety-Six; enrolled June 11, '98; mustered in June 15, '98; transferred to Co. F August 23, '98.
64. FRANCIS M. COOPER, private, Easley; enrolled July 26, '98; mustered in July 26, '98; transferred to Co. I August 23, '98.
65. ARTHUR COCKEREL, 23 years, private, laborer, Richardsonville; enrolled June 8, '98; mustered in June 15, '98; transferred to Co. I August 23, '98.
66. OSCAR M. CURETON, 23 years, private, student, Greenville; enrolled June 8, '98; mustered in June 15, '98; transferred to Co. I August 23, '98.
67. WELCOM J. DAVID, 22 years, private, machinist, Columbia; enrolled June 15, '98; mustered in June 15, '98; transferred to Co. C June 26, '98.
68. THOS. M. DANTZLER, 18 years, private, farmer, St. Matthews; enrolled June 6, '98; mustered in June 15, '98; transferred to Co. C June 21, '98.
69. THOS. T. DAVIS, private, Pelzer; enrolled July 27, '98; mustered in July 27, '98; transferred to Hospital Corps October 1, '98.

70. JNO. DAVIS, 24 years, private, lineman, Augusta, Ga.; enrolled June 6, '98; mustered in June 15, '98; transferred to Heavy Battery August 5, '98.
71. JNO. D. DUNAWAY, 42 years, private, laborer, Spartanburg; enrolled June 13, '98; mustered in June 15, '98; transferred to Hospital Corps November 14, '98.
72. AIKEN DUNCAN, private, Piedmont; enrolled July 27, '98; mustered in July 27, '98; transferred to Co. I August 23, '98.
73. ISAAC ESTRIDGE, 20 years, private, laborer, Columbia; enrolled June 6, '98; mustered in June 15, '98; transferred to Co. I August 23, '98.
74. OLIN FRAZIER, 36 years, private, blacksmith, St. Matthews; enrolled June 7, '98; mustered in June 15, '98; transferred to Co. I August 23, '98.
75. WM. W. FULLER, 25 years, Sergeant, teacher, Longmires; enrolled June 1, '98; mustered in June 15, '98; promoted Quartermaster Sergeant August 5, '98.
76. WM. F. GOODSON, 23 years, private, weaver, Columbia; enrolled June 11, '98; mustered in June 15, '98; transferred to Co. A June 26, '98.
77. BERKLEY GIBSON, 18 years, private, clerk, Orangeburg; enrolled June 15, '98; mustered in June 15, '98; transferred to Co. C June 21, '98.
78. CHAS. E. GRIFFIN, 27 years, private, weaver, Pacolet; enrolled June 13, '98; mustered in June 15, '98; transferred to Co. I August 23, '98.
79. VIRGIL T. GREGORY, 19 years, private, weaver, Cross Keys; enrolled June 8, '98; mustered in June 15, '98; transferred to Co. I August 23, '98.
80. GEO. HARVEY, 19 years, private, harness maker, Atlanta, Ga.; enrolled June 10, '98; mustered in June 15, '98; transferred to banw August 23, '98.
81. WM. E. HENDRIX, 19 years, private, farmer, Columbia; enrolled June 6, '98; mustered in June 15, '98; transferred to Co. I August 23, '98.
82. WM. HOSEY, 22 years, private, farmer, Greenville; enrolled June 8, '98; mustered in June 15, '98; transferred to Co. I August 23, '98.
83. ARCHIE P. HOWIE, 18 years, private, clerk, Columbia; enrolled June 15, '98; mustered in June 15, '98; transferred to Co. F August 23, '98.
84. FRED. K. JOHNSON, private, Bennettsville; enrolled July 30, '98; mustered in July 30, '98; transferred to Co. I August 23, '98.
85. PAUL H. JOYNER, 18 years, private, railroad employee, Columbia; enrolled June 15, '98; mustered in June 15, '98; transferred to Co. I August 23, '98.
86. CHAS. M. JESSEN, 18 years, private, book-keeper, Charleston; enrolled June 9, '98; mustered in June 15, '98; transferred to Co. I August 23, '98.
87. ETHEL H. JAMES, private, Greenville; enrolled July 27, '98; mustered in July 27, '98; transferred to Hospital Corps October 21, '98.
88. THEO. G. MAY, 18 years, private, blacksmith, Charleston; enrolled June 9, '98; mustered in June 15, '98; transferred to Co. I August 23, '98.
89. WADE P. MILES, private, Columbia; enrolled August 3, '98; mustered in August 3, '98; transferred to Co. I August 23, '98.
90. WM. C. MCABEE, 19 years, private, laborer, Spartanburg; enrolled June 10, '98; mustered in June 15, '98; transferred to Co. I August 23, '98.

91. WM. M. MOODY, private, Pelzer; enrolled July 27, '98; mustered in July 27, '98; transferred to Co. I August 23, '98.
92. LAWRENCE POWELL, private, Augusta, Ga.; enrolled June 26, '98; mustered in June 26, '98; transferred to Co. I August 23, '98.
93. GARY F. ROSE, 26 years, private, laborer, Columbia; enrolled June 6, '98; mustered in June 15, '98; transferred to Co. I August 23, '98.
94. JNO. F. RITTER, private, Walhalla; enrolled August 8, '98; mustered in August 8, '98; transferred to Co. I August 23, '98.
95. JEFF SMITH, private, Greenville; enrolled July 27, '98; mustered in July 27, '98; transferred to Band September 2, '98.
96. GEO. A. SLOANE, 22 years, private, printer, Columbia; enrolled June 14, '98; mustered in June 15, '98; transferred to Co. C June 21, '98.
97. EUGENE E. STONE, 19 years, Corporal, laborer, Greenville; enrolled June 8, '98; mustered in June 15, '98; transferred to Co. F August 23, '98.
98. WM. THOMAS, private, Pacolet; enrolled July 13, '98; mustered in July 13, '98; transferred to Co. I August 23, '98.
99. LEONARD H. WHITEHEAD, 23 years, private, laborer, Greenville; enrolled June 8, '98; mustered in June 15, '98; transferred to Co. M August 23, '98.
100. JAS. A. WALKER, 21 years, private, agent, Orangeburg; enrolled June 13, '98; mustered in June 15, '98; transferred to Co. C June 21, '98.
101. ARTHUR B. ZEIGLER, 21 years, Corporal, carpenter, Blackville; enrolled May 5, '98; mustered in June 15, '98; transferred to Co. I August 23, '98.
102. JNO. W. CHASTEEN, 19 years, private, farmer, Anderson; enrolled June 6, '98; mustered in June 15, '98.
103. OSSIE CHILDERS, 23 years, private, laborer, Greenville; enrolled June 8, '98; mustered in June 15, '98.
104. GEO. FORD, 23 years, private, mason; enrolled June 8, '98; mustered in June 15, '98.
105. JNO. GREEN, private, Landrum; enrolled August 8, '98; mustered in August 8, '98.
106. THOS. G. HAWKINS, 21 years, private, laborer, Anderson; enrolled June 8, '98; mustered in June 15, '98.
107. JNO. HOSEY, private, Greenville; enrolled July 23, '98; mustered in July 23, '98.
108. BEN. A. PATTERSON, 20 years, private, farmer, Cherokee Falls; enrolled June 9, '98; mustered in June 15, '98.
109. WM. H. PRICE, 21 years, private, flagman, Garlandsville, Ga.; enrolled June 13, '98; mustered in June 15, '98.
110. TEXAS L. SCOTT, private, Kingstree; enrolled July 15, '98; mustered in July 15, '98.
111. THOS. M. SCOTT, private, Pelzer; enrolled July 27, '98; mustered in July 27, '98.
112. JAS. R. TAYLOR, 38 years, private, weaver, Union; enrolled June 8, '98; mustered in June 15, '98.
113. OSCAR W. WILLIAMSON, 28 years, private, clerk, Greenville; enrolled June 6, '98; mustered in June 15, '98.

Capt. D. O. Herbert.

Lieut. O. B. Rosenger.

Lieut. H. L. Spahr.

Company C, Second Regiment

1. DAN'L O. HERBERT, 40 years, Captain, lawyer, Orangeburg; enrolled May 5, '98; mustered in May 20, '98.

1. OTTO B. ROSENGER, 36 years, First Lieutenant, artist, Orangeburg; enrolled May 5, '98; mustered in May 20, '98.

1. HERMAN L. SPAHR, 22 years, Second Lieutenant, teacher, Orangeburg; enrolled May 5, '98; mustered in May 20, '98.

1. JOS. J. MACKEY, 26 years, First Sergeant, farmer, Orangeburg; enrolled May 5, '98; mustered in May 20, '98; promoted First Sergeat September 1, '98.

1. LEVI BROWN, 24 years, Quartermaster Sergeant, carpenter, Aiken; enrolled May 5, '98; mustered in May 20, '98; promoted from private February 15, '99.

1. TILDEN T. AYERS, 21 years, Sergeant, clerk, Orangeburg; enrolled May 5, '98; mustered in May 20, '98; promoted from Corporal August 1, '98.

2. JNO. W. FAIREY, JR., 19 years, Sergeant, book-keeper, Orangeburg; enrolled May 5, '98; mustered in May 20, '98; promoted from Corporal August 23, '98.
3. ERNEST H. HEIDTMAN, 21 years, Sergeant, clerk, Orangeburg; enrolled May 5, '98; mustered in May 20, '98; promoted from Corporal Septemper 1, '98.
4. HENRY J. RAST, 29 years, Sergeant, policeman, Charleston; enrolled May 5, '98; mustered in May 20, '98; promoted from private October 15, '98.

1. EMMET C. DIBBLE, 20 years, Corporal, farmer, Orangeburg; enrolled May 5, '98; mustered in May 20, '98; promoted from private August 1, '98.
2. WM. C. OWEN, 18 years, Corporal, student, Orangeburg; enrolled May 13, '98; mustered in May 20, '98; promoted from private August 1, '98.
3. EDWIN O. SMITH, 22 years, Corporal, salesman, Copes; enrolled May 5, '98; mustered in May 20, '98; promoted from private August 1, '98.
4. ORIN L. CRUM, 20 years, Corporal, clerk, Rowesville; enrolled May 19, '98; mustered in May 20, '98; promoted from private September 1, '98.
5. FRED F. POOSER, 27 years, Corporal, farmer, Cameron; enrolled May 9, '98; mustered in May 20, '98; promoted from private September 1, '98.
6. WADE H. ZEIGLER, 20 years, Corporal, carpenter, St. Mathews; enrolled May 16, '98; mustered in May 20, '98; promoted from private November 15, '98.
7. GEO. W. DANNELLY, 20 years, Lance Corporal, farmer, North; enrolled May 5, '98; mustered in May 20, '98; promoted from private November 15, '98.

1. ERNEST H. MOBLEY, 22 years, private, carpenter, Augusta, Ga.; enrolled May 5, '98; mustered in May 20, '98.
2. JAS. W. CANNON, 22 years, private, clerk, Orangeburg; enrolled May 5, '98; mustered in May 20, '98.
3. GOVAN BAXTER, 24 years, private, conductor, Orangeburg; enrolled May 5, '98; mustered in May 20, '98.
4. GEO. W. HUNT, 30 years, private, farmer, Branchville; enrolled May 19, '98; mustered in May 20, '98.
5. WM. D. AUTLEY, private, Cordova; enrolled June 25, '98; mustered in June 25, '98.
6. DANTZLER T. AYERS, 21 years, private, farmer, Orangeburg; enrolled May 5, '98; mustered in May 20, '98.
7. ROSS AYERS, 18 years, private, student, Orangeburg; enrolled May 5, '98; mustered in May 20, '98.
8. RAY P. BALDWIN, 23 years, private, farmer, Orangeburg; enrolled May 5, '98; mustered in May 20, '98.
9. AUBREY M. BATES, private, St. Mathews; enrolled July 12, '98; mustered in July 12, '98.
10. PERRY E. BRANDENBURG, private, St. Mathews; enrolled July 23, '98; mustered in June 23, '98.

11. JNO. W. CHAMPY, 25 years, private, carpenter, Bowman; enrolled May 5, '98; mustered in May 20, '98.
12. WM. W. CRUM, private, Rowesville; enrolled July 28, '98; mustered in July 29, '98.
13. EDWARD L. CROUCH, private, Leesville; enrolled July 15, '98; mustered in July 17, '98.
14. GEO. R. CURTIS, 24 years, private, farmer, Cordova; enrolled May 13, '98; mustered in May 20, '98.
15. THOS. M. DANTZLER, private, St. Mathews; enrolled June 6, '98; mustered in June 15, '98.
16. FRED L. DEMARS, private, Orangeburg; enrolled June 25, '98; mustered in June 25, '98.
17. DAVID H. DEWITT, private, Branchville; enrolled July 11, '98; mustered in July 11, '98.
18. ROBT. W. EVANS, private, Cameron; enrolled June 16, '98; mustered in June 17, '98.
19. OLIN P. EVANS, 18 years, private, carpenter, Bowman; enrolled May 13, '98; mustered in May 20, '98.
20. ANDREW L. GARICK, 25 years, private, farmer, Norway; enrolled May 5, '98; mustered in May 20, '98.
21. BERKLEY O. GIBSON, private, Norway; enrolled June 15, '98; mustered in June 15, '98.
22. HASKELL GORTMAN, 25 years, private, sawyer, North; enrolled May 19, '98; mustered in May 20, '98.
23. ALBERT L. HAMMETT, 22 years, private, drummer, Mercer; enrolled May 5, '98; mustered in May 20, '98.
24. FRED. A. HAPPOLDT, 23 years, private, printer, Spartanburg; enrolled May 5, '98; mustered in May 20, '98.
25. GARY B. HARLEY, 20 years, private, farmer, Orangeburg; enrolled May 9, '98; mustered in May 20, '98.
26. AVERY M. HEATON, JR., 18 years, private, student, Orangeburg; enrolled May 9, '98; mustered in May 20, '98.
27. CHAS. M. HERLONG, 19 years, private, farmer, St. Matthews; enrolled May 16, '98; mustered in May 20, '98.
28. HAMPTON L. HERLONG, private, St. Matthews; enrolled August 5, '98; mustered in August 6, '98.
29. ROBT. C. HOWELL, 22 years, private, farmer, St. Georges; enrolled May 18, '98; mustered in May 20, '98.
30. GEO. A. HUTTO, 22 years, private, farmer, Norway; enrolled May 11, '98; mustered in May 20, '98.
31. ARTHUR E. JERNIGAN, 23 years, private, merchant, Cordova; enrolled May 5, '98; mustered in May 20, '98.
32. JAKE JERNIGAN, 18 years, private, millman, Orangeburg; enrolled May 5, '98; mustered in May 20, '98.
33. JULIUS J. JONES, 25 years, private, farmer, Elloree; enrolled May 5, '98; mustered in May 20, '98.
34. AURELIAN V. KENERLY, 25 years, private, clerk, Cordova; enrolled May 5, '98; mustered in May 20, '98.
35. AUGUS J. KITRELL, private, Cope; enrolled August 24, '98; mustered in August 24, '98.

36. MIKE K. KNOTTS, 19 years, private, millman, Knotts; enrolled May 17, '98; mustered in May 20, '98.
37. WM. A. LIVINGSTON, 18 years, private, clerk, Cope; enrolled May 5, '98; mustered in May 20, '98.
38. CLARENCE A. LUCAS, 19 years, private, student, Orangeburg; enrolled May 5, '98; mustered in May 20, '98.
39. JNO. E. MCKEOWN, Orangeburg; enrolled June 21, '98; mustered in June 23, '98.
40. NICHOLAS W. MILLER, 24 years, private, student, Orangeburg; enrolled May 5, '98; mustered in May 20, '98.
41. ALEXANDER M. PALMER, 19 years, private, clerk, Orangeburg; enrolled May 18, '98; mustered in May 20, '98.
42. THEO. G. ROBINSON, 22 years, private, sawyer, Rowesville; enrolled May 5, '98; mustered in May 20, '98.
43. ALFRED A. SCOTT, 33 years, private, laborer, Orangeburg; enrolled May 5, '98; mustered in May 20, '98.
44. ALEXANDER SMITH, private, Dantzler; enrolled June 25, '98; mustered in June 25, '98.
45. JULIUS E. SMOAK, 24 years, private, wheelwright, Orangeburg; enrolled May 5, '98; mustered in May 20, '98.
46. SAM'L W. SNELL, 20 years, private, farmer, Elloree; enrolled May 5, '98; mustered in May 20, '98.
47. HAMPTON M. STROCK, 22 years, private, farmer, Elloree; enrolled May 5, '98; mustered in May 20, '98.
48. ROBT. S. TILLMAN, private, Van Wyck; enrolled December 18, '98; mustered in December 27, '98.
49. CHAS. M. WACTOR, 26 years, private, farmer, St. Mathews; enrolled May 5, '98; mustered in May 20, '98.
50. CHAS. B. WILLIAMSON, 24 years, private, farmer, Orangeburg; enrolled May 5, '98; mustered in May 20, '98.
51. GEO. W. WIMBERLY, private, Branchville; enrolled July 11, '98; mustered in July 11, '98.
52. THOS. WIMBERLY, 25 years, private, farmer, St. Mathews; enrolled May 18, '98; mustered in May 20, '98.
53. EDGAR J. WOLFE, private, Rowesville; enrolled July 28, '98; mustered in July 29, '98.
54. GEO. ZEIGLER, 22 years, private, carpenter, St. Mathews; enrolled May 6, '98; mustered in May 20, '98.
55. JASPER ULMER, 19 years, private, farmer, Elloree; enrolled August 15, '98; mustered in August 16, '98; transferred from Co. G October 5, '98.
56. ADAM. H. MOSS, 27 years, Second Lieutenant, lawyer, Orangeburg; enrolled May 5, '98; mustered in May 20, '98; discharged to accept commission as Captain.
57. NORMAN H. BULL, 40 years, Sergeant, clerk, Orangeburg; enrolled May 5, '98; mustered in May 26, '98; discharged July 17, '98, to accept commission.
58. SAM'L DIBBLE, 29 years, Corporal, civil engineer, Orangeburg; enrolled May 5, '98; mustered in May 20, '98; discharged to accept commission.

59. HERMAN L. SPAHR, 22 years, First Sergeant, teacher, Orangeburg; enrolled May 5, '98; mustered in May 20, '98; discharged to accept commission.
60. CHAS. D. LIDE, 25 years, private, machinist, Orangeburg; enrolled May 5, '98; mustered in May 20, '98; discharged from service October 29, '98.
61. JAS. P. DOYLE, 26 years, private, horse trader, Orangeburg; enrolled May 5, '98; mustered in May 20, '98; discharged from hospital December 23, '98.
62. JACKSON C. RICE, private, Orangeburg; enrolled June 25, '98; mustered in June 25, '98; discharged from service August 17, '98.
63. WM. O. SHULER, 21 years, private, farmer, Elloree; enrolled May 5, '98; mustered in May 20, '98; discharged from service December 8, '98.
64. JAS. L. HARLEY, 26 years, private, farmer, Orangeburg; enrolled May 5, '98; mustered in May 20, '98; discharged from service January 30, '99.
65. ALEX. C. DOYLE, 19 years, private, student, Orangeburg; enrolled May 5, '98; mustered in May 20, '98; discharged from service January 26, '99.
66. WM. T. MCKEWN, 24 years, Quartermaster Sergeant, railroad employee, Orangeburg; enrolled May 5, '98; mustered in May 20, '98; discharged from service February 14, '99.
67. THAD. C. WILLIAMSON, 34 years, private, farmer, North; enrolled May 5, '98; mustered in May 20, '98; discharged from service February 14, '99.
68. CLAUDE M. BARTON, private, St. Mathews; enrolled June 18, '98; mustered in June 20, '98; discharged from service March 6, '98.
69. THOS. H. TATUM, 19 years, Sergeant, student, Cope; enrolled May 5, '98; mustered in May 20, '98; promoted Sergeant Major August 23, '98.
70. JOS. A. BERRY, 21 years, Corporal, lawyer, Branchville; enrolled May 5, '98; mustered in May 20, '98; transferred to Co. K August 23, '98.
71. ALBERT J. WHEELER, 26 years, Corporal, teacher, Fair, Iowa; enrolled May 5, '98; mustered in May 20, '98; transferred to Co. I August 23, '98.
72. THOS. L. BUYCK, 28 years, Corporal, clerk, St. Mathews; enrolled May 5, '98; mustered in May 20, '98; promoted from private August 1, '98.
73. WM. P. STROMAN, 23 years, Corporal, farmer, Orangeburg; enrolled May 5, '98; mustered in May 20, '98; promoted from private August 1, '98.
74. FRANK S. PAULLING, 20 years, Corporal, farmer, St. Mathews; enrolled May 5, '98; mustered in May 20, '98; promoted from private August 1, '98.
75. JESSE E. BELL, 20 years, private, farmer, Orangeburg; enrolled May 9, '98; mustered in May 20, '98; transferred to Co. I August 23, '98.
76. HEBRON BERRY, 20 years, private, farmer, Branchville; enrolled May 5, '98; mustered in May 20, '98; transferred to Co. L August 23, '98.
77. JOS. B. BOWYER, 18 years, private, blacksmith, Branchville; enrolled July 11, '98; mustered in July 11, '98; transferred to Co. I August 23, '98.

78. WM. C. BRADLEY, private, Camden; enrolled July 14, '98; mustered in July 15, '98; transferred to Co. I August 23, '98.
79. GEO. M. COLLIER, 35 years, private, farmer, Elloree; enrolled May 5, '98; mustered in May 20, '98; transferred to Co. I August 23, '98.
80. WM. COTTON, private, Ridgeway; enrolled July 21, '98; mustered in July 23, '98; transferred to Co. I August 23, '98.
81. WELCOME J. DAVID, 22 years, private, machinist, Columbia; enrolled June 15, '98; mustered in June 15, '98; transferred from Co. B June 26, '98.
82. ROBT. L. FAIREY, 19 years, private, farmer, Rowesville; enrolled May 13, '98; mustered in May 20, '98; transferred to Co. I August 23, '98.
83. WILLIE HAYES, private, Beulaville; enrolled June 10, '98; mustered in June 10, '98; transferred to Co. I August 23, '98.
84. JAS. B. HOLMAN, 20 years, private, clerk, Sumter; enrolled May 5, '98; mustered in May 19, '98; transferred from Co. M, 1st. S. C. V. I, June 17, '98.
85. HENRY H. HUGHES, 21 years, private, farmer, Orangeburg; enrolled May 16, '98; mustered in May 20, '98; transferred to Co. I August 23, '98.
86. LEWIS L. JONES, 27 years, private, laborer, Piroway, N. C.; enrolled May 16, '98; mustered in May 20, '98; transferred to Co. I August 23, '98.
87. JNO. LAMBERT, 25 years, private, mill hand; Darlington; enrolled May 7, '98; mustered in May 20, '98; transferred to Co. I August 23, '98.
88. GEO. A. SLOANE, 22 years, private, printer, Columbia; enrolled June 14, '98; mustered in June 15, '98; transferred from Co. B to C, then to Co. I, August 23, '98.
89. LOUIS A. WHITTLE, private, Salleys; enrolled July 17, '98; mustered in July 18, '98; transferred to Co. I August 23, '98.
90. ZACHARIAH WOOTEN, private, Timmonsville; enrolled June 23, '98; mustered in June 25, '98; transferred to Co. M August 23, '98.
91. ARTHUR M. MCCULLOUGH, 30 years, private, farmer, Union; enrolled May 19, '98; mustered in May 20, '98; transferred to Co. M August 23, '98.
92. HAMILTON O. SHULER, 39 years, private, farmer, Wells; enrolled May 5, '98; mustered in May 20, '98; transferred to Co. M August 23, '98.
93. JNO. LEUTZ, 25 years, private, carpenter, Orangeburg; enrolled May 5, '98; mustered in May 20, '98; transferred to hospital November 1, '98.
94. LAWTON H. WANNAMAKER, 21 years, Corporal, P. O. clerk, Orangeburg; enrolled May 5, '98; mustered in May 20, '98; promoted from private and transferred to hospital November 1, '98.
95. ST. CLAIR BOONE, private, Rowesville; enrolled July 28, '98; mustered in August 6, '98; transferred to Co. I August 23, '98.
96. FRANK W. FREDERICK, 36 years, Sergeant, civil engineer, Orangeburg; enrolled May 5, '98; mustered in May 20, '98; transferred to N. C. Staff October 15, '98.
97. THOS. E. LIGHTFOOT, 26 years, private, laundryman, Orangeburg; enrolled May 19, '98; mustered in May 20, '98; transferred to Band September 1, '98.

98. JAS. A. WALKER, 21 years, private, agent, Greensboro, N. C.; enrolled June 13, '98; mustered in June 15, '98; transferred from Co. B June 21, '98.
99. INSLEE T. BENNETT, 24 years, private, clerk, Aiken; enrolled May 5, '98; mustered in May 20, '98; transferred to Co. L December 1, '98.
100. JAS. M. CORTEZ, 21 years, private, carpenter, Aiken; enrolled May 5, '98; mustered in May 20, '98; transferred to Co. I January 21, '99.
101. ROBT. COVINGTON, private, Columbia; enrolled July 25, '98; mustered in July 25, '98; died in Florida of fever, October 22, '98.

Capt. W. C. Davis.

Lieut. A. C. Davis.

Lieut. J. E. Kelly.

Company D, Second Regiment

1. WM. C. DAVIS, 28 years, Captain, lawyer, Manning; enrolled May 5, '98; mustered in May 21, '98.
1. ALEX. C. DAVIS, 26 years, First Lieutenant, merchant, Manning; enrolled May 5, '98; mustered in May 21, '98.
1. JAS. E. KELLY, 30 years, Second Lieutenant, farmer, Manning; enrolled May 5, '98; mustered in May 21, '98.
1. WM. W. JOHNSON, 24 years, First Sergeant, farmer, Manning; enrolled May 5, '98; mustered in May 21, '98.
1. CHAS. D. JOYNER, 24 years, Quartermaster Sergeant, clerk, Lake City; enrolled May 10, '98; mustered in May 21, '98; promoted from private August 23, '98.
1. JNO. H. JUNE, 27 years, Sergeant, farmer, Jordan; enrolled May 5, '98; mustered in May 21, '98; promoted from Corporal July 1, '98.
2. WM. J. TILLER, 23 years, Sergeant, millman, Chesterfield; enrolled May 20, '98; mustered in May 21, '98; promoted from private August 14, '98.

South Carolina Troops in the War with Spain   181

3. THOS. P. BROWN, 22 years, Sergeant, farmer, Packsville; enrolled May 5, '98; mustered in May 14, '98; promoted from private October 12, '98.
4. RICHARD S. KEMP, 25 years, Sergeant, farmer, Kirksey; enrolled May 7, '98; mustered in May 21, '98; promoted from private December 12, '98.

1. WM. B. GRIESHABER, 32 years, Corporal, farmer, Wallaceville; enrolled May 11, '98; mustered in May 21, '98.
2. WADE H. JOHNSON, 23 years, Corporal, printer, Florence; enrolled May 16, '98; mustered in May 21, '98; promoted from private August 1, '98.
3. REUBEN F. RIDGEWAY, 25 years, Corporal, farmer, Manning; enrolled May 5, '98; mustered in May 21, '98; promoted from private October 12, '98.
4. EVAN E. HODGE, 30 years, Corporal, farmer, Alcolu; enrolled May 5, '98; mustered in May 14, '98; transferred from Co. A as private, Corporal December 12, '98.
5. ROBT. T. GARDENER, 21 years, Corporal, millman, Lucile; enrolled May 15, '98; mustered in May 21, '98; promoted from private December 15, '98.
6. THOS. W. VAUGH, Corporal, Nelsons; enrolled August 15, '98; mustered in August 15, '98; promoted from private December 15, '98.

1. EDWIN M. RODGERS, 19 years, private, farmer, Lake City; enrolled May 10, '98; mustered in May 21, '98.
2. FRED W. HORNE, 21 years, private, farmer, Lucile; enrolled May 15, '98; mustered in May 21, '98.
3. BURGESS A. DRAYTON, 20 years, private, wheelwright, Packsville; enrolled May 5, '98; mustered in May 21, '98.
4. LAURENCE F. WILSON, 28 years, private, millman, Greelyville; enrolled May 5, '98; mustered in May 21, '98.
5. GEO. A. BACOT, 35 years, private, lumberman, Darlington; enrolled May 16, '98; mustered in May 21, '98.
6. MILEY G. BONEHILL, 19 years, private, farmer, Johnsonville; enrolled May 5, '98; mustered in May 21, '98.
7. WM. A. BROWN, 20 years, private, millman, Greelyville; enrolled May 5, '98; mustered in May 21, '98.
8. EDWARD B. CLARKE, 18 years, private, farmer, Foreston; enrolled May 10, '98; mustered in May 21, '98.
9. STEPHEN A. CLARKE, private, Foreston; enrolled August 1, '98; mustered in August 1, '98.
10. NEWTON B. COCKERELL, 21 years, private, hosier, Manning; enrolled May 5, '98; mustered in May 21, '98.
11. ISAAC T. DAVIS, private, Packsville; enrolled August 1, '98; mustered in August 1, '98.
12. ANGLO DUBOSE, 20 years, private, farmer, Manning; enrolled May 5, '98; mustered in May 21, '98.
13. FLEETWOOD DUBOSE, private, Manning; enrolled August 1, '98; mustered in August 1, '98.

14. HAYNE C. EDENS, private, Tatum; enrolled June 8, '98; mustered in June 8, '98.
15. JAS. B. EDENS, private, Tatum; enrolled January 3, '99; mustered in January 14, '99.
16. ARMINIOUS L. EPPS, private, Kingstree; enrolled July 13, '98; mustered in July 13, '98.
17. JNO. J. EPPS, 23 years, private, farmer, Sardinas; enrolled May 5, '98; mustered in May 21, '98.
18. MARION O. GARDINER, 21 years, private, hostler, Eutawville; enrolled May 5, '98; mustered in May 14, '98; transferred from Co. A June 17, '98.
19. JOS. S. GRANT, private, Walterboro; enrolled July 8, '98; mustered in July 8, '98.
20. GEO. A. HAIN, 22 years, private, farmer, Lucile; enrolled May 16, '98; mustered in May 21, '98.
21. GEO. HASELDEN, private, Lake City; enrolled December 31, '98; mustered in December 31, '98.
22. JAS. G. HICKS, 18 years, private, farmer, Spartanburg; enrolled May 20, '98; mustered in May 21, '98.
23. JNO. F. HODGE, private, Manning; enrolled August 1, '98; mustered in August 1, '98.
24. JOS. F. HODGE, private, Manning; enrolled August 1, '98; mustered in August 1, '98.
25. CHAS. L. JAMES, 40 years, private, carpenter, Panola; enrolled May 5, '98; mustered in May 21, '98.
26. CHAS. F. JANKINSON, private, Manning; enrolled July 2, '98; mustered in July 2, '98.
27. ARCHIE M. JOHNSON, 18 years, private, millman, Spartanburg; enrolled May 20, '98; mustered in May 21, 98.
28. DAVID B. JONES, 22 years, private, farmer, Manning; enrolled May 5, '98; mustered in May 21, '98.
29. ROBT. J. JONES, 19 years, private, farmer, Mooresville, Mo.; enrolled May 15, '98; mustered in May 21, '98.
30. JNO. H. JOYNER, 28 years, private, turpentine, Lake City; enrolled May 4, '98; mustered in May 21, '98.
31. JNO. JENNINGS, 34 years, private, carpenter, Spartanburg; enrolled May 20, '98; mustered in May 21, '98.
32. OSCAR S. KELLY, 20 years, private, laborer, Lake City; enrolled May 4, '98; mustered in May 21, '98.
33. JAS. A. KING, 19 years, private, millman, Manning; enrolled May 5, '98; mustered in May 21, '98; transferred from Co. A.
34. CHAS. A. LEWIS, 27 years, private, farmer, Manning; enrolled May 5, '98; mustered in May 21, '98.
35. HARRY A. McCALL, 26 years, private, clerk, Cross; enrolled May 9, '98; mustered in May 21, '98.
36. JAS. R. McCARTER, 37 years, private, farmer, Spartanburg; enrolled May 20, '98; mustered in May 21, '98.
37. HUGH McDONALD, 25 years, private, farmer, Lake City; enrolled May 20, '98; mustered in May 21, '98.
38. WM. H. McELWEEN, private, Lake City; enrolled July 15, '98; mustered in July 15, '98.

39. Jno. T. Moore, 21 years, private, dairyman, McCall; enrolled May 20, '98; mustered in May 21, '98.
40. Peter C. Minus, private, Florence; enrolled August 3, '98; mustered in August 3, '98.
41. Rufus L. Minus, 19 years, private, farmer, Florence; enrolled May 16, '98; mustered in May 21, '98.
42. Wyatt Nettles, 21 years, private, farmer, Lake City; enrolled May 17, '98; mustered in May 21, '98.
43. Andrew D. Norris, private, Chadburn, N. C.; enrolled June 9, '98; mustered in June 9, '98.
44. Jno. W. Norton, private, Florence; enrolled August 3, '98; mustered in August 3, '98.
45. Jos. Norton, private, Florence; enrolled July 29, '98; mustered in July 29, '98.
46. Lorenzo D. Player, 19 years, private, student, Workman; enrolled May 5, '98; mustered in May 21, '98.
47. David C. Potter, 21 years, private, farmer, Chadburn, N. C.; enrolled May 15, '98; mustered in May 21, '98.
48. Cuthbert Pritchard, private, Sumter; enrolled August 1, '98; mustered in August 1, '98.
49. Wm. M. Reams, 27 years, private, farmer, Manning; enrolled May 5, '98; mustered in May 21, '98.
50. Jas. W. Russell, 21 years, private, farmer, St. Stevens; enrolled May 19, '98; mustered in May 21, '98.
51. Jas. A. Sellers, 25 years, private, farmer, Chesterfield; enrolled May 16, '98; mustered in May 21, '98.
52. Frank Smith, private, Kingstree; enrolled July 18, '98; mustered in July 18, '98.
53. Walter E. Spigner, 19 years, private, hosier, Alcolu; enrolled May 5, '98; mustered in May 21, '98.
54. Norman K. Timmons, 22 years, private, farmer, Manning; enrolled May 5, '98; mustered in May 21, '98.
55. Benj. T. Tobias, 30 years, private, farmer, Manning; enrolled May 5, '98; mustered in May 21, '98.
56. Wm. H. Touchberry, 19 years, private, farmer, Manning; enrolled May 5, '98; mustered in May 21, '98.
57. Jos. F. Turbeville, private, Florence; enrolled July 12, '98; mustered in July 12, '98.
58. Donald M. White, private, Manning; enrolled August 1, '98; mustered in August 1, '98.
59. Thos. M. Tisdale, 25 years, Sergeant, farmer, Packsville; enrolled May 5, '98; mustered in May 21, '98; discharged October 12, '98.
60. Thos. J. Stukes, 25 years, Sergeant, farmer, Jordan; enrolled May 5, '98; mustered in May 21, '98; discharged December 8, '98.
61. Enos D. Cockerell, 21 years, private, Manning; enrolled May 8, '98; mustered in May 21, '98; discharged October 29, '98.
62. Wm. H. Grant, private, Walterboro; enrolled July 8, '98; mustered in July 8, '98; discharged April 2, '99.
63. Jenkins D. Hinson, 19 years, private, farmer, Tatum; enrolled May 20, '98; mustered in May 21, '98; discharged October 24, '98.

64. ROBT. C. HUGGINS, private, Darlington; enrolled July 7, '98; mustered in July 7, '98; discharged February 28, '99.
65. MARVIN B. INGRAM, 21 years, private, farmer, Sumter; enrolled May 5, '98; mustered in May 21, '98; discharged April 4, '99.
66. SAML. S. MALPUSO, private, Alcolu; enrolled July 29, '98; mustered in July 29, '98; discharged January 19, '99.
67. LEWIS H. SMITH, 28 years, private, carpenter, Augusta, Ga.; enrolled May 6, '98; mustered in May 21, '98; discharged December 5, '98.
68. GEO. W. TURNER, private, Boykin; enrolled August 15, '98; mustered in August 15, '98; discharged March 2, '99.
69. ARCHIE W. THOMSON, 43 years, private, farmer, Georgetown; enrolled May 5, '98; mustered in May 14, '98; transferred from Co. B June 17, '98.
70. CHAS. J. EPPS, 25 years, Quartermaster Sergeant, pharmacist, Kingstree; enrolled May 16, '98; mustered in May 21, '98; promoted from Sergeant July 1, '98.
71. MARION M. CLARK, 18 years, Corporal, editor, Fernandina; enrolled May 8, '98; mustered in May 21, '98; transferred to Co. I August 23, '98.
72. WM. D. PADGETT, 35 years, Corporal, machinist, Cloud's Creek; enrolled May 5, '98; mustered in May 21, '98; transferred to Co. I August 23, '98.
73. THOS. E. CARROLL, 25 years, private, farmer; Packsville; enrolled May 5, '98; mustered in May 21, '98; transferred to Co. I August 23, '98.
74. JNO. S. BOYD, 22 years, private, teacher, Manning; enrolled May 14, '98; mustered in May 21, '98; transferred to Co. I August 23, '98.
75. CHAS. C. WHITE, 19 years, private, farmer, Manning; enrolled May 5, '98; mustered in May 21, '98; transferred to Co. I August 23, '98.
76. HENRY APPELT, 37 years, private, clerk, Darlington; enrolled May 5, '98; mustered in May 21, '98; transferred to Co. A June 17, '98.
77. WM. H. BAKER, 28 years, private, farmer, Alcolu; enrolled May 5, '98; mustered in May 21, '98; transferred to Co. I August 23, '98.
78. WM. J. BODIFORD, private, Greelyville; enrolled July 17, '98; mustered in July 17, '98; transferred to Co. I August 23, '98.
79. LUCIEN M. COCKERELL, 22 years, private, farmer, Manning; enrolled May 5, '98; mustered in May 21, '98; transferred to Co. I August 23, '98.
80. WM. T. COOPER, private, Rock Hill; enrolled July 27, '98; mustered in July 27, '98; transferred to Co. I August 23, '98.
81. RUFUS COVINGTON, 20 years, private, farmer, Bennettsville; enrolled May 20, '98; mustered in May 21, '98; transferred to Co. I August 23, '98.
82. CHAS. W. DISHER, 21 years, private, farmer, Workman; enrolled May 5, '98; mustered in May 21, '98; transferred to Co. I August 23, '98.
83. CHAS. E. EPPS, 21 years, private, farmer, Mouzons; enrolled May 5, '98; mustered in May 21, '98; transferred to Hospital Corps October 29, '98.
84. ARGUILE GILBERT, 23 years, private, farmer, Darlington; enrolled May 5, '98; mustered in May 21, '98; transferred to Co. A June 17, '98.
85. WM. P. GODWIN, private, Lake City; enrolled July 14, '98; mustered in July 14, '98; transferred to Co. I August 23, '98.
86. RENALDA G. GRAHAM, teacher, Lake City; enrolled July 13, '98; mustered in July 13, '98; transferred to Co. I August 23, '98.

87. VAUGHN M. GRIMSLEY, 24 years, private, sawyer, McCarthers, N. C.; enrolled May 5, '98; mustered in May 21, '98; transferred to Co. I August 23, '98.
88. SOUTHERN C. HATCHELL, private, Effingham; enrolled August 3, '98; mustered in August 3, '98; transferred to Co. I August 23, '98.
89. HILLERY B. HOLLMAN, 22 years, private, fireman, Greelyville; enrolled May 5, '98; mustered in May 21, '98; transferred to Co. I August 23, '98.
90. ROBT. F. JACKSON, 25 years, private, machinist, Graniteville; enrolled May 6, '98; mustered in May 21, '98; transferred to Co. L August 10, '98.
91. MATHEW KITCHEN, 23 years, private, farmer, Branchville; enrolled May 15, '98; mustered in May 21, '98; transferred to Co. I August 23,'98.
92. WM. L. LAWHORN, private, Timmonsville; enrolled August 3, '98; mustered in August 3, '98; transferred to Co. M September 4, '98.
93. LAMPLEY D. NETTLES, 21 years, private, clerk, Forreston; enrolled May 8, '98; mustered in May 21, '98; transferred to Co. I August 23, '98.
94. WADE H. NEIL, 21 years, private, farmer, Darlington; enrolled May 16, '98; mustered in May 21, '98; transferred to Co. A June 17, '98.
95. JNO. ODOM, 20 years, private, farmer, Darlington; enrolled May 16, '98; mustered in May 21, '98; transferred to Co. A June 17, '98.
96. EDWARD G. ORRELL, private, Darlington; enrolled June 29, '98; mustered in June 29, '98; transferred to Co. I August 23, '98.
97. LUTHER M. PRICE, 26 years, private, millman, Stokes Bridge; enrolled May 5, '98; mustered in May 21, '98; transferred to Co. A June 17, '98.
98. MARTIN A. ROYALS, 26 years, private, farmer, Conway; enrolled May 15, '98; mustered in May 21, '98; transferred to Co. I August 23, '98.
99. HEDGEMAN B. SIMS, 21 years, private, millman, Graniteville; enrolled May 6, '98; mustered in May 21, '98; transferred to Co. L, 1st S. C. V. I., August 10, '98.
100. GEO. D. THOMAS, private, Lambert; enrolled June 15, '98; mustered in June 21, '98; transferred to Co. I August 23, '98.
101. THOS. C. WEATHERBY, 18 years, private, clerk, Bennettsville; enrolled May 17, '98; mustered in May 21, '98; transferred to Co. I August 23, '98.
102. ISAAC WHITE, 19 years, private, farmer, Chadburn, N. C.; enrolled May 15, '98; mustered in May 21, '98; transferred to Co. I August 23, '98.
103. JAS. H. WINDHAM, 26 years, private, millman, Manning; enrolled May 14, '98; mustered in May 21, '98; transferred to Co. I August 23,'98.
104. JOS. P. MCLEOD, 20 years, private, farmer, Davis; enrolled May 5, '98; mustered in May 21, '98; died Columbia, pneumonia, June 3, '98.
105. JOS. F. STUKES, 23 years, private, salesman, Brogden; enrolled May 5, '98; mustered in May 21, '98; died fever, at home, July 27, '98.

Capt. W. W. Wannamaker.

Lieut. J. W. Culler.

Lieut. C. S. Cummings.

Company E, Second Regiment

1. WM. W. WANNAMAKER, 25 years, Captain, lawyer, Orangeburg; enrolled July 8, '98; mustered in August 15, '98.

1. JULIAN W. CULLER, 26 years, First Lieutenant, clerk, Orangeburg; enrolled July 8, '98; mustered in July 8, '98; promoted from Second Lieutenant August 15, '98.

1. CHAS. S. CUMMINGS, 24 years, Second Lieutenant, watchmaker, Orangeburg; enrolled July 11, '98; mustered in July 11, '98; promoted from First Sergeant September 12, '98.

1. EMILE E. PASSAILAIGUE, 21 years, First Sergeant, salesman, Charleston; enrolled August 10, '98; mustered in August 10, '98; promoted from Corporal September 10, '98.

1. JNO. M. TRULUCK, 21 years, Quartermaster Sergeant, operator, Florence; enrolled July 28, '98; mustered in July 31, '98; promoted from Sergeant November 1, '98.

1. JNO. B. HUGHES, 18 years, Sergeant, clerk, Orangeburg; enrolled July 9, '98; mustered in July 9, '98.

South Carolina Troops in the War with Spain 187

2. Jno. P. Moseley, 18 years, Sergeant, salesman, Orangeburg; enrolled July 9, '98; mustered in July 9, '98.
3. David L. Kaminer, 25 years, Sergeant, carpenter, Sandy Run; enrolled July 9, '98; mustered in July 9, '98.
4. Alfred J. Gannon, 21 years, private, brakeman, Charleston; enrolled May 25, '98; mustered in May 25, '98; promoted from Corporal November 1, '98.

1. David P. O. Cain, 28 years, Corporal, farmer, Orangeburg; enrolled May 9, '98; mustered in May 9, '98.
2. Gabriel E. Summers, 21 years, Corporal, farmer, Ehneys; enrolled August 14, '98; mustered in August 14, '98.
3. Jerry M. Fogle, 22 years, Corporal, teacher, Middlepen; enrolled August 13, '98; mustered in August 13, '98; promoted from private September 1, '98.
4. Wm. O. Lewis, 31 years, Corporal, salesman, West Clarksville, N. Y.; enrolled August 12, '98; mustered in August 12, '98; promoted from private September 10, '98.
5. Jno. S. Bissell, 28 years, Corporal, clerk, Charleston; enrolled July 25, '98; mustered in July 25, '98; promoted from private November 1, '98.
6. Israel O. Edmunds, 33 years, Corporal, salesman, New York; enrolled May 23, '98; mustered in May 23, '98; transferred as private from Co. L, 1st S. C. V. I.
7. Stoll D. Tomlinson, 21 years, Lance Corporal, farmer, Max; enrolled August 13, '98; mustered in August 13, '98; appointed December 1, '98.

1. Shellie B. Hall, 21 years, private, farmer, Orangeburg; enrolled July 9, '98; mustered in July 9, '98.
2. Leander A. Moorer, 21 years, private, farmer, Orangeburg; enrolled July 9, '98; mustered in July 9, '98.
3. Jas. S. Neal, 21 years, private, foundryman, Clemson College; enrolled July 16, '98; mustered in July 18, '98.
4. Chas. A. Davis, 24 years, private, farmer, Ruples; enrolled July 9, '98; mustered in July 9, '98.
5. Chas. T. Paxton, private, Vicksburg, Miss.; enrolled December 27, '98; mustered in January 2, '99.
6. Jno. M. Autley, private, Jamison; enrolled December 16, '98; mustered in December 21, '98.
7. Hillary A. Baker, 22 years, private, farmer, Magnolia; enrolled August 13, '98; mustered in August 13, '98.
8. Jos. S. Barker, 20 years, private, farmer, Gillisonville; enrolled August 12, '98; mustered in August 23, '98.
9. Henry M. Bedgood, 20 years, private, stone cutter, Augusta, Ga.; enrolled August 13, '98; mustered in August 13, '98.
10. Chas. R. Brown, 24 years, private, farmer, St. Georges; enrolled July 15, '98; mustered in July 15, '98.
11. Chas. S. Capers, 21 years, private, plumber, Charleston; enrolled July 26, '98; mustered in July 26, '98.

12. Jno. S. Caughman, 24 years, private, farmer, Silver Springs; enrolled August 8, '98; mustered in August 8, '98.
13. Allen O. Chavis, 18 years, private, farmer, Livingston; enrolled July 11, '98; mustered in July 11, '98.
14. Clinton B. Clark, 18 years, private, farmer, St. Mathews; enrolled July 11, '98; mustered in July 12, '98.
15. Albert B. Dunn, 22 years, private, farmer, Livingston; enrolled July 9, '98; mustered in July 9, '98.
16. Acey E. Evins, 22 years, private, farmer, Magnolia; enrolled August 10, '98; mustered in August 10, '98.
17. Dennis S. Fogle, 22 years, private, farmer, Springfield; enrolled August 7, '98; mustered in August 7, '98.
18. Jas. Z. Gantt, 22 years, private, farmer, Orangeburg; enrolled July 9, '98; mustered in July 9, '98.
19. Jacob L. Gleaton, 19 years, private, farmer, Orangeburg; enrolled July 11, '98; mustered in July 11, '98.
20. Lorenzo T. Gleaton, 21 years, private, farmer, Livingston; enrolled July 11, '98; mustered in July 11, '98.
21. Saml. E. Gardner, 22 years, private, farmer, Cartersville; enrolled August 13, '98; mustered in August 13, '98.
22. Wm. A. Harrell, 26 years, private, laborer, Charleston; enrolled July 25, '98; mustered in July 25, '98.
23. Jos. H. Hearn, 23 years, private, weaver, Columbia; enrolled August 2, '98; mustered in August 2, '98.
24. Jas. L. Harvey, 21 years, private, farmer, Gillisonville; enrolled August 11, '98; mustered in August 12, '98.
25. Jesse H. Heise, 22 years, private, carpenter, Columbia; enrolled August 16, '98; mustered in August 16, '98.
26. Steven C. Hill, 21 years, private, farmer, Magnolia; enrolled August 10, '98; mustered in August 10, '98.
27. Glanton R. Holmes, 21 years, private, farmer, Cartersville; enrolled August 13, '98; mustered in August 15, '98.
28. Fletcher G. Hoover, 18 years, private, farmer, Witts Mill; enrolled August 16, '98; mustered in August 18, '98.
29. Jefferson L. Hoover, 21 years, private, farmer, Witts Mill; enrolled August 7, '98; mustered in August 7, '98.
30. Lawrence S. Hutto, 18 years, private, farmer, Orangeburg; enrolled July 11, '98; mustered in July 12, '98.
31. Walter Hutto, 21 years, private, farmer, Cope; enrolled August 7, '98; mustered in August 7, '98.
32. Absalom V. Inabinet, 22 years, private, carpenter, Middlepen; enrolled August 13, '98; mustered in August 13, '98.
33. Jas. L. Johnson, 21 years, private, farmer, Salley's; enrolled August 7, '98; mustered in August 7, '98.
34. Jno. W. Johnson, 18 years, private, farmer, Salley's; enrolled August 7, '98; mustered in August 7, '98.
35. Wilton P. Johnson, 23 years, private, farmer, Salley's; enrolled August 7, '98; mustered in August 7, '98.
36. Wm. E. Jordan, 21 years, private, farmer, Florence; enrolled August 10, '98; mustered in August 10, '98.

South Carolina Troops in the War with Spain 189

37. WM. H. KNIGHT, 19 years, private, laborer, Orangeburg; enrolled July 9, '98; mustered in July 9, '98.
38. JAS. T. LEMON, 43 years, private, laborer, Orangeburg; enrolled July 15, '98; mustered in August 8, '98.
39. ATTICUS A. LIVINGSTON, 23 years, private, farmer, Livingston; enrolled August 7, '98; mustered in August 7, '98.
40. PHILLIP E. MARTIN, 23 years, private, farmer, Ehney; enrolled August 14, '98; mustered in August 14, '98.
41. GEO. F. MEARS, 22 years, private, laborer, Weimers; enrolled August 8, '98; mustered in August 8, '98.
42. ROBT. Q. MOORE, 21 years, private, farmer, Max; enrolled August 10, '98; mustered in August 10, '98.
43. EDWARD G. MOSELEY, 22 years, private, laborer, Camden; enrolled August 13, '98; mustered in August 13, '98.
44. THOS. A. O. CAIN, 21 years, private, farmer, Orangeburg; enrolled July 9, '98; mustered in July 9, '98.
45. JOS. B. PLAYER, 21 years, private, farmer, Shiloh; enrolled August 13, '98; mustered in August 13, '98.
46. MORGAN L. POSEY, 21 years, private, farmer, Springfield; enrolled August 7, '98; mustered in August 7, '98.
47. GEO. W. PRICE, 23 years, private, farmer, Silver Springs; enrolled August 7, '98; mustered in August 7, '98.
48. GEO. H. ROUSE, 18 years, private, farmer, Rowesville; enrolled July 9, '98; mustered in August 2, '98.
49. JNO. W. SAULS, 21 years, private, millman, Orangeburg; enrolled August 13, '98; mustered in August 13, '98.
50. EUGENE T. SMITH, 21 years, private, weaver, Columbia; enrolled August 5, '98; mustered in August 6, '98.
51. ARTIS U. STEVENSON, 18 years, private, farmer, Nieses; enrolled July 9, '98; mustered in July 9, '98.
52. ROBT. L. STOKES, 21 years, private, millman, Orangeburg; enrolled August 13, '98; mustered in August 13, '98.
53. JAS. TAYLOR, 21 years, private, millman, Orangeburg; enrolled August 13, '98; mustered in August 13, '98.
54. WM. WATTS, 25 years, private, millman, Orangeburg; enrolled August 8, '98; mustered in August 8, '98.
55. GEO. WICKS, 26 years, private, farmer, Ruples; enrolled July 9, '98; mustered in July 9, '98.
56. FRANK M. AYERS, 22 years, Corporal, farmer, Orangeburg; enrolled July 9, '98; mustered in July 9, '98; discharged November 30, '98, S. O.
57. HERBERT L. AYERS, 22 years, Lance Corporal, farmer, Nichols; enrolled August 12, '98; mustered in August 12, '98; discharged November 22, '98, S. O. 59.
58. ERNEST L. BALDWIN, 38 years, Corporal, farmer, Orangeburg; enrolled July 9, '98; mustered in July 9, '98; discharged February 23, '99, S. O. 47.
59. HENRY M. JENKINS, 18 years, private, farmer, Rowesville; enrolled August 1, '98; mustered in August 6, '98; discharged December 13, '98; S. O. 76.

60. FRANK WELSH, 26 years, private, farmer, Magnolia; enrolled August 13, '98! mustered in August 13, '98; discharged March 30, '99, S. O. 74.
61. DAVID R. CLAYTON, 26 years, private, painter, Columbia; enrolled August 10, '98; mustered in August 11, '98; transferred to Band September 20, '98.
62. THURSTON O. McGEE, 22 years, private, blacksmith, Timmonsville; enrolled August 17, '98; mustered in August 17, '98; transferred to Hospital Corps October 27, '98.
63. FRANK M. NUNNAMAKER, 22 years, private, farmer, Irmo; enrolled August 15, '98; mustered in August 15, '98; transferred to Hospital Corps October 27, '98.
64. WM. B. SMELTZER, 26 years, private, broker, Columbia; enrolled August 9, '98; mustered in August 9, '98; transferred to Band September 20, '98.
65. GOLPHIN BARTON, 21 years, private, farmer, Rowesville; enrolled August 1, '98; mustered in August 2, '98; died of fever November 11, '98, in hospital.
66. JAS. W. BLEWER, 21 years, private, farmer, Bowman; enrolled August 13, '98; mustered in August 13, '98; died of fever October 26, '98, in hospital.
67. EDWARD A. HOPKINS, 27 years, Quartermaster Sergeant, operator, Creston; enrolled July 9, '98; mustered in July 9, '98; died of fever October 30, '98, in hospital.
68. WADE H. BAILEY, 21 years, private, farmer, Walkersville; enrolled August 5, '98; mustered in August 5, '98.
69. CHAS. HOWARD, 22 years, private, weaver, Columbia; enrolled August 3, '98; mustered in August 13, '98.
70. BELTON D. JEFFCOAT, 21 years, private, clerk, North; enrolled July 9, '98; mustered in July 9, '98.

Company F, Second Regiment

1. WM. P. CRAWFORD, 29 years, Captain, editor, Chester; enrolled July 29, '98; mustered in August 17, '98.
1. HORATIO M. KENT, 41 years, First Lieutenant, farmer, Lenoir, N. C.; enrolled July 20, '98; mustered in August 20, '98.
1. THOS. C. HOWZE, 30 years, Second Lieutenant, farmer, Bascomville; enrolled May 4, '98; mustered in August 17, '98; promoted by transfer from 1st S. C. V. I.
1. JAS W. THOMPSON, 20 years, First Sergeant, farmer, Liberty Hill; enrolled July 20, '98; mustered in July 20, '98.
1. ISAAC M. HYATT, 31 years, Quartermaster Sergeant, farmer, Fort Lawn; enrolled July 29, '98; mustered in July 29, '98.
1. CHAS. D. CUNNINGHAM, 21 years, Sergeant, farmer, Liberty Hill; enrolled July 20, '98; mustered in July 20, '98.
2. McPHERSON B. BROOKS, 19 years, Sergeant, clerk, Ninety-Six; enrolled June 11, '98; mustered in June 11, '98; promoted from Corporal August 28, '98.
3. EDWARD J. GOULEY, 23 years, Sergeant, shoemaker, Worcester, Mass.; enrolled July 23, '98; mustered in July 23, '98.
4. EUGENE E. STONE, 19 years, Sergeant, laborer, Greenville; enrolled June 8, '98; mustered in June 8, '98; promoted from Corporal August 23, '98.
1. JOS. J. WILLIAMS, 25 years, Corporal, laborer, Richburg; enrolled July 20, '98; mustered in July 20, '98.
2. ARCHIE P. HOWIE, 18 years, Corporal, clerk, Columbia; enrolled June 15, '98; mustered in June 15, '98; promoted from Corporal August 23, '98.
3. WILLETT S. MILLER, 26 years, Corporal, merchant, Todd, N. C.; enrolled July 29, '98; mustered in July 29, '98.
4. JACOB C. BOWMAN, 18 years, Corporal, merchant, Granite Falls, N. C.; enrolled July 20, '98; mustered in July 20, '98.
5. THOS. D. LAND, 28 years, Corporal, merchant, Mount Zion, N. C.; enrolled August 10, '98; mustered in August 10, '98.
6. ANDREW J. HUGGINS, 25 years, Corporal, blacksmith, Boom, N. C.; enrolled July 29, '98; mustered in July 29, '98.
1. ROBT. LEFEVER, 21 years, private, farmer, Gamewell, N. C.; enrolled August 10, '98; mustered in August 10, '98.
2. ANDREW J. STOGNER, 21 years, private, farmer, Bacornville; enrolled July 20, '98; mustered in July 20, '98.
3. GEO. C. MASSEY, 28 years, private, farmer, Lancaster; enrolled August 16, '98; mustered in August 16, '98.

4. WM. L. ROBINSON, 38 years, private, carpenter, Chester; enrolled July 20, '98; mustered in July 20, '98.
5. WM. T. CLAWSON, 22 years, private, farmer, Todd, N. C.; enrolled July 29, '98; mustered in July 29, '98.
6. JNO. E. ARNEY, 19 years, private, blacksmith, Hartland, N. C.; enrolled July 20, '98; mustered in July 20, '98.
7. WM. F. AUSTIN, 21 years, private, laborer, Lenoir, N. C.; enrolled July 29, '98; mustered in July 29, '98.
8. WM. O. BARNETT, 24 years, private, farmer, Mt. Zion, N. C.; enrolled August 10, '98; mustered in August 10, '98.
9. GAITHER F. BARNETT, 21 years, private, farmer, Mt. Zion, N. C.; enrolled August 10, '98; mustered in August 10, '98.
10. CHAS. BOYER, 21 years, private, farmer, Chester; enrolled July 20, '98; mustered in July 20, '98.
11. FRANK S. BRUICE, 18 years, private, laborer, Chester; enrolled July 20, '98; mustered in July 20, '98.
12. WM. CAMMERON, 20 years, private, farmer, Smiths Turnout; enrolled July 29, '98; mustered in July 29, '98.
13. JAS. I. CAMMERON, 23 years, private, farmer, Cornwell; enrolled July 20, '98; mustered in July 20, '98.
14. JAS. F. CARROLL, 21 years, private, farmer, Triplet, N. C.; enrolled August 10, '98; mustered in August 10, '98.
15. THOS. S. CARTER, 21 years, private, farmer, Chester; enrolled July 20, '98; mustered in July 20, '98.
16. EUGENE CARLTON, 21 years, private, farmer, Stony Fork, N. C.; enrolled August 10, '98; mustered in August 10, '98.
17. ERNEST CAUTHEN, 22 years, private, millhand, Lancaster; enrolled August 10, '98; mustered in August 10, '98.
18. WM. CHALK, 21 years, private, farmer, Chester; enrolled July 23, '98; mustered in July 23, '98.
19. RENES DORSTER, 21 years, private, farmer, Smiths Turnout; enrolled July 30, '98; mustered in July 30, '98.
20. JOS. EARNEST, 18 years, private, laborer, Lenoir, N. C.; enrolled July 20, '98; mustered in July 20, '98.
21. ROBT. M. ERWIN, 23 years, private, laborer, Newton, N. C.; enrolled July 29, '98; mustered in July 29, '98.
22. JNO. L. FOX, 22 years, private, mill hand, Lenoir, N. C.; enrolled August 10, '98; mustered in August 10, '98.
23. SILAS A. FURR, 18 years, private, farmer, Chester; enrolled July 20, '98; mustered in July 20, '98.
24. JNO. B. GOBLE, 21 years, private, farmer, Wellridge; enrolled July 29, '98; mustered in July 29, '98.
25. GEO. GREER, 21 years, private, farmer, Triplett, N. C.; enrolled August 10, '98; mustered in August 10, '98.
26. ROY L. GROSS, 21 years, private, machinist, Hickory, N. C.; enrolled July 20, '98; mustered in July 20, '98.
27. JNO. B. HALL, 25 years, private, farmer, Mt. Zion, N. C.; enrolled August 10, '98; mustered in August 10, '98.
28. MART L. HILDERBRAND, 18 years, private, farmer, Morganton, N. C.; enrolled August 10, '98; mustered in August 10, '98.

South Carolina Troops in the War with Spain   193

29. Henry Hudspeth, 22 years, private, laborer, Gamewell, N. C.; enrolled July 20, '98; mustered in July 20, '98.
30. Walter S. Jones, 21 years, private, news agent, Seneca; enrolled August 5, '98; mustered in August 5, '98.
31. Milton W. Kelsey, 23 years, private, farmer, Fort Lawn; enrolled July 20, '98; mustered in July 20, '98.
32. Jas. E. Knight, 25 years, private, farmer, Tradesville; enrolled August 10, '98; mustered in August 10, '98.
33. Wm. B. Knight, 21 years, private, farmer, Tradesville; enrolled August 10, '98; mustered in August 10, '98.
34. Wm. R. Lane, 25 years, private, farmer, Morganton, N. C.; enrolled July 29, '98; mustered in July 29, '98.
35. Chas. Leonard, 21 years, private, farmer, Collettsville, N. C.; enrolled July 29, '98; mustered in July 29, '98.
36. Jno. Lewis, 21 years, private, farmer, Meet Camp, N. C.; enrolled July 29, '98; mustered in July 29, '98.
37. Thos. A. Marshall, 21 years, private, farmer, Lowesville, N. C.; enrolled July 20, '98; mustered in July 20, '98.
38. Chas. R. Minors, 18 years, private, farmer, Landsford; enrolled July 29, '98; mustered in July 29, '98.
39. Wm. D. Mitchell, 23 years, private, farmer, Hendrix, N. C.; enrolled August 10, '98; mustered in August 10, '98.
40. Wm. R. Nelson, 21 years, private, laborer, Patterson, N. C.; enrolled July 20, '98; mustered in July 20, '98.
41. Jno. R. Parker, 21 years, private, millhand, Patterson, N. C.; enrolled August 10, '98; mustered in August 10, '98.
42. Pink A. Rockett, 21 years, private, farmer, Chambers, N. C.; enrolled August 10, '98; mustered in August 10, '98.
43. Dan. W. Setzer, 21 years, private, laborer, Patterson, N. C.; enrolled August 10, '98; mustered in August 10, '98.
44. Abraham Smith, 29 years, private, farmer, Morganton, N. C.; enrolled August 18, '98; mustered in August 18, '98.
45. Wm. H. Suddeth, 24 years, private, farmer, Morganton, N. C.; enrolled July 29, '98; mustered in July 29, '98.
46. Jas. W. Todd, Jr., 21 years, private, farmer, Todd, N. C.; enrolled July 29, '98; mustered in July 29, '98.
47. Solomon E. Townsend, 21 years, private, millman, Vallecrusis, N. C.; enrolled July 29, '98; mustered in July 29, '98.
48. Chas. R. Wilkes, 27 years, private, farmer, Baton Rouge; enrolled July 20, '98; mustered in July 20, '98.
49. Wm. H. Smith, 30 years, Corporal, laborer, Lancaster; enrolled July 20, '98; mustered in July 20, '98; discharged December 19, '98.
50. Jas. Williams, 25 years, private, farmer, Lenoir; enrolled August 10, '98; mustered in August 10, '98; discharged December 26, '98.
51. Jos. C. Keenan, 21 years, private, farmer, Lewis, S. C.; enrolled July 30, '98; mustered in July 30, '98; discharged December 29, '98.
52. Sam'l H. Massey, 23 years, private, farmer, Tradesville; enrolled August 10, '98; mustered in August 10, '98; discharged January 16, '99.
53. Robt. D. McNinch, 33 years, private, carpenter, Chester; enrolled July 20, '98; mustered in July 20, '98; discharged January 16, '99.

54. WM. M. WHEELER, 21 years, private, farmer, Triplett; enrolled August 10, '98; mustered in August 10, '98; discharged January 26, '99.
55. JNO. L. ROCKETT, 22 years, private, farmer, Chambers, N. C.; enrolled August 10, '98; mustered in August 10, '98; discharged February 13, '99.
56. DAVID M. WILSON, 38 years, private, carpenter, Southerland, N. C.; enrolled July 20, '98; mustered in July 20, '98; discharged February 13, '99.
57. FRANK H. MULL, 21 years, private, farmer, Morganton, N. C.; enrolled August 12, '98; mustered in August 12, '98; discharged February 2, '99.
58. DAVID S. WILSON, 42 years, private, farmer, Table Rock, N. C.; enrolled July 29, '98; mustered in July 29, '98; discharged February 16, '99.
59. CHAS. F. HUFFMAN, 18 years, private, farmer, Morganton, N. C.; enrolled August 10, '98; mustered in August 10, '98; discharged March 6, '99.
60. SAM'L L. GREEN, 21 years, private, farmer, Mt. Zion, N. C.; enrolled August 10, '98; mustered in August 10, '98; discharged March 7, '99.
61. BENJ. F. HERMAN, 21 years, private, farmer, Granite Falls, N. C.; enrolled July 20, '98; mustered in July 20, '98; discharged November 29, '98.
62. DALLAS A. SETZER, 24 years, private, laborer, Newton, N. C.; enrolled July 20, '98; mustered in July 20, '98; discharged December 22, '98.
63. LAVE L. LOUDERMILK, 24 years, private, weaver, Gastonia, N. C.; enrolled July 29, '98; mustered in July 29, '98; transferred to Band September 2, '98.
64. SILVERY H. CUNNINGHAM, 21 years, private, farmer, Liberty Hill; enrolled July 20, '98; mustered in July 20, '98; transferred to Hospital Corps October 27, '98.
65. SAM'L C. MILLER, 22 years, private, weaver, Williamston, Pa.; enrolled July 20, '98; mustered in July 20, '98; transferred to Hospital Corps January 16, '99.
66. ALBERT SMITH, 21 years, Corporal, farmer, Stony Fork, N. C.; enrolled August 10, '98; mustered in August 10, '98; died of fever October 25, '98, hospital.
67. THOS. S. TRIVETT, 21 years, private, laborer, Virgil, N. C.; enrolled August 10, '98; mustered in August 10, '98; died of fever February 20, '99, hospital.
68. GEO. P. COOPER, 27 years, private, weaver, Swansea; enrolled August 12, '98; mustered in August 12, '98.

Capt. S. J. McCaughrin.

Lieut. E. C. Horton.

Company G, Second Regiment

1. SILAS J. MCCAUGHRIN, 32 years, Captain, farmer, Newberry; enrolled July 23, '98; mustered in August 19, '98.
1. EDWIN C. HORTON, 26 years, First Lieutenant, druggist, Clinton; enrolled July 23, '98; mustered in August 19, '98.
1. ROBT. F. DUKES, 25 years, Second Lieutenant, merchant, Branchville; enrolled August 9, '98; mustered in August 19, '98.
1. CALDWELL E. FANT, 22 years, First Sergeant, clerk, Newberry; enrolled August 8, '98; mustered in August 24, '98.
1. GEO. S. NOLAND, 45 years, Quartermaster Sergeant, clerk, Newberry; enrolled August 8, '98; mustered in August 8, '98.
1. HERMAN P. AULL, 20 years, Sergeant, farmer, Newberry; enrolled June 14, '98; mustered in June 14, '98; promoted from private October 10, '98.
2. ANDREW B. STOUDEMIRE, 28 years, Sergeant, overseer, Peaks; enrolled August 10, '98; mustered in August 10, '98.
3. GEO. H. BALLENTINE, 21 years, tinner, Laurens; enrolled August 8, '98; mustered in August 9, '98; promoted from Corporal October 30, '98.

4. WM. J. MILLER, 22 years, Sergeant, book-keeper, Newberry; enrolled August 8, '98; mustered in August 9, '98; promoted from Corporal October 21, '98.

1. LEONARD B. CUMMINGS, 24 years, Corporal, railroad employee, Oswego; enrolled August 16, '98; mustered in August 16, '98; promoted from private September 1, '98.
2. GEO. F. TURNER, 21 years, Corporal, farmer, Newberry; enrolled August 13, '98; mustered in August 14, '98; promoted from private September 21, '98.
3. OLLIE O. EARGLE, 21 years, Corporal, farmer, Peak; enrolled July 23, '98; mustered in July 24, '98; promoted from private October 1, '98.
4. JACKSON J. ABRAMS, 29 years, Corporal, farmer, Whitmire; enrolled August 8, '98; mustered in August 8, '98; promoted from private October 10, '98.
5. SNYDER J. PARROTT, 20 years, Corporal, stenographer, Clinton; enrolled August 9, '98; mustered in August 9, '98; promoted from private October 21, '98.
6. WILBUR C. HIPP, 25 years, Corporal, carpenter, Pomaria; enrolled August 8, '98; mustered in August 8, '98; promoted from private October 30, '98.

1. ROBT. L. KIBLER, private, Newberry; enrolled December 13, '98; mustered in December 17, '98.
2. WATSON M. CONNOR, 25 years, private, farmer, Branchville; enrolled August 9, '98; mustered in August 9, '98.
3. WM. J. SLOAN, 21 years, private, farmer, Laurens; enrolled August 16, '98; mustered in August 17, '98.
4. JAS. N. SLIGH, 25 years, private, machinist, Newberry; enrolled August 8, '98; mustered in August 8, '98.
5. JAS. S. CHALMERS, 30 years, private, farmer, Newberry; enrolled August 8, '98; mustered in August 8, '98.
6. KEMBLE P. BAILEY, 21 years, private, farmer, Laurens; enrolled August 19, '98; mustered in August 19, '98.
7. ARTHUR J. BAIR, 21 years, private, farmer, Branchville; enrolled August 13, '98; mustered in August 19, '98.
8. JNO. J. BARRS, 22 years, private, brakeman, Branchville; enrolled August 13, '98; mustered in August 13, '98.
9. WM. W. BARRS, 20 years, private, farmer, Branchville; enrolled August 9, '98; mustered in August 9, '98.
10. WM. A. BOYD, 22 years, private, farmer, Laurens; enrolled August 9, '98; mustered in August 9, '98.
11. ELMORE G. BRAMLETT, 21 years, private, farmer, Laurens; enrolled August 9, '98; mustered in August 9, '98.
12. CHAS. H. BROUGHTON, 21 years, private, carpenter, Newberry; enrolled August 22, '98; mustered in August 22, '98.
13. FRANK J. BYRD, 23 years, private, farmer, Branchville; enrolled August 9, '98; mustered in August 9, '98.
14. SAM'L B. CAUBLE, 31 years, private, painter, Salisbury, N. C.; enrolled August 8, '98; mustered in August 11, '98.

15. KISLER COLLINS, 21 years, private, farmer, Branchville; enrolled August 13, '98; mustered in August 13, '98.
16. JULIUS J. CONNELLY, 23 years, private, farmer, Branchville; enrolled August 9, '98; mustered in August 9, '98.
17. JNO. C. CONNOR, 22 years, private, weaver, Clinton; enrolled August 9, '98; mustered in August 9, '98.
18. GEO. B. COOK, 43 years, private, farmer, Prosperity; enrolled August 8, '98; mustered in August 8, '98.
19. JNO. DAVIS, 22 years, private, weaver, Newberry; enrolled August 9, '98; mustered in August 9, '98.
20. RANSOM DEWITT, 26 years, private, farmer, Branchville; enrolled August 13, '98; mustered in August 13, '98.
21. WM. DEWITT, 18 years, private, farmer, Branchville; enrolled August 13, '98; mustered in August 13, '98.
22. WM. D. DIVER, 30 years, private, carpenter, Helena; enrolled August 8, '98; mustered in August 8, '98.
23. FRANK W. FANT, 42 years, private, lawyer, Newberry; enrolled July 23, '98; mustered in July 23, '98.
24. CLAUDE P. FINLEY, 21 years, private, farmer, Madden; enrolled August 19, '98; mustered in August 19, '98.
25. GIFF H. FINLEY, 21 years, private, farmer, Madden; enrolled August 19, '98; mustered in August 19, '98.
26. JOHN L. FINLEY, 24 years, private, farmer, Madden; enrolled August 9, '98; mustered in August 9, '98.
27. JAS. FLAKE, 23 years, private, millman, Orangeburg; enrolled August 8, '98; mustered in August 8, '98.
28. JNO. D. GLYNN, 22 years, private, farmer, Clinton; enrolled August 9, '98; mustered in August 9, '98.
29. WM. M. GLYNN, 20 years, private, farmer, Clinton; enrolled August 15, '98; mustered in August 17, '98.
30. EDWARD GROVES, 20 years, private, machinist, Clinton; enrolled August 9, '98; mustered in August 9, '98.
31. ARTHUR HANEY, 21 years, private, laborer, Winston, N. C.; enrolled August 9, '98; mustered in August 9, '98.
32. PATRICK H. HARGROVE, 21 years, private, farmer, Newberry; enrolled August 8, '98; mustered in August 8, '98.
33. JAS. F. HINTON, 19 years, private, farmer, Lykesland; enrolled August 16, '98; mustered in August 16, '98.
34. ARMAND P. HINTON, 18 years, private, student, Newberry; enrolled August 8, '98; mustered in August 8, '98.
35. WM. HUIETT, 23 years, private, farmer, Newberry; enrolled August 15, '98; mustered in August 15, '98.
36. WM. O. JORDAN, 19 years, private, weaver, Clinton; enrolled August 9, '98; mustered in August 9, '98.
37. DAVID MALONE, 21 years, private, farmer, Laurens; enrolled August 19, '98; mustered in August 19, '98.
38. WM. D. MAYBIN, 22 years, private, farmer, Maybinton; enrolled August 22, '98; mustered in August 22, '98.
39. MADISON D. MILAN, 20 years, private, farmer, Clinton; enrolled August 9, '98; mustered in August 9, '98.

40. JAS. G. MILLER, 36 years, private, farmer, Newberry; enrolled August 14, '98; mustered in August 15, '98.
41. WM. McGARVY, 21 years, private, farmer, Laurens; enrolled August 9, '98; mustered in August 9, '98.
42. GEO. A. McKINNEY, 27 years, private, millman, Spartanburg; enrolled August 8, '98; mustered in August 8, '98.
43. LEON M. MYERS, 18 years, private, farmer, Branchville; enrolled August 16, '98; mustered in August 16, '98.
44. HENRY PITTS, 23 years, private farmer, Laurens; enrolled August 9, '98; mustered in August 9, '98.
45. FORD ROPER, 21 years, private. farmer, Laurens; enrolled August 9, '98; mustered in August 9, '98.
46. OWENS P. SAXON, 38 years, private, merchant, Newberry; enrolled August 8, '98; mustered in August 8, '98.
47. WM. J. SMITH, 31 years, private, millman, Newberry; enrolled August 12, '98; mustered in August 12, '98.
48. HUGO S. SPELL, 21 years, private, farmer, Branchville; enrolled August 13, '98; mustered in August 13, '98.
49. GEO. J. SPATTS, 21 years, private, farmer, Newberry; enrolled August 8, '98; mustered in August 8, '98.
50. EDGAR W. TEAGUE, 21 years, private, farmer, Laurens; enrolled August 9, '98; mustered in August 9, '98.
51. JNO. H. TODD, 37 years, private, farmer, Newberry; enrolled August 8, '98; mustered in August 8, '98.
52. JAS. R. TUCKER, 20 years, private, farmer, Clinton; enrolled August 10, '98; mustered in August 10, '98.
53. THOS. F. TURNER, 22 years, private, farmer, Clinton; enrolled August 9, '98; mustered in August 10, '98.
54. JAS. A. WATSON, 23 years, private, brakeman, Branchville; enrolled August 9, '98; mustered in August 9, '98.
55. JAS. B. WATSON, 21 years, private, brakeman, Branchville; enrolled August 9, '98; mustered in August 9, '98.
56. THOS. H. WATSON, 21 years, private, brakeman, Branchville; enrolled August 9, '98; mustered in August 9, '98.
57. HUGO W. WEATHERS, 22 years, private, farmer, Branchville; enrolled August 16, '98; mustered in August 16, '98.
58. JNO. H. WHITSELL, 22 years, private, farmer, Branchville; enrolled August 13, '98; mustered in August 13, '98.
59. GEO. J. WILSON, 21 years, private, baker, Newark, O.; enrolled August 10, '98; mustered in August 10, '98.
60. JAS. M. WILSON, 20 years, private, farmer, Branchville; enrolled August 13, '98; mustered in August 13, '98.
61. THOS. WOODALL, 21 years, private, weaver, Clinton; enrolled August 9, '98; mustered in August 9, '98.
62. WALTER A. SYFRETT, 32 years, private, farmer, Reevesville; enrolled August 9, '98; mustered in August 9, '98; discharged December 17, '98, Savannah.
63. JNO. L. GOFF, 21 years, private, laborer, Wilkesborough, N. C.; enrolled August 19, '98; mustered in August 19, '98; discharged January 6, '99, at hospital.

64. CHAS. E. GLENN, 24 years, private, farmer, Clinton; enrolled August 12, '98; mustered in August 12, '98; discharged February 6, '99, at Whitmires.
65. JAS. W. HAWKINS, 23 years, private, farmer, Pleasant; enrolled August 16, '98; mustered in August 16, '98; discharged March 2, '99, at Bookmans, S. C.
66. MORGAN T. MOONEY, 25 years, Sergeant, operator, Branchville; enrolled August 9, '98; mustered in August 9, '98; died Florida, October 21, '98.
67. JASPER ULMER, 19 years, private, farmer, Elloree; enrolled August 15, '98; mustered in August 15, '98; transferred to Co. C October 5, '98.
68. DUGAN HARGROVE, 21 years, private, moulder, Laurens; enrolled August 12, '98; mustered in August 13, '98; transferred to Band October 27, '98.
69. ABE PEARLSTINE, 22 years, Corporal, book-keeper, Branchville; enrolled August 9, '98; mustered in August 9, '98; discharged September 2, '98.

Capt. J. L. Perrin.

Lieut. J. C. Cheatham.

Company H, Second Regiment

1. JNO. L. PERRIN, 37 years, Captain, merchant, Abbeville; enrolled July 21, '98; mustered in August 19, '98.

1. ROBT. F. WOODS, 27 years, First Lieutenant, student, Darlington; enrolled May 5, '98; mustered in May 5, '98; promoted from private August 25, '98.

1. JAS. C. CHEATHAM, 22 years, Second Lieutenant, student, Watts; enrolled July 2, '98; mustered in August 7, '98; promoted from Sergeant February 2, '99.

1. AUGUSTUS C. JOHNSON, 23 years, First Sergeant, jeweler, Darlington; enrolled August 10, '98; mustered in August 10, '98; promoted from Sergeant February 3, '99.

1. EUGENE C. HUNTER, 30 years, Quartermaster Sergeant, deputy sheriff, Bamberg; enrolled August 16, '98; mustered in August 16, '98.

1. JAS. N. KING, 26 years, Sergeant, mechanic, Ninety-Six; enrolled July 21, '98; mustered in July 21, '98.

2. WM. D. BLUME, 18 years, Sergeant, clerk, Bamberg; enrolled July 19, '98; mustered in July 19, '98; promoted from Corporal December 8, '98.

3. ROBT. L. MOORE, 23 years, Sergeant, tinner, Darlington; enrolled August 13, '98; mustered in August 13, '98; promoted from Corporal December 22, '98.
4. JNO. B. GIBERT, 21 years, Sergeant, farmer, Abbeville; enrolled August 13, '98; mustered in August 13, '98; promoted from private February 4, '99.

1. WM. J. NICKELS, 19 years, Corporal, student, Due West; enrolled July 21, '98; mustered in July 21, '98.
2. RUDY REED, 25 years, Corporal, horse trader, Winston, N. C.; enrolled August 10, '98; mustered in August 10, '98.
3. JNO. I. TAYLOR, 27 years, Corporal, salesman, Darlington; enrolled August 10, '98; mustered in August 10, '98; promoted from private December 8, '98.
4. LINDSAY M. PRATT, 20 years, Corporal, farmer, Ninety-Six; enrolled July 21, '98; mustered in July 27, '98; promoted from private December 22, '98.
5. JNO. W. HUGHES, 23 years, Corporal, farmer, Hodges; enrolled July 21, '98; mustered in July 21, '98; promoted from private January 16, '99.
6. WM. MATHERS, 27 years, Corporal, farmer, Govan; enrolled July 19, '98; mustered in July 19, '98; promoted from private February 4, '99.

1. BENJ. E. EVANS, 18 years, private, farmer, Abbeville; enrolled August 6, '98; mustered in August 6, '98.
2. RAVENEL BRAVEBRY, 23 years, private, laborer, Scranton; enrolled August 16, '98; mustered in August 16, '98.
3. BENTLEY BOWLES, 35 years, private, laborer, Darlington; enrolled August 10, '98; mustered in August 10, '98.
4. WM. B. GOINGS, 37 years, private, policeman, Abbeville; enrolled August 6, '98; mustered in August 6, '98.
5. SAM'L W. HILL, 21 years, private, farmer, Dover; enrolled July 21, '98; mustered in July 21, '98.
6. WM. F. BESSINGER, 20 years, private, farmer, Govan; enrolled August 17, '98; mustered in August 17, '98.
7. EUGENE E. BLACKMAN, 26 years, private, farmer, Darlington; enrolled August 13, '98; mustered in August 17, '98.
8. DONNIE L. BRICKLE, 21 years, private, farmer, Cardova; enrolled August 16, '98; mustered in August 16, '98.
9. GELZER C. CARTER, 20 years, private, farmer, Lydia; enrolled August 10, '98; mustered in August 10, '98.
10. THOS. C. CALVIN, 42 years, private, blacksmith, Darlington; enrolled August 13, '98; mustered in August 13, '98.
11. ALEX. A. DELAUGHTER, 23 years, private, farmer, Poverty Hill; enrolled August 16, '98; mustered in August 16, '98.
12. THOS. C. DOWLING, 21 years, private, clerk, Barnwell; enrolled August 19, '98; mustered in August 19, '98.
13. CHARLETON L. FARMER, 23 years, private, farmer, Effingham; enrolled August 10, '98; mustered in August 10, '98.

14. DAVID G. FELDER, 18 years, private, farmer, Bamberg; enrolled August 14, '98; mustered in August 14, '98.
15. ISOM GOODWIN, 31 years, private, farmer, Bamberg; enrolled July 19, '98; mustered in July 19, '98.
16. JESSE C. GORDON, 22 years, private, farmer, Abbeville; enrolled August 6, '98; mustered in August 6, '98.
17. CHAS. GRIFFIN, 23 years, private, weaver, Bamberg; enrolled July 19, '98; mustered in July 19, '98.
18. WM. B. GRIFFITH, 21 years, private, farmer, Saluda; enrolled July 29, '98; mustered in July 29, '98.
19. FRANK A. HADWIN, 22 years, private, millman, Bamberg; enrolled August 17, '98; mustered in August 17, '98.
20. JNO. W. HENDERSON, 21 years, private, farmer, Princeton; enrolled August 16, '98; mustered in August 16, '98.
21. MUNSEY W. JAMES, 18 years, private, farmer, Scranton; enrolled August 16, '98; mustered in August 16, '98.
22. WM. J. LANCASTER, 21 years, private, farmer, Barnwell; enrolled August 13, '98; mustered in August 13, '98.
23. CHAS. H. LINK, 21 years, private, farmer, Abbeville; enrolled August 6, '98; mustered in August 6, '98.
24. BARNEY S. LOYD, 21 years, private, farmer, Lydia; enrolled August 10, '98; mustered in August 10, '98.
25. JULIUS S. MANN, 22 years, private, farmer, Abbeville; enrolled July 21, '98; mustered in July 21, '98.
26. NEWTON P. MITCHAM, 21 years, private, farmer, Smoak; enrolled August 9, '98; mustered in August 9, '98.
27. SAM'L A. MOODY, 32 years, private, farmer, Darlington; enrolled August 10, '98; mustered in August 10, '98.
28. JEFFERSON F. MORRIS, 21 years, private, farmer, Bamberg; enrolled August 13, '98; mustered in August 13, '98.
29. CHAS. H. MCINVILLE, 22 years, private, farmer, Hartsville; enrolled August 10, '98; mustered in August 10, '98.
30. WM. A. MCKNIGHT, 21 years, private, clerk, Timmonsville; enrolled August 10, '98; mustered in August 10, '98.
31. JEROME P. MCLENDON, 20 years, private, farmer, Cypress; enrolled August 15, '98; mustered in August 15, '98.
32. ROBT. J. MIMMONS, 28 years, private, farmer, Govan; enrolled July 26, '98; mustered in July 26, '98.
33. ERWIN PARKS, 21 years, private, operator, Pacolet; enrolled August 6, '98; mustered in August 6, '98.
34. WM. W. PATRICK, 19 years, private, farmer, Bamberg; enrolled July 19, '98; mustered in July 19, '98.
35. WADE H. RAINES, 21 years, private, farmer, Philadelphia, S. C.; enrolled August 13, '98; mustered in August 13, '98.
36. WM. F. ROWLAND, private, Donalds; enrolled December 16, '98; mustered in December 16, '98.
37. ROBT. E. SCHRAUN, 18 years, private, farmer, Abbeville; enrolled July 21, '98; mustered in July 22, '98.
38. GEO. A. SHILITO, 20 years, private, tinner, Clinton; enrolled August 9, '98; mustered in August 9, '98.

39. WM. SIMPSON, 21 years, private, farmer, Arion; enrolled August 16, '98; mustered in August 16, '98.
40. HOMER V. SMITH, 23 years, private, farmer, Anderson; enrolled August 6, '98; mustered in August 6, '98.
41. FLENOR SMOAK, 25 years, private, millman, Bamberg; enrolled August 17, '98; mustered in August 17, '98.
42. ABRAM J. STEEDLEY, 23 years, private, farmer, Hartzog; enrolled August 18, '98; mustered in August 18, '98.
43. ARTHUR STRADLEY, 21 years, private, painter, Bamberg; enrolled July 19, '98; mustered in July 19, '98.
44. HENRY TEEL, 21 years, private, farmer, Hartsville; enrolled August 10, '98; mustered in August 10, '98.
45. WALTER J. WARR, 23 years, private, farmer, Swift Creek; enrolled August 13, '98; mustered in August 13, '98.
46. WM. H. WORRELL, 27 years, private, farmer, Effingham; enrolled August 16, '98; mustered in August 16, '98.
47. FRANK WHITLEY, 26 years, private, farmer, Darlington; enrolled August 15, '98; mustered in August 15, '98.
48. PINK WILSON, 25 years, private, farmer, Govan; enrolled August 22, '98; mustered in August 22, '98.
49. JAS. E. ZEIGLER, 25 years, private, farmer, Farrell Cross Roads; enrolled July 19, '98; mustered in July 19, '98.
50. HENRY S. DOWLING, 23 years, Second Lieutenant, lawyer, Bamberg; enrolled July 19, '98; mustered in August 20, '98; resigned September 2, '98.
51. JAS. C. CHEATHAM, 22 years, First Sergeant, student, Watts; enrolled July 21, '98; mustered in August 7, '98; discharged February 2, '99, to accept commission.
52. ALEX. S. BARTON, 30 years, Sergeant, machinist, Bamberg; enrolled August 18, '98; mustered in August 18, '98; discharged September 7, '98, at Savannah, Ga.
53. JAS. T. BARNES, 24 years, Sergeant, teacher, Ellenton; enrolled August 18, '98; mustered in August 18, '98; discharged December 21, '98, at Savannah, Ga.
54. RICHARD E. PLOWDEN, 20 years, Corporal, student, Darlington; enrolled May 5, '98; mustered in May 5, '98; discharged December 15, '98, at Savannah, Ga.
55. BURRELL L. JONES, 42 years, Corporal, farmer, Smoak; enrolled August 9, '98; mustered in August 9, '98; discharged January 16, '99, at Havana, Cuba.
56. LONNY B. CROMER, 18 years, private, farmer, Ninety Six; enrolled July 21, '98; mustered in July 31, '98; discharged November 20, '98.
57. JNO. S. GARNER, 23 years, private, machinist, Syracuse; enrolled August 10, '98; mustered in August 10, '98; discharged February 10, '99, Havana, Cuba.
58. CHAS. H. GARRIS, 18 years, private, farmer, Hartzog; enrolled August 13, '98; mustered in August 19, '98; discharged December 27, '98, Savannah, Ga.

59. Jos. T. Grobusky, 21 years, private, farmer, Aaron; enrolled August 13, '98; mustered in August 13, '98; discharged December 14, '98, Savannah, Ga.
60. Marcus Jones, 21 years, private, farmer; Branchville; enrolled August 13, '98; mustered in August 13, '98; discharged December 22, '98, Savannah, Ga.
61. Stoll C. James, 22 years, private, farmer, Scranton; enrolled August 16, '98; mustered in August 16, '98; discharged January 25, '99, Havana, Cuba.
62. Pierce L. Tribble, 22 years, private, farmer, Donalds; enrolled August 13, '98; mustered in August 13, '98; discharged February 14, '99, from hospital.
63. Walter F. White, 39 years, private, farmer, Florence; enrolled August 10, '98; mustered in August 10, '98; discharged December 13, '98, at Savannah, Ga.
64. Andrew C. Armstrong, 21 years, private, millman, Piedmont; enrolled August 13, '98; mustered in August 13, '98; transferred to Hospital Corps October 29, '98.
65. Jno. R. Dunn, 21 years, private, farmer, Donalds; enrolled August 13, '98; mustered in August 13, '98; transferred to Hospital Corps October 27, '98.
66. Jas. W. Wilson, 25 years, private, farmer, Branchville; enrolled July 19, '98; mustered in July 19, '98; transferred to Band September 1, '98.
67. Wm. Finley, 21 years, private, farmer, Troy; enrolled July 21, '98; mustered in July 21, '98; died November 29, '98, tuberculosis.
68. Jas. P. Connerly, 21 years, private, farmer; Barnwell; enrolled August 22, '98; mustered in August 22, '98.
69. Andrew R. Gardiner, 21 years, private, farmer, Darlington; enrolled August 10, '98; mustered in August 10, '98.
70. Robt. L. Hiers, 25 years, private, farmer, Ehrhardt's; enrolled July 19, '98; mustered in July 19, '98.

Capt. W. E. Gonzales.

Lieut. E. R. Tompkins.

Lieut. C. J. Epps.

Company I, Second Regiment

1. WM. E. GONZALES, 32 years, Captain, journalist, Columbia; enrolled May 21, '98; mustered in August 23, '98.

1. EDWARD R. TOMPKINS, First Lieutenant, Rock Hill; enrolled September 10, '98; mustered in September 10, '98; promoted from Sergeant Major September 10, '98.

1. CHAS J. EPPS, 25 years, Second Lieutenant, pharmacist, Kingstree; enrolled September 10, '98; mustered in September 10, '98; promoted from Sergeant September 10, '98.

1. WALTER M. WILSON, 21 years, First Sergeant, clerk, Florence; enrolled May 5, '98; mustered in May 14, '98; transferred from Co. A August 23, '98.

1. ABRAM E. BRUNSON, 23 years, Quartermaster Sergeant, agent, Holly Hill; enrolled May 5, '98; mustered in May 14, '98; promoted from Corporal January 26, '99.

1. JAS. B. HOLLMAN, 20 years, Sergeant, clerk, Sumter; enrolled May 5, '98; mustered in May 19, '98.

2. ALBERT J. WHEELER, 26 years, Sergeant, teacher, Traer, Iowa; enrolled May 5, '98; mustered in May 19, '98.
3. THOS. E. CARROLL, 25 years, Sergeant, farmer, Packsville; enrolled May 5, '98; mustered in May 21, '98.
4. ARTHUR B. ZEIGLER, 21 years, Sergeant, carpenter, Blackville; enrolled May 5, '98; mustered in June 15, '98; promoted from Corporal August 23, '98.

1. WM. D. PADGETT, 35 years, Corporal, machinist, Saluda; enrolled May 5, '98; mustered in May 21, '98.
2. LAMPLEY D. NETTLES, 21 years, Corporal, clerk, Foreston; enrolled May 8, '98; mustered in May 21, '98.
3. WM. A. FARS, 20 years, Corporal, merchant, Dillon; enrolled August 22, '98; mustered in August 22, '98; promoted from private November 1, '98.
4. JOS. M. AUTIBUS, 19 years, Corporal, plumber, Charleston; enrolled June 15, '98; mustered in June 15, '98; promoted from private November 1, '98.
5. GEO. A. SLOANE, 22 years, Corporal, printer, Columbia; enrolled June 14, '98; mustered in June 15, '98; promoted from private January 26, '99.
6. LEWIS P. FOGLE, 21 years, Corporal, farmer, Orangeburg; enrolled August 18, '98; mustered in August 18, '98; promoted from private January 26, '99.

1. WM. C. MCABEE, 19 years, private, laborer, Spartanburg; enrolled June 10, '98; mustered in June 13, '98; transferred from Co. B August 23, '98.
2. ISAAC WHITE, 19 years, private, farmer, Chadburn; enrolled May 15, '98; mustered in May 21, '98; transferred from Co. D August 23, '98.
3. OLIN FRAZIER, 36 years, private, blacksmith, St. Matthews; enrolled June 7, '98; mustered in June 15, '98; transferred from Co. B August 23, '98.
4. WELCOM J. DAVID, 22 years, private, machinist, Columbia; enrolled June 15, '98; mustered in June 15, '98; transferred from Co. C August 23, '98.
5. CHAS. C. WHITE, 19 years, private, farmer, Tindalls; enrolled May 5, '98; mustered in May 21, '98; transferred from Co. D August 23, '98.
6. WM. H. BAKER, 28 years, private, farmer, Midway; enrolled May 5, '98; mustered in May 21, '98; transferred from Co. D August 23, '98.
7. WM. J. BODIFORD, 20 years, private, farmer, Greelyville; enrolled July 17, '98; mustered in July 17, '98; transferred from Co. D August 23, '98.
8. JESSE E. BELL, 20 years, private, farmer, Orangeburg; enrolled May 9, '98; mustered in May 20, '98; transferred from Co. C August 23, '98.
9. JOS. BOWER, 18 years, private, blacksmith, Branchville; enrolled July 11, '98; mustered in July 11, '98; transferred from Co. C August 23, '98.

South Carolina Troops in the War with Spain   207

10. JNO. S. BOYD, 22 years, private, teacher, Manning; enrolled May 14, '98; mustered in May 21, '98; transferred from Co. C August 23, '98.
11. WM. C. BRADLEY, 40 years, private, carpenter, Columbia; enrolled July 14, '98; mustered in July 14, '98; transferred from Co. C August 23, '98.
12. GEO. M. COLLIER, 35 years, private, farmer, Elloree; enrolled May 5, '98; mustered in May 20, '98; transferred from Co. C August 23, '98.
13. WM. T. COOPER, 18 years, private, painter, Greenwood; enrolled July 27, '98; mustered in July 27, '98; transferred from Co. D August 23, '98.
14. JAS. M. CORTEZ, 21 years, private, carpenter, Graniteville; enrolled May 5, '98; mustered in May 20, '98; transferred from Co. C January 21, '99.
15. WM. COTTON, 21 years, private, farmer, Columbia; enrolled July 21, '98; mustered in July 21, '98; transferred from Co. C August 23, '98.
16. RUFUS COVINGTON, 20 years, private, farmer; Bennettsville; enrolled May 20, '98; mustered in May 21, '98; transferred from Co. D August 23, '98.
17. JNO. R. COX, 23 years, private, farmer, Kingstree; enrolled July 14, '98; mustered in July 14, '98; transferred from Co. A August 23, '98.
18. CHAS. W. DISHER, 21 years, private, farmer, Workman; enrolled May 5, '98; mustered in May 21, '98; transferred from Co. D August 23, '98.
19. ROBT. L. FAIREY, 19 years, private, farmer, Rowesville; enrolled May 13, '98; mustered in May 20, '98; transferred from Co. C August 23, '98.
20. WM. P. GOODWIN, 23 years, private, laborer, Lake City; enrolled July 14, '98; mustered in July 14, '98; transferred from Co. D August 23, '98.
21. RENALDER G. GRAHAM, 18 years, private, farmer, Lake City; enrolled July 13, '98; mustered in July 13, '98; transferred from Co. D August 23, '98.
22. VIRGIL T. GREGORY, 19 years, private, weaver, Cross Keys; enrolled June 8, '98; mustered in June 15, '98; transferred from Co. B August 23, '98.
23. CHAS. E. GRIFFIN, 27 years, private, weaver, Pacolet; enrolled July 13, '98; mustered in June 15, '98; transferred from Co. B August 23, '98.
24. NEAL R. HATCHELL, 21 years, private, lineman, Florence; enrolled July 12, '98; mustered in July 12, '98; transferred from Co. A August 23, '98.
25. SOUTHERN C. HATCHELL, 18 years, private, farmer, Effingham; enrolled August 3, '98; mustered in August 3, '98; transferred from Co. D August 23, '98.
26. WM. HAYES, 21 years, private, farmer, St. Matthews; enrolled June 10, '98; mustered in June 10, '98; transferred from Co. C August 23, '98.

27. WM. E. HENDRIX, 19 years, private, farmer, Columbia; enrolled June 6, '98; mustered in June 15, '98; transferred from Co. B August 23, '98.
28. HILLERY B. HOLLEMAN, 22 years, private, farmer, Greelyville; enrolled May 5, '98; mustered in May 21, '98; transferred from Co. D August 23, '98.
29. WM. HOSEY, 32 years, private, farmer, Greenville; enrolled June 8, '98; mustered in June 15, '98; transferred from Co. B August 23, '98.
30. HENRY H. HUGHES, 21 years, private, farmer, Orangeburg; enrolled May 16, '98; mustered in May 20, '98; transferred from Co. C August 23, '98.
31. CHAS. N. JESSEN, 18 years, private, book-keeper, Charleston; enrolled June 9, '98; mustered in June 15, '98; transferred from Co. B August 23, '98.
32. FREDERICK JOHNSON, 19 years, private, farmer, Bennettsville; enrolled July 30, '98; mustered in July 30, '98; transferred from Co. B August 23, '98.
33. LOUIS L. JONES, 27 years, private, laborer, St. Mathews; enrolled May 16, '98; mustered in May 20, '98; transferred from Co. C August 23, '98.
34. PAUL H. JOYNER, 18 years, private, railroad employee, Columbia; enrolled June 15, '98; mustered in June 15, '98; transferred from Co. B August 23, '98.
35. JNO. LAMBERT, 25 years, private, millman, Langley; enrolled May 7, '98; mustered in May 20, '98; transferred from Co. C August 23, '98.
36. THEO. G. MAY, 18 years, private, blacksmith, Charleston; enrolled June 9, '98; mustered in June 15, '98; transferred from Co. B August 23, '98.
37. CHAS. H. MCCLUNG, 18 years, private, carpenter, Columbia; enrolled July 22, '98; mustered in July 22, '98; transferred from Co. A August 23, '98.
38. WM. ODOM, 18 years, private, farmer, Hartsville; enrolled May 5, '98; mustered in May 14, '98; transferred from Co. A August 23, '98.
39. LAURENCE POWELL, 24 years, private spinner, Augusta, Ga.; enrolled June 26, '98; mustered in June 26, '98; transferred from Co. B August 23, '98.
40. OBIDAR S. PATE, 19 years, private, farmer, Mar's Bluff; enrolled July 29, '98; mustered in July 29, '98; transferred from Co. A August 23, '98.
41. JNO. F. RITTER, 39 years, private, millman, Walhalla; enrolled August 8, '98; mustered in August 8, '98; transferred from Co. B August 23, '98.
42. GARY F. ROSE, 26 years, private, laborer, Columbia; enrolled June 6, '98; mustered in June 15, '98; transferred from Co. B August 23, '98.
43. MARTIN A. ROYALS, 26 years, private, farmer, Mixonville; enrolled May 15, '98; mustered in May 21, '98; transferred from Co. B August 23, '98.
44. GEO. D. THOMAS, 19 years, private, millman, Cade's; enrolled July 15, '98; mustered in July 15, '98; transferred from Co. D August 23, '98.

45. LOUIS S. WHITTLE, 19 years, private, farmer, Salleys; enrolled July 17, '98; mustered in July 17, '98; transferred from Co. C August 23, '98.
46. CHAS. W. WIGGINS, private, Marion; enrolled December 22, '98; mustered in December 24, '98.
47. HENRY APPELT, 37 years, private, clerk, Darlington; enrolled May 5, '98; mustered in May 21, '98; discharged January 26, '99.
48. JNO. F. REID, 22 years, Sergeant, book-keeper, Sumter; enrolled May 5, '98; mustered in May 19, '98; discharged October 5, '98.
49. MARION M. CLARK, 18 years, Corporal, editor, Lake City; enrolled May 8, '98; mustered in May 21, '98; discharged September 3, '98.
50. FRANCES M. COOPER, 28 years, Corporal, carpenter, Greenwood; enrolled July 23, '98; mustered in July 26, '98; discharged November 13, '98.
51. ST. CLAIR BOONE, 18 years, private, student, Rowesville; enrolled July 28, '98; mustered in July 28, '98; discharged December 28, '98.
52. CULL BRASINGTON, 18 years, private, clerk, Bennettsville; enrolled May 5, '98; mustered in May 14, '98; discharged November 19, '98.
53. ARTHUR COCKERELL, 23 years, private, laborer, Richardsonville; enrolled June 8, '98; mustered in June 15, '98; discharged September 4, '98.
54. OSCAR CURETON, 18 years, private, student, Greenville; enrolled June 8, '98; mustered in June 15, '98; discharged September 29, '98.
55. CHAS. J. EPPS, 25 years, private, pharmacist, Kingstree; enrolled May 15, '98; mustered in May 21, '98; discharged September 9, '98.
56. VON M. GRIMSLEY, 24 years, private, sawyer, McCartha, N. C.; enrolled May 15, '98; mustered in May 21, '98; discharged February 6, '99.
57. DAN'L M. MCCALL, 26 years, private, clerk, Clio; enrolled May 14, '98; mustered in May 14, '98; discharged November 13, '98.
58. WADE P. MILES, 31 years, private, clerk, Columbia; enrolled August 3, '98; mustered in August 3, '98; discharged October 26, '98.
59. THOS. C. WEATHERSBY, 18 years, private, Bennettsville; enrolled May 17, '98; mustered in May 21, '98; discharged September 3, '98.
60. JAS. H. WINDHAM, 26 years, private, millman, Manning; enrolled May 14, '98; mustered in May 21, '98; discharged October 26, '98.
61. DAN'L R. BLACKMAN, 29 years, private, machinist, Darlington; enrolled May 5, '98; mustered in May 14, '98; transferred to Band September 2, '98.
62. GEO. A. BRISTOW, 20 years, private, printer, Kingstree; enrolled May 12, '98; mustered in May 14, '98; transferred to Hospital Corps October 1, '98.
63. EDWARD G. ORRELL, 27 years, private, drug clerk, Darlington; enrolled June 29, '98; mustered in June 29, '98; transferred to Hospital Corps October 20, '98.
64. LUTHER M. PRICE, 26 years, private, millman, Tindall; enrolled May 5, '98; mustered in May 21, '98; transferred to Band September 2, '98.
65. MATHEW KITCHEN, 23 years, private, farmer, Branchville; enrolled May 15, '98; mustered in May 21, '98; died in hospital, meningitis, December 10, '98.
66. JOS. ALFRED, 29 years, private, weaver, Greenville; enrolled July 29, '98; mustered in July 29, '98.

67. AIKEN DUNCAN, 21 years, private, weaver, Piedmont; enrolled July 27, '98; mustered in July 27, '98.
68. WM. J. BODIFORD, 20 years, private, farmer, Greenville; enrolled July 17, '98; mustered in July 17, '98.
69. LUCIAN M. COCKERELL, 22 years, private, farmer, Manning; enrolled May 5, '98; mustered in May 21, '98.
70. ISAAC ESTRIDGE, 20 years, private, laborer, Columbia; enrolled June 6, '98; mustered in June 15, '98.
71. HILLERY B. HOLLMAN, 22 years, private, fireman, Greenville; enrolled May 5, '98; mustered in May 21, '98.
72. WM. HOSEY, 32 years, private, farmer, Greenville; enrolled June 8, '98; mustered in June 15, '98.
73. WM. M. MOODY, 23 years, private, weaver, Pelzer; enrolled July 27, '98; mustered in July 27, '98.
74. WM. THOMAS, 26 years, private, farmer, Pacolet; enrolled July 13, '98; mustered in July 13, '98.

Capt. I. M. Mauldin.

Lieut. J. M. Bowden.

Lieut. W. N. Scott.

Company K, Second Regiment

1. IVY M. MAULDIN, 21 years, Captain, lawyer, Pickens; enrolled July 15, '98; mustered in August 23, '98.

1. JAS. M. BOWDEN, 34 years, First Lieutenant, merchant, Spartanburg; enrolled August 23, '98; mustered in August 23, '98.

1. WALTER N. SCOTT, 20 years, Second Lieutenant, farmer, Brushy Creek; enrolled August 6, '98; mustered in August 6, '98; promoted from private September 13, '98.

1. JOS. A. BERRY, 21 years, First Sergeant, lawyer, Orangeburg; enrolled May 5, '98; mustered in May 5, '98; promoted from Corporal August 23, '98.

1. JAS. C. JENNINGS, 40 years, Quartermaster Sergeant, hotel manager, Pickens; enrolled July 15, '98; mustered in July 15, '98; promoted from private August 23, '98.

1. WM. P. MEARES, 23 years, Sergeant, farmer, Pelzer; enrolled July 21, '98; mustered in July 21, '98.

2. GEO. R. HENDRIX, 24 years, Sergeant, teacher, Pickens; enrolled August 12, '98; mustered in August 12, '98.

3. ALONZO BROWN, 38 years, Sergeant, carpenter, Gaffney; enrolled August 16, '98; mustered in August 16, '98.
4. AMBROSE E. GRIFFIN, 37 years, Sergeant, farmer, Pickens; enrolled July 16, '98; mustered in July 16, '98; promoted from Corporal August 23, '98.

1. GEO. B. SMALLEY, 20 years, Corporal, farmer, Pickens; enrolled July 15, '98; mustered in July 15, '98.
2. JNO. P. GRIFFIN, 22 years, Corporal, farmer, Belton; enrolled August 6, '98; mustered in August 6, '98; promoted from private October 1, '98.
3. WM. H. FIELD, 21 years, Corporal, farmer, Pindar; enrolled August 19, '98; mustered in August 19, '98; promoted from private December 1, '98.
4. LUTHER D. SMITH, 21 years, Corporal, farmer, Pickens; enrolled August 11, '98; mustered in August 11, '98; promoted from private October 1, '98.
5. WM. M. HENDERSON, 26 years, Corporal, farmer, Pelzer; enrolled August 15, '98; mustered in August 15, '98; promoted from private October 1, '98.
6. AUGUSTUS WEBBER, JR., 23 years, Corporal, farmer, Anderson; enrolled July 21, '98; mustered in July 21, '98; promoted from private December 1, '98.

1. FRED. W. HOWLAND, 30 years, private, engineer, Spartanburg; enrolled August 6, '98; mustered in August 6, '98.
2. WALTER E. MAYFIELD, 21 years, private, farmer, Honea Path; enrolled August 5, '98; mustered in August 5, '98.
3. WALTER A. HESTER, 21 years, private, printer, Pickens; enrolled August 20, '98; mustered in August 20, '98.
4. WM. B. KEASLER, 26 years, private, brick-layer, Anderson; enrolled July 28, '98; mustered in July 28, '98.
5. CHAS. C. HILL, 32 years, private, operator, Ennoree; enrolled July 18, '98; mustered in July 18, '98.
6. JOEL ADAMS, 18 years, private, mill hand, Spartanburg; enrolled August 6, '98; mustered in August 6, '98.
7. CLAUDE ALLISON, 23 years, private, printer, Pickens; enrolled August 19, '98; mustered in August 19, '98.
8. JAS. M. ALLISON, 19 years, private, farmer, Pickens; enrolled August 12, '98; mustered in August 12, '98.
9. ROBT. ANTHONY, 20 years, private, farmer, Pickens; enrolled August 19, '98; mustered in August 19, '98.
10. WM. A. BANKS, 27 years, private, weaver, Pelzer; enrolled August 16, '98; mustered in August 16, '98.
11. DAVID H. BOYCE, 22 years, private, farmer, Princeton; enrolled August 15, '98; mustered in August 15, '98.
12. ZACHARIA T. BRACKETT, 35 years, private, carpenter, Henrietta, N. C.; enrolled August 16, '98; mustered in August 16, '98.
13. HENRY C. BROWN, 29 years, private, farmer, Glendale; enrolled August 17, '98; mustered in August 17, '98.

South Carolina Troops in the War with Spain 213

14. WM. M. BURBANKS, 30 years, private, laborer, Fort Mill; enrolled July 28, '98; mustered in July 28, '98.
15. JNO. W. CAPPS, 37 years, private, shoemaker, Pickens; enrolled July 16, '98; mustered in July 16, '98.
16. SAM'L P. CASE, 21 years, private, farmer, Baxter, N. C.; enrolled July 18, '98; mustered in July 18, '98.
17. JNO. E. CLAY, 37 years, private, carpenter, Spartanburg; enrolled August 11, '98; mustered in August 11, '98.
18. THOS. D. CURTIS, 28 years, private, farmer, Grambling; enrolled August 16, '98; mustered in August 16, '98.
19. MEDICUS F. DAY, 21 years, private, farmer, Pickens; enrolled July 15, '98; mustered in July 15, '98.
20. AMOS DODGENS, 19 years, private, farmer, Pickens; enrolled August 19, '98; mustered in August 19, '98.
21. ERNEST ELLIS, 19 years, private, millman, Gaffney; enrolled August 16, '98; mustered in August 16, '98.
22. WM. ELLISON, 19 years, private, farmer, Wares; enrolled August 6, '98; mustered in August 6, '98.
23. THOS. H. EMORY, 18 years, private, weaver, Clifton; enrolled August 16, '98; mustered in August 16, '98.
24. HENRY FORTNER, 21 years, private, weaver, Pelzer; enrolled August 16, '98; mustered in August 16, '98.
25. WM. L. GELSTRAP, 26 years, private, farmer, Pickens; enrolled July 16, '98; mustered in July 16, '98.
26. SILAS B. GRIFFIN, 19 years, private, farmer, Belton; enrolled August 6, '98; mustered in August 6, '98.
27. WM. M. GRUBB, 28 years, private, farmer, Gaffney; enrolled August 16, '98; mustered in August 16, '98.
28. JAS. W. HESTER, 18 years, private, farmer, Pickens; enrolled July 28, '98; mustered in July 28, '98.
29. JESSE C. JENNINGS, 18 years, private, farmer, Pickens; enrolled July 15, '98; mustered in July 15, '98.
30. HAMILTON R. JUSTICE, 28 years, private, weaver, Pelzer; enrolled July 21, '98; mustered in July 21, '98.
31. ROBT. E. LABOON, 22 years, private, farmer, Brushy Creek; enrolled August 5, '98; mustered in August 5, '98.
32. CHAS. C. MABRY, 26 years, private, farmer, Asbury; enrolled July 18, '98; mustered in July 18, '98.
33. WILLIE MILLER, 18 years, private, farmer, Easley; enrolled August 12, '98; mustered in August 12, '98.
34. JNO. B. MOORE, 18 years, private, student, Waterloo; enrolled August 12, '98; mustered in August 12, '98.
35. CLARENCE D. SEXTON, 18 years, private, clerk, Union; enrolled August 16, '98; mustered in August 16, '98.
36. ROBT. SMITH, 22 years, private, millman, Enoree; enrolled August 11, '98; mustered in August 11, '98.
37. CHAS. M. SMITH, 19 years, private, farmer, Belton; enrolled August 6, '98; mustered in August 6, '98.
38. THOS. P. SEAY, 27 years, private, farmer, Inman; enrolled July 18, '98; mustered in July 18, '98.

39. CHAS. E. SULLIVAN, 22 years, private, farmer, Belton; enrolled August 15, '98; mustered in August 15, '98.
40. CHAS. WARREN, 24 years, private, millman, Pickens; enrolled August 19, '98; mustered in August 19, '98.
41. ALFRED T. WILLIS, 18 years, private, student, Landrum; enrolled August 10, '98; mustered in August 10, '98.
42. HENRY E. WHITED, 25 years, private, millman, Orangeburg; enrolled August 13, '98; mustered in August 13, '98.
43. JNO. T. WILSON, 26 years, private, millman, Brushy Creek; enrolled August 5, '98; mustered in August 5, '98.
44. JNO. F. WILLBANKS, 26 years, private, farmer, Mauldin; enrolled August 15, '98; mustered in August 15, '98.
45. WALTER N. SCOTT, 20 years, private, farmer, Brushy Creek; enrolled August 6, '98; mustered in August 6, '98; discharged to accept commission September 12, '98.
46. MARION COTHRAN, 19 years, private, farmer, Cooley's Bridge; enrolled August 15, '98; mustered in August 15, '98; discharged September 19, '98.
47. JEROME PALMER, 19 years, private, printer, Pickens; enrolled August 12, '98; mustered in August 12, '98; discharged December 23, '98.
48. WM. M. BOGGS, 35 years, private, farmer, Liberty; enrolled August 12, '98; mustered in August 12, '98; discharged January 3, '99.
49. JAS. R. MABRY, 22 years, private, farmer, Boiling Springs; enrolled August 17, '98; mustered in August 17, '98; discharged January 3, '99.
50. GEO. GOUTHRO, 25 years, private, farmer, Spartanburg; enrolled August 6, '98; mustered in August 6, '98; discharged January 15, '99.
51. JNO. W. FULLER, 22 years, private, millman, Union; enrolled August 10, '98; mustered in August 10, '98; discharged January 15, '99.
52. WM. H. GILSTROP, 30 years, private, farmer, Fields; enrolled August 12, '98; mustered in August 12, '98; discharged January 15, '99.
53. ROWLAND W. EMORY, 20 years, private, farmer, Clifton; enrolled August 16, '98; mustered in August 16, '98; discharged January 26, '99.
54. EUGENE WEBB, 28 years, private, farmer, Anderson; enrolled July 21, '98; mustered in July 21, '98; discharged March 23, '99.
55. ALBERT BELCHER, 21 years, private, farmer, Fairforest; enrolled August 6, '98; mustered in August 6, '98; discharged December 22, '98.
56. JOS. C. BLACKWOOD, 21 years, private, farmer, Obed; enrolled August 16, '98; mustered in August 16, '98; transferred to Hospital Corps October 6, '98.
57. JACOB A. PICKLE, 25 years, private, farmer, Pickens; enrolled August 20, '98; mustered in August 20, '98; transferred to Hospital Corps October 21, '98.
57. ARTHUR EPTON, 21 years, private, blacksmith, Spartanburg; enrolled August 11, '98; mustered in August 11, '98; died of disease at Columbia September 25, '98.
58. JAKE E. HOLLINGSWORTH, 18 years, private, weaver, Pelzer; enrolled August 16, '98; mustered in August 16, '98.
59. JNO. M. KIRBY, 28 years, private, millman, Spartanburg; enrolled August 16, '98; mustered in August 16, '98.

60. SAM'L O. COOLEY, 23 years, private, weaver, Odessa; enrolled August 5, '98; mustered in August 5, '98.
61. CHAS. M. SMITH, 19 years, private, farmer, Belton; enrolled August 6, '98; mustered in August 6, '98.
62. JOS. BROCK, 21 years, private, policeman, Pickens; enrolled August 12, '98; mustered in August 12, '98.
63. DAVIS J. COOPER, 26 years, private, farmer, Pickens; enrolled August 12, '98; mustered in August 12, '98.
64. ABRAM BLACK, 32 years, private, salesman, Spartanburg; enrolled August 16, '98; mustered in August 16, '98.
65. DAWSON A. BELL, 24 years, private, flagman, Greenville; enrolled August 16, '98; mustered in August 16, '98.
66. GEO. W. MCKINNY, 21 years, private, weaver, Pacolet; enrolled July 18, '98; mustered in July 18, '98.
67. BENJ. P. HOWELL, 31 years, private, farmer, Saluda, N. C.; enrolled July 18, '98; mustered in July 18, '98.
68. JNO. D. KEYS, 24 years, private, farmer, Belton; enrolled July 21, '98; mustered in July 21, '98.

Capt. A. H. Moss.

Lieut. T. S. Moorman, Jr.

Lieut. L. J. Bristow.

Company L, Second Regiment

1. ADAM H. MOSS, 27 years, Captain, lawyer, Orangeburg; enrolled May 5, '98; mustered in May 5, '98; promoted from First Lieutenant November 14, '98.

1. THOS. S. MOORMAN, JR., 23 years, First Lieutenant, dairyman, Columbia; enrolled August 6, '98; mustered in August 6, '98.

1. LOUIS J. BRISTOW, 22 years, Second Lieutenant, editor, Kingstree; enrolled May 5, '98; mustered in May 5, '98; promoted from Sergeant September 10, '98.

1. WM. J. HAMER, JR., 26 years, First Sergeant, farmer, Chesterfield; enrolled May 5, '98; mustered in May 5, '98; transferred as private from Co. A.

1. THOS. L. BUYCK, 28 years, Quartermaster Sergeant, clerk, St. Mathews; enrolled May 5, '98; mustered in May 5, '98.

1. FRANK F. PAULDING, 20 years, Sergeant, farmer, St. Mathews; enrolled May 5, '98; mustered in May 5, '98.

2. HENRY A. ATKINSON, 21 years, Sergeant, railroad employee, Florence; enrolled August 8, '98; mustered in August 8, '98.

3. Jos. W. Hanna, 22 years, Sergeant, clerk, Chesterfield; enrolled June 24, '98; mustered in June 24, '98; promoted from Corporal September 1, '98.
4. Hebron Berry, 20 years, Sergeant, farmer, Branchville; enrolled May 5, '98; mustered in May 5, '98; promoted from Corporal December 26, '98.

1. Jno. S. Bellinger, 22 years, Corporal, farmer, Orangeburg; enrolled July 9, '98; mustered in July 9, '98.
2. Sterling G. Jordan, 23 years, Corporal, agent, Charleston; enrolled July 26, '98; mustered in July 26, '98.
3. Henry W. Kortjohn, 21 years, Sergeant, book-keeper, Orangeburg; enrolled July 8, '98; mustered in July 8, '98.
4. McDonough M. Wilson, 21 years, Corporal, farmer, Magnolia; enrolled August 11, '98; mustered in August 11, '98.
5. David M. Haithcock, 22 years, Corporal, teacher, Eastover; enrolled August 16, '98; mustered in August 16, '98.
6. Oscar H. Pratt, 21 years, Corporal, farmer, Monroe, N. C.; enrolled August 18, '98; mustered in August 18, '98.

1. Ernest C. Fairey, 18 years, private, farmer, Orangeburg; enrolled July 9, '98; mustered in July 9, '98.
2. Jno. M. Barbee, 21 years, private, weaver, Durham, N. C.; enrolled July 19, '98; mustered in July 19, '98.
3. Jas. M. Mangum, 18 years, private, printer, Chesterfield; enrolled August 18, '98; mustered in August 18, '98.
4. Jno. D. Jolly, 22 years, private, farmer, Hinson; enrolled August 15, '98; mustered in August 15, '98.
5. Willie G. Lecons, 36 years, private, laborer, Columbia; enrolled August 10, '98; mustered in August 10, '98.
6. Jesse L. Baker, 21 years, private, farmer, Magnolia; enrolled August 13, '98; mustered in August 13, '98.
7. Elliot H. Bissell, 21 years, private, farmer, Norway; enrolled August 7, '98; mustered in August 7, '98.
8. Edward B. Carter, 25 years, private, farmer, Orangeburg; enrolled August 22, '98; mustered in August 22, '98.
9. Richard A. Chavis, 33 years, private, millman, Orangeburg; enrolled August 13, '98; mustered in August 13, '98.
10. Jno. W. Fisher, 19 years, private, farmer, Granite Falls, N. C.; enrolled July 20, '98; mustered in July 20, '98.
11. Henry Fraser, 18 years, private, weaver, Columbia; enrolled August 6, '98; mustered in August 6, '98.
12. Jno. M. Garrick, 23 years, private, farmer, Norway; enrolled August 20, '98; mustered in August 20, '98.
13. Wm. B. Gulledge, 21 years, private, farmer, Morven, N. C.; enrolled August 18, '98; mustered in August 18, '98.
14. Albert P. Hatchell, 25 years, private, farmer, Cartersville; enrolled August 13, '98; mustered in August 13, '98.
15. Geo. W. Hayden, 21 years, private, farmer, Orangeburg; enrolled August 14, '98; mustered in August 14, '98.

16. GEO. HENKEL, 20 years, private, machinist, Hickory; enrolled July 20, '98; mustered in July 20, '98.
17. LUCIUS B. HUGHES, 21 years, private, farmer, Livingston; enrolled August 7, '98; mustered in August 7, '98.
18. CLARENCE J. INABINET, 18 years, private, farmer, Orangeburg; enrolled August 2, '98; mustered in August 2, '98.
19. JAS. M. JACKSON, 18 years, private, farmer, Longtown; enrolled August 6, '98; mustered in August 6, '98.
20. THOS. F. LOFTIN, 24 years, private, laborer, Columbia; enrolled August 6, '98; mustered in August 6, '98.
21. LAURENCE H. LYLES, 21 years, private, millman, Columbia; enrolled August 7, '98; mustered in August 7, '98.
22. PETER C. MATHEWS, 18 years, private, farmer, Kingstree; enrolled August 16, '98; mustered in August 16, '98.
23. JOS. T. MAREE, 25 years, private, farmer, Monck's Corner; enrolled August 10, '98; mustered in August 10, '98.
24. HENRY M. MYERS, 28 years, private, carpenter, Charleston; enrolled August 10, '98; mustered in August 10, '98.
25. MILLARD B. MITCHUM, 21 years, private, farmer, Salters; enrolled August 20, '98; mustered in August 20, '98.
26. HENRY C. MOORE, 18 years, private, laborer, Columbia; enrolled August 6. '98; mustered in August 6, '98.
27. SAM'L B. McCLEARY, 18 years, private, farmer, Lane's; enrolled August 20, '98; mustered in August 20, '98.
28. NEWMAN McCOLLUM, 21 years, private, farmer, Baton Rouge; enrolled August 16, '98; mustered in August 16, '98.
29. JNO. H. PERKINS, 21 years, private, farmer, Chesterfield; enrolled August 18, '98; mustered in August 18, '98.
30. THOS. L. PEAY, 20 years, private, farmer, Longtown; enrolled August 6, '98; mustered in August 6, '98.
31. JNO. J. POWERS, 21 years, private, farmer, Charleston; enrolled August 16, '98; mustered in August 16, '98.
32. HIRAL A. POOLE, 23 years, private, farmer, Mayesville; enrolled August 13, '98; mustered in August 13, '98.
33. JNO. T. PROCTOR, 21 years, private, photographer, Dillon; enrolled August 16, '98; mustered in August 16, '98.
34. WM. P. RAINES, 20 years, private, farmer, Columbia; enrolled August 9, '98; mustered in August 9, '98.
35. JAS. R. RICHARDS, 21 years, private, farmer, Charleston; enrolled August 20, '98; mustered in August 20, '98.
36. HARRY ROBINSON, 35 years, private, laborer, Arthens; enrolled August 6, '98; mustered in August 6, '98.
37. WM. D. RUSS, 27 years, private, farmer, Salters; enrolled August 20, '98; mustered in August 20, '98.
38. EDWARD J. SHIVER, 21 years, private, farmer, Gourdin's; enrolled August 16, '98; mustered in August 16, '98.
39. GEO. W. SMITH, 21 years, private, farmer, North; enrolled August 7, '98; mustered in August 7, '98.
40. WM. F. SMITH, 21 years, private, farmer, Baton Rouge; enrolled August 10, '98; mustered in August 10, '98.

South Carolina Troops in the War with Spain 219

41. SHELTON R. SMOAK, 18 years, private, farmer, Orangeburg; enrolled August 13, '98; mustered in August 13, '98.
42. WM. L. STUBBS, 22 years, private, farmer, Mowin, N. C.; enrolled August 18, '98; mustered in August 18, '98.
43. ROBT. H. TISDALE, 24 years, private, farmer, Kingstree; enrolled August 16, '98; mustered in August 16, '98.
44. JNO. TUBERVILLE, 21 years, private, laborer, Hannah; enrolled August 15, '98; mustered in August 15, '98.
45. EDWARD G. VANCLEVE, 21 years, private, newsboy, Columbia; enrolled August 4, '98; mustered in August 4, '98.
46. RICHARD D. WALKER, 20 years, private, farmer, Ridgeway; enrolled August 6, '98; mustered in August 6, '98.
47. HENRY E. WATSON, 21 years, private, farmer, Mowin, N. C.; enrolled August 18, '98; mustered in August 18, '98.
48. ROSSER B. WATTS, 21 years, private, laborer, Blythewood; enrolled August 18, '98; mustered in August 18, '98.
49. ALBERT Y. WILEY, 34 years, private, farmer, Hickory, N. C.; enrolled July 23, '98; mustered in July 23, '98.
50. JOS. WEST, 21 years, private, farmer, Sutton; enrolled August 16, '98; mustered in August 16, '98.
51. WM. E. MCINTOSH, 21 years, private, farmer, Magnolia; enrolled August 10, '98; mustered in August 10, '98; discharged October 15, '98.
52. BREVARD S. GORDON, 18 years, private, weaver, Weaver; enrolled July 20, '98; mustered in July 20, '98; discharged November 29, '98.
53. WM. P. STROMAN, 23 years, Sergeant, farmer, Orangeburg; enrolled May 5, '98; mustered in May 5, '98; discharged December 5, '98.
54. INSLEE T. BENNETT, 24 years, private, clerk, New York; enrolled May 5, '98; mustered in May 5, '98; discharged January 25, '99.
55. WALTER O. THOMAS, 21 years, private, farmer, Mouzon; enrolled August 16, '98; mustered in August 16, '98; discharged February 3, '99.
56. ARTHUR GRAHAM, 20 years, private, farmer, Gourdins; enrolled August 16, '98; mustered in August 16, '98; discharged November 26, '98.
57. CHAS. P. MCCANTS, 26 years, private, musician, Columbia; enrolled August 8, '98; mustered in August 8, '98; transferred to Band September 20, '98.
58. GEO. H. MASON, 24 years, private, farmer, Copes; enrolled August 20, '98; mustered in August 20, '98; transferred to Hospital Corps October 1, '98.
59. LEONARD E. GARICK, 21 years, private, farmer, Norway; enrolled August 20, '98; mustered in August 20, '98; transferred to Hospital Corps October 27, '98.
60. JAS. A. SHULER, 42 years, private, operator, St. Stevens; enrolled August 15, '98; mustered in August 15, '98; transferred to Signal Corps December 1, '98.
61. MEEK M. LYLES, 21 years, private, farmer, Mowin, N. C.; enrolled August 18, '98; mustered in August 18, '98; died October 28, '98, Jacksonville.
62. RENALDO L. WARD, 21 years, private, farmer, Benson; enrolled August 16, '98; mustered in August 16, '98; died November 3, '98, Jacksonville, Fla.

63. JACOB A. EPTING, 21 years, private, Newberry; enrolled August 20, '98; mustered in August 20, '98; died February 19, '99, Havana, Cuba.
64. RORT. N. MCKAY, 29 years, private, farmer, Ridgeway; enrolled August 9, '98; mustered in August 9, '98; died March 30, '99, Havana, Cuba.
65. JOS. F. BERRIER, 27 years, private, laborer, Columbia; enrolled August 6, '98; mustered in August 6, '98.
66. RICHARD CHAVIS, 33 years, private, millhand, Orangeburg; enrolled August 13, '98; mustered in August 13, '98.
67. JOS. FLOYD, 21 years, private, laborer, Mott's Bridge; enrolled August 10, '98; mustered in August 10, '98.
68. ALONZO F. FULLER, 22 years, private, laborer, Columbia; enrolled August 15, '98; mustered in August 15, '98.

Lieut. J. D. West.

Lieut. W. T. Ellerbe.

Company M, Second Regiment

1. BENJ. A. ROGERS, 58 years, Captain, farmer, Bennettsville; enrolled August 3, '98; mustered in August 23, '98.

1. JOS. D. WEST, 29 years, First Lieutenant, teacher, Socaste; enrolled May 12, '98; mustered in September 10, '98; promoted from private September 10, '98.

1. WM. T. ELLERBE, 25 years, Second Lieutenant, farmer, Jordanville; enrolled August 24, '98; mustered in August 24, '98.

1. SIMON F. PARROTT, 24 years, First Sergeant, editor, Darlington; enrolled May 5, '98; mustered in May 14, '98; promoted from private August 23, '98.

1. JAS. K. MCMILLAN, 37 years, Quartermaster Sergeant, farmer, Toddsville; enrolled August 6, '98; mustered in August 6, '98.

1. WM. L. GILLESPIE, 23 years, Sergeant, farmer, Kollock; enrolled August 18, '98; mustered in August 18, '98.

2. EDWARD A. VAUGHT, 23 years, Sergeant, farmer, Bucksville; enrolled August 6, '98; mustered in August 6, '98.

3. WM. W. IRBY, 27 years, Sergeant, farmer, Smithville; enrolled August 18, '98; mustered in August 18, '98; promoted from private December 19, '98.

4. CHARLEY M. LONG, 21 years, Sergeant, farmer, Conway; enrolled August 20, '98; mustered in August 20, '98; promoted from Corporal November 14, '98.

1. JNO. M. HUNTER, 22 years, Corporal, farmer, Midway; enrolled July 19, '98; mustered in July 19, '98.
2. SEBA E. CANNON, 21 years, Corporal, farmer, Dongola; enrolled August 6, '98; mustered in August 6, '98.
3. HENRY C. CANNON, 25 years, Corporal, farmer, Haskell; enrolled August 8, '98; mustered in August 8, '98; promoted from private November 14, '98.
4. JAS. W. DRIGGERS, 22 years, Corporal, farmer, Smithville; enrolled August 18, '98; mustered in August 18, '98; promoted from private January 27, '99.
5. ROBT. L. OLIVER, 23 years, Corporal, farmer, Toddsville; enrolled August 6, '98; mustered in August 6, '98; promoted from private December 14, '98.
6. WILEY J. RHODES, 21 years, Corporal, printer, Darlington; enrolled August 13, '98; mustered in August 13, '98; promoted from private April 1, '99.

1. MAHEM W. WILSON, 28 years, private, sawyer, Toddsville; enrolled August 6, '98; mustered in August 6, '98.
2. AUGUSTUS R. HARRELSON, 29 years, private, farmer, Howard; enrolled August 20, '98; mustered in August 20, '98.
3. SAML. C. LONG, 19 years, private, farmer, Conway; enrolled August 20, '98; mustered in August 20, '98.
4. HENLEY J. BROWN, 19 years, private, farmer, Withers; enrolled August 6, '98; mustered in August 6, '98.
5. JNO. W. RUSH, 27 years, private, engineer, Cobbs; enrolled August 12, '98; mustered in August 13, '98.
6. ROLAND C. ATKINSON, 18 years, private, farmer, Swift Creek; enrolled August 13, '98; mustered in August 13, '98.
7. ANSEL BRIDGES, 18 years, private, farmer, Brownsville; enrolled August 4, '98; mustered in August 4, '98.
8. WM. A. BRIDGES, 42 years, private, farmer, Brownsville; enrolled August 4, '98; mustered in August 4, '98.
9. RUFUS B. BRUTON, 23 years, private, farmer, Forney; enrolled August 12, '98; mustered in August 12, '98.
10. WALTER W. BRUTON, 27 years, private, laborer, Forney; enrolled August 12, '98; mustered in August 12, '98.
11. WM. F. CANNON, 22 years, private, farmer, Gideon; enrolled August 8, '98; mustered in August 8, '98.
12. WESTON G. COLLINS, 19 years, private, farmer, Socaste; enrolled August 6, '98; mustered in August 6, '98.
13. JAS. H. COVINGTON, 39 years, private, farmer, Covington; enrolled August 4, '98; mustered in August 4, '98.
14. GEO. E. DUSENBURY, 21 years, private, farmer, Conway; enrolled August 6, '98; mustered in August 6, '98.
15. MYRIC DUSENBURY, 21 years, private, farmer, Socaste; enrolled August 8, '98; mustered in August 8, '98.

16. WM. D. EDWARDS, 19 years, private, farmer, Conway; enrolled August 6, '98; mustered in August 6, '98.
17. GEO. ELLENBURG, 21 years, private, farmer, Pelzer; enrolled August 5, '98; mustered in August 5, '98.
18. WM. H. GRANGER, 22 years, private, farmer, Harold; enrolled August 12, '98; mustered in August 12, '98.
19. RETURN P. HARDWICK, 21 years, private, farmer, Adrian; enrolled August 20, '98; mustered in August 20, '98.
20. OLIVER M. HARRELSON, 23 years, private, farmer, Conway; enrolled August 20, '98; mustered in August 20, '98.
21. CHAS. H. HOLSENBACK, 21 years, private, machinist, Langley; enrolled August 16, '98; mustered in August 16, '98.
22. ALLISON JACOBS, 27 years, private, farmer, Bennettsville; enrolled August 4, '98; mustered in August 4, '98.
23. HYMAN P. JEFFCOAT, 21 years, private, farmer, Witts Mill; enrolled August 17, '98; mustered in August 17, '98.
24. MATHEW T. JORDAN, 18 years, private, farmer, Haskell; enrolled August 11, '98; mustered in August 11, '98.
25. JNO. S. LEE, 24 years, private, farmer, Conway; enrolled August 20, '98; mustered in August 20, '98.
26. FREDERICK C. LEWIS, 19 years, private, laborer, Adrian; enrolled August 12, '98; mustered in August 12, '98
27. JABEZ H. LONG, 26 years, private, farmer, Adrian; enrolled August 8, '98; mustered in August 8, '98.
28. ROBT. J. LUNNEY, 20 years, private, student, Darlington; enrolled May 5, '98; mustered in May 14, '98; transferred from Co. A August 23, '98.
29. CHAS. H. MURRELL, 23 years, private, laborer, Conway; enrolled August 8, '98; mustered in August 8, '98.
30. ED. W. MCCRACKEN, 20 years, private, farmer, Conway; enrolled August 8, '98; mustered in August 8, '98.
31. THOS. A. MCQUAGE, 29 years, private, farmer, Bennettsville; enrolled August 4, '98; mustered in August 4, '98.
32. JESSE E. NIXON, 27 years, private, farmer, Nixonville; enrolled August 20, '98; mustered in August 20, '98.
33. JAS. W. NORRIS, 20 years, private, farmer, Chadburn, N. C.; enrolled August 6, '98; mustered in August 8, '98.
34. GEO. T. OLLIVER, 21 years, private, farmer, Toddsville; enrolled August 6, '98; mustered in August 6, '98.
35. WM. A. SESSIONS, 30 years, private, farmer, Adrian; enrolled August 20, '98; mustered in August 20, '98.
36. JAS. W. SHIRAH, 21 years, private, farmer, Harrell; enrolled August 2, '98; mustered in August 2, '98.
37. WM. T. SPRINGS, 18 years, private, farmer, Loris; enrolled August 20, '98; mustered in August 20, '98.
38. JNO. G. STANLEY, 20 years, private, farmer, Lois; enrolled August 12, '98; mustered in August 12, '98.
39. JESSE W. STANSELL, 32 years, private, farmer, Port Shoals; enrolled July 21, '98; mustered in July 21, '98.

40. WM. M. STEADLEY, 21 years, private, farmer, Colson; enrolled August 8, '98; mustered in August 8, '98.
41. ALBERT R. TEDDER, 20 years, private, farmer, Kollock; enrolled August 18, '98; mustered in August 18, '98.
42. MURRAY L. TEDDER, 18 years, private, farmer, Kollock; enrolled August 18, '98; mustered in August 18, '98.
43. MORGAN TINDAL, 23 years, private, farmer, Smiths Mill; enrolled August 11, '98; mustered in August 11, '98.
44. HOSEY M. TODD, 21 years, private, farmer, Hammond; enrolled August 20, '98; mustered in August 20, '98.
45. JOS. R. TUCKER, 19 years, private, farmer, Conway; enrolled August 6, '98; mustered in August 6, '98.
46. MOSES P. TYLER, 28 years, private, farmer, Bayboro; enrolled August 20, '98; mustered in August 20, '98.
47. GEO. W. WATTS, 22 years, private, laborer, Conway; enrolled August 20, '98; mustered in August 20, '98.
48. THOS. E. WISE, 19 years, private, farmer, Conway; enrolled August 6, '98; mustered in August 6, '98.
49. ZACHARIAH WOOTEN, 30 years, private, machinist, Timmonsville; enrolled August 23, '98; mustered in August 23, '98.
50. ISAAC C. BROWN, 26 years, private, farmer, Withers; enrolled August 20, '98; mustered in August 20, '98; discharged Havana January 16, '99.
51. SOLAN F. HUGHES, 25 years, Corporal, farmer, Chadburn, enrolled August 8, '98; mustered in August 8, '98; discharged Savannah December 17, '98.
52. SAML. E. HUGHES, 26 years, private, farmer, Chadburn; enrolled August 6, '98; mustered in August 6, '98; discharged Fort McPherson February 4, '99.
53. LAMAR HUNTER, 21 years, private, farmer, Darlington; enrolled August 15, '98; mustered in August 15, '98; discharged Savannah December 18, '98.
54. CONLEY MELTON, 27 years, private, farmer, Smithville; enrolled August 18, '98; mustered in August 18, '98; discharged Savannah December 26, '98.
55. HENRY PREVOST, 33 years, private, farmer, Smoaks; enrolled August 18, '98; mustered in August 18, '98; discharged Savannah December 12, '98.
56. JAS. M. PREVOST, 24 years, private, farmer, Smoaks; enrolled August 17, '98; mustered in August 17, '98; discharged Branchville March 11, '99.
57. JAS. W. THORP, 23 years, Corporal, blacksmith, Marlow; enrolled August 20, '98; mustered in August 20, '98; discharged Marlow, S. C., March 29, '99.
58. WALTER K. WEST, 25 years, Sergeant, farmer, Socaste; enrolled May 14, '98; mustered in May 14, '98; discharged Savannah, Ga., December 14, '98.
59. WM. B. HARRON, 22 years, private, laborer, Bamberg; enrolled August 13, '98; mustered in August 13, '98; discharged Savannah, Ga., October 30, '98.

60. WM. L. LAWHORN, 27 years, private, farmer, Timmonsville; enrolled August 10, '98; mustered in August 10, '98; discharged Washington, D. C., December 14, '98.
61. FREDERICK E. GIBSON, 20 years, private, printer, Bennettsville; enrolled May 12, '98; mustered in May 14, '98; discharged Columbia September 12, '98.
62. ARTHUR McCULLOUGH, 30 years, private, farmer, Walhalla; enrolled May 19, '98; mustered in May 20, '98; discharged Jacksonville, Fla., '98.
63. BEN. MAGIL, 28 years, private, farmer, Due West; enrolled August 5, '98; mustered in August 5, '98; transferred to band September 20, 98.
64. JNO. E. McBRIDE, 19 years, private, book-keeper, Abbeville; enrolled May 5, '98; mustered in May 14, '98; transferred from Co. A August 23, '98.
65. HAMILTON O. SHULER, 39 years, private, farmer, Wells; enrolled May 5, '98; mustered in May 20, '98; transferred from Co. C August 23, '98.
66. RASMUS STEVENS, 21 years, private, farmer, Smoaks; enrolled August 13, '98; mustered in August 13, '98; transferred to Co A September 20, '98.
67. GEO. W. STOKES, 23 years, private, farmer, Lamar; enrolled May 5, '98; mustered in May 14, '98; transferred to U. S. Hospital October 6, '98.
68. FRANK P. SWAN, 28 years, private, farmer, Effingham; enrolled May 13, '98; mustered in May 14, '98; transferred to Hospital Corps October 30, '98.
69. ERVIN W. METTS, 22 years, private, farmer, Izlar; enrolled August 16, '98; mustered in August 16, '98; died of disease November 7, '98.
70. JESSE FULLER, 20 years, private, mill hand, Spartanburg; enrolled August 6, '98; mustered in August 6, '98.
71. JNO. W. KING, 34 years, private, laborer, Bayboro; enrolled August 11, '98; mustered in August 11, '98.
72. LEONARD H. WHITEHEAD, 23 years, private, laborer, Greenville; enrolled June 8, '98; mustered in June 8, '98; transferred from Co. B August 23, '98.

Officers of Heavy Battery

Capt. Edw. Anderson.

Lieut. L. C. Moore.

Lieut. J. M. Ward.

Lieut. R. H. Allen.

The Heavy Battery, South Carolina Volunteer Artillery.

When the President of the United States made his first call for volunteers for the Spanish-American War, Governor Ellerbe called a conference of the Brigadier Generals and Colonels of the State Troops at Columbia, April 27th, and stated that South Carolina was expected to furnish one Regiment and one Battalion of Infantry and one Battery of Heavy Artillery. At this conference the duty of raising the Battery of Heavy Artillery was assigned to General Edward Anderson, of Charleston, then commanding the Fourth Brigade of State Troops. Upon his return from Columbia, Gen. Anderson called a meeting of the officers of the Brigade, and stated that the Governor expected Charleston to furnish the Battery, and asked their assistance in raising it. Finding the officers lukewarm, Gen. Anderson immediately issued a call through the newspapers, asking for volunteers without regard to whether or not they had been members of militia organizations, which met with a ready response, and on the evening of May 3d, at a meeting held at the Carolina Rifles Armory, the Battery was organized by the election of the following officers:

Edward Anderson, Captain.
Leonard C. Moore, First Lieutenant.
J. Moultrie Ward, Second Lieutenant.
Richard H. Allan, Second Lieutenant.

Captain Anderson is a graduate of the South Carolina Military Academy (class of 1886), had served for twelve years in the State Militia, and at the time of his resignation from the State service was the senior Brigadier General (the ranking officer) in the State.

Lieutenant Moore had been for five years a member of the Sumter Guards, and held the position of Sergeant at the time he volunteered.

Lieutenant Ward had been for a number of years interested in the militia of the State, serving with marked ability as Captain of the Moultrie Guards.

Lieutenant Allan attended the South Carolina Military Academy for two years, and had been a member of the Carolina Rifles, and afterwards of the Sumter Guards.

Among those who volunteered were a few men who had been members of the Sumter Guards, Carolina Rifles, Washington Light Infantry, and the Irish Volunteers, but the great majority were not familiar with the use of arms.

There was one group of men from Walterboro, under James M. Patterson, a graduate of the South Carolina Military Academy (class of 1888), and another from Camden, Kershaw County, under James T. Burdell, also a Citadel man (class of 1890); and indeed, before the Battery was mustered into service, nearly every county in the State was represented in its ranks.

On the morning of May 5th, at 9 o'clock, the Battery assembled on Marion Square, and under an escort composed of the Confederate Veterans and the corps of Cadets of the South Carolina Military Academy, marched to the South Carolina and Georgia Railway station and took a special train for Columbia, the State rendezvous. The camp at the Fair Grounds was reached about 3 o'clock.

The Surgeons being busy examining the volunteers at Hyatt's Park, it was May 9th before the Battery came up for the physical examination.

The examination was very severe, only 64 men passing of the 171 who presented themselves.

Both Captain Anderson and Lieutenant Ward were rejected, but Governor Ellerbe telegraphed the President, and succeeded in having them admitted.

Many rejections were on account of weight, the Charleston men being generally small, spare built men, but capable of great endurance.

Some of the rejected men entered the 1st S. C. Regiment, quite a number went into the 2d S. C. Regiment, a dozen or more enlisted in the 3d Immunes, at least fifteen went with the Naval Reserves, and some even enlisted in the regular service.

Men who preferred the Artillery branch of the service continued to volunteer from all parts of the State, until on the afternoon of May 21st, at 5.17 o'clock, after presenting fully 350 to 400 men to be examined, the Battery (144 strong) was mustered into the service of the United States by Captain Fuller, U. S. Army.

The following telegram was received on May 22d:

Capt. Edward Anderson, Heavy Battery, U. S. V., Columbia, S. C.:
Report by telegraph to Commanding Officer, Department of the Gulf, Atlanta, Ga., for assignment and duty.
By order Secretary of War.
H. C. CORBIN,
Adjutant General.

In accordance with this order the following telegram was sent:
General Commanding Department of the Gulf, Atlanta, Ga.:

Am ordered by Secretary of War to report to you for assignment to station for duty. Am ununiformed and unequipped.

EDWARD ANDERSON,
Captain Heavy Battery.

On May 25th, the Battery moved from the Fair Grounds and pitched camp at Geiger's Springs, about a mile from the limits of the city of Columbia, in a beautiful grove of pines, of which the owner, Mr. Newman, had kindly offered the use. There the regular camp duties of sentry, police, etc., were entered into, and there the Battery remained until May 28th, when orders having been received from the General Commanding the Department of the Guilf to report to the Post at Sullivan's Island for "station and instruction," camp was broken at 5 A. M., and the Battery marched to the South Carolina and Georgia Railroad station and took a special train for Charleston. Sullivan's Island was reached at 6.15 P. M.

Upon reaching Sullivan's Island, Capt. Anderson reported to Lieut. Col. Jacob B. Rawls, 1st U. S. Art., Commanding the Post, and was ordered to pitch camp on the parade ground back of Fort Moultrie, alongside Co. "E," 5th U. S. Infantry.

A week after reaching camp, the Battery was presented with a handsome regimental flag by citizens of Charleston, through the following Committee: J. Elmore Martin, B. I. Simmons, Henry Fraser Walker, Henry P. Williams, W. Gibbes Whaley, Hasell W. Crouch, Harry F. Miler, James H. Moore, Henry B. Jennings, W. M. Muckenfuss.

David M. Ramsey, D. D., the Pastor of the Citadel Square Baptist Church of Charleston, made an eloquent presentation address, and Miss Alice R. Taylor, the Sponsor, with her Maid of Honor, Miss Lila B. Pickens, turned over the flag to Capt. Anderson, with a few well chosen words.

Capt. Anderson thanked the Committee, assured them that the Battery would faithfully guard the flag, and calling up Sergt. J. Monroe Johnson, Jr., appointed him Acting Color Sergeant, should circumstances ever cause the Battery to be on detached duty and in a position to fly a flag.

In a few days a school of instruction was opened for the officers by 2d Lieut. Johnson Hagood, 1st Artillery, detailed for this purpose, and very soon three officers from the 2d North Carolina Regiment (Infantry), 1st Lieut. C. H. White, 2d Lieut. John B. Tillinghast, 2d Lieut. Lyman Deal, and three from the 3d Texas Infantry, 1st Lieut. Sanford E. Gantt, 2d Lieut. Robert E. Donoho, 2d Lieut. Milo B.

Matthews, were detailed to join the officers of the Battery in their studies.

The subjects taken up were "Artillery Tactics, particularly those relating to Sea Coast Guns," "Exterior and Interior Ballistics," Composition of Gunpowder and other Explosives, etc.

These studies, with drilling the men and serving on Courts Martial, not only on those cases originating at the Post, but also those from several posts farther South, which were sent to Sullivan's Island for trial, kept the officers quite busy.

The uniforms and rifles arriving soon, the men were instructed in the "Manual of Arms," "School of the Soldier," "Guard Duties," "Articles of War," and also in handling the 10-inch rifles at Battery Jasper and the 12-inch mortars at Battery Capron.

In a short time the men were put on guard duty, and during the remainder of their enlistment performed every duty of garrison life, exactly as the regular soldiers of Batteries "C" and "M," 1st U. S. Artillery, stationed at the Post.

The second call for volunteers having been issued, Capt. Anderson was ordered by the War Department, on June 10th, to recruit to full strength. He accordingly issued the following order:

HEAVY BATTERY, S. C. VOL. ARTILLERY,
SULLIVAN'S ISLAND, S. C., June 11th, 1898.

I. In compliance with par. 3, G. O. No. 61, A. G. O., Washington, D. C., June 1st, 1898, 2d Lieutenant J. M. Ward, H. B., S. C. V. A., is hereby detailed as recruiting officer and acting assistant Quartermaster.

II. A recruiting party, consisting of 2d Lieutenant J. M. Ward, H. B., S. C. V. A., and Private H. G. Jennings, H. B., S. C. V. A., will proceed as soon as practicable to Charleston, S. C., and to such other points in the State of South Carolina as in the opinion of the recruiting officer are deemed necessary.

Lieut. Ward will be governed by instructions contained in G. O. No. 61, A. G. O., June 1st, 1898, and circular letter of June 3d, 1898, A. G. O.

EDWARD ANDERSON,
Capt. Heavy Battery, S. C. Vol. Artillery.

Sergt. Theo. D. Jervey was afterwards ordered to report to Lieut. Ward and assist in recruiting.

Lieut. Ward remained on detached service until early in August, when having recruited the Battery to full war strength (200), he reported back for duty.

The first death to occur in the Battery (and the only one from disease) was on July 24th, when Private William T. Addison succumbed to typhoid fever.

The Battery being well drilled and disciplined, repeated efforts were made through both Senators and Congressmen to have the Battery take part in active service, but, like many another volunteer organization, without avail.

The continued rains of July and August caused the parade ground to assume the condition of a swamp and threatened the health of the men, so on August 13th permission was obtained from Lieut. Col. Rawles, and the Battery moved camp to the Isle of Palms, where ten days was spent.

The owners of the property were not only kind enough, through their President, Dr. Lawrence, to give the use of the island for camping purposes, but transported the Battery to and from the island, and erected kitchens and other buildings.

OFFICE OF POST COMMANDER,
SULLIVAN'S ISLAND, MOULTRIEVILLE, S, C., August 20, 1898.

Special Orders No. 101.

Pursuant to instructions from Headquarters, Department of the Gulf, dated August 16, 1898, 1st Lieut. Leonard C. Moore, Heavy Battery, S. C. Vol. Artillery, with six Sergeants, three Corporals, and forty-one privates from the Heavy Battery, S. C. Vol. Artillery, will proceed on Wednesday, August 24th, 1898, by the Steamer Pilot Boy, to Hilton Head, Port Royal Harbor, S. C., to go into camp thereat, and take charge of and guard the battery of 8-inch breech-loading rifled guns at that point.

By order of Lieut. Col. Rawles.

GEO. W. VAN DEUSEN,
1st Lieut. and Adjutant 1st Artillery, Adjutant.

On August 24th, in compliance with the foregoing order, Lieut. Moore and fifty enlisted men proceeded to Hilton Head, and upon arrival thereat, August 26th, P. M., went into camp on the site of old Fort Walker, where a temporary battery of two guns had been mounted, and remained there until orders were received, September 13th, to take command of Land's End, St. Helena Island, relieving two companies of the 2d N. C. Volunteer Infantry, under command of Maj. Dixon, who were ordered home for muster-out.

The fortifications at Land's End consisted of a battery of 2, 4,

7-inch Armstrong rapid-fire guns, and emplacements for three 10-inch rifles were in course of construction.

From this date to January 10th, 1899, when ordered back to Sullivan's Island to be mustered out, this detachment constituted the sole garrison of both Hilton Head and Land's End, except a brief intermission, when Battery "B," 1st Artillery, Capt. Merrill, was stationed at Hilton Head.

The balance of the Battery moved from the Isle of Palms on August 23d, and camped on the lot surrounding the Presbyterian Church, on Sullivan's Island, and the lot next west, the property of Edward W. Hughes, the use of which was kindly given.

Private Theodore P. Godfrey was shot on King street, near Princess, by an unknown negro, on the 6th of September. Godfrey was standing on King street, talking with some comrades; the negro used profane language, and as some ladies were passing, Godfrey remonstrated with him. The negro drew a pistol, and after interchanging a few words, shot Godfrey through the abdomen. Godfrey was carried to the City Hospital and lingered until the 9th, where he died. The negro was never captured by the police.

Secretary of War Alger visited the Post on September 27th. The entire garrison, at this time numbering nearly seven hundred men, were inspected and passed in review, and were congratulated on their steady marching and their soldierly appearance.

OFFICE OF POST COMMANDER,
SULLIVAN'S ISLAND, MOULTRIEVILLE, S. C., October 2d, 1898.

Special Order No. 126.

2. Under the provisions of G. O. No. 80, A. G. O., 1898, Captain Edward Anderson, S. C. V. Artillery, is hereby appointed as a Summary Court for this Post, for the trial of offences cognizable under that order.

By order of Lieut. Col. Rawles,

GEO. W. VAN DEUSEN,
1st Lieut. and Adjutant 1st Artillery, Adjutant.

Capt. Anderson continued as Summary Court, until relieved by 1st Lieut. F. S. Harlow, 1st Artillery, on January 29th, 1899.

When orders were received at the Post in regard to mustering out the Battery, Col. Rawles wrote the Adjutant General the following letter showing his idea of the value of the Battery to the Government:

OFFICE OF POST COMMANDER,
SULLIVAN'S ISLAND, MOULTRIEVILLE, S. C., December 31st, 1898.
The Adjutant General U. S. Army, Washington, D. C.

Sir: Referring to the muster out of the Heavy Battery, South Carolina Volunteer Artillery, now serving at Sullivan's Island and Land's End, South Carolina, which was yesterday directed by telegram to take place as soon as it can be accomplished, it is my desire to respectfully make known somewhat the services this organization has rendered and is still rendering the Government, as well as the possibility of its being most useful under certain conditions, during some months to come. The strength of the Battery now is 154 enlisted men, 45 of whom are in charge, under a Lieutenant, of the defensive works at Land's End and Hilton Head, S. C. The latter have been doing excellent work in the care of the valuable armament at those stations, and will have to be replaced by other artillerymen. At Sullivan's Island, the main strength of the Battery has become versed in the duties of Artillery soldiers, and are of very material assistance in the garrisoning of this post.

The announcement of the termination of war conditions by a peace proclamation will be attended with heavy loss in the strength of the regular garrison here, because of the numerous discharges that will occur, and it will be found that much embarrassment will follow for some time to come because of an inadequate garrison. The Captain of the Volunteer Battery (Anderson) informs me that the discontented element of his command has been about eliminated, and there no longer exists much dissatisfaction concerning retention in the United States service.

Because of all circumstances presented, and the extensive armament of this Post, embracing that of Forts Capron, Moultrie and Battery Jasper, and the six-inch rapid-fire battery, now partially constructed, each requiring persistent effort and ample men for their care and preservation, it occurs to me that could the muster-out of this Battery be deferred, during the transition state that is about to take place because of the discharge of very many men from the regulars and re-enlistment of others for a definite and prolonged period, it would prove to be a measure decidedly in the interest of the service.

I have thus written upon this subject because of a wish to make known the good services of this Volunteer Battery in the past, and the apparent value that would attach to a continuation of such service for a time in the future; and I would be glad to see a reconsideration of the decision to muster them out, although in so expressing myself, I trust it will not be considered that I am suggesting what is beyond my province to make mention of.

Very respectfully, your obedient servant,

J. B. RAWLES,
Lieut. Col. 1st Artillery, Commanding Post.

Early in January, the temporary barracks near Battery Jasper having been completed, the Battery moved into them, and there remained until mustered out on February 4th, having completed exactly nine months of service. The discipline of the Battery was maintained throughout the entire time.

The following letter of Col. Rawles to Capt. Anderson, shows his appreciation of the services of the Battery while under his command:

OFFICE OF POST COMMANDER,
SULLIVAN'S ISLAND, MOULTRIEVILLE, S. C., February 4th, 1899.
Captain Edward Anderson, Heavy Battery, S. C. V. Artillery, Sullivan's Island, S. C.

My Dear Captain: It is a gratification for me as Commanding Officer to make favorable mention of the Heavy Battery, South Carolina Volunteer Artillery, which has been at this station, under your immediate command, since May 29th, 1898. The personal association, both official and otherwise, with the officers of the Battery has been characterized by the most harmonious relations and conditions between them and the Post Commander. They have performed their duties, generally, with commendable zeal and efficiency, and with an integrity of purpose worthy of gentlemen and befitting the rank they have held as commissioned officers in the service of the United States. As an organization, the Battery has done valuable and, in the line of many duties, most efficient service. It must have become apparent to all that to secure highly efficient conditions in this arm of the service requires persistent application and prolonged effort. Time had accomplished much in this direction, and the Battery at the date of muster-out, February 4th, 1899, was on the road to a degree of efficiency as an Artillery organization which would, had it been continued in the service, have made it a most desirable component in the defensive system of the coast of the United States.

Very respectfully,

J. B. RAWLES,
Lieut. Col. 1st Artillery, U. S. Army.

Itinerary Heavy Battery, S. C. V. A.

The Heavy Battery, U. S. Vol. Artillery, was organized at Charleston, S. C., and reported at rendezvous at Columbia, S. C., May 3d, 1898; was mustered into service May 21, 1898, by Capt. Exra B. Fuller, 7th U. S. Cavalry, chief mustering officer. The Battery reported for duty at Sullivan's Island station, May 28, 1898, and there remained in service until February 4, 1899, when it was mustered out of service by 1st Lieut. Geo. W. Van Deusen, 1st Artillery, mustering officer.

Roster of Heavy Battery, S. C. V. A.

1. EDWARD ANDERSON, 31 years, Captain, secretary, Charleston; enrolled May 5, '98; mustered in May 21, '98.
1. LEONARD C. MOORE, 23 years, First Lieutenant, clerk, Charleston; enrolled May 5, '98; mustered in May 21, '98.
1. JNO. M. WARD, 23 years, Second Lieutenant, government clerk, Summerville; enrolled May 5, '98; mustered in May 21, '98.
2. RICHARD H. ALLEN, 20 years, Second Lieutenant, clerk, Charleston; enrolled May 5, '98; mustered in May 21, '98.
1. HOWARD JACKSON, JR., 26 years, First Sergeant, book-keeper, Charleston; enrolled May 5, '98; mustered in May 21, '98.
1. HERBERT T. MOORE, 38 years, Sergeant, farmer, Darlington; enrolled May 5, '98; mustered in May 21, '98.
2. SOLOMON L. CLARK, 27 years, Sergeant, clerk, Charleston; enrolled May 5, '98; mustered in May 21, '98.
3. WM. E. KEELS, 34 years, Sergeant, farmer, Summerton; enrolled May 5, '98; mustered in May 21, '98.
4. VINCENT A. BISSELL, 24 years, Sergeant, mechanic, Charleston; enrolled May 5, '98; mustered in May 21, '98.
5. THEO. D. JERVEY, 20 years, Sergeant, clerk, Charleston; enrolled May 5, '98; mustered in May 21, '98.
6. WM. M. LAROCHE, 23 years, private, millman, Charleston; enrolled May 5, '98; mustered in May 21, '98.
7. JNO. E. MOORE, 36 years, Sergeant, contractor, Walterboro; enrolled May 5, '98; mustered in May 21, '98.
8. JOSIAH S. MIXON, 20 years, Sergeant, clerk, Allendale; enrolled May 5, '98; mustered in May 21, '98.
9. WM. F. MOSELEY, 28 years, Sergeant, clerk, Camden; enrolled May 5, '98; mustered in May 21, '98.
10. WM. McK. DEHON, 23 years, Sergeant, salesman, Summerville; enrolled May 5, '98; mustered in May 21, '98.
11. JAS. R. WORSHAM, 23 years, Sergeant, lawyer, Mt. Pleasant; enrolled May 5, '98; mustered in May 21, '98.
12. EDWARD S. DINGLE, 25 years, Sergeant, reporter, Charleston; enrolled May 5, '98; mustered in May 21, '98.
13. WM. W. WINKLER, 21 years, Sergeant, druggist, Summerville; enrolled May 5, '98; mustered in May 21, '98.
14. WILLIS P. ABBEY, 22 years, private, P. O. Dept., St. Georges; enrolled May 5, '98; mustered in May 21, '98; promoted from Corporal December 1, '98.
15. PORTER K. WINKLER, 23 years, Sergeant, clerk, Summerville; enrolled May 5, '98; mustered in May 21, '98; promoted from Corporal December 1, '98.

SOUTH CAROLINA TROOPS IN THE WAR WITH SPAIN 287

16. JNO. E. WIERMAN, 23 years, Sergeant, butcher, Charleston; enrolled May 5, '98; mustered in May 21, '98; promoted from Corporal December 15, '98.
17. EDWARD H. RAWLS, 20 years, Sergeant, farmer, Lexington; enrolled May 5, '98; mustered in May 21, '98; promoted from Corporal December 15, '98.
18. ARTHUR L. WATKINS, 21 years, Sergeant, clerk, Camden; enrolled May 5, '98; mustered in May 21, '98; promoted from Corporal December 1, '98.
19. FRED W. BULCKEN, 20 years, Sergeant, conductor, Charleston; enrolled May 5, '98; mustered in May 21, '98; promoted from Corporal December 15, '98.
20. ARTHUR L. BURNETT, 18 years, Sergeant, clerk, Camden; enrolled May 21, '98; mustered in May 21, '98; promoted from private August 20, '98.
21. JACK WILSON, 22 years, Sergeant, upholsterer, Pittsburg, Pa.; enrolled May 5, '98; mustered in May 21, '98; promoted from Corporal January 1, '99.
22. BARNETT S. LIPSCOMB, 25 years, Sergeant, salesman, Gaffney; enrolled May 17, '98; mustered in May 21, '98; promoted from Corporal January 1, '99.

1. ARNOLD A. CAPERS, Corporal, Walterboro; enrolled July 2, '98; mustered in July 2, '98; promoted from private December 1, '98.
2. GILLIS C. CLYBURN, 23 years, Corporal, farmer, Camden; enrolled May 12, '98; mustered in May 21, '98; promoted from private December 1, '98.
3. ARTHUR H. GIBBES, 24 years, Corporal, laborer, Charleston; enrolled May 12, '98; mustered in May 21, '98; promoted from private December 1, '98.
4. JAS. W. SMYLY, Corporal, Colleton; enrolled August 6, '98; mustered in August 6, '98; promoted from private December 1, '98.
5. FRED W. VON SPRECKELSEN, 23 years, Corporal, clerk, Charleston; enrolled May 5, '98; mustered in May 21, '98; promoted from private December 15, '98.
6. JNO. H. ORTMANN, 23 years, Corporal, clerk, Charleston; enrolled May 5, '98; mustered in May 21, '98; promoted from private December 15, '98.
7. JNO. HOPKINS, 23 years, Corporal, jobber, Portland, Me.; enrolled May 5, '98; mustered in May 21, '98; promoted from private January 1, '99.
8. PERRY G. SMITH, 24 years, Corporal, blacksmith, Walterboro; enrolled May 12, '98; mustered in May 21, '98; promoted from private January 1, '99.
9. EUGENE S. BETHEA, 22 years, Corporal, book-keeper, Marion; enrolled May 5, '98; mustered in May 21, '98; promoted from private January 1, '99.
10. SAML. L. STEIN, Corporal, Charleston; enrolled June 28, '98; mustered in June 28, '98; promoted from private January 1, '99.

1. GEO. H. VIOHL, private, Charleston, enrolled May 5, '98; mustered in May 21, '98.
2. HANLEY KUHUE, 19 years, private, clerk, Hamburg, Ger.; enrolled May 12, '98; mustered in May 21, '98.
3. DOMINCO TRINCHERO, 30 years, private, clerk, San Dominge, Italy; enrolled May 5, '98; mustered in May 21, '98.
4. WM. SYLVESTER, 33 years, private, engineer, Detroit, Mich.; enrolled May 5, '98; mustered in May 21, '98.
5. WM. F. ADAIR, private, Charleston; enrolled July 26, '98; mustered in July 26, '98.
6. JAS. ADDISON, private, Pelzer; enrolled August 10, '98; mustered in August 10, '98.
7. JAS. ALLEN, 23 years, private, millman, Langley; enrolled May 21, '98; mustered in May 21, '98.
8. ALONZO J. AXSON, private, Charleston; enrolled August 13, '98; mustered in August 13, '98.
9. JOS. BALDWIN, private, Laurens; enrolled August 9, '98; mustered in August 9, '98.
10. JOS. H. BECK, 20 years, private, news agent, Grahamville; enrolled May 5, '98; mustered in May 21, '98.
11. JESSE M. BENNETT, 22 years, private, farmer, Baldoc; enrolled May 5, '98; mustered in May 21, '98.
12. WM. L. BENSON, private, Marion; enrolled July 7, '98; mustered in July 7, '98.
13. GUS BIERMAN, 23 years, private, baker, Charleston; enrolled May 5, '98; mustered in May 21, '98.
14. STAINSLANS J. BOUNAVICY, 22 years, private, salesman, Kobogne, Russia; enrolled May 5, '98; mustered in May 21, '98.
15. PHILLIP E. BRAID, private, Charleston; enrolled August 17, '98; mustered in August 17, '98.
16. LAURENCE BREWER, 24 years, private, farmer, Brownsville; enrolled May 5, '98; mustered in May 21, '98.
17. CASINO E. BROCKINTON, Kingstree; enrolled July 10, '98; mustered in July 10, '98.
18. ARTHUR A. BURN, 20 years, private, wrecker, Charleston; enrolled May 5, '98; mustered in May 21, '98.
19. DAVID C. CABLE, 24 years, private, carpenter, Charleston; enrolled May 5, '98; mustered in May 21, '98.
20. JNO. J. CALDER, 23 years, private, butcher, Charleston; enrolled May 12, '98; mustered in May 21, '98.
21. FRED B. CAMPBELL, 21 years, private, carpenter, Aiken; enrolled May 21, '98; mustered in May 21, '98.
22. JNO. L. CAPERS, 18 years, private, news agent, Walterboro; enrolled May 16, '98; mustered in May 21, '98.
23. FRANK E. CARTER, 22 years, private, agent, Charleston; enrolled May 5, '98; mustered in May 21, '98.
24. WILLARD R. CHANDLER, 23 years, private, engineer, Sumter; enrolled May 12, '98; mustered in May 21, '98.
25. WM. CHURCHILL, 22 years, private, plumber, Charleston; enrolled May 15, '98; mustered in May 21, '98.

SOUTH CAROLINA TROOPS IN THE WAR WITH SPAIN 239

26. MOUZON F. CLOY, 25 years, private, carpenter, Allendale; enrolled May 16, '98; mustered in May 21, '98.
27. WM. J. CONNOR, 26 years, clerk, St. George's; enrolled May 17, '98; mustered in May 21, '98.
28. RANDOLPH D. CREECH, 37 years, farmer, Bennettsville; enrolled May 17, '98; mustered in May 21, '98.
29. IRWIN ST. C. CROFT, 18 years, private, clerk, Charleston; enrolled May 5, '98; mustered in May 21, '98.
30. HENRY B. CROSBY, 30 years, private, laborer, Ruffins; enrolled May 12, '98; mustered in May 12, '98.
31. JOS. CROSBY, private, Walterboro; enrolled July 29, '98; mustered in July 29, '98.
32. WM. E. CRAVEN, private, Charleston; enrolled July 3, '98; mustered in July 3, '98.
33. TIM G. DARGAN, 21 years, private, horseman, Darlington; enrolled May 3, '98; mustered in May 16, '98; transferred from Co. A, 2d S. C. V. I., June 26, '98.
34. JNO. DAVIS, 24 years, private, lineman, Greenville; enrolled June 6, '98; mustered in June 6, '98; transferred from Co. B, 2d S. C. V. I., August 3, '98.
35. CHAS. P. DISEKER, private, Spartanburg; enrolled July 25, '98; mustered in July 25, '98.
36. JAS. C. DEVEAUX, 19 years, private, salesman, Summerville; enrolled May 5, '98; mustered in May 23, '98.
37. BENJ. H. EARHART, 38 years, private, farmer, Brooks; enrolled May 18, '98; mustered in May 21, '98.
38. JNO. J. FARMER, private, Pelzer; enrolled August 9, '98; mustered in August 9, '98.
39. GEO. GABEL, 29 years, private, carpenter, Montz, Germany; enrolled May 5, '98; mustered in May 21, '98.
40. CLAUDE L. GAFFNEY, 18 years, private, student, Gaffney; enrolled May 17, '98; mustered in May 21, '98.
41. JAS. S. GIBBES, private, Charleston; enrolled July 7, '98; mustered in July 7, '98.
42. WILLIE B. GROVES, 18 years, private, farmer, Walterboro; enrolled May 17, '98; mustered in May 21, '98.
43. JOS. HARMON, 24 years, private, farmer, Summerville; enrolled May 16, '98; mustered in May 21, '98.
44. WALTER S. HARMON, 25 years, private, millman, Lucydale; enrolled May 16, '98; mustered in May 21, '98.
45. CHAS. T. HART, private, Spartanburg; enrolled August 2, '98; mustered in August 2, 98.
46. ROBT. L. HARVIN, private, Sumter; enrolled July 12, '98; mustered in July 12, '98.
47. JOS. A. HANCK, 19 years, private, stonecutter, Charleston; enrolled May 5, '98; mustered in May 21, '98.
48. CHAS. D. HAWKINS, 23 years, private, carpenter, Lexington; enrolled May 12, '98; mustered in May 21, '98.
49. CARSTEN HEISSER, 23 years, private, clerk, Charleston; enrolled May 5, '98; mustered in May 21, '98.

50. LUTHER HIERS, 18 years, private, farmer, Walterboro; enrolled May 17, '98; mustered in May 21, '98.
51. HENRY HILL, 22 years, private, clerk, Ridgeville; enrolled May 5, '98; mustered in May 21, '98.
52. ARTHUR HELSON, private, Charleston; enrolled August 19, '98; mustered in August 19, '98.
53. ZED HOPE, 18 years, private, barber, Gaffney; enrolled May 17, '98; mustered in May 21, '98.
54. WM. E. HUGGINS, private, Blackville; enrolled June 27, '98; mustered in June 27, '98.
55. DOLPHUS H. HUNSINGER, 22 years, private, farmer, Spartanburg; enrolled May 5, '98; mustered in May 21, '98.
56. HARRY L. JERVEY, 20 years, private, clerk, Charleston; enrolled May 5, '98; mustered in May 21, '98.
57. CHAS. D. KING, 28 years, private, cigar maker, Winston, N. C.; enrolled May 5, '98; mustered in May 21, '98.
58. RICHARD P. KNIGHT, private, Springfield; enrolled June 27, '98; mustered in June 27, '98
59. GEO. W. KOON, 23 years, farmer, Fairbanks; enrolled May 17, '98; mustered in May 21, '98.
60. JNO. W. LAWRENCE, 25 years, private, farmer, Hendersonville; enrolled May 17, '98; mustered in May 21, '98.
61. CHAS. LADSHAW, 32 years, private, clerk, Conatta; enrolled May 12, '98; mustered in May 21, '98.
62. OSCAR H. LIMEHOUSE, 21 years, private, farmer, Summerville; enrolled May 5, '98; mustered in May 21, '98.
63. STATES L. LOCKWOOD, private, Charleston; enrolled June 30, '98; mustered in June 30, '98.
64. CHAS. MACKINNON, 19 years, private, salesman, Montreal, Canada; enrolled May 5, '98; mustered in May 21, '98.
65. THOS. P. MARTIN, 22 years, private, farmer, Holly Hill; enrolled May 17, '98; mustered in May 21, '98.
66. WM. McK. MARTIN, 27 years, private, farmer, Holly Hill; enrolled May 17, '98; mustered in May 21, '98.
67. JOS. MINNIS, 20 years, private, clerk, Yemassee; enrolled May 5, '98; mustered in May 21, '98.
68. LOUIS MARKUS, private, Hungary; enrolled July 29, '98; mustered in July 29, '98.
69. FRANKLIN L. McCULLOUGH, private, Kingstree; enrolled July 5, '98; mustered in July 5, '98.
70. PAUL W. McDOWELL, 18 years, private, miller, Camden; enrolled May 12, '98; mustered in May 21, '98.
71. RICHARD A. MOUSSEAU, private, Charleston; enrolled July 9, '98; mustered in July 9, '98.
72. WM. E. NANTZ, 22 years, private, painter, Gaffney; enrolled May 5, '98; mustered in May 21, '98.
73. THOS. P. NAPIER, 21 years, private, spinner, Graniteville; enrolled May 21, '98; mustered in May 21, '98.
74. LUTE F. ODOM, private, Blackville; enrolled June 29, '98; mustered in June 29, '98.

75. CALVIN H. OWENS, 20 years, private, conductor, Charleston; enrolled May 5, '98; mustered in May 21, '98.
76. JOS. P. PADGETT, 21 years, private, clerk, Walterboro; enrolled May 17, '98; mustered in May 21, '98.
77. WM. E. PADGETT, private, Spartanburg; enrolled July 23, '98; mustered in July 23, '98.
78. WM. E. PAULS, 21 years, private, tinner, Charleston; enrolled May 5, '98; mustered in May 21, '98.
79. HENRY C. PAZAN, 23 years, private, laborer, Columbia; enrolled May 12, '98; mustered in May 21, '98.
80. BENJ. F. PETERS, 23 years, private, laborer, Charleston; enrolled May 16, '98; mustered in May 21, '98.
81. GEO. PETERSON, private, Charleston; enrolled July 12, '98; mustered in July 12, '98.
82. THOS. M. PINCKNEY, private, Yemassee; enrolled July 29, '98; mustered in July 29, '98.
83. THOS. H. RAWLS, 31 years, private, farmer, Lexington; enrolled May 12, '98; mustered in May 21, '98.
84. CHAS. D. RICE, private, Walterboro; enrolled August 9, '98; mustered in August 9, '98.
85. JNO. H. ROPER, private, Spartanburg; enrolled July 27, '98; mustered in July 27, '98.
86. WM. S. ROBINSON, 21 years, private, plumber, Charleston; enrolled May 5, '98; mustered in May 21, '98.
87. JNO. J. RUGGERS, 19 years, private, baker, Charleston; enrolled May 5, '98; mustered in May 21, '98.
88. BENJ. F. RUSSELL, private, Williamston; enrolled August 10, '98; mustered in August 10, '98.
89. HENRY RION, 26 years, private, printer, Savannah, Ga.; enrolled May 5, '98; mustered in May 21, '98.
90. HARVEY F. SHULER, private, Sumter; enrolled July 15, '98; mustered in July 15, '98.
91. JOS. A. SCOTT, 18 years, private, laborer, Charleston; enrolled May 5, '98; mustered in May 21, '98.
92. JAS. F. SHAW, 21 years, private, electrician, Charleston; enrolled May 5, '98; mustered in May 21, '98.
93. MONGIN F. SMITH, private, Charleston; enrolled July 12, '98; mustered in July 12, '98.
94. WALLACE B. STEWMAN, private, McMinnville, Tenn.; enrolled August 9, '98; mustered in August 9, '98.
95. LUTHER STRICKLAND, private, Pelzer; enrolled August 10, '98; mustered in August 10, '98.
96. HALVOR S. SUENDSEN, JR., 20 years, private, clerk, Charleston; enrolled May 19, '98; mustered in May 21, '98.
97. JNO. J. SWEENEY, 40 years, private, policeman, Charleston; enrolled May 17, '98; mustered in May 21, '98.
98. HENRY T. TAYLOR, 22 years, private, farmer, Covington, S. C.; enrolled May 16, '98; mustered in May 21, '98.
99. MARION THIGPEN, 19 years, private, laborer, Sumter; enrolled May 5, '98; mustered in May 21, '98.

100. WM. R. THOMAS, 22 years, private, farmer, Bamberg; enrolled May 17, '98; mustered in May 21, '98.
101. ROBT. L. THOMPSON, private, Columbia; enrolled June 23, '98; mustered in June 23, '98.
102. GEO. D. THOMPSON, private, Spartanburg; enrolled August 1, '98; mustered in August 1, '98.
103. ABRAHAM WADSWORTH, 27 years, private, liveryman; Charleston; enrolled May 5, '98; mustered in May 21, '98.
104. JAS. R. WALKER, private, Columbia; enrolled June 17, '98; mustered in June 17, '98.
105. STEVEN T. WALLACE, 21 years, private, laborer, Darlington; enrolled May 12, '98; mustered in May 21, '98.
106. WM. F. WALLACE, 23 years, private, fireman, Port Royal; enrolled May 12, '98; mustered in May 21, '98.
107. JAS. E. WATERS, 27 years, private, farmer, Camden; enrolled May 17, '98; mustered in May 21, '98.
108. SIMON P. WEED, 23 years, private, farmer, Lexington; enrolled May 12, '98; mustered in May 21, '98.
109. LOUIS D. WESSEL, 21 years, private, miller, Charleston; enrolled May 5, '98; mustered in May 21, '98.
110. EUGENE F. WEST, 35 years, private, upholsterer, Charleston; enrolled May 16, '98; mustered in May 21, '98.
111. BEN N. WHALEY, private, Blackville; enrolled June 27, '98; mustered in June 27, '98.
112. MUSE WHITE, private, Pelzer; enrolled August 9, '98; mustered in August 9, '98.
113. ANDREW G. WHITTAKER, 20 years, private, clerk, Camden; enrolled May 5, '98; mustered in May 21, '98.
114. RICHARD D. WINNINGHAM, private, Springfield; enrolled July 2, '98; mustered in July 2, '98.
115. WM. K. WOOD, private, Pelzer; enrolled August 10, '98; mustered in August 10, '98.
116. WM. WIDNER, 23 years, private, miller, Aiken; enrolled May 21, '98; mustered in May 21, '98.
117. WM. H. GATES, private, Sumter; enrolled July 11, '98; mustered in July 11, '98.
118. DANL. ZEIGLER, 18 years, private, farmer, Walterboro; enrolled May 17, '98; mustered in May 21, '98.
119. JNO. W. WIDNER, 27 years, private, miller, Bath; enrolled May 21, '98; mustered in May 21, '98; discharged July 15, '98.
120. HOWARD A. LITTLEJOHN, 25 years, private, clerk, Gaffney; enrolled May 5, '98; mustered in May 21, '98; discharged September 29, '98.
121. CHARLIE BOPPE, 33 years, private, butcher, Charleston; enrolled May 5, '98; mustered in May 21, '98; discharged October 10, '98.
122. JNO. M. VOGEL, private, Spartanburg; enrolled August 2, '98; mustered in August 2, '98; discharged October 22, '98.
123. HENRY N. WIERMAN, 24 years, private, grocer, Charleston; enrolled May 5, '98; mustered in May 21, '98; discharged October 26, '98.
124. EDWARD D. TILTON, 39 years, private, machinist, San Mateo, Fla.; enrolled May 5, '98; mustered in May 21, '98; discharged October 26, '98.

125. Jos. Bellinger, 27 years, private, insurance, Charleston; enrolled May 5, '98; mustered in May 21, '98; discharged October 28, '98.
126. Wm. E. Reese, 22 years, private, farmer, Congaree; enrolled May 5, '98; mustered in May 21, '98; discharged October 27, '98.
127. Jno. M. McCrackin, private, clerk, Spartanburg; enrolled July 29, '98; mustered in July 29, '98; discharged November 18, '98.
128. David E. O'Brien, private, Sullivan's Island; enrolled June 21, '98; mustered in June 21, '98; discharged Nov. 18, '98.
129. Chas. Toff, private, Pelzer; enrolled August 9, '98; mustered in August 9, '98; discharged November 18, '98.
130. Jno. M. Johnson, Jr., 20 years, Sergeant, student, Marion; enrolled May 5, '98; mustered in May 21, '98; discharged October 9, '98.
131. Rene R. Jervey, 23 years, private, conductor, Charleston; enrolled May 5, '98; mustered in May 21, '98; discharged October 9, '98.
132. Harry G. Jennings, 20 years, private, clerk, Charleston; enrolled May 5, '98; mustered in May 21, '98; discharged October 16, '98.
133. Leroy Lee, private, Sumter; enrolled July 11, '98; mustered in July 11, '98; discharged October 16, '98.
134. Wm. F. Rowland, 39 years, private, painter, Donalds; enrolled May 5, '98; mustered in May 21, '98; discharged October 16, '98.
135. Milton S. Kyzer, 20 years, private, farmer, Lexington; enrolled May 5, '98; mustered in May 21, '98; discharged October 20, '98.
136. Fred W. McKerall, private, Marion; enrolled July 7, '98; mustered in July 7, '98; discharged October 20, '98.
137. Robt. T. Davis, private, Pelzer; enrolled August 10, '98; mustered in August 10, '98; discharged September 20, '98.
138. Eustace St. P. Bellinger, 23 years, Sergeant, book-keeper, Walterboro; enrolled May 5, '98; mustered in May 21, '98; discharged October 26, '98.
139. Edmund C. Bellinger, 18 years, private, farmer, Walterboro; enrolled May 5, '98; mustered in May 21, '98; discharged October 26, '98.
140. Gustav McWilliams, 30 years, private, trainman, Charleston; enrolled May 5, '98; mustered in May 21, '98; discharged October 26, '98.
141. Darling P. Patterson, 18 years, private, policeman, Walterboro; enrolled May 5, '98; mustered in May 21, '98; discharged October 26, '98.
142. Jas. L. Jervey, 23 years, Sergeant, broker, Charleston; enrolled May 5, '98; mustered in May 21, '98; discharged November 4, '98.
143. Wm. St. J. Jervey, 25 years, Sergeant, broker, Charleston; enrolled May 5, '98; mustered in May 21, '98; discharged November 7, '98.
144. Jos. A. Storfer, 29 years, Corporal, merchant, Charleston; enrolled May 5, '98; mustered in May 21, '98; discharged November 8, '98.
145. Jas. T. Bendell, 29, Sergeant, civil engineer, Camden; enrolled May 5, '98; mustered in May 21, '98; discharged December 9, '98.
146. Jas. M. Patterson, 30 years, Sergeant, civil engineer, Walterboro; enrolled May 5, '98; mustered in May 21, '98; discharged December 11, '98.
147. Wm. R. Fuller, 29 years, private, engineer, Walterboro; enrolled May 5, '98; mustered in May 21, '98; discharged November 4, '98.

148. GEO. H. MOORE, 24 years, Sergeant, clerk, Hendersonville; enrolled May 5, '98; mustered in May 21, '98; discharged December 11, '98.
149. PERCY C. BLACKMAN, private, Sullivan's Island; enrolled June 22, '98; mustered in June 22, '98; discharged December 11, '98.
150. ARTHUR ABEL, private, Blackville, enrolled July 4, '98; mustered in July 4, '98; discharged December 9, '98.
151. JACOB EDMUNDS, 41 years, private, artisan, Charleston; enrolled May 5, '98; mustered in May 21, '98; discharged December 18, '98.
152. FRED H. GRIFFIN, 29 years, private, farmer, Holly Hill; enrolled May 5, '98; mustered in May 21, '98; discharged December 15, '98.
153. THADEUS C. REMLEY, 19 years, private, farmer, Walterboro; enrolled May 5, '98; mustered in May 21, '98; discharged December 11, '98.
154. JNO. H. CLIFTON, private, Sumter; enrolled July 15, '98; mustered in July 15, '98; discharged June 5, '98.
155. FRANK R. FROST, 34 years, Sergeant, lawyer, Charleston; enrolled May 10, '98; mustered in May 21, '98; discharged May 26, '98.
156. CURTIS M. TIMMERMAN, private, Pelzer; enrolled August 10, '98; mustered in August 10, '98; discharged December 14, '98.
157. THEO. P. GODFREY, private, Sullivan's Island; enrolled July 5, '98; mustered in July 5, '98; died Charleston Hospital September 9, '98.
158. WM. T. ADDISON, 35 years, private, laborer, Heath Springs; enrolled May 5, '98; mustered in May 21, '98; died Sullivan's Island, fever, July 24, '98.
159. OSCAR C. BOWICK, 22 years, Corporal, laborer, Charleston; enrolled May 5, '98; mustered in May 21, '98.
160. JNO. COLEY, 21 years, private, farmer, Cairy, Ga.; enrolled May 18, '98; mustered in May 21, '98.
161. CHAS. QUICK, 27 years, private, machinist, Bennettsville; enrolled May 17, '98; mustered in May 21, '98.
162. GEO. W. JOHNSON, 20 years, private, plumber, Charleston; enrolled May 5, '98; mustered in May 21, '98.
163. GEO. F. BROWN, private, Blackville; enrolled July 3, '98; mustered in July 3, '98.
164. HERMAN W. JONES, 24 years, private, painter, Charleston; enrolled May 5, '98; mustered in May 21, '98.
165. HENRY PRICE, private, Pelzer; enrolled August 10, '98; mustered in August 10, '98.
166. WM. MOORE, 24 years, private, upholsterer, Hendersonville; enrolled May 5, '98; mustered in May 21, '98.

Officers of Naval Militia

Com. R. H. Pinckney.

Lieut. J. J. Igoe.

Lieut. N. G. Morrall.

Lieut. J. A. Patjens.

Officers of Naval Militia

Lieut. Wm. Elliott, Jr.

Lieut. Geo. Swann.

Lieut. C. S. McKinley.

Lieut. W. H. Touchstone.

Sketch of the Naval Militia.

HEADQUARTERS SO. CA. NAVAL MILITIA,
CHARLESTON, S. C., November 25th, 1899.

General J. W. Floyd, Adjutant and Inspector General of South Carolina, Columbia, S. C.

Sir: In response to your request for a correct and condensed record of the part the Naval Militia of South Carolina took in the late war with the Kingdom of Spain, I respectfully submit the following as addenda to the report, and also the roster previously sent your office:

Number of officers 21 and men 302—in active organization at outbreak of hostilities. Total 323—increased by 102 reserve members joining and enlisting as active members within ten days after declaration of war, making total of 425 officers and men in the force.

Number of commissioned officers 18, warrant officers 6, men 187—who were mustered into the Naval Service of the United States. Total 211 in United States Navy.

The Naval Militia of South Carolina supplied 18 commissioned officers, 6 warrant officers, and 187 men to the Naval Service. Of this number, the following list will show the disposition of both men and officers and the service in which engaged:

6 commissioned officers, 80 men, manned U. S. S. "Celtic."

5 commissioned officers, 40 men, manned naval batteries at Port Royal.

3 commissioned officers, 20 men, manned Coast Signal Stations 4th District.

1 commissioned officer, 15 men, manned U. S. S. "Chickasaw."
1 commissioned officer, 15 men, manned U. S. S. "Cheyenne."
1 commissioned officer, 15 men, manned U. S. S. "Waban."
1 commissioned officer was detailed at Naval Station, Port Royal.
1 warrant officer was detailed on U. S. S. "Hercules."
1 warrant officer was detailed on U. S. S. "Massasoit."
4 warrant officers were detailed at U. S. Navy Yard, New York.
2 men were detailed on U. S. S. "Morrill."
24 officers, 187 men—total 211 in U. S. Navy.
In addition to above, the Naval Militia furnished:
12 men for Charleston Heavy Battery, U. S. Vol. Army.
2 men for Bamberg Guards, U. S. Vol. Army.
2 men for Manning Guards, U. S. Vol. Army.

16 total in army—making a grand total of 227 men in service, and leaving 198 men who were not called out, but who were ready and anxious to volunteer their services to their country for the honor of their State.

After the 227 men were in service, I wired the Secretary of Navy that the South Carolina Naval Militia could and would furnish from 100 to 200 more men if they were needed to man any vessel and to go anywhere. Special mention of this offer was made in the official report of Captain Bartlett, U. S. N., Chief of the U. S. Coast Defense Service, to the Government. But there was no further necessity or call.

They all served with intelligence, fidelity and zeal, notwithstanding that to a large number, being men of education, the work was far different from anything that they had ever been accustomed to. They met the issue as a duty, in such manner as to merit the approval and commendation of their superior officers, and earn the enviable record of "work well done." Where all did so well, it is hardly fair to make any special mention; but only to show the value of the Coast Signal Service to the Government, I will cite as an index the details of one piece of work, from among many, performed by the crews of the Morris Island and Charleston Signal Stations. On the night before the arrival of the U. S. Ships "Columbia" and "Yale" off the bar, at 12 1-2 o'clock, a dispatch was received at the Signal Headquarters requesting that the Chief Quartermaster of Camp Alger, Va., be notified immediately on arrival of Cruisers "Columbia" and "Yale" off Charleston bar, and to communicate with Captain Sands, U. S. N., as to when he will be ready to receive troops on board. I immediately caused Morris Island Station to be called, and signalled instructions to keep lookout at mast-head and report approach of any vessel from southward. At 3 o'clock, Morris Island called Headquarters by signal lights (they are five miles apart), and reported "Cruiser 'Columbia' coming up from south." I told the signal man at Charleston Station to ask him, "How do you know it is 'Columbia?'" He replied instantly, "Four smoke-stacks." The station at Morris Island had not been told what vessels were expected, and the answer showed how thoroughly they knew by looks each and every vessel in our Navy, and also in that of our enemy. In about half an hour Morris Island reported, "'Yale' coming up from south." These vessels when first seen were fifteen miles at sea; they were recognized instantly, however, and that at night and at such a distance. The information thus obtained was instantly wired to Camp Alger, and as soon as the two cruisers anchored, which they did beyond the lightship, nine miles off shore and away from the station, they were signalled by the Morris Island crew, who called for Captain Sands, commanding the "Columbia," and flashed the message across nine miles of midnight sea; it was received, and the answer came back as follows: "Ready now for troops, or as soon as they can get here;" and coupled with the request that he be informed as to how many were coming and when they would arrive. This message was immediately sent to Camp Alger, and notice of arrival was at same time sent to Washington, and in half an hour reply that troops numbered 2,700— half would arrive forenoon and half afternoon of the following day, and that they bring 18 horses; all of this was flashed to Captain Sands. The next morning the first section of train rolled down on the East Shore Terminal tracks loaded with troops. General Garrison immediately came to the Headquarters Office and requested a message of an entire sheet of foolscap to be at once sent to Captain Sands; it was transmitted from Charleston Station to Morris Island, and thence to the "Columbia," nine miles away, and inside of thirty minutes the answer was handed General Garrison. When the other sections of train arrived, bringing General Wilson, he sent a message also, and received the answer with equal promptitude. The service rendered was so well done as to merit and receive the commendations of Generals Garrison and Wilson, also of Captain Sands and Captain Wise on the ships; and when it is further stated that during the entire time of service the Morris Island Station never missed discovering and reporting each and every vessel of whatever description which came into this port day or night, and also all those which passed outside either north or south, if they were within reach of the powerful telescopes of the station, all of this was most valuable to the National Government; hence, the Department's desire that the Naval Militias continue to practice the Signal Codes.

There were many other instances of work done by the Signal Stations at Charleston and Morris Island at critical times and when of vital importance to the Government.

The men and officers of the Naval Militia of South Carolina who went on the ships "Celtic," "Chickasaw," "Cheyenne," and "Waban," and also those who manned the naval batteries at Port Royal, did their duty well and to the entire satisfaction of their commanding officers, who have testified in writing to the several Departments the high appreciation of the intelligence, patriotism and zeal of the South Carolina Naval Militia. And further, when it is borne in mind that the Naval Militia was the only command in the State who were ready at a moment's notice, and who supplied every demand made upon them on the instant, without having to open books for enlistment, their value to their native State is apparent.

The needs of the Naval Militia are very different from those of the other State troops, and while the National Government makes an appropriation for them, it can only be used in obtaining arms and ammunition. They have always had to provide their own uniforms, while the other troops are supplied by the State out of its national appropriation. They have also had to pay their own expenses for transportation, food and lodging, when assembled at Charleston for the annual cruises.

It would, therefore, be but a fitting tribute for the State to show its appreciation of its blue jackets by making a small and special appropriation for the use and maintenance of the Naval Militia.

I have the honor to be, yours respectfully,

R. H. PINCKNEY,
Commander South Carolina Naval Militia.

HEADQUARTERS S. C. NAVAL MILITIA,
CHARLESTON, S. C.

General J. W. Floyd, Adjutant and Inspector General of South Carolina, Columbia, S. C.

Sir: I herewith submit the following report of the South Carolina Naval Militia, which I have the honor to command, first, as State troops and subsequently in the service of the United States, just prior to and during the war with the Kingdom of Spain.

On March 28th, 1898, I received orders from your office to put the Battalion in readiness to answer any sudden call of the President for their services. Upon receipt of this order, I left my business in North Carolina, where I was then engaged, and returned to Charleston, and at once issued the necessary orders putting the entire command in constant drilling and training for any call which might be made upon it. Also received through your office letter of Navy Department, requesting detailed information of vessels belonging to the seaports of the State suitable for transformation into improvised gun vesels, rams or torpedo boats, and the necessary blanks on which to make such report, together with the order to comply with desire as expressed in letter of Department. This order was obeyed after ten days hard and continuous work, the papers forwarded to Department, and under date of April 15th, the acknowledgment of their receipt and the thanks of the Department were received, with instructions to report to Commander C. H. Arnold, U. S. N., in charge 6th District Coast Defense, Headquarters Charleston, S. C., and to give him any further information I might obtain. I reported to Commander Arnold April 18th, and he so endorsed my order.

On April 20th, received from your office copy of letter from Navy Department to Governor, requesting that Naval Militia officers be permitted to receive instructions and orders direct from Capt. Goodrich, U. S. N., or such other officer as should be appointed as Superintendent of Coast Signal Service on the breaking out of war. Also, the official order to me to comply with above request. Thereafter the following orders were received direct:

Received order dated April 21st: "Commander Pinckney, kindly forward estimates immediately. (Signed) Goodrich." Order obeyed, all estimates and bids for construction of Signal Stations along the coast, and for the full and entire equipment of same having been previously secured, were forwarded. When it is remembered that these Signal Stations were all on the seaward side of far outlying islands, miles away from any railroad facilities, and only approachable by small boats, the details of visiting the several localities and selecting the most advantageous sites required time, care and considerable expense, which was borne personally by me, and which cannot be refunded by the National Government unless Congress passes an Act authorizing Secretary of Navy to pay such claims to the Governor as reimbursement; it will be seen what difficulties were met and overcome promptly by the Naval Militia.

Received order, dated April 22d: "Commander Pinckney, establish and man Coast Signal Stations already determined on. Lowest bids, greatest economy, most speed necessary. (Signed) Goodrich." This order was executed with utmost dispatch, so that by May 2d, the stations had houses built, signal masts 100 feet high, with 40-foot yard arm 65 feet from ground erected, with all necessary halyards for lanterns and flags, consisting of 12 large Fresnal lens lanterns, 6 white and 6 red, complete sets of all signal and code flags, telescopes, binoculars, rockets, mess outfits, stoves, chairs, tables, charts, and secret codes and books, all supplied; the men enlisted and armed; stations, all of them, manned and in working order; telegraph and telephone lines and cables connecting the various stations with the headquarters stations at Charleston, were then being rapidly erected and were subsequently completed; the men being thoroughly proficient in all the various and necessary knowledge of signaling in any and every way, performed such valuable service to the National Government as to merit the following very complimentary extract from letter of Capt. John R. Bartlett, U. S. N., Superintendent of U. S. Coast Signal Service and Chief of Auxiliary Naval Force of United States, to wit:

"Express to the officers and men of the Signal Service under your command, my appreciation of their excellent services, and that I consider that they have served their country just as efficiently and rendered just as valuable service as if they had been at the front.

"(Signed) JNO. R. BARTLETT, U. S. N.,
"Supt. Coast Signal Service, Washington, D. C."

Received order, dated April 22d: "Commander Pinckney, please nominate an officer as assistant to Commander Arnold, in charge 4th District, Coast Signal Service. He will be commissioned an Ensign. (Signed) Goodrich." I nominated Ensign C. S. McKinley, of 2d Division, one of the best signal officers in the corps, who reported for duty immediately, was examined and commissioned, and served until honorably discharged after termination of war.

Received order, April 30th: "Commander R. H. Pinckney: The Department orders me to request that you nominate a second officer of Naval Militia to act as assistant 4th District Coast Signal Service. He will be commissioned an Ensign U. S. N. (Signed) C. H. Arnold, Commander U. S. N., in charge 4th District Coast Signal Service." I nominated Ensign E. A. Darby, of 1st Division, who at once reported for duty, and was subsequently examined and commissioned, and served until honorably discharged after termination of war.

Received order from Assistant Secretary of Navy, T. Roosevelt, "to furnish 105 officers and men to go to Wilmington, N. C., and man U. S. S. 'Nantucket,' and take her to Port Royal, S. C., and to notify him if I could fill quota, and when." Under same date I wired Department as follows: "Naval Militia of South Carolina ready and qualified to man Nantucket now. Can furnish quota, send lists for crew."

The next day this order was countermanded, and the Naval Militia of North Carolina, who were then in charge of the vessel, were assigned to this duty. Thereupon, I again tendered unconditionally the services of the South Carolina Naval Militia to the Secretary of the Navy, to man any vessel and to go anywhere, and on May 4th received communication from Navy Department, asking that I detail 40 men and nominate 5 officers of Naval Militia for assignment to duty at Port Royal, to man the Naval Batteries there. I nominated N. G. Morrall as Lieutenant, William Elliott, Jr., and E. J. Burn as Lieutenants Junior Grade; H. S. Townsend as Ensign, and Dr. T. O. Hutson as Assistant Surgeon—all officers of 3d Division, S. C. N. M. They were so commissioned, and detailed 40 petty officers and men of 3d Division at Beaufort for above service. They served until honorably discharged after termination of war.

On May 8th, several of the men of the Naval Militia, being disheartened at the countermanding of the order to man "Nantucket," requested permission to go to Columbia to join the "Heavy Battery" being then organized. I granted their request, and 12 men of the Naval Militia joined said Battery, 2 more joined "Bamberg Guards," and 2 "Manning Guards," and were enlisted in U. S. Volunteer Army with these commands.

Received order, May 19th, from Chief of Bureau of Navigation at Washington, D. C., to report to Commander Roxwell, U. S. N., at Port Royal, S. C., for examination for commission as a Lieutenant in U. S. Navy. I obeyed the order, reporting May 21st, was examined and commissioned, and ordered to assume charge of the 4th District Coast Signal Service, extending from North Carolina to Florida, with headquarters at Charleston, and served in that capacity until honorably discharged after termination of war, and after winding up all the affairs of the various stations in said District.

Received, May 25th, order of Secretary of Navy: "To furnish 6 officers and 80 men to go to New York and man the U. S. S. 'Celtic,' and to notify him where and when a recruiting officer could meet and enlist men." I wired as follows: "Crew ready. Recruiting officer can meet men here as soon as he can get here."

With only twelve hours time allowed to select and enlist crew, it was done, the officers nominated as follows: J. J. Igoe, Lieutenant; J. A. Patjens and T. F. Webb, Lieutenants Junior Grade; W. M. Bostick and W. F. Webb, Ensigns; W. H. Touchstone, Assistant Engineer, rank of Ensign. They were all examined and subsequently commissioned, and with the 80 petty officers and men left Charleston May 26th, 1898, for New York. They manned the vessel and took her to Santiago de Cuba, being attached to the North Atlantic squadron, and there they were present and took part in the grandest naval victory of modern times, the entire destruction of Cervera's fleet by Admiral W. S. Schley. They were honorably discharged after termination of war.

Received orders, June 15th, from Commander C. H. Arnold, U. S. N., in charge 6th District Coast Defense: To furnish three crews of 15 men each and 3 officers, to man auxiliary cruisers "Cheyenne," "Chickasaw," and "Waban," as soon as they were refitted by Government. This was done, the 45 men enlisted, with three officers nominated by me, viz: George H. Swann, Lieutenant Junior Grade, J. E. Relyea and John Wickart, Ensigns, were commissioned. The three vessels sailed from Charleston on July 27th for Key West and other places. These men served until honorably discharged after termination of war.

The detailed list of the names of officers and men, the positions each and every one of them held, the service in which each was engaged, and the vessels on which they served, and the Naval Militia Division from which each came, will more fully and completely appear in the Roster of Naval Militia in the Spanish War, which has already been forwarded to your office.

I have the honor to be, very respectfully,

R. H. PINCKNEY,
Commander S. C. Naval Militia, and late Lieutenant U. S. Navy.

ROSTER

Of Commissioned Officers, Petty Officers and enlisted men of the South Carolina Naval Militia, who served in the United States Navy during the War with the Kingdom of Spain, 1898. Showing the positions held by each in U. S. N., and the service in which engaged, as well as the vessels on which they served, and the number and name of the Naval Militia Division to which each belonged.

ROBERT HOWE PINCKNEY, Lieutenant U. S. N., in charge of 4th District Coast Signal Service, extending from North Carolina to Florida; commander S. C. Naval Militia, 2d Division S. C. N. M. (Chicora Co.)

JAS. J. IGOE, Lieutenant U. S. N., U. S. S. "Celtic," 1st Division S. C. N. M. (Lafayette Co.)

NORMAN G. MORRALL, Lieutenant U. S. N., naval batteries Port Royal, S. C., 3d Division S. C. N. M. (Beaufort Co.)

J. A. PATJENS, Lieutenant (J. G.) U. S. N., U. S. S. "Celtic," 2d Division S. C. N. M. (Chicora Co.)

THOS. F. WEBB, Lieutenant (J. G.) U. S. N., U. S. S. "Celtic," 2d Division S. C. N. M. (Chicora Co.)

WM. ELLIOTT, Lieutenant (J. G.) U. S. N., naval batteries, Port Royal, S. C., 3d Division S. C. N. M. (Beaufort Co.)

E. J. BURN, Lieutenant (J. G.) U. S. N., naval batteries, Port Royal, S. C., 3d Division S. C. N. M. (Beaufort, Co.)

GEORGE SWANN, Lieutenant (J. G.) U. S. N., commanding the U. S. S. "Cheyenne," 2d Division S. C. N. M. (Chicora Co.)

CHAS. S. MCKINLEY, Ensign U. S. N., Coast Signal Service and Pensacola Navy Yard, 4th District, 2d Division S. C. N. M. (Chicora Co.)

H. S. TOWNSEND, Ensign U. S. N., naval batteries, Port Royal, S. C., 3d Division S. C. N. M. (Beaufort Co.)

WM. M. BOSTICK, Ensign U. S. N., U. S. S. "Celtic," 1st Division S. C. N. M. (Lafayette Co.)

WADE F. WEBB, Ensign U. S. N., U. S. S. "Celtic," 2d Division S. C. N. M. (Chicora Co.)

W. H. TOUCHSTONE, Assistant Engineer and Ensign U. S. N., U. S. S. "Celtic." 2d Division S. C. N. M. (Chicora Co.)

E. A. DABRY, Ensign U. S. N., Coast Signal Service, 4th District, 1st Division S. C. N. M. (Lafayette Co.)

ISAAC E. RELYEA, Ensign U. S. N., U. S. S. "Waban," 2d Division S. C. N. M. (Chicora Co.)

JNO. WICHART, Ensign U. S. N., U. S. S. "Chickasaw," 2d Division S. C. N. M. (Chicora Co.)

ALLEN STUART, Assistant Surgeon U. S. N., naval station Port Royal, 3d Division S. C. N. M. (Beaufort Co.)

T. OGIER HUTSON, Assistant Surgeon U. S. N., naval batteries Port Royal, S. C., 3d Division S. C. N. M. (Beaufort Co.)

WARRANT OFFICERS.

J. H. Hainsworth, mate U. S. N., U. S. S. "Hercules," 3d Division S. C. N. M. (Beaufort Co.)
Micah Jenkins, mate U. S. N., U. S. S. "Massasoit," 3d Division S. C. N. M. (Beaufort Co.)
Peter L. Lea, mate U. S. N., navy yard New York, 3d Division S. C. N. M. (Beaufort Co.)
J. M. Murray, mate U. S. N., navy yard New York, 3d Division S. C. N. M. (Beaufort Co.)
Jno. O'Brien, mate U. S. N., navy yard New York, 3d Division S. C. N. M. (Beaufort Co.)
W. H. E. Van Harten, mate U. S. N., navy yard New York, 3d Division S. C. N. M. (Beaufort Co.)

PETTY OFFICERS.

Thos. B. Hays, chief master at arms, U. S. S. "Celtic," 1st Division S. C. N. M. (Lafayette Co.)
Edward M. Royal, chief yeoman, Coast Signal Service 4th District, 2d Division S. C. N. M. (Chicora Co.)
Priestly C. Coker, chief quartermaster, Coast Signal Service 4th District, 2d Division S. C. N. M. (Chicora Co.)
Joel W. Frampton, chief quartermaster, Coast Signal Service 4th District, 2d Division S. C. N. M. (Chicora Co.)
Frank J. McKinley, chief quartermaster mate, Coast Signal Service 4th District, 2d Division S. C. N. M. (Chicora Co.)
A. M. Lewis, chief quartermaster mate, U. S. S. "Celtic," 2d Divivion S. C. N. M. (Chicora Co.)
H. A. Torck, chief boatswain mate, U. S. S. "Celtic," 2d Division S. C. N. M. (Chicora Co.)
M. Meyers, chief carpenter mate, U. S. S. "Celtic," 1st Division S. C. N. M. (Lafayette Co.)
O. E. Erisksen, chief machinist, U. S. S. "Waban," 2d Division S. C. N. M. (Chicora Co.)
W. S. Adair, chief machinist, U. S. S. "Chickasaw," 2d Division S. C. N. M. (Chicora Co.)
Angus Smith, chief machinist, U. S. S. "Cheyenne," 2d Division S. C. N. M. (Chicora Co.)
Thos. Hancock, chief machinist, U. S. S. "Celtic," 2d Division S. C. N. M. (Chicora Co.)
J. J. O'Connor, chief machinist, U. S. S. "Celtic," 2d Division S. C. N. M. (Chicora Co.)
C. B. Scanlon, chief machinist, U. S. S. "Celtic," 2d Division S. C. N. M. (Chicora Co.)
S. J. Mazyck, chief machinist, U. S. S. "Celtic," 2d Division S. C. N. M. (Chicora Co.)
Hugh Taylor, 1st class machinist, U. S. S. "Celtic," 2d Division S. C. N. M. (Chicora Co.)

C. Atkinson, 1st class machinist, U. S. S. "Celtic," 1st Division S. C. N. M. (Lafayette Co.)

W. A. Webb, quartermaster mate, 1st class, U. S. S. "Celtic," 2d Division S. C. N. M. (Chicora Co.)

T. J. Aldret, quartermaster mate, 1st class, U. S. S. "Celtic," 2d Division S. C. N. M. (Chicora Co.)

J. T. Pigot, quartermaster mate, 1st class, U. S. S. "Chickasaw," 2d Division S. C. N. M. (Chicora Co.)

T. Danielson, quartermaster mate, 1st class, U. S. S. "Waban," 2d Division S. C. N. M. (Chicora Co.)

Charles Swann, quartermaster mate, 1st class, U. S. S. "Cheyenne," 2d Division S. C. N. M. (Chicora Co.)

John Alley, boatswain's mate, 1st class, U. S. S. "Cheyenne," 2d Division S. C. N. M. (Chicora Co.)

A. J. Watson, boatswain's mate, 1st class, U. S. S. "Waban," 1st Division S. C. N. (Lafayette Co.)

C. B. Wallace, boatswain's mate, 1st class, U. S. S. "Chickasaw," 2d Division S. C. N. M. (Chicora Co.)

J. Q. Phillips, master-at-arms, 1st class, naval batteries Port Royal, 3d Division S. C. N. M. (Beaufort Co.)

L. R. Calder, gunner's mate, 1st class, naval batteries Port Royal, 3d Division S. C. N. M. (Beaufort Co.)

J. P. Minus, quartermaster's mate, 2d class, Coast Signal Service, 4th District, 2d Division S. C. N. M. (Chicora Co.)

L. S. Jervey, Jr., quartermaster's mate, 2d class, Coast Signal Service, 4th District, 2d Division S. C. N. M. (Chicora Co.)

C. P. Langley, quartermaster's mate, 2d class, Coast Signal Service, 4th District, 2d Division S. C. N. M. (Chicora Co.)

J. P. Langley, quartermaster's mate, 2d class, Coast Signal Service, 4th District, 2d Division S. C. N. M. (Chicora Co.)

T. L. Hanna, quartermaster's mate, 2d class, Coast Signal Service, 4th District, 2d Division S. C. N. M. (Chicora Co.)

D. L. Whitesides, quartermaster's mate, 2d class, Coast Signal Service, 4th District, 2d Division S. C. N. M. (Chicora Co.)

E. T. Coleman, quartermaster's mate, 2d class, Coast Signal Service, 4th District, 2d Division S. C. N. M. (Chicora Co.)

V. G. Lewis, quartermaster's mate, 2d class, Coast Signal Service, 4th District, 2d Division S. C. N. M. (Chicora Co.)

A. G. Miscally, quartermaster's mate, 2d class, Coast Signal Service, 4th District, 1st Division S. C. N. M. (Lafayette Co.)

A. J. Axson, quartermaster's mate, 2d class, Coast Signal Service, 4th District, 1st Division S. C. N. M. (Lafayette Co.)

T. A. Mather, quartermaster's mate, 2d class, Coast Signal Service, 4th District, 1st Division S. C. N. M. (Lafayette Co.)

H. L. Sanders, quartermaster's mate, 2d class, naval batteries, Port Royal, 3d Division S. C. N. M. (Beaufort Co.)

A. R. Haig, Jr., quartermaster's mate, 2d class, naval batteries, Port Royal, 3d Division S. C. N. M. (Beaufort Co.)

E. E. Lengnick, quartermaster's mate, 2d class, naval batteries, Port Royal, 3d Division S. C. N. M. (Beaufort Co.)

W. T. WIGGIN, quartermaster's mate, 2d class, naval batteries, Port Royal, 3d Division S. C. N. M. (Beaufort Co.)

CHAS. M. BRISTOL, gunner's mate, 2d class, naval batteries, Port Royal, 3d Division S. C. N. M. (Beaufort Co.)

J. T. RUTLEDGE, gunner's mate, 2d class, U. S. S. "Morrill," 2d Division S. C. N. M. (Chicora Co.)

S. H. RODGERS, JR., gunner's mate, 2d class, naval batteries, Port Royal, 3d Division S. C. N. M. (Beaufort Co.)

H. W. RICHARDSON, JR., boatswain's mate, 2d class, naval batteries, Port Royal, 3d Division S. C. N. M. (Beaufort Co.)

B. B. PAUL, boatswain's mate, 2d class, naval batteries, Port Royal, 3d Division S. C. N. M. (Beaufort Co.)

W. C. BELLOWS, JR., carpenter's mate, 2d class, naval batteries, Port Royal, 3d division S. C. N. M. (Beaufort Co.)

W. G. BAILEY, machinist, 2d class, U. S. S. "Celtic," 2d Division S. C. N. M. (Chicora Co.)

GEORGE RIVERS, machinist, 2d class, U. S. S. "Morrill," 2d Division S. C. N. M. (Chicora Co.)

F. B. BRAID, machinist, 2d class, U. S. S. "Celtic," 1st Division S. C. N. M. (Lafayette Co.)

A. P. JONES, machinist, 2d class, U. S. S. "Chickasaw," 2d Division S. C. N. M. (Chicora Co.)

J. DAVIN, machinist, 2d class, U. S. S. "Cheyenne," 1st Division S. C. N. M. (Lafayette Co.)

T. KEITHLEY, machinist, 2d class, U. S. S. "Waban," 2d Division S. C. N. M. (Chicora Co.)

JNO. DIX, carpenter's mate, 3d class, U. S. S. "Celtic," 2d Division (Chicora Co.)

E. H. BEE, yeoman, 3d class, naval batteries, Port Royal, 3d Division (Beaufort Co.)

J. H. H. LUNDEN, master-at-arms, 3d class, U. S. S. "Celtic," 2d Division (Chicora Co.)

T. J. GANTT, electrician and gunner's mate, U. S. S. "Celtic," 1st Division (Lafayette Co.)

J. C. O'CONNOR, electrician and gunner's mate, U. S. S. "Celtic," 1st Division (Lafayette Co.)

H. S. GAILLARD, electrician and gunner's mate, U. S. S. "Celtic," 2d Division (Chicora Co.)

H. C. RHODES, oiler, U. S. S. "Celtic," 2d Division (Chicora Co.)

C. H. GREGORIE, oiler, U. S. S. "Celtic," 1st Division (Lafayette Co.)

R. W. WARREN, oiler, U. S. S. "Celtic," 1st Division (Lafayette Co.)

ROBERT BAKER, blacksmith, U. S. S. "Celtic," 2d Division (Chicora Co.)

F. J. FOSBERRY, plumber and fitter, U. S. S. "Celtic," 2d Division (Chicora Co.)

J. J. COLEMAN, boilermaker, U. S. S. "Celtic," 1st Division (Lafayette Co.)

J. CANTWELL, coppersmith, U. S. S. "Celtic," 1st Division (Lafayette Co.)

P. L. WEBB, fireman, 1st class, U. S. S. "Celtic," 2d Division (Chicora Co.)

E. J. DORAN, fireman, 1st class, U. S. S. "Celtic," 2d Division (Chicora Co.)

J. J. WHITE, fireman, 1st class, U. S. S. "Celtic," 1st Division (Lafayette Co.)

J. C. MEGGETT, fireman, 1st class, U. S. S. "Celtic," 1st Division (Lafayette Co.)
J. A. PINNER, fireman, 1st class, U. S. S. "Celtic," 1st Division (Lafayette Co.)
G. W. H. MCDONALD, fireman, 1st class, U. S. S. "Cheyenne," 1st Division (Lafayette Co.)
P. MCINTYRE, fireman, 1st class, U. S. S. "Cheyenne," 1st Division (Lafayette Co.)
JAMES BYRNES, fireman, 1st class, U. S. S. "Waban," 1st Division (Lafayette Co.)
G. KANING, fireman, 1st class, U. S. S. "Waban," 1st Division (Lafayette Co.)
CHARLES WOLKE, fireman, 1st class, U. S. S. "Chickasaw," 1st Division (Lafayette Co.)
J. JONES, fireman, 1st class, U. S. S. "Chickasaw," 1st Division (Lafayette Co.)
J. L. BROUGHTON, fireman, 2d class, U. S. S. "Chickasaw," 1st Division (Lafayette Co.)
S. HALL, fireman, 2d class, U. S. S. "Chickasaw," 1st Division (Lafayette Co.)
J. COSGROVE, fireman, 2d class, U. S. S. "Waban," 1st Division (Lafayette Co.)
F. SINEATH, fireman, 2d class, U. S. S. "Waban," 2d Division (Chicora Co.)
W. PRAUSER, fireman, 2d class, U. S. S. "Cheyenne," 2d Division (Chicora Co.)
D. MORAN, fireman, 2d class, U. S. S. "Cheyenne," 1st Division (Lafayette Co.)
M. MILLIGAN, fireman, 2d class, U. S. S. "Celtic," 2d Division (Chicora Co.)
R. E. O'BRIEN, fireman, 2d class, U. S. S. "Celtic," 2d Division (Chicora Co.)
GEORGE ALDRET, fireman, 2d class, U. S. S. "Celtic," 2d Division (Chicora Co.)
T. R. BOLCHOZ, fireman, 2d class, U. S. S. "Celtic," 1st Division (Lafayette Co.)
H. SNOWDEN, coxswain, U. S. S. "Celtic," 2d Division (Chicora Co.)
F. G. SWAFFIELD, coxswain, U. S. S. "Celtic," 1st Division (Lafayette Co.)
J. B. EVANS, coxswain, naval batteries, Port Royal, 3d Division (Beaufort Co.)
W. M. STENMEYER, coxswain, naval batteries, Port Royal, 3d Division (Beaufort Co.)
E. P. LAWTON, jack of dust, U. S. S. "Celtic," 1st Division (Lafayette Co.)
A. W. ECKEL, apothecary, U. S. S. "Celtic," 1st Division (Lafayette Co.)
W. J. HOWELL, bayman, U. S. S. "Celtic," 1st Division (Lafayette Co.)
L. G. WARING, seaman, U. S. S. "Celtic," 2d Division (Chicora Co.)
J. A. TRUESDALE, seaman, U. S. S. "Celtic," 2d Division (Chicora Co.)
C. A. DOAR, seaman, U. S. S. "Celtic," 2d Division (Chicora Co.)
H. W. CROUCH, JR., seaman, U. S. S. "Celtic," 2d Division (Chicora Co.)
J. MILLIGAN, seaman, U. S. S. "Celtic," 2d Division (Chicora Co.)
E. F. REDELL, seaman, U. S. S. "Celtic," 2d Division (Chicora Co.)
C. M. HARLEY, seaman, U. S. S. "Celtic," 2d Division (Chicora Co.)
J. L. KENNEDY, seaman, U. S. S. "Celtic," 2d Division (Chicora Co.)
R. C. KINTZEN, seaman, U. S. S. "Celtic," 2d Division (Chicora Co.)
R. D. CARTER, seaman, U. S. S. "Celtic," 2d Division (Chicora Co.)
W. C. LOTZ, seaman, U. S. S. "Celtic," 1st Division (Lafayette Co.)
T. J. LEITCH, seaman, U. S. S. "Celtic," 1st Division (Lafayette Co.)

M. MITCHUM, seaman, U. S. S. "Celtic," 1st Division (Lafayette Co.)
A. McBRIDE, seaman, U. S. S. "Celtic," 1st Division (Lafayette Co.)
C. D. PINNER, seaman, U. S. S. "Celtic," 1st Division (Lafayette Co.)
J. E. WEBB, seaman, U. S. S. "Celtic," 1st Division (Lafayette Co.)
J. S. BEAUDROT, seaman, U. S. S. "Celtic," 1st Division (Lafayette Co.)
J. A. GURNEY, seaman, U. S. S. "Celtic," 1st Division (Lafayette Co.)
J. F. POWERS, seaman, U. S. S. "Celtic," 1st Division (Lafayette Co.)
J. F. PILLS, seaman, U. S. S. "Celtic," 1st Division (Lafayette Co.)
J. W. PARRY, seaman, U. S. S. "Celtic," 1st Division (Lafayette Co.)
H. DECON, seaman, U. S. S. "Celtic," 1st Division (Lafayette Co.)
M. H. OWENS, seaman, U. S. S. "Celtic," 1st Division (Lafayette Co.)
C. OEHMIG, seaman, U. S. S. "Celtic," 2d Division (Chicora Co.)
M. KAIN, seaman, U. S. S. "Waban," 2d Division (Chicora Co.)
J. ERISKEN, seaman, U. S. S. "Waban," 2d Division (Chicora Co.)
M. LINDSAY, seaman, U. S. S. "Waban," 2d Division (Chicora Co.)
C. CARTER, seaman, U. S. S. "Waban," 2d Division (Chicora Co.)
P. JACOBSEN, seaman, U. S. S. "Waban," 2d Division (Chicora Co.)
J. SICGEE, seaman, U. S. S. "Cheyenne," 1st Division (Lafayette Co.)
F. McCOY, seaman, U. S. S. "Cheyenne," 1st Division (Lafayette Co.)
C. PERRY, seaman, U. S. S. "Cheyenne," 2d Division (Chicora Co.)
C. JOHNSON, seaman, U. S. S. "Cheyenne," 2d Division (Chicora Co.)
T. ALLEY, seaman, U. S. S. "Cheyenne," 2d Division (Chicora Co.)
W. WILLIAMS, seaman, U. S. S. "Chickasaw," 2d Division (Chicora Co.)
S. OLSEN, seaman, U. S. S. "Chickasaw," 2d Division (Chicora Co.)
T. A. HOLTER, seaman, U. S. S. "Chickasaw," 2d Division (Chicora Co.)
J. MISSROON, seaman, U. S. S. "Chickasaw," 2d Division (Chicora Co.)
J. DEANTONIA, seaman, U. S. S. "Chickasaw," 1st Division (Lafayette Co.)
E. J. DACOSTA, seaman, naval batteries, Port Royal, 3d Division (Beaufort Co.)
T. H. HARMS, JR., seaman, naval batteries, Port Royal, 3d Division (Beaufort Co.)
H. H. HAY, seaman, naval batteries, Port Royal, 3d Division (Beaufort Co.)
M. E. LOPEZ, JR., seaman, naval batteries, Port Royal, 3d Division (Beaufort Co.)
W. G. MARBERT, seaman, naval batteries, Port Royal, 3d Division (Beaufort Co.)
C. L. PAUL, JR., seaman, naval batteries, Port Royal, 3d Division (Beaufort Co.)
J. O. H. SANDERS, JR., seaman, naval batteries, Port Boyal, 3d Division (Beaufort Co.)
H. E. SCHEPER, seaman, naval batteries, Port Royal, 3d Division (Beaufort Co.)
S. R. STONEY, JR., seaman, naval batteries, Port Royal, 3d Division (Beaufort Co.)
W. W. VINCENT, seaman, naval batteries, Port Royal, 3d Division (Beaufort Co.)
F. C. CHAPLIN, ordinary seaman, naval batteries, Port Royal, 3d Division (Beaufort Co.)
W. M. DAVIS, ordinary seaman, naval batteries, Port Royal, 3d division (Beaufort Co.)

W. A. JERNIGAN, ordinary seaman, naval batteries, Port Royal, 3d Division (Beaufort Co.)
J. M. H. MCKENZIE, ordinary seaman, naval batteries, Port Royal, 3d Division (Beaufort Co.)
W. B. SKILLINGS, ordinary seaman, naval batteries, Port Royal, 3d Division (Beaufort Co.)
C. S. STENMEYER, ordinary seaman, naval batteries, Port Royal, 3d Division (Beaufort Co.)
J. E. YOUMANS, ordinary seaman, naval batteries, Port Royal, 3d Division (Beaufort Co.)
S. M. BENTON, landsman, naval batteries, Port Royal, 3d Division (Beaufort Co.)
W. S. CHAPLIN, landsman, naval batteries, Port Royal, 3d Division (Beaufort Co.)
R. M. DAVIDSON, landsman, naval batteries, Port Royal, 3d Division (Beaufort Co.)
J. M. FRY, landsman, naval batteries, Port Royal, 3d Division (Beaufort Co.)
P. D. GIVENS, landsman, naval batteries, Port Royal, 3d Division (Beaufort Co.)
W. J. RILEY, landsman, naval batteries, Port Royal, 3d Division (Beaufort Co.)
W. D. VINCENT, landsman, naval batteries, Port Royal, 3d Division (Beaufort Co.)
E. L. YOUMANS, landsman, naval batteries, Port Royal, 3d Division (Beaufort Co.)
JNO. YOUMANS, landsman, naval batteries, Port Royal, 3d Division (Beaufort Co.)
L. R. BABER, landsman, Coast Signal Service, 2d Division (Chicora Co.)
F. SMITH, landsman, Coast Signal Service, 1st Division (Lafayette Co.)
JNO. WILSON, landsman, Coast Signal Service, 2d Division (Chicora Co.)
W. G. BARRON, landsman, Coast Signal Service, 2d Division (Chicora Co.)
C. SCHUMAKER, ship's cook, U. S. S. "Waban," 1st Division (Lafayette Co.)
N. ST. CLAIR, ship's cook, U. S. S. "Cheyenne," 1st Division (Lafayette Co.)
W. F. A. BECKER, ship's cook, U. S. S. "Chickasaw," 2d Division (Chicora Co.)
E. J. QUINBY, cabin cook, U. S. S. "Celtic," 1st Division (Lafayette Co.)
L. E. ROBERTS, cabin steward, U. S. S. "Celtic," 1st Division (Lafayette Co.)
R. E. BIZE, ward room steward, U. S. S. "Celtic," 1st Division (Lafayette Co.)
ISAAC HARRIS, ward room cook, U. S. S. "Celtic," 2d Division (Chicora Co.)
J. E. COOPER, ship's cook, 1st class, U. S. S. "Celtic, 1st Division (Lafayette Co.)
W. SCHULTZ, cabin mess attendant, U. S. S. "Celtic," 2d Division (Chicora Co.)
W. J. BURKE, ward room mess attendant, U. S. S. "Celtic," 1st Division (Lafayette Co.)
J. G. MAGWOOD, ward room mess attendant, U. S. S. "Celtic," 1st Division (Lafayette Co.)
C. H. TAVEL, ward room mess attendant, U. S. S. "Celtic," 1st Division (Lafayette Co.)

F. BURKHARDT, ward room mess attendant, U. S. S. "Celtic," 2d Division (Chicora Co.)

L. M. FINE, ward room mess attendant, U. S. S. "Chickasaw," 1st Division (Lafayette Co.)

THOS. FLYNN, ward room mess attendant, U. S. S. "Cheyenne, 1st Division (Lafayette Co.)

JNO. MEYER, ward room mess attendant, U. S. S. "Waban," 1st Division (Lafayette Co.)

W. L. BEAUDROT, coal passer, U. S. S. "Celtic," 1st Division (Lafayette Co.)

E. R. McDONALD, coal passer, U. S. S. "Celtic," 1st Division (Lafayette Co.)

J. E. CHURCHILL, coal passer, U. S. S. "Celtic," 1st Division (Lafayette Co.)

G. B. S. SEYLE, coal passer, U. S. S. "Celtic," 1st Division (Lafayette Co)

J. W. DAVIS, coal passer, U. S. S. "Celtic," 1st Division (Lafayette Co.)

J. W. H. WEATHERHORN, coal passer, U. S. S. "Celtic," 1st Division (Lafayette Co.)

Total, 211 men in U. S. Navy from S. C. Naval Militia, and 16 men in U. S. Volunteer Army, Naval Militia. Grand total, 227 men.

1st Division (Lafayette Co.) furnished 72 men in U. S. Navy; 1st Division (Lafayette Co.) furnished 14 men in U. S. Army—86 men. Total for 1st Division, 86 men.

2d Division (Chicora Co.) furnished 87 men in U. S. Navy; 2d Division (Chicora Co.) furnished 2 men in U. S. Army—89 men. Total for 2d Division, 89 men.

3d Division (Beaufort Co.) furnished 52 men in U. S. Navy. Total for 3d Division, 52 men—227 men.

Signing of the Protocol

The protocol between the United States and Spain was signed on the 12th day of August, 1898, when hostilities immediately ceased. The treaty of peace was signed at Paris on the 10th day of December, 1898, followed by the ratification of same by our government on February 6th, 1899, and by the Spanish government on March the 19th, 1899. Peace declared and the treaty signed, it at once became incumbent upon the President to carry into execution the Acts of Congress, passed April 22d and 26th, 1898, which required that at the end of the war the entire volunteer forces should be immediately discharged from the service and the Regular Army be reduced to a peace basis. The President, however, did not act with that promptness that the volunteers expected, and considerable time elapsed before the mustering out of the forces commenced. Such apathy by the government caused great restlessness and clamor among the troops, because the war at an end they could see no apparent reason or necessity for their detention. They felt that they had enlisted to fight in defense of their country, and while hostilities continued, they were ready and anxious to do battle in her cause; but when the war was over and their services no longer needed, they naturally grew impatient and weary of the monotony of camp life, preferring to return to their homes, families and civil occupations which they had left, because duty, patriotism and country demanded it.

Before I conclude I may say that the limits of the book have very far exceeded the intention of the writer, and yet suggestions of matter that might be added to the interest of the reader constantly intrude as I near the end. Many of South Carolina's distinguished sons were in the war that were not members of the volunteer troops, that comprise the subject matter in hand. I would like to extend its scope on that account, but from lack of data, or the place to seek it, I shall only mention from memory some of their names. In the volunteer service outside of the State was Gen. M. C. Butler, hero and veteran of two wars, who was Major General throughout the trouble; Capt. Alfred Hampton, aide upon the staff of Gen. Butler; and Capt. Micah Jenkins of the Regiment of Rough Riders, who, Col. Roosevelt, the commander, in the battle of Santiago, denominated "The coolest and bravest man in the regiment." And in far away California, I find another Carolinian, Col. Johnstone Jones, brother of Col. Wilie Jones, who was Colonel of the 1st California Regiment Volunteer Cavalry. In the Regular Army was Maj. E.

A. Garlington, Capt. M. C. Butler, Capt. Richard McMaster (who won his promotion from the ranks), Lieut. John Jenkins and Lieut. George H. McMaster. In the Regular Navy was Lieut. Bryson Patton, Lieut. J. Miller Moore and Lieut. Victor Blue, whose daring exploit in locating the Spanish squadron in the harbor of Santiago, won for him the nation's highest praise and gratitude. The foregoing are a few of the native Carolinians who held commissions of rank, and though not immediately with the volunteer troops of the State, were valiantly doing their duty in other and more distant parts of the field of war, winning fame for themselves and adding lustre and glory to their mother State.

CONCLUSION.

I feel constrained to say that every effort has been made in the compilation of this work to have it correct and exact in every detail, and to carry to print before it is forgotten and lost in the lapse of years, only substantial and valuable material by which some one, at some time in the future, may be assisted in adding another chapter to South Carolina's incomparable history of the past. And now, as I reach the end, I am very humbly reminded of one sentence, in that eloquent outburst of the immortal Webster, delivered during that critical epoch of the nation's history, in which the intellectual giants of Massachusetts and South Carolina became engaged in the most profound and deeply interesting contest ever heard in the halls of the American Congress, and in Webster's own words, substituting South Carolina for Masachusetts, I am led to exclaim, "South Carolina needs no encomium at my hands." Her prominence in the conception and creation of the American Republic; the heroic deeds and sacrifices of her patriots in the seven years struggle that sealed its birth; the undying devotion and patient suffering of her women for the cause; the purity and zeal of her clergy; the convincing logic and eloquence of her orators and statesmen; the legal learning and power of her "bench and bar;" the strength and brilliancy of her authors of history, fiction and poetry; the generalship, courage and bravery of her soldiers upon every battlefield of the nation's conflicts, and the gallantry and chivalry of her people, illumine every page of our country's history, and there it will shine in effulgent glory "forever and forever." J. W. FLOYD.

South Carolinians of the Third U. S. Volunteer Engineers in the Spanish-American War.

Colonel David DuBose Gaillard, Winnsboro, S. C.
Major Henry C. Davis, Winnsboro, S. C.
First Lieutenant Fingal C. Black, Spartanburg, S. C.
Second Lieutenant Alfred Hampton, S. C.
Second Lieutenant Sam'l Dibble, Jr., Orangeburg, S. C.
First Lieut. St. C. B. Gwinn, Spartanburg, S. C.
Second Lieutenant Ralph E. Boggs, Spartanburg, S. C.
Regimental Quartermaster Sergeant E. H. McCullough, Walhalla, S. C.
Sergeant Wm. J. Robinson, Chester, S. C.
Sergeant James S. Elder, Winnsboro, S. C.
Corporal E. F. Pagan, Walhalla, S. C.
Private Geo. W. Ready, Aiken, S. C.
Private Harry Burbage, Spartanburg, S. C.
Private Geo. A. Condrey, Spartanburg, S. C.
Private Chas. E. Morgan, Fair Forest, S. C.
Private Henry O. Ayers, Orangeburg, S. C.
Private Mart G. Ayers, Orangeburg, S. C. Died at Lexington, Ky.
Private James H. Cope, Orangeburg, S. C.
Private Barnwell W. Palmer, Orangeburg, S. C.
Private Geo. Zeigler, Orangeburg, S. C.
Private J. H. Carson, Spartanburg, S. C.

Colonel David D. Gaillard was born in Clarendon County, then a portion of Sumter District, S. C., September 4, 1859, and was appointed to West Point by Congressman Richardson after a competitive examination in which more than twenty applicants participated. In 1884, he graduated fifth in his class, and was assigned to the Corps of Engineers. He assisted in the improvement of the St John's River and was second in command in the Mexican Boundary Commission. After this he was sent on a special mission to Alaska, to locate and build certain storehouses on the border. At the beginning of hostilities, Capt. Gaillard was in charge of the aqueduct and water supply of Washington City. He was commissioned Colonel of the Third Engineers in the summer of 1898. As the head of this organization, he made it one of the best drilled and best disciplined regiments in either the regular or volunteer army. Colonel Gaillard was in personal command of the regiment at Macon, Ga., when, under orders of General Wilson, this regiment disarmed the Sixth Virginia Regiment (colored). This is possibly the first instance in the history of the government of the disarming of United States troops by United States troops. Colonel Gaillard's foreign service was in Santa Clara Province, Cuba, with headquarters at Cienfuegos, Cuba. In addition to his duties with the regiment, he was chief engineer officer of Santa Clara Province on the staff of Gen. John C. Bates, and under his direction much important engineering work was done, including topographical survey and map of the Spanish defences in and around Cienfuegos; cleaning the city of Cienfuegos and other places; investigation and report on the railroad facilities of the Province, with map and report on same; inspection and reports on the condition of the military barracks of the Province; investigation and reports on the sewer and water supply systems of the city of Cienfuegos; triangulations, soundings and borings in the inner harbor of Cienfuegos; repairing of the government wharf; the construction of tide gauges and report on the tide in the harbor of Cienfuegos; a complete series of levels and the establishment of permanent bench marks for the city, with map of their locations, etc. Colonel Gaillard was mustered out of the volunteer service at Atlanta, Ga., May 17, 1899, and reported for duty with the Engineer Corps of the regular army. He is now (1901) again in charge of the water supply of Washington, D. C.

Major Henry Clarence Davis was born in Fairfield County, S. C., September 15th, 1857, and was appointed to the West Point Military Academy by Congressman J. H. Evins, after a competitive examination, over twenty-three competitors. He graduated fifth in the class of 1883, and was assigned to the 3d Artillery, at Mt. Vernon Barracks, Ala. At the request of Gen. Stephen D. Lee, he was detailed as Commandant and Professor of Mathematics of the Mississippi Agricultural College in 1887-8-9. After three years more in the School of Ordnance, Lieutenant Davis rejoined his regiment at San Antonio, Tex. In 1896, he was appointed Assistant Professor of Natural Philosophy at West Point. While serving there he was commissioned Major of the 3d Volunteer Engineers, in the summer of 1898, and acted as recruiting officer until September; then he joined the regiment at Jefferson Barracks, Mo., going actively to work organizing, equipping, disciplining and drilling the Second Battalion. The progress made by this battalion, and the high state of efficiency attained by it, speak well for the thoroughness of its early training by Major Davis. Unfortunately for the regiment, Major Davis' services in the National Military Academy were too valuable at this time for him to be detailed on duty with troops in the field, and upon the reopening of the Academy in the autumn, he was forced to resign his commission in the Engineers and resume his scholastic work. He is now (1901) detailed as an instructor in the Officers' School at Fort Monroe.

First Lieut. Fingal C. Black was born at Euharlee, Bartow County, Ga., but has been in South Carolina since 1874. He attended the South Carolina College in 1885 and 1886; entered the South Carolina Military Academy October, 1886, and graduated in 1890. He taught in the public schools of the State two years, then commenced the practice of engineering. At the beginning of hostilities he was County Engineer of Spartanburg County. Lieutenant Black was examined in Atlanta, Ga., July 5, and having satisfactorily passed the required examination, was commissioned First Lieutenant of the 3d Engineers, July 13, 1898. He was appointed Enrolling Officer for the regiment, with headquarters at Spartanburg, where he was on duty until September, when he joined the regiment at Jefferson Barracks, Mo. He was in command of Co. H, 3d Engineers, when this company, with five other companies of the regiment, marched from Young's High Bridge, Ky., to Camp Hamilton, Ky., a distance of twenty-eight miles, in heavy marching order. This is said to be the longest distance marched by such a large body of troops in heavy marching order during the war. Lieutenant Black was in command of Co. H, at Macon, Ga., when the Sixth Virginia Regiment (colored) were disarmed by the 3d Engineers, and his company took charge of the prisoners as soon as the arms were secured. In this connection it might be well to state that the call for this duty was sounded between 11 and 12 o'clock at night, and that the regiment was armed and equipped for battle in twenty minutes. Lieutenant Black's foreign service was in and around Cienfuegos, Cuba, where, in addition to his duties as commanding officer of Co. H (Captain Thomas of Co. H being on detached duty during the entire stay of the company in Cuba), he had charge of the topographical survey of the Spanish defences in and around Cienfuegos, made a map of this territory, and repaired the government wharf at Cienfuegos. Lieutenant Black served with the regiment until it was mustered out of the service at Atlanta, Ga., May 17, 1899, after which he resumed the practice of his profession.

Second Lieutenant Alfred Hampton, son of Gen. Wade Hampton, served on the staff of Major General M. C. Butler.

Second Lieutenant Sam'l Dibble, Jr., after performing duty as Enrolling Officer at Orangeburg, S. C., reported for duty with the regiment in September, 1898. He did foreign service at Pinar Del Rio, Cuba, and was mustered out of the service at Atlanta, Ga., May 17, 1899.

First Lieutenant St. C. B. Gwinn was enrolled at Spartanburg, S. C., and reported for duty with the regiment at Jefferson Barracks, Mo., in July. Lieutenant Gwinn saw foreign service at Matanzas, Cuba, and was mustered out of the service at Atlanta, Ga., May 17, 1899.

Second Lieutenant Ralph E. Boggs was enrolled at Spartanburg, S. C., and reported for duty with the regiment at Jefferson Barracks, Mo., in September, 1899. Lieutenant Boggs did foreign service at Cienfuegos, Cuba, and was mustered out of the service at Atlanta, Ga., May, 1899.

Quartermaster Sergeant F. H. McCullough, Sergeant Wm. J. Robinson and Private Geo. W. Ready served with the regiment from its muster in at Jefferson Barracks, Mo., to its muster out at Atlanta, Ga., and saw foreign service at and around Cienfuegos, Cuba.

Sergeant James Elder served with the regiment both in the States and at Matanzas, Cuba.

The other South Carolinians mentioned in this paper served with the regiment in the States and Cuba, except Mart G. Ayers, who after a short service at Jefferson Barracks, Mo., died in the line of duty at Camp Hamilton, near Lexington, Ky.

Of the South Carolinians in this arm of the service, not one was ever in the guard house—a record not attained by the sons of any other State.

www.ingramcontent.com/pod-product-compliance
Lightning Source LLC
Chambersburg PA
CBHW020644300426
44112CB00007B/237